The Descent of Christ

Biblical Studies Library

The Descent of Christ: Ephesians 4:7–11 and Traditional Hebrew Imagery,
W. Hall Harris III

Marriage as a Covenant: Biblical Law and Ethics as Developed from Malachi, Gordon P. Hugenberger

The Structure of Hebrews: A Text-Linguistic Analysis, George H. Guthrie

The Descent of Christ

Ephesians 4:7–11
and Traditional Hebrew Imagery

W. Hall Harris III

Baker Books

A Division of Baker Book House Co
Grand Rapids, Michigan 49516

© 1996 by E. J. Brill, Leiden, The Netherlands

Published by Baker Books
a division of Baker Book House Company
P.O. Box 6287, Grand Rapids, MI 49516-6287

First cloth edition published 1996 by E. J. Brill as volume 32 in Arbeiten zur Geschichte des Antiken Judentums und des Urchristentums.

First paperback edition published 1998 by Baker Books.

Printed in the United States of America

Library of Congress Cataloging-in-Publication Data

Harris, W. Hall.
      The descent of Christ : Ephesians 4:7–11 and traditional Hebrew imagery / by W. Hall Harris III.
      p.   cm. — (Biblical studies library)
   Originally published: Leiden; New York: E.J. Brill, 1996, in series: Arbeiten zur Geschichte des antiken Judentums und des Urchristentums.
      Includes bibliographical references and indexes.
      ISBN: 0-8010-2191-X (pbk.)
      1. Bible. N.T. Ephesians IV, 7–11—Criticism, interpretation, etc. 2. Bible. O.T. Psalms LXVIII, 19—Criticism, interpretation, Psalms. 4. Bible. O.T. Psalms LXVIII, 19—Relation to Ephesians. I. Title. II. Series.
   [BS2695.2.H34   1998]
   227′.506—dc21   98-35376

To Ursula

CONTENTS

PREFACE

This book began as a doctoral dissertation presented to the Department of Biblical Studies at the University of Sheffield in the summer of 1988. Although I have long been interested in the publication of the results of that research, other commitments have repeatedly managed to take priority over the revisions and improvements necessary to achieve this. Now it has finally been updated in considerable detail to keep abreast of recent developments, but it remains essentially unchanged in its basic assertions and conclusions.

There are many people who deserve my heartfelt thanks for their kind assistance in the pursuit of this research over the years. Above all are Dr. Bruce Chilton, my original *Doktorvater* at Sheffield, from whom I acquired an appreciation for the rabbinic literature which plays such a significant role in the present study, and Dr. Andrew T. Lincoln, under whose supervision I finished this work, and whose expertise in Ephesians contributed immeasurably to its quality and depth. I also owe many thanks to Professor John Rogerson of Sheffield, who was always available to encourage and to offer helpful suggestions, as were others in the department, notably Dr. David Clines and Dr. Philip Davies.

I would like to thank my own institution, Dallas Theological Seminary, for allowing me two years of study leave to pursue this research, and to my department chairman, Dr. Harold Hoehner, who contributed much not only to my professional development but also to my exegetical skill and to my interest in Ephesians. I would also like to express my gratitude to Rev. Derek Jefferson and Dr. Mary Jefferson of Sheffield, whose friendship and help made my stay in Britain so much more pleasant, and to Dr. David Orton, with whom I enjoyed many an interesting conversation while we were postgraduate students in the Biblical Studies Department, and whose continuing assistance has finally resulted in the publication of this book. I am grateful to Mr. Daniel Buck for his kind assistance in proofreading the final copy. Finally I would like especially to thank my wife Ursula, whom I met on a trip to Germany and married in the course of this research, for her constant encouragement and patient toleration which have seen me through many a difficult spot to the completion of the present book.

Needless to say, the shortcomings in the present work cannot be attributed to anyone but myself.

W. Hall Harris III
Dallas Theological Seminary

ABBREVIATIONS

1. General Abbreviations

BCE	Before the Common Era	MT	Masoretic Text
CE	Common Era	NT	New Testament
LXX	Septuagint	OT	Old Testament

2. Abbreviations of the Names of Pseudepigraphical Books

Ep. Arist.	Epistle of Aristeas	T. Benj.	Testament of Benjamin
Jub.	Jubilees	T. Dan	Testament of Dan
T. 12 Patr.	Testaments of the Twelve Patriarchs	T. Levi	Testament of Levi, etc.

3. Abbreviations of Targumic Material

Tg.	Targum	Tg. Neof.	Targum Neofiti I
Tg. Onq.	Targum Onqelos	Tg. Psalms	Targum to the Psalms

4. Abbreviations of Rabbinic Material

Abot R. Nat.	Abot de Rabbi Nathan	Pal.	Palestinian
Ag. Ber.	Aggadat Bereshit	Pesiq. R.	Pesiqta Rabbati
Mek.	Mekilta	Pirqe R. El.	Pirqe de Rabbi Eliezer
Mek. Bah.	Mek. Bahodesh	Rab.	Rabbah
Mek. R. Ish.	Mekilta de Rabbi Ishmael	Shem. Rab.	Shemot Rabbah
Midr.	Midrash	Shir. Rab.	Shir haShirim Rabbah
Midr. Teh.	Midrash Tehillim	Sof.	Soferim

5. Abbreviations of Periodicals, Reference Works, and Serials

AB	Anchor Bible	ATR	Anglican Theological Review
AbBC	Abingdon Bible Commentary	BAGD	W. Bauer, W. F. Arndt, F. W. Gingrich, and F. W. Danker, A Greek-English Lexicon of the New Testament and Other Early Christian Literature
ACW	Ancient Christian Writers		
AGJU	Arbeiten zur Geschichte des Antiken Judentums und des Urchristentums		
AnBib	Analecta biblica	BBC	The Broadman Bible Commentary
ANS	Auslegung neutestamentlicher Schriften		
		BDB	F. Brown, S. R. Driver, and C. A. Briggs, A Hebrew and English Lexicon of the Old Testament
APOT	R. H. Charles (ed.), The Apocrypha and Pseudepigrapha of the Old Testament in English		
AqSS	Aquinas Scripture Series	BDF	F. Blass, A. Debrunner, and R. W. Funk, A Greek Grammar of the New Testament and Other Early Christian Literature
ASeign	Assemblées du Seigneur		
ASNU	Acta seminarii neotestamentici upsaliensis		
ATANT	Abhandlungen zur Theologie des Alten und Neuen Testaments	BHS	Biblia hebraica stuttgartensia

BHT	Beiträge zur historischen Theologie	*JSJ*	*Journal for the Study of Judaism in the Persian,*
Bib	*Biblica*		*Hellenistic and Roman Period*
BiTod	*Bible Today*	*JSNT*	*Journal for the Study of the*
BJS	Brown Judaic Studies		*New Testament*
BNTC	Black's New Testament Commentaries	JSNTSup	JSNT—Supplement Series
		JTS	*Journal of Theological Studies*
BTH	Bibliothèque de théologie historique	KEK	Kritisch-exegetischer Kommentar über das Neue Testament
BSac	*Bibliotheca Sacra*	KNT	Kommentar zum Neuen
BZ	*Biblische Zeitschrift*		Testament herausgegeben von
BZAW	Beihefte zur *ZAW*		Theodor Zahn
CSion	Cahiers sioniens	LCL	Loeb Classical Library
CBC	Cambridge Bible Commentary	LD	Lectio divina
CBQ	*Catholic Biblical Quarterly*	*LTJ*	*Lutheran Theological Journal*
CChr	Corpus Christianorum	MHT	J. H. Moulton, W. F. Howard,
CNT	Commentaire du Nouveau Testament		and N. Turner (eds.), *A Grammar of New Testament*
CNT(K)	Commentaar op het Nieuwe Testament		*Greek*
		MNTC	Moffatt New Testament Commentary
CR	Corpus Reformatorum		
DR	*Downside Review*	*Mus*	*Muséon*
EGT	W. R. Nicoll (ed.), *The Expositor's Greek Testament*	*MH*	*Museum Helveticum*
		NA27	K. Aland et al., (eds.), Nestle-
EKKNT	Evangelisch-katholischer Kommentar zum Neuen Testament		Aland *Novum Testamentum graece*, 27th ed. rev.
		NASB	New American Standard Bible
EpPC	Epworth Preachers' Commentaries	*NBl*	*New Blackfriars*
		NCB	New Century Bible
ExpTim	*Expository Times*	*NCHS*	C. Gore, H. L. Goudge, and A.
GCS	Die griechischen christlichen Schriftsteller der ersten Jahrhunderte		Guillaume (eds.), *A New Commentary on Holy Scripture including the Apocrypha*
Hermeneia	Hermeneia—A Critical and Historical Commentary on the Bible	NClarB	New Clarendon Bible
		NICNT	New International Commentary on the New Testament
HKNT	Handkommentar zum Neuen Testament	*NKZ*	*Neue kirchliche Zeitschrift*
		NovT	*Novum Testamentum*
HNT	Handbuch zum Neuen Testament	NovTSup	Novum Testamentum, Supplements
HNTC	Harper's New Testament Commentaries		
		NTC	New Testament Commentary
HSNT	Die heiligen Schriften des Neuen Testaments	NTD	Das Neue Testament Deutsch
		NTS	*New Testament Studies*
HTKNT	Herders theologischer Kommentar zum Neuen Testament	NTTS	New Testament Tools and Studies
		OJRS	*Ohio Journal of Religious Studies*
HTR	*Harvard Theological Review*		
HTS	Harvard Theological Studies	ÖTBK	Ökumenischer Taschenbuchkommentar zum Neuen Testament
HUCA	*Hebrew Union College Annual*		
IB	*Interpreter's Bible*		
ICC	International Critical Commentary	OTP	J. H. Charlesworth (ed.), *The Old Testament Pseudepigrapha*
JBC	R. E. Brown, J. A. Fitzmyer, and R. E. Murphy (eds.), *The Jerome Biblical Commentary*	PCB	M. Black and H. H. Rowley (eds.), *Peake's Commentary on the Bible*
JBL	*Journal of Biblical Literature*	PG	Migne, J.-P. (ed.), *Patrologiae cursus completus, series graeca*
JJS	*Journal of Jewish Studies*		
JQR	*Jewish Quarterly Review*		

PL	Migne, J.-P. (ed.), *Patrologiae cursus completus, series latina*	TBC	Torch Bible Commentaries
PMS	Publications in Medieval Studies	*TDNT*	G. Kittel and G. Friedrich (eds.), *Theological Dictionary of the New Testament*
PNTC	Pelican New Testament Commentaries	*TLZ*	*Theologische Literaturzeitung*
PVTG	Pseudepigrapha Veteris Testamenti graece	TNTC	Tyndale New Testament Commentaries
RB	*Revue biblique*	*TSFBul*	*TSF Bulletin*
REJ	*Revue des études juives*	*TTK*	*Tidsskrift for Teologi og Kirke*
RevExp	*Review and Expositor*	TU	Texte und Untersuchungen zur Geschichte der altchristlichen Literatur
RHPR	*Revue d' histoire et de philosophie religieuses*		
RivB	*Revista biblica*	*TZ*	*Theologische Zeitschrift*
RNT	Regensburger Neues Testament	*UBSGNT*	United Bible Societies *Greek New Testament*
RSR	*Recherches de science religieuse*	*VD*	*Verbum domini*
RSTh	Regensburger Studien zur Theologie	*VT*	*Vetus Testamentum*
		VTSup	Vetus Testamentum, Supplements
SANT	Studien zum Alten und Neuen Testament	WBC	Word Biblical Commentary
SBT	Studies in Biblical Theology	WC	Westminster Commentaries
SBJ	*La sainte bible de Jérusalem*	WStB	Wuppertaler Studienbibel
SCS	Septuagint and Cognate Studies	WPC	Westminster Pelican Commentaries
SE	*Studia Evangelica I, II, III* (= TU 73 [1959], 87 [1964], 88 [1964], etc.)	*WTJ*	*Westminster Theological Journal*
SEÅ	*Svensk exegetisk årsbok*	*WiWeis*	*Wissenschaft und Weisheit*
SJLA	Studies in Judaism in Late Antiquity	YJS	Yale Judaica Series
		ZBK	Zürcher Bibelkommentare
SNTSMS	Society for New Testament Studies Monograph Series	*ZKG*	*Zeitschrift für Kirchengeschichte*
SPB	Studia postbiblica	*ZNW*	*Zeitschrift für die neutestamentliche Wissenschaft*
ST	*Studia Theologica*		
SVTP	Studia in Veteris Testamenti Pseudepigrapha	*ZWT*	*Zeitschrift für wissenschaftliche Theologie*

INTRODUCTION

What follows is the detailed story of a New Testament text—including the Old Testament quotation which it contains—and of the underlying traditions that shaped its imagery and influenced its author to adapt that Old Testament text to convey his own christological understanding.

This study began a number of years ago as an attempt to investigate the problems associated with the descent of Christ in Eph 4:7-11. Through an examination of the evidence for the differing views, one interpretation has emerged as the most probable, and this is the position that is defended in the pages which follow. This interpretation itself is not new; it can be found as long ago as the third century CE in the writings of Origen. In modern times it was proposed at the end of the last century by H. *Frhr.* von Soden and endorsed not long afterwards by the British scholar T. K. Abbott. To their credit as exegetical scholars, both von Soden and Abbott argued for this interpretation primarily on the basis of the internal logic and the argument-flow within the passage itself. Since their time much new information has surfaced regarding ascent and descent imagery and traditions associated with Moses and the giving of the Torah at Sinai. These Moses-traditions, particularly in terms of their association with Psalm 68, provide crucial clues to a proper understanding of the nature and time of Christ's descent with respect to the ascent mentioned in the psalm quotation (Eph 4:8). If the Moses-traditions appearing in the (later) rabbinic interpretations of Psalm 68 can be shown to lie behind the use of that psalm in Eph 4:8, it would strongly suggest that the author of Ephesians envisioned a subsequent descent of Christ to distribute to his church the spiritual gifts described in Eph 4:11-16, since Moses, following his ascent of Mt. Sinai to receive the Torah, descended to deliver it to the Israelites encamped below. Such a sequence, which places the descent after the ascent, would provide the answer to two questions often overlooked by recent interpreters of the passage: (a) why did the author of Ephesians find it necessary to infer a descent from the ascent mentioned in the psalm, and (b) why did the author need to stress the identity of "the one who descended" with "the one who ascended" as he does in Eph 4:9-10? The Moses-traditions associated with Psalm 68 in later rabbinic writings, if known to the author of Ephesians, would have naturally led him to assume a subsequent descent involving the distribution of the gifts. But it was still necessary for the author to affirm the identity of the Christ who ascended victoriously according to the psalm with the Christ who descended to his church to distribute spiritual gifts, for such an identification would not be immediately obvious to the readers.

More than once the rabbinic interpretation of Ps 68:19 has been cited as proof for a reconstruction of the meaning of Eph 4:8-10 without adequate attempts to establish with a reasonable degree of certainty the date of the traditions in question. Such temptation must be resisted, however, and thus Chapter Three of this book is devoted to the examination of early rabbinic and non-rabbinic interpretations of Ps 68:19 in order to determine what may or may not be said with certainty about the use of such Moses-traditions by the author of Ephesians. Chapter Four then goes on to examine further the ascent traditions connected with Moses aside from Psalm 68.

Another area of particular interest with regard to the use of Ps 68:19 by the author of Ephesians concerns the connection of the psalm with the feast of Pentecost as a celebration of the giving of the Torah at Sinai. Such connections, if they can be shown to exist early enough to have influenced the composition of Ephesians, would provide additional evidence associating the psalm with the giving of spiritual gifts to the early church. This in turn would indicate a link with Christ's gift to the church of the gifts (or gifted individuals) mentioned in Eph 4:11-16. Chapter Five of this work investigates several lines of evidence which point to a relationship between Eph 4:7-11 and the giving of the Spirit.

The contextual argument for a subsequent descent of Christ in the passage, which formed the primary basis for the arguments of both von Soden and Abbott, is developed at length in Chapter Six. Consideration is also given to the theological implications of identifying the ascended Christ as the Spirit who returned to distribute gifts to his church.

In addition, there has never before been a comprehensive attempt to trace the history of interpretation of Eph 4:7-11. Thus Chapter One provides the basic framework for such an investigation, by placing the present discussion within a historical tradition, and at the same time by demonstrating how the various current interpretations of the passage came into existence. Chapter Two provides necessary lexical and syntactical background related to the locus of Christ's descent in the passage. The primary purpose of this book, however, is to articulate and defend a particular interpretation as thoroughly as possible, with consideration of other interpretive possibilities as necessary. I harbor no illusions that the material presented here will win immediate and widespread acceptance as the definitive solution to the problems of the passage. Nor is the present work intended to provide a comprehensive treatment of all the interpretive problems in Eph 4:7-11; some details which are not directly relevant to the basic interpretation are not discussed at all. But I do hope that the issues discussed here will provide a sound basis upon which future discussions of the problems of the passage may proceed, and that a consensus of opinion as to its general meaning will eventually emerge.

CHAPTER ONE

THE *DESCENSUS AD INFEROS* AND EPH 4:7-11

As early as the middle of the 15th century Reginald Pecock, bishop of St. Asaph (1444) and later of Chichester (1450), rejected the doctrine of the Descent to Hell and denied apostolic authorship of the 'Apostles' Creed'.[1] Whether or not the doctrine of the *descensus* can be found in the Epistle to the Ephesians is of course the primary subject of our investigation. But before we turn to the exegesis of Eph 4:7-11 and the examination of related background issues, a brief survey of the history of the doctrine of the *descensus* will set the stage for the modern debate over the meaning of the passage.

A. THE DOCTRINE OF THE *DESCENSUS*

The belief that Christ spent the *triduum* (the interval between his death on the cross and his resurrection) in the underworld was common in Christian teaching from the earliest times. It may have been in the background of a number of NT passages, as A. T. Hanson recently sought to prove.[2] The doctrine did not appear in credal formulations until 359 CE, when it was mentioned in the 'Fourth Formula of Sirmium': the Lord "died, and descended to the underworld [εἰς τὰ καταχθόνια κατελθόντα], and regulated things there, Whom the gatekeepers of hell saw and shuddered."[3] But the tradition of a descent of Christ to the underworld between his death and resurrection is far older. It is mentioned frequently among the post-apostolic fathers: Ignatius (110 CE)[4] apparently alluded to the doctrine (Πρὸς Μαγνησιεῖς 9.3),[5] and so did Poly-

---

[1] J. N. D. Kelly, *Early Christian Creeds*, 3rd ed. (London: Longman, 1972) 5.

[2] A. T. Hanson, *The New Testament Interpretation of Scripture* (London: SPCK, 1980) 122-56.

[3] J. N. D. Kelly, *Early Christian Creeds*, 378. The only scriptural passage mentioned in support is Job 38:17.

[4] This and subsequent dates for the post-apostolic fathers are dates of death unless otherwise indicated.

[5] Ignatius' actual statement reads, "and therefore, he whom they [the prophets] rightly awaited, when he came, raised them from the dead" (καὶ διὰ τοῦτο, ὃν δικαίως ἀνέμενον, παρὼν ἤγειρεν αὐτοὺς ἐκ νεκρῶν). The Greek text of Ignatius' Epistle to the Magnesians is from the Βιβλιοθηκη Ἑλληνων Πατερων και Ἐκκλησιαστικων Συγγραφεων, 2: Κλημης ὁ Ρωμης—Διδαχη των Δωδεκα Ἀποστολων—Βαρναβα Ἐπιστολη—ἡ προς Διογνητον Ἐπιστολη—Ἰγνατιος (Athens: Apostolic Diaconate of the Church of Greece, 1955) 270. While this could imply belief in a *descensus ad inferos*, it may be no more than an allusion to Matt 27:52.

carp (156 CE) in Πρὸς Φιλιππησίους 1.2.[6] Irenaeus (202 CE) made repeated mention of the *descensus* (*Adversus haereses* 4.27.2, 5.31.1, and
5.33.1). Among the earliest to elaborate the doctrine was Tertullian (220
CE), who stated in *De anima* 55.2:

> Nor did he ascend into the heights of heaven before descending into the
> lower regions of the earth ["in inferiora terrarum"], that he might there
> make the patriarchs and prophets partakers of himself.[7]

A reference to the *descensus* occurs seven or eight times in the *Homilies
of Aphraates* (ca. 337-345 CE), twice in the 3rd century *Acts of Thomas*,[8] at least once in Ephraim the Syrian's (373 CE) *On our Lord*, and in
the Edessene document contained in the *Doctrine of Addai* which was
quoted by Eusebius (*Hist. eccl.* 1.13.20, ἐσταυρώθη, καὶ κατέβη εἰς τὸν
ᾄδην).[9]

From these early references to the doctrine of the *descensus* it was
only a few short steps to more elaborate formulations. Christ was active

---

6 The phrase in Polycarp is, "to our Lord Jesus Christ, who on behalf of our sins suffered
to the point of death, 'whom God raised from the dead, having loosed the pains of Hades.'"
The Greek text reads as follows: εἰς τὸν κύριον ἡμῶν Ἰησοῦν Χριστόν, ὃς ὑπέμεινεν ὑπὲρ
τῶν ἁμαρτιῶν ἡμῶν ἕως θανάτου καταντῆσαι, «ὃν ἤγειρεν ὁ θεὸς λύσας τὰς ὠδῖνας τοῦ
ᾄδου·» (Βιβλιοθηκη Ἑλληνων Πατερων και Ἐκκλησιαστικων Συγγραφεων, 3: Πολυκαρπος Σμυρνης—Ἑρμας—Παπιας—Κοδρατος—Ἀριστειδης—Ἰουστινος [Athens: Apostolic Diaconate of the Church of Greece, 1955] 15). The phrase λύσας τὰς ὠδῖνας τοῦ ᾄδου is
quoted from Acts 2:24, in a form also found in a few manuscripts of the so-called "Western"
text (e.g., D [05, codex Bezae or Cantabrigiensis], most of the Itala manuscripts, the Vulgate,
and the Peshitta). The great majority of NT manuscripts read τοῦ θανάτου for τοῦ ᾄδου. Polycarp quoted the text without elaboration, but it seems likely that anyone who followed the
reading of codex D [05] et al. in Acts 2:24 would have held to some sort of doctrine of a *descensus*, because the text itself virtually requires it. Since Polycarp did not comment on the
reading, it probably did not originate with him, but represents an even earlier variant reading.

7 My translation from the text of *De anima* 55 in *Tertulliani Opera*, CChr 2 (Turnhout:
Brepols, 1954) 862. For discussion of this text, and whether Tertullian was alluding to the OT
text of Ps 68:19 or to Eph 4:8 (the NT quotation of Ps 68:19) see below, ch. 3, 118-20.

8 *Acts of Thomas* 10 addressed Christ as "ambassador sent from the height who didst descend even to Hell, who having opened the doors didst bring up thence those who for many
ages had been shut up in the treasury of darkness, and show them the way that leads up to the
height..." (E. Hennecke, *New Testament Apocrypha*, ed. W. Schneemelcher, trans. and ed. R.
McL. Wilson [Philadelphia: Westminster, 1965] 2.448). This passage was understood to refer
to the *descensus* by W. Foerster (*Die Gnosis*, 1: *Zeugnisse der Kirchenväter* [Zürich and
Stuttgart: Artemis, 1969] 347). However, it should be noted that J. A. MacCullagh suggested
that in this passage 'Hell' may not have constituted a reference to the underworld, but rather
referred to the earth itself (*The Harrowing of Hell: A Comparative Study of an Early Christian Doctrine* [Edinburgh: Clark, 1930] 305).

9 Eusebius' *Hist. eccl.* 1.13.20 as published in Βιβλιοθηκη Ἑλληνων Πατερων και
Ἐκκλησιαστικων Συγγραφεων, 19: Τιτος Βοστρων—Θεοδωρος—Ἡρακλειας—Ἀλεξαν-
δρος Λυκοπολεως—Ἐυσεβιος Καισαρειας (Athens: Apostolic Diaconate of the Church of
Greece, 1959) 222. Many of the Eastern sources were discussed by R. H. Connolly ("The Early
Syriac Creed," *ZNW* 7 [1906] 202-223) and included in W. Cureton (*Ancient Syriac Docu-
ments* [London, n.p., 1864; reprint ed., Amsterdam: Oriental, 1967]). The statement quoted by
Eusebius from the *Doctrine of Addai* is also found (in English translation) in Cureton
(*Documents* 5).

during the three days between his death and resurrection preaching salvation to the souls in Hades, or alternatively, performing a triumphant act of liberation on their behalf and defeating Satan in the process. Hippolytus (235 CE) added the idea that John the Baptist was Jesus' forerunner in the underworld just as he was on earth,[10] while Hermas proposed that the apostles and teachers who themselves had died carried on the Lord's ministry in the underworld and baptized their converts.[11] Interpretations involving preaching and/or baptism were usually inferred from 1 Pet 3:19-22, while those involving a triumphant liberation of captives were based on Eph 4:7-10. But it seemed scarcely credible that the OT saints, who had foreseen Christ's coming, should need to be enlightened concerning his person, and gradually, as it came to be believed that an offer to the unconverted dead of a second opportunity for repentance in the nether world was inappropriate, the view of the *descensus* which emphasized the deliverance of the saints and the defeat of Satan gained prominence in the West. By the time of Augustine (died 430 CE) the view that Christ had liberated from Hades any persons other than those who had foreseen his coming and kept his precepts by anticipation was branded heretical.[12]

B. A BRIEF HISTORY OF THE INTERPRETATION OF EPH 4:7-11

The doctrine of the *descensus ad inferos*, as we have seen, was well established in the early church. Turning to the interpretation of Eph 4:7-11 the picture is less clear.[13] Early ecclesiastical writers who affirmed their belief in the doctrine of a *descensus* did not always trouble themselves to offer a scriptural reference in support of their view, especially in cases where they assumed it to be commonly held. The first credal formulation

---

[10] *De Christo et anti-Christo* 45, where after quoting John 1:29 ("Behold, the Lamb of God who takes away the sin of the world"), Hippolytus added, "οὗτος προέφθασε καὶ τοῖς ἐν ᾅδῃ προευαγγελίσασθαι, ἀναιρεθεὶς ὑπὸ Ἡρώδου" (Βιβλιοθηκη Ἑλληνων Πατερων και Ἐκκλησιαστικων Συγγραφεων, 6: Ἱππολυτος [Athens: Apostolic Diaconate of the Church of Greece, 1956] 212).

[11] *Similitudes* 9.16.6 of the *Shepherd of Hermas*; the passage in question reads:"...these apostles and teachers who preached the name of the Son of God, after they had fallen asleep in the power and faith of the Son of God, preached also to them that had fallen asleep before them, and themselves gave unto them the seal of the preaching. Therefore they went down with them into the water and came up again. But these went down alive [and again came up alive]; whereas the others that had fallen asleep before them went down dead and came up alive" (J. B. Lightfoot, *Apostolic Fathers* [London, Macmillan, 1891; reprint ed., Grand Rapids: Baker, 1956] 232).

[12] Augustine, *De haeresibus* 79, in *Aurelii Augustini Opera*, CChr 46 (Turnhout: Brepols, 1969) 336.

[13] A brief but helpful survey of the history of interpretation of the passage in question is found in E. Haupt (*Die Gefangenschaftsbriefe*, KEK 8 [Göttingen: Vandenhoeck, 1899] 141-50).

to refer explicitly to the doctrine of the *descensus*, the Fourth Formula of Sirmium (359 CE), gave only a single scriptural reference in support of the doctrine. That reference—to Job 38:17—was far less clear than references to either of the two NT passages commonly associated with the *descensus* would have been. Such tendencies make it difficult to say with certainty what a given writer would have believed about Eph 4:7-11 (or any other specific biblical passage concerned with a possible *descensus*).

1. *The Descent in Eph 4:7-11 as a* Descensus ad Inferos

Nevertheless, in spite of the difficulties associated with any attempt to determine the view of a given Father on the descent of Christ in Eph 4:7-11, it appears that a number of early commentators understood this passage to contain a reference to Christ's descent to the underworld. Tertullian's statement in *De anima* 55.2 almost certainly reflects such an understanding of Eph 4:9-10 because of the reference to Christ ascending "into the heights of heaven" following a descent "into the lower regions of the earth."[14] The purpose of Christ's descent according to Tertullian was "to make the patriarchs and prophets partakers of himself." This suggests that Tertullian may have interpreted the phrase ᾐχμαλώτευσεν αἰχμαλωσίαν in the quotation from Ps 68:19 (Eph 4:8) as a reference to OT saints redeemed by Christ from Hades and led up from there by Christ upon his victorious ascent. Likewise (at about the same time as Tertullian) Irenaeus interpreted Eph 4:9-10 to refer to a *descensus ad inferos* which Christ made on behalf of his disciples.[15] In the fourth century Ambrosiaster in his comments on Eph 4:9 stated that Christ, triumphing over the devil, "descended into the heart of the earth" ("descendit in cor terrae"), that is, to the underworld, before his triumphal ascent above all the heavens.[16] Victorinus was another early commentator who held to a *descensus* in Eph 4:7-11.[17] During the late fourth century Chrysostom interpreted the descent in Eph 4:9-10 as a descent of Christ to Hades, citing in this connection Gen 44:29 (εἰς

---

14 See the text of the quotation from *De anima* 55.2 above, 2.

15 *Adversus haereses* 4.22.1. In context Christ's finding the disciples asleep in Gethsemane two times was interpreted as symbolic of his two comings, where in the first instance he did not awaken the disciples, but the second time he made them stand up. Thus at his first coming Christ did not awaken the dead who are asleep in the lower parts of the earth, although he did descend there to look upon them. After this Irenaeus quoted Eph 4:9 and said that Christ's descent was on behalf of his disciples.

16 *In Epistolam B. Pauli ad Ephesios*, ch. 4 (*PL* 17, col. 387). The works written by Ambrosiaster and attributed to St Ambrose are thought to have been written during the reign of Pope Damasus (366-84 CE).

17 M. Barth, *Ephesians: Translation and Commentary on Chapters 4-6*, AB 34A (Garden City, NY: Doubleday, 1974) 433, n. 45.

ᾅδου) and Ps 142:7 (εἰς λάκκον). The 'captives' led captive, according to Chrysostom, were the devil (τὸν διάβολον), death (τὸν θάνατον), the curse (τὴν ἀράν), and sin (τὴν ἀμαρτίαν).[18] At the beginning of the fifth century Pelagius held that Christ descended to hell with his spirit ("qui descendit cum anima in infernum"), but ascended to heaven with both body and spirit.[19] Jerome, writing about the same time, apparently saw in the descent of Christ in Eph 4:9-10 a reference both to the incarnation and to a descent to the underworld. He assumed that the descent was prior to the ascent ("propterea ascendit, quia ante descenderat"), and cited John 3:13, which suggests a possible allusion to the incarnation. Jerome went on to state, however, that the locus of Christ's descent was the underworld ("inferiora autem terrae, infernus accipitur ad quem Dominus noster Salvatorque descendit...," and "Quod autem infernus in inferiori parte terrae sit, et Psalmista testatur..."). Pss 103:17 and 54:16 were then quoted as proof of this point.[20] Theodoret, writing in the mid-fifth century, was aware that while Eph 4:8 spoke of 'giving' gifts (ἔδωκε δόματα), the text of Ps 68:19 read differently (ἔλαβε δόματα). He explained that Christ 'received' the faith of men and 'gave' gifts in return. The descent itself he interpreted as a reference to Christ's death (κατώτερα γὰρ μέρη τῆς γῆς τὸν θάνατον ἐκάλεσεν).[21] Oecumenius, in the sixth century, quoted Gen 42:38 and Ps 27:1 in his interpretation of the descent in Eph 4:9-10 to prove that Christ's descent was to Hades, that is, the underworld (λέγει δὲ τὸν ᾅδην). He added that the Nestorians made the heretical and blasphemous assertion that the one who descended and the one who ascended was the same (Ὁ αὐτός, φησὶν, ἐστὶν ὁ καταβὰς καὶ ὁ ἀναβάς). Oecumenius went on to explain that what the Nestorians were actually asserting was that Christ "descended into the flesh as God, but ascended (ἀναβαίνει) as a man, while he descended into Hades as a man, but arose (ἀνίσταται) as God."[22]

By the later medieval period the views of the earlier Fathers had become more or less accepted. Theophylact, in his eleventh century commentary on Ephesians, affirmed like others before him that Christ descended to Hades (εἰς τὸν ᾅδην), and cited Gen 24:38 and Ps 27:1 as scriptural support.[23] Aquinas' understanding of Eph 4:7-11 is typical of the period, insofar as he repeated the opinions of his predecessors, but

---

[18] *In Epistolam ad Ephesios Homilia XI* (*PG* 62, cols. 81-82).

[19] A. Souter, *Pelagius' Expositions of Thirteen Epistles of St Paul: Text and Apparatus Criticus* (Cambridge: Cambridge University Press, 1926) 2.364.

[20] *Commentariorum in Epistolam ad Ephesios*, book 2, ch. 4 (*PL* 26, cols. 498-99).

[21] *Interpretatio Epistolae ad Ephesios*, ch. 4 (*PG* 82, cols. 533-35).

[22] *Pauli Apostoli ad Ephesios Epistola*, ch. 6 (*PG* 118, cols. 1215-20).

[23] *Theophylacti Commentarius in Epistolam ad Ephesios*, ch. 4 (*PG* 124, cols. 1083-84). Ps 27:1 was also quoted in support of a *descensus ad inferos* by Oecumenius (see above).

he apparently held to multiple meanings for the descent itself. The captives which were led captive (according to the quotation from Ps 68:19 in Eph 4:8) were those saints who had died before Christ's coming and were being held like prisoners by the devil in limbo. These persons Christ liberated and brought with himself to heaven. Yet Aquinas did not stop with this interpretation of the captives; he added that the captives led captive by Christ did not refer only to those already dead, but also to the living, who were held under the bondage of sin until liberated by Christ. To these who were rescued alive from the power of the devil Christ had also given the (spiritual) gifts referred to in the quotation from Ps 68:19. With regard to the ascent and descent mentioned in Eph 4:9-10, Aquinas apparently understood the ὅτι which introduces the reference to the descent in Eph 4:9 (ὅτι καὶ κατέβη εἰς τὰ κατώτερα μέρη τῆς γῆς) as causal rather than epexegetical or explanatory. Thus Aquinas saw the reason for the ascent of Christ in his (prior) descent: had he not descended first, Christ could not have ascended. This suggests the possibility of understanding Christ's descent in terms of his incarnation rather than a descent to the underworld. In fact, Aquinas saw both meanings present in the passage. He first understood the phrase τὰ κατώτερα μέρη τῆς γῆς as a reference to the parts of the earth itself which were inhabited by men, lower than the heavens and the atmosphere. Phil 2:7 was quoted to show that Christ humbled himself at the incarnation by becoming like the rest of humanity. But Aquinas went on to give a second interpretation of τὰ κατώτερα μέρη τῆς γῆς which understood the phrase to refer to parts lower than the earth itself, namely, hell. This he saw to agree with the phrase in the quotation from Ps 68:19 which spoke of leading captivity captive, which he had previously understood to refer to Christ's liberation of those who were held as prisoners of the devil. Thus it appears that while Aquinas was aware of an interpretation of the descent in Eph 4:9-10 which referred it to Christ's incarnation, he preferred to understand it as a reference to a *descensus ad inferos* (or more properly, *ad infernos*). Aquinas went on to assert the identity in Eph 4:10 of "the one who descended" (ὁ καταβάς) with "the one who ascended" (ὁ ἀναβάς), since he saw this as an affirmation of the unity of person in the two natures of Christ, the divine and the human.[24]

1.1. *The Traditional View in Modern Times*
The views of the Reformers on the interpretation of Eph 4:9-10 are not always entirely clear, as a number of examples will demonstrate. Luther

---

[24] St. Thomas Aquinas, *Commentary on Saint Paul's Epistle to the Ephesians*, trans. M. L. Lamb, AqSS 2 (Albany, NY: Magi Books, 1966) 159-61.

apparently made no recorded comments on verses 7-9 of the passage. His comments on Eph 4:10 concern only the exaltation of Christ to fill all things and give no clue to his interpretation of the *descensus*.[25] Based on Luther's translation of Eph 4:9 ("Daß er aber aufgefahren ist, was ist das andres, als daß er auch hinuntergefahren ist in die untersten Örter der Erde?")[26] it is probable that he held to the traditional view that Christ descended to the underworld during the period between his death and resurrection, but this is not absolutely certain.

Another of the early Reformers, H. Zwingli, wrote no commentary on Ephesians, but his marginal annotations on Greek manuscripts of the Pauline epistles he had copied by hand himself have survived. These copies of the Pauline epistles in Greek were made from Erasmus' 1516 edition (known as the *Novum Instrumentum*) and included Erasmus' own annotations and marginal glosses. They were probably done by Zwingli between 1516 and 1519. Apart from Erasmus, Zwingli used other sources for his marginal annotations. For the letter to the Ephesians these were the works of Ambrosiaster, Chrysostom, and Jerome.[27] Over the word κατώτερα in Eph 4:9 appears the gloss "infimas" (the superlative of *inferus*). Following this is another gloss attributed to Jerome (the abbreviation used is "Hiero" [= Hieronymus]): "inferiora terre intelligit inferos" ("'the lower parts of the earth' is understood by the term 'underworld'").[28] Zwingli apparently picked up both of these notes from Erasmus, but he gave no indication of a dissenting opinion. Thus it is very probable that Zwingli himself understood the descent in Eph 4:9-10 to refer to Christ's descent to the underworld, that is, the traditional interpretation of the passage.

Over two centuries later, J. A. Bengel (1742) likewise understood the passage in Eph 4:9-10 to refer to a *descensus ad inferos*.[29] H. A. W. Meyer, in the first edition of his commentary (1843), understood the descent mentioned in Eph 4:9 to refer not to a descent to the underworld as such (since the subsequent ascent was from the earth itself), but to Christ's 'descent' to death and the grave ("Durch die Widerlegung der

---

[25] M. Luther, *D. Martin Luthers Epistel-Auslegung*, ed. E. Ellwein, 3: *Die Briefe an die Epheser, Philipper und Kolosser* (Göttingen: Vandenhoeck u. Ruprecht, 1973) 40-59.

[26] *Lutherbibel erklärt: Die Heilige Schrift in der Übersetzung Martin Luthers mit Erläuterungen für die bibellesende Gemeinde* (Stuttgart: Württembergische Bibelanstalt, 1974) 389.

[27] H. Zwingli, *Huldreich Zwinglis Sämtliche Werke*, ed. E. Egli, G. Finsler, W. Köhler, O. Farner, F. Blanke, and L. von Muralt, 12: *Randglossen Zwinglis zu biblischen Schriften*, CR 99.1 (Leipzig: Heinsius, 1941; reprint ed., Zürich: Theologischer Verlag Zürich, 1982) 1-2, 7.

[28] Zwingli, *Huldreich Zwinglis Sämtliche Werke*, 81.

[29] J. A. Bengel, *Gnomon Novi Testamenti* (Tübingen: Schramm, 1742) 779. Bengel stated that the phrase ᾐχμαλώτευσεν αἰχμαλωσίαν in Eph 4:8 presupposed a descent into the "lower parts of the earth" ("in inferiores terrae partes").

Erklärung von der Höllenfahrt fallen auch die Beziehungen auf *den Tod und das Begräbniss* Christi").[30] Later, in the fourth edition of his commentary (1862), Meyer apparently changed his opinion. In this later edition he now preferred a descent to the underworld as the most probable interpretation of Eph 4:9-10. The object of the author, according to Meyer, was to present Christ as the one who filled the entire universe, having previously passed through the whole world. He descended from heaven into the utmost depths of Hades, and from there to the utmost heights of heaven. This realm through which Christ passed had to extend not merely to earth, but to the underworld, because the author of Ephesians had the two utmost limits of the universe in view, as the *terminus a quo* and *ad quem* of Christ's triumphal progress. The expression εἰς τὰ κατώτερα τῆς γῆς could only be accounted for when it pointed the reader to a region lower than the earth, that is, Hades.

Meyer also considered the objection that Christ ascended to heaven not from Hades but from earth to be insignificant because Christ at the point of his ascension from earth had already returned, arisen, and ascended from Hades, thus making Hades the deepest *terminus a quo* of his ascension, as it had been the *terminus ad quem* of his descent.[31]

More recent interpreters writing at the turn of the century, such as B. F. Westcott (1906) and J. A. Robinson (1904), continued to hold (more or less) the traditional view of Eph 4:7-11, that the passage referred to some sort of descent between Christ's death and resurrection, either to Hades or more simply to Sheol, the grave.[32] E. Bröse (1898) argued for a *descensus ad inferos* on the basis of the phrase τὰ κατώτερα τῆς γῆς in Eph 4:9, which referred to places "under the earth" rather than on the earth itself because it was contrasted with the phrase ὑπεράνω πάντων τῶν οὐρανῶν, which specified the locus of Christ's ascent as "above all the heavens." In this connection Bröse compared τὰ κατώτερα τῆς γῆς with καταχθονίων in Phil 2:10, which clearly reflected a 'three-storied' cosmology. He also insisted that Paul never used καταβαίνω to refer to the incarnation as John did, and pointed out that ἵνα πληρώσῃ τὰ πάντα in Eph 4:10 must include Hades.[33] Certainly Bröse's observation about Paul's use of καταβαίνω is well taken; this is a major obstacle for the view that sees the descent in Eph 4:9-10 as a reference to the incarna-

---

[30] H. A. W. Meyer, *Kritisch-exegetisches Handbuch über den Brief an die Epheser* (Göttingen: Vandenhoeck u. Ruprecht, 1843) 161-62 [emphasis his].

[31] H. A. W. Meyer, *Critical and Exegetical Handbook to the Epistle to the Ephesians*, trans. from the 4th German ed. by M. J. Evans, rev. and ed. by W. P. Dickson (New York: Funk & Wagnalls, 1884) 450-51.

[32] B. F. Westcott, *St. Paul's Epistle to the Ephesians* (London: Macmillan, 1906; reprint ed., Minneapolis: Klock & Klock, 1978); J. A. Robinson, *St. Paul's Epistle to the Ephesians*, 2d ed. (London: Macmillan, 1904; reprint ed., Grand Rapids: Kregel, 1979) 180.

[33] E. Bröse, "Der descensus ad inferos Eph. 4, 8-10," *NKZ* 9 (1898) 447-55.

tion.[34] However, the assumption that πληρόω in 4:10 must refer to 'filling' in the sense of 'occupying' is open to question. Eph 1:20-23 suggests a more non-spatial sense for πληρόω, namely, the 'filling' of the church by Christ, a meaning also supported by the use of πληρόω in Eph 5:18 where it is the Spirit who is to do the 'filling'.[35]

In the twentieth century a number of scholars still interpreted Eph 4:9-10 as some form of a *descensus ad inferos*. W. Bousset (1913) endorsed such a view as an attempt to explain the early Christian κύριος-cult in terms of an adaptation to the worship of hellenistic deities.[36] Another scholar who argued for the traditional concept of a *descensus ad inferos* in Eph 4:9-10 was J.-M. Vosté (1921). Vosté's discussion of the problems in Eph 4:7-11 was fairly complete, beginning with the OT context of Ps 68:19 (quoted in Eph 4:8). Although the psalm was originally an ascent-psalm of Yahweh, Paul made some changes in the form of the citation and applied the psalm to Christ. Vosté considered the addition of the word πρῶτον in the Greek text of Eph 4:9 (*primum* in the Vulgate text) dubious, although he agreed with the sense of the addition (which necessitated a descent of Christ prior to the ascent mentioned in the psalm). In his discussion of the nature of the descent itself, Vosté mentioned the three major interpretive possibilities: (a) a descent from heaven at the incarnation; (b) a descent to the underworld ("ad inferos, in sheôl"); or (c) a descent for the distribution of the gifts and for the indwelling of the Spirit in the souls of the just. The latter view was attributed to Abbott, following von Soden, although Vosté rejected it without lengthy consideration as being contrary to Pauline logic, which would have necessitated a prior descent. As far as the two remaining possibilities were concerned, Vosté considered the determining factor to be the identification of the "inferiores partes terrae" (in Greek, τὰ κατώτερα μέρη τῆς γῆς). He discussed the possible interpretations of the genitive τῆς γῆς and concluded that a partitive genitive, indicating the locus of the descent as Sheol or the underworld ("inferos"), was preferable. This was supported by the analogy of scripture (Ps 62 [63]:10 and Ps 138 [139]:15 are mentioned), by doctrinal and literary analogies with Rom 10:7, Acts 2:27, 1 Pet 3:19 and 4:6, and by the logic of the context, which mentioned the locus of Christ's ascent as "super omnes coelos"

---

[34] This view is discussed below, 14-23.

[35] See below, ch. 6, 181, n. 28, for bibliography related to the problems of the πλήρωμα terminology in Eph 1:20-23, most of which are beyond the scope of the present work.

[36] W. Bousset, *Kyrios Christos: A History of the Belief in Christ from the Beginning of Christianity to Irenaeus*, trans. J. E. Steely (Nashville: Abingdon, 1970) 30-31. The 1st German ed. appeared in 1913; the 4th German ed. was published in Göttingen in 1935 by Vandenhoeck u. Ruprecht.

(ὑπεράνω πάντων τῶν οὐρανῶν).[37]

H. Odeberg (1934) also argued for a traditional understanding of the *descensus ad inferos*, although his analysis proceeded along lines that were more philosophical than linguistic or grammatical. He noted that an acceptance of Christ's descent into the underworld was not bound up with any idea of the liberation of imprisoned or condemned spirits.[38] The main argument Odeberg offered in favor of such a descent was that Christ must have been victorious over all the evil cosmic powers of the universe, and this implied he pursued them to the farthest and deepest recesses of their activity:

> He [Christ] must, hence, go beyond the surface-world, in which fallen mankind dwells, to the depths of Darkness, the utmost sphere of the authority of evil.[39]

Odeberg apparently overlooked the significant fact that the author of Ephesians did not locate the evil powers in the underworld, but in the air, where they were subject to defeat upon Christ's victorious ascent (cf. Eph 1:21, 2:2, 3:10, and 6:12). Therefore to overcome the powers a *descensus ad inferos* would not be required. Another scholar who supported such a traditional view of the *descensus* in Eph 4:9-10 was P. Benoit, in an article on the Pauline perspective demonstrated by the Epistle to the Ephesians (1937).[40]

E. F. Ströter (1952) also understood the descent of Christ in Eph 4:9-10 to be a descent to the underworld. During this time Christ preached to the imprisoned spirits, as described at greater length in 1 Pet 3:18-21. Ströter differed from many interpreters in thinking that this descent was not made during the *triduum* but after Christ's resurrection on the third day. At that time (and not before) Christ was given the keys of Hades and death and had unhindered access into and out of the underworld. He went there not as a dead person, himself bound by death, but as the one who had been dead and was now alive for ever and ever, holding the key to the realm of shadows.[41]

F. W. Beare (1953) acknowledged the associations of Psalm 68 with Pentecost in the early church, but still managed to assert (with surprising dogmatism) that the phrase εἰς τὰ κατώτερα μέρη τῆς γῆς in Eph 4:9 "cannot mean simply the earth as lower than the heavens. It is certainly

---

[37] J.-M. Vosté, *Commentarius in epistolam ad Ephesios* (Paris: Gabalda, 1921) 182-84.

[38] H. Odeberg, *The View of the Universe in the Epistle to the Ephesians* (Lund: Gleerup, 1934) 17-18.

[39] Odeberg, *The View of the Universe*, 19.

[40] P. Benoit, "L'horizon paulinien de l'épître aux Éphésiens," *RB* 46 (1937) 348.

[41] E. F. Ströter, *Die Herrlichkeit des Leibes Christi: Der Epheserbrief*, 2d ed. (Gümligen-Bern: Siloah, 1952) 99-100.

a reference—the earliest in Christian literature—to the descent of Christ into Hades."[42] Beare gave no evidence to support his contention in spite of the certainty with which he asserted it. Another influential advocate of this 'traditional' interpretation of Eph 4:9 is F. Büchsel, whose *TDNT* article on κατώτερος has become well known.[43] Büchsel mentioned that καταβαίνειν might be a technical term for descent to the underworld, although he wisely acknowledged that this did not prove determinative for its use in Eph 4:7-10. Neither was the use of the genitive phrase τῆς γῆς conclusive, although a partitive genitive following μέρη would have been simpler as an explanation for the use of the genitive here. Büchsel believed the strongest argument in favor of a descent of Christ to the place of the dead was the antithesis to the descent found in Eph 4:10: the one who descended "into the lower parts of the earth" (εἰς τὰ κατώτερα μέρη τῆς γῆς) in Eph 4:9 was described as "the one who ascended above all the heavens" (ὁ ἀναβὰς ὑπεράνω πάντων τῶν οὐρανῶν). For Büchsel, as for E. Bröse, these phrases denoted the outer limits of Christ's journey.[44] Since the locus of his ascent was at God's right hand in the height of heaven, the logical antithesis would not be the earth itself, but under the earth, i. e., the sphere of the underworld, the place of the dead. J. Schneider in his *TDNT* article on μέρος acknowledged his debt to Büchsel; on account of Büchsel's article on κατώτερος he modified his own view of the descent in Eph 4:9-10.[45] Schneider stated in this article on μέρος that he had been persuaded by Büchsel's arguments that the locus of Christ's descent was the realm of the dead. In a previous *TDNT* article Schneider had endorsed the view that Christ's descent in Eph 4:9-10 referred to his incarnation.[46]

Yet another recent advocate of the *descensus ad inferos* in Eph 4:7-10 was A. T. Hanson (1980), who examined at length the scriptural background of the doctrine of the *descensus*.[47] Hanson surveyed a considerable number of other interpreters with regard to their views on the *descensus* in Eph 4:9-10, citing with approval the arguments of Bröse and Büchsel and rejecting those of Schlier[48] and Caird.[49] Hanson concluded that the author of Ephesians held that Christ made the *descensus ad inferos*, and this lay behind Eph 4:9-10. Finding in the quotation he cited from Ps 68:19 a reference to Christ's victorious ascent, and hold-

---

42 F. W. Beare, "The Epistle to the Ephesians," *IB* 10 (New York: Abingdon, 1953) 689.
43 F. Büchsel, s.v. "κατώτερος," *TDNT* 3.641-42.
44 See the discussion of Bröse's view above, 8.
45 J. Schneider, s.v. "μέρος," *TDNT* 4.597-98.
46 S.v. "καταβαίνω," *TDNT* 1.523.
47 A. T. Hanson, *The New Testament Interpretation of Scripture* (London: SPCK, 1980) 135-150.
48 H. Schlier's view is discussed below, 15-16.
49 See below, 27-28, for a description of G. B. Caird's view.

ing to a doctrine of the *descensus* as well, the author of Ephesians wrote
verses 9-10 in order to introduce a reference to the *descensus* into the
context. What Hanson did not explain adequately was why the author
of Ephesians would have felt compelled to introduce such a reference to
the *descensus* into the context of Eph 4:7-10 (assuming that he did hold
to such a belief).[50]

Still another interpreter whose view of Eph 4:9-10 was apparently influenced by Büchsel was J. D. G. Dunn (1980). Dunn essentially followed Büchsel's arguments: (1) the phrase τὰ κατώτερα μέρη τῆς γῆς
was most naturally read as a synonym for Hades, as indicated by references like Ps 63:9 [LXX Ps 62:10]; (2) a genitive following μέρη was
most likely partitive, not appositive; and (3) the logical antithesis of
"above all the heavens" in Eph 4:10 was "underneath the earth."[51]
Thus Dunn saw Eph 4:9-10 as a variation of the common NT association
of Christ's death with his resurrection.

1.2. *A Modern Variation on the Traditional Interpretation*

A further variation of the traditional view (that the descent of Christ in
Eph 4:9-10 was a *descensus ad inferos*) deserves brief mention. It is becoming increasingly common among recent interpreters to relate the locus of the descent to Sheol, the place of the dead, without attempting to
specify what Christ did there (if anything) or whom he encountered
while there (if anyone). With this interpretation the *descensus* in Eph
4:9-10 was simply a way of referring to Jesus' physical death, without
introducing speculation about any activities he may have conducted in
the underworld during the *triduum*. G. H. P. Thompson (1967) preferred
this understanding of Christ's descent in Eph 4:9-10. He suggested that
the "slight alterations" Paul made to the quotation from Ps 68:19 indicated he might be following a "Jewish paraphrase," by which Thompson probably meant *Targum* Psalms.[52] Since the commentary was on the
text of the New English Bible, Thompson discussed briefly the possibility that the descent of Eph 4:9-10 referred to the incarnation (the NEB
renders τὰ κατώτερα μέρη τῆς γῆς as an appositive genitive: "he descended to the lowest level, down to the very earth"). But Thompson
concluded that the alternative translation (NEB footnote: "descended
to the regions beneath the earth") was to be preferred. This, said

---

[50] A. T. Hanson's arguments in favor of a *descensus ad inferos* in Eph 4:9-10 are critiqued
at much greater length in ch. 2 of the present work. See below, 59-61.

[51] J. D. G. Dunn, *Christology in the Making: A New Testament Inquiry into the Origins of
the Doctrine of the Incarnation* (London: SCM, 1980) 186-87.

[52] G. H. P. Thompson, *The Letters of Paul to the Ephesians, to the Colossians, and to
Philemon*, CBC (Cambridge: Cambridge University Press, 1967) 67-68. It was the editorial
policy of the series to avoid technical references to extra-biblical literature (General Editor's
Preface, v).

Thompson, was a way of describing physical death, and thus stressed that Jesus became involved in the full range of human experience— even death itself—not as an outside observer, but as an insider.

This was essentially the same position taken by N. Hugedé (1973). He attributed the inference of a descent in the midrashic exegesis (Eph 4:9-10) of the quotation from Ps 68:19 (Eph 4:8) to Paul's preference for strong antitheses. Hugedé mentioned the possibility that the genitive in the phrase εἰς τὰ κατώτερα μέρη τῆς γῆς may be an appositive referring to the earth itself as opposed to heaven ("Aux cieux s'oppose la terre, qui sont les deux aspects de la carrière du Christ"). Thus the descent of Christ in Eph 4:9-10 could refer to his incarnation, and this corresponded perfectly to the author's intention, which was to establish a relationship between the psalm quotation and the redemptive career of Christ considered in its two antithetical aspects, earth and heaven. Although Hugedé found much in favor of such an interpretation, he ultimately preferred (after briefly examining the evidence for understanding τῆς γῆς as partitive genitive) to understand τὰ κατώτερα μέρη τῆς γῆς as a reference to the regions below the earth itself ("les parties inférieures de la terre"). In the formula κατέβη εἰς τὰ κατώτερα μέρη τῆς γῆς he saw an allusion to Christ's death on the cross ("la fin tragique du Christ") and his sojourn among the dead ("son séjour parmi les morts"). Hugedé made it clear that he did not consider this a reference to the *descensus ad inferos* in the traditional sense because he specifically dismissed the idea that Christ between his death and his resurrection paid a visit "in spirit" to the dead in Hades. Such a belief, expressed by certain of the Fathers, was too dependent upon Greek mythology and today had been abandoned.[53]

Another recent interpreter whose view of the descent probably belongs in this category was F. Rienecker (1961). Rienecker's actual view is very difficult to determine; he quoted Luther's translation of Eph 4:9 with approval (which would seem to imply an understanding of the descent in terms of the 'traditional' view, as Luther did) but he then stated that this descent of Christ to the lowest parts of the earth was connected to the reality and completeness of his incarnation. In what appears to be an attempt to relate the passage to contemporary experience, Rienecker stated how Christ descended to the uttermost depths of human experience as well as to the deepest part of the earth, that is, the last, deepest depth of all:

---

[53] N. Hugedé, *L'Épître aux Éphésiens* (Geneva: Labor et Fides, 1973) 152-54. Hugedé stated his rejection of the 'traditional' concept of the *descensus ad inferos* in n. 49, 153, where he added that such ideas were probably transferred to Eph 4:9-10 from existing interpretations of 1 Pet 3:19-20 and 4:6.

In den letzten Tiefen hat Christus gekämpft, und da hat Er gesiegt. In den letzten Tiefen ist Er gewesen bis zur Gottverlassenheit, damit aus Ihm heraus die Neuschöpfung einer Menschheit kommen könnte, die sich darstellt in der Gemeinde. In diesen letzten Tiefen ist die Sünde gesühnt, in diesen tiefsten Tiefen ist der Fall überwunden, es ist der Schlange der Kopf zertreten, der Tod überwunden und der Gewalthaber des Todes, der Teufel, besiegt. Und der, der hinuntergefahren ist in diese letzten Tiefen, ist siegreich zurückgekehrt.[54]

Here Rienecker dealt not so much with the original meaning of the text of Eph 4:9-10 as with its theological significance, especially in terms of the human condition.

Still another recent writer who related the descent to the death of Christ was F. Mußner (1982), although he acknowledged the difficulty of resolving the precise meaning of the phrase εἰς τὰ κατώτερα μέρη τῆς γῆς in Eph 4:9.[55] Against the view that the descent was a reference to Christ's incarnation, he pointed out that the author of Ephesians could simply have written "he descended to the earth" rather than introducing the reference to the "lower regions" of the earth. Since in the letter to the Ephesians the demonic and satanic 'powers' were located in the realm of the air (2:2, 6:12), it was more probable that the author meant by the phrase "the lower parts of the earth" a reference to Sheol, the place of the dead. Mußner admitted that nowhere else in Ephesians was there a reference to Sheol; if the phrase in 4:9 described the realm of the dead it was the only place in the letter to do so. Nevertheless, this was most probably what was intended, or else behind Eph 4:9 was a reference to the more traditional idea of a descent to the underworld (*ad inferos*). According to Mußner, the question could not be resolved with certainty in the final analysis.

2. The Descent in Eph 4:7-11 as the Incarnation

Within the last century two other significant interpretations have gained popularity, and each of these has seriously challenged the traditional view (with its variations). The more widely held of these alternative views understands the descent in Eph 4:9-10 as a reference to the incarnation. Such an understanding of the descent motif in Ephesians 4 is not new; in substance it dates back at least as far as Theodore of Mopsuestia (428 CE).[56] In the later medieval period P. Abelard, in the twelfth century, apparently held such a view. The descent of Christ, according

---

[54] F. Rienecker, *Der Brief des Paulus an die Epheser*, WStB 8 (Wuppertal: R. Brockhaus, 1961) 143.

[55] F. Mußner, *Der Brief an die Epheser*, ÖTBK 10 (Gütersloh: Gerd Mohn, 1982) 123.

[56] Theodore of Mopsuestia, "Ad Ephesios," *In Epistolas B. Pauli Commentarii*, ed. H. B. Swete (Cambridge: Cambridge University Press, 1880) 1.112-96.

to Abelard, referred to his humiliation when he entered human existence at the incarnation; the "lower parts of the earth" ("inferiores partes terre") described the humble and poorer region of the earth itself to which Christ came.[57] Even Aquinas, who ultimately preferred to interpret Eph 4:9-10 as a *descensus ad inferos*, demonstrated a knowledge of the view that the descent referred to Christ's incarnation.[58] During the period of the Reformation a somewhat similar view which saw in the descent a reference to the crucifixion as Christ's supreme humiliation was held by J. Calvin, apparently following Chrysostom.[59] More recently such a view was endorsed by J. Macpherson, who in his *Commentary on St Paul's Epistle to the Ephesians* (1892) held that the descent of Eph 4:9-10 referred to the incarnation, including Christ's earthly sufferings and his death on the cross.[60]

In general, those who hold this view must understand the genitive τῆς γῆς in Eph 4:9 as an appositive genitive. In this case the genitive further specifies the preceding phrase which it modifies: the expression τὰ κατώτερα μέρη τῆς γῆς is equivalent to "the lower regions, namely, the earth." Such an understanding of the genitive phrase τῆς γῆς has become increasingly popular among interpreters and grammarians in the twentieth century.[61]

H. Schlier (1930) saw Eph 4:9-10 as a reference to the descent and ascent of the redeemer (he was to develop this view more fully in his 1957 commentary, see below).[62] W. L. Knox (1939) understood 4:9-10 as a reference both to the incarnation and to the ascension.[63] Following

---

[57] A. Landgraf, *Commentarius Cantabrigiensis in Epistolas Paule e Schola Petri Abaelardi: 2. in Epistolam ad Corinthios, I^am et II^am ad Galatas et ad Ephesios*, PMS 2 (Notre Dame, IN: University of Notre Dame, 1939) 415-16.

[58] St. Thomas Aquinas, *Commentary on Saint Paul's Epistle to the Ephesians*, 160-61. For a fuller discussion of Aquinas' views, see above, 5-6.

[59] J. Calvin, *Commentarius in epistolam ad Ephesios*, CR 15 (Brunswick: Schwetschke, 1895), cols. 141-240. How Calvin derived this understanding of the *descensus* from Chrysostom is not clear, since Chrysostom clearly understood the *descensus* in Eph 4:9-10 to refer to a descent of Christ to Hades (see above, 6). Furthermore, G. B. Caird stated that Calvin understood the descent of Christ in Eph 4:9-10 to refer to the incarnation ("The Descent of Christ in Ephesians 4, 7-11," *SE* 2 [= TU 87], ed. F. L. Cross [Berlin: Akademie, 1964] 536). Presumably Calvin himself saw the descent as referring to the crucifixion, but as the lowest, most humiliating aspect of the incarnation, and this may have given rise to the apparently differing formulations of Calvin's view.

[60] J. Macpherson, *Commentary on St Paul's Epistle to the Ephesians* (Edinburgh: Clark, 1892) 302-3.

[61] For a survey of modern scholars who have understood τῆς γῆς in Eph 4:9 as an appositive genitive, see ch. 2, 50-54.

[62] H. Schlier, *Christus und die Kirche im Epheserbrief*, BHT 6 (Tübingen: Mohr, 1930). The view was repeated and expanded in his commentary, *Der Brief an die Epheser* (Düsseldorf: Patmos-Verlag, 1957), discussed more fully below.

[63] W. L. Knox, *St. Paul and the Church of the Gentiles* (Cambridge: Cambridge University Press, 1939) 194ff.

Schlier, E. Percy (1946) took the phrase κατώτερα μέρη τῆς γῆς to refer
only to the earth itself as the lower regions, in comparison with heaven.
But rather than a reference to a heavenly redeemer myth involving a descent and ascent, Percy saw in Eph 4:9-10 (as Knox did) a reference to
the incarnation.[64]

H. Bietenhard (1951) acknowledged that Paul in Eph 4:8 quoted the
same psalm which the rabbis used to refer to Moses' ascension to heav-
en, but Paul interpreted it as a reference to Jesus Christ. Yet Eph 4:9 did
not speak of a descent to Hades, for such an idea would be superfluous
in this context. So the phrase κατώτερα μέρη τῆς γῆς described not the
underworld, but the earth, which in the cosmos was 'under' heaven.[65]
Bietenhard did not explain why a reference to the incarnation in this
context would be any less superfluous that a reference to a descent to
the underworld.

M. Dibelius (1953) mentioned von Soden's view,[66] observing that
the "descent" was related to the "giving of gifts." But he rejected von
Soden's interpretation because he considered such a meaning for καταβαίνειν remote, and added that ἔδωκεν δόματα proved nothing because
it appeared in the quotation. Quoting Theodore of Mopsuestia, Dibelius
took the view that Eph 4:9-10 referred to the incarnation, although he
believed the addition of πρῶτον in 4:9 to be a later scribal gloss.[67]

H. Schlier (1957) understood the passage in light of the Gnostic
'redeemed Redeemer' mythology ("der Urmensch-Erlösermythus"),
comparing καταβῆναι to the Johannine usage (John 6:62, 20:17, et al.).
The phrase τῆς γῆς was therefore understood as an appositive genitive,
confirmed by the observation that elsewhere in Ephesians the evil
'powers' were not in Hades or Sheol but in 'heaven'. Schlier understood the descent itself in 4:9 to refer to the incarnation. The insertion of
πρῶτον (the major textual variant in Eph 4:9) was rejected because it
was somehow indicative of the 'descensus ad inferos' view. It is not
clear how this connection was made since the inclusion of πρῶτον in
Eph 4:9 would be perfectly compatible with Schlier's own view.[68]

F. W. Grosheide (1960) also interpreted the descent of Christ in Eph
4:9-10 as a reference to the incarnation. The use of the verb ἀναβαίνειν
in the quotation from Ps 68:19 suggested also καταβαίνειν, a related descent similar to the descent and ascent mentioned in John 3:13; this was

[64] E. Percy, *Die Probleme der Kolosser- und Epheserbriefe* (Lund: Gleerup, 1946) 274.

[65] H. Bietenhard, *Die himmlische Welt im Urchristentum und Spätjudentum* (Tübingen: Mohr, 1951) 237.

[66] H. von Soden's view is discussed below, 24.

[67] M. Dibelius, *An die Kolosser, Epheser, an Philemon*, HNT 12 (Tübingen: Mohr, 1953) 80.

[68] H. Schlier, *Der Brief an die Epheser* (Düsseldorf: Patmos-Verlag, 1957) 192.

introduced by the author of Ephesians in 4:9. The phrase εἰς τὰ κατώ-τερα μέρη τῆς γῆς in Eph 4:9 did not describe the parts lower than the earth itself, but the earth as the region lower than heaven. Grosheide mentioned several alternative explanations for the passage, including the traditional view that Christ descended to hell, a reference to Christ's incarnation, or merely a reference to his death and burial. Because verse 10 speaks of an ascension to heaven Grosheide thought the descent most likely referred to Christ's descent to earth at the incarnation. He understood τῆς γῆς as a genitive of apposition, citing additional examples of this usage in 2 Cor 5:5, Rom 4:11, and Rom 8:23.[69]

Basing his view on the application by *Targum* Psalms of Ps 68:19 to Moses, J. Cambier (1963) argued that Paul had made an analogous application of the Psalm to Christ: he descended to earth (the incarnation) and then ascended to heaven (the resurrection and ascension) to affirm his universal sovereignty. Cambier further asserted that *'monter au ciel'* in Paul was never used to describe the ascension, but referred to Christ's glorification. In Cambier's opinion it was even less probable that the descent in Eph 4:9 involved a descent of the Holy Spirit or a descent to hell or at the parousia.[70] Actually Cambier's own reconstruction of the argument favored a subsequent descent (at Pentecost), but he did not appear to be aware of this. Neither did he discuss the textual problem with the insertion or deletion of πρῶτον in 4:9, nor the fact that his own view relegated the midrashic expansion found in 4:9-10 to a mere parenthesis in the argument of Ephesians 4.

F. Foulkes (1963) understood the descent of Eph 4:9 to refer to either the incarnation or the death of Christ. He did not state a clear preference for one view over the other, although it appears from the discussion following that Foulkes was inclined to interpret the descent as a reference to the incarnation. The passage stressed the universality of Christ's presence (there was no place in existence, in earth or heaven, where his presence was not known or felt) and the identity of the one who ascended with the one "who came down and lived among men, sharing their sorrows, trials, and temptations."[71] Foulkes also rejected the notion of a subsequent descent at Pentecost on the grounds that the

---

[69] F. W. Grosheide, *De Brief van Paulus aan de Efeziërs*, CNT(K) (Kampen: Kok, 1960) 65-66.

[70] J. Cambier, "La signification christologique d'Éph. IV.7-10," *NTS* 9 (1963) 262-75. Cambier did not indicate whether some other scholar proposed the view he mentioned, that the descent in Eph 4:9 referred to the descent of Christ at the parousia (275); I have been unable to locate any other reference to such a position. Cambier's own view was reiterated in his exposition of Ephesians published three years later (*Vie Chrétienne en Église: L'Épître aux Éphésiens lue aux chrétiens d'aujourd'hui* [Paris: Desclée, 1966] 127-29).

[71] F. Foulkes, *The Epistle of Paul to the Ephesians: An Introduction and Commentary*, TNTC (London: Tyndale, 1963) 116-17.

giving of gifts to men was associated in the text with the ascent, not the descent.[72]

M. Zerwick (1963) also took the position that the locus of Christ's descent was the earth itself and the descent referred to the incarnation. Zerwick observed that in Paul's quotation from Ps 68:19 the very point the apostle had wished to make was missing, since the psalm spoke not of giving gifts to men, but of accepting gifts from men. Paul, said Zerwick, was following a rabbinic interpretation of the psalm, which applied the verse in question to Moses who ascended Mt. Sinai to receive the law and bring it down to men as a gift. Zerwick did not mention the source of this rabbinic interpretation of Ps 68:19 or its occurrence in *Tg. Psalms*, nor did he comment on the difficulties in dating the rabbinic sources. In the midrashic explanation which followed the quotation (verses 9-10), Zerwick understood Paul to be attempting to prove that the only one who could have ascended to heaven was Jesus Christ, the one who had first descended from heaven. Although Zerwick did not cite any text in support of this view, his language is suggestive of John 3:13, and it is clear that he subscribed to a prior descent at the incarnation.[73]

G. Johnston (1967) called Ps 68:19 a lection for Pentecost (without citing any proof); the alteration from 'receiving' to 'giving' in Eph 4:8 was described as "deliberate." Johnston mentioned briefly B. Lindars' view that the psalm was deliberately modified in the interest of doctrine on the model of the Qumrân prophetic commentaries on OT texts. As far as the descent itself was concerned, Johnston understood it as a descent to the earth itself, not the underworld, because he interpreted Ephesians in light of a gnostic heresy.[74] Thus it is clear (although not explicitly stated) that he understood the descent of Christ in Eph 4:9-10 as a reference to the incarnation.

J. Ernst (1970) noted the difficulty of establishing the connection of all the elements of Eph 4:8-13. He also observed that the relation of ἀναβάς to the ascension and κατέβη to the incarnation was disputed, as was the meaning of τὰ κατώτερα κ.τ.λ. as a reference to the earth as the realm of humanity or to a descent to the underworld. Ernst did not offer any detailed critique of the various positions, nor any significant defense of his own view. He only stated in passing that a reference to the incarnation was more probable than any other interpretation.[75] The pos-

---

[72] Foulkes, *The Epistle of Paul to the Ephesians*, 117.

[73] M. Zerwick, *The Epistle to the Ephesians*, trans. K. Smyth (New York: Herder & Herder, 1969) 106-7.

[74] G. Johnston, *Ephesians, Philippians Colossians and Philemon*, NCB (London: Thomas Nelson, 1967) 18-19.

[75] J. Ernst, *Pleroma und Pleroma Christi: Geschichte und Deutung eines Begriffs der*

sibility of a subsequent descent was not mentioned, despite the appearance of G. B. Caird's article arguing for such an interpretation some six years earlier.[76]

R. N. Longenecker (1970) believed that Eph 4:8-10 probably incorporated a traditional understanding among early Christians, since both the citation of Ps 68:19 and the parenthetical comment which followed it were given as though commonly assumed. What Longenecker called "a statement of the obvious" was made in order to bridge the gap in the argument from the "gift of Christ" in Eph 4:7 to a discussion of Christ's gifts in 4:11-16. Thus the references to Christ's descent and ascent reflected an earlier tradition; they were not original with Paul. The original motif probably had to do only with the humiliation of Christ's incarnation, servitude, temptation, and death, themes which occur in a number of NT passages like Phil 2:6-11, John 1:1-18, 3:13, 6:62, Heb 2:5-18, and 5:1-10. Soon it was apparently extended to include a *descensus ad inferos* as held in the second century (if not already present in 1 Pet 3:19 and 4:6).[77] Although Longenecker did not explicitly state his view concerning the interpretation of Eph 4:8-10, he would probably have related the descent in 4:9-10 to Christ's incarnation (and possibly to his death also).

J. Gnilka (1971) acknowledged that Psalm 68 and Exodus 19 were the Jewish synagogue lessons for Pentecost, and that Christians, reflecting upon this tradition, could have set the work of the ascended Christ and the 'ascended' Moses in parallel. However, this did not mean that one could already assume the existence, at the time Ephesians was written, of a Christian Pentecost.[78] Did the descent, then, refer to the incarnation or to the sending of the Holy Spirit (i.e., at Pentecost)? Gnilka thought that in light of Eph 4:10, which established the full identity between the one who ascended and the one who descended, only a reference to the incarnation was possible.[79]

---

paulinischen Antilegomena (Regensburg: Friedrich Pustet, 1970) 136.

[76] This article by G. B. Caird ("The Descent of Christ in Ephesians 4, 7-11," *SE* 2 [= TU 87], ed. F. L. Cross [Berlin: Akademie, 1964] 535-435) will be discussed in more detail below; see 27-28.

[77] R. N. Longenecker, *The Christology of Early Jewish Christianity*, SBT, 2d ser., 17 (London: SCM, 1970) 60.

[78] J. Gnilka, *Der Epheserbrief*, HTKNT (Freiburg: Herder, 1971) 208. Gnilka meant by a 'Christian' Pentecost a celebration of Pentecost parallel to the Jewish celebration in which the descent of the Spirit (or of Christ in the person of the Spirit) was celebrated. This was almost certainly an allusion to G. B. Caird's article ("The Descent of Christ in Ephesians 4, 7-11," *SE* 2 [= TU 87], ed. F. L. Cross [Berlin: Akademie, 1964] 535-45) which will be discussed in more detail below; see 27-28.

[79] Gnilka pointed out in n. 8 (208) that the identity here affirmed between the one who ascended and the one who descended was something *other* than the identification of the *works* of the Lord (κύριος) and the Spirit (πνεῦμα) found in 2 Cor 3:17 (*contra* Caird).

Like Gnilka, H.-J. Klauck (1973) saw the identification between the one who ascended and the one who descended in Eph 4:10 as suggesting a reference to the incarnation. Klauck argued that the genitive τῆς γῆς in Eph 4:9 should be understood as appositional or epexegetic, not as comparative or partitive. Although by form a comparative, κατώτερος in the phrase τὰ κατώτερα μέρη τῆς γῆς could in later Greek be used as a superlative or even a positive. Thus the statement in Eph 4:9 (paraphrased) could mean, "Er stieg herab zur Erde, die (vom Himmel aus gesehen) tief unten liegt."[80] Klauck also saw in the cosmology of Ephesians further evidence that the earth was the destination of Christ in his descent, rather than the underworld. The 'stories' described by the author of Ephesians were not underworld, earth, and heaven, but earth, an intermediate zone ("Zwischenbereiche"), and heaven. It was in this 'intermediate zone' between earth and heaven that the cosmic powers were located according to the author of Ephesians (cf. Eph 1:21; 2:2; 3:10; and 6:12). These powers were overcome by Christ at his ascent to heaven from earth, not during a supposed descent to the underworld. Thus for Klauck the descent in Eph 4:9-10 was best understood as a reference to the incarnation.

R. Schnackenburg (1973) stated that a subsequent descent of Christ (by the Spirit at Pentecost) in Ephesians 4 was ruled out for two main reasons. First, verses 9 and 10 did not easily lend themselves to such an interpretation. Even if 4:9 allowed it, 4:10 would rule it out because the latter verse emphasized the ascent again (with the final ἵνα clause) rather than the descent. Second, the portrayal of the procession of the Spirit at Pentecost as a descending of Christ would be unique in the NT. A total identification of Christ with the Spirit (which Schnackenburg thought this view would necessitate) was foreign both to Paul (including 2 Cor. 3:17) and John (John 14:16-20 and 20:22).[81] Schnackenburg concluded that there were two remaining explanations possible for Eph 4:9: a descent to the underworld or the incarnation. He favored the second alternative: the author of Ephesians interpreted ἀναβάς from the quotation in 4:9 and applied it to Christ using Jewish methods.[82] This would be easily understood if the author were opposing a Jewish exegetical tradition which referred Ps 68:19 to Moses.[83] But why intro-

---

[80] H.-J. Klauck, "Das Amt in der Kirche nach Eph 4, 1-16," *WiWeis* 36 (1973) 81-110. His paraphrase of Eph 4:9 is found on p. 94.

[81] R. Schnackenburg, "Christus, Geist und Gemeinde (Eph. 4:1-16)" in *Christ and Spirit in the New Testament*, ed. B. Lindars and S. Smalley (Cambridge: Cambridge University Press, 1973) 279-96. References to Eph 4:9-10 are found on pp. 287ff.

[82] Probably Schnackenburg was referring to a form of midrash here, although in the article cited he did not explicitly state what method of Jewish exegesis he had in mind.

[83] Jewish traditions associating Moses with Ps 68:19 as background to Eph 4:7-11 will be examined thoroughly in chapter 3 of the present work. In his later commentary (discussed be-

duce a reference to the descent? Schnackenburg explained that it was probably because the writer wished to show Christ, who had ascended on high, in his exalted place (cf. Eph 1:20-23). The phrase τὰ κατώτερα κ.τ.λ. was best explained from christological concepts like those of Chrysostom on Phil 2:6-11. But this need not involve a descent to the underworld. If the purpose of the descent-ascent as given in Eph 4:10 was that "all be filled," we should expect to find a reference to a 'power' in the underworld. But according to the cosmology of Ephesians, the powers were located not in the underworld but in the air.[84] This led Schnackenburg to conclude that an allusion to the Christian celebration of Pentecost in the passage was unlikely. The quotation from Ps 68:19 may have been suitable to Pentecost, but this did not seem likely because the Spirit was not directly mentioned in Eph 4:9-10.

M. Barth (1974) thought (like Schnackenburg) that Eph 4:8-10 placed more emphasis on the ascent than on the descent.[85] The descent itself was not a *descensus ad inferos* for a number of reasons: (1) the LXX used terminology to describe Sheol which differed from that of Eph 4:9;[86] (2) other references to the spiritual 'powers' in Eph 2:2, 6:12, and (possibly) 3:15 did not locate them "under the earth"; (3) in Ephesians the victory of Christ was achieved in his exaltation (cf. 1:19-21), not in a descent to the underworld;[87] (4) a descent to hell would be a second descent following Christ's descent to earth, but the text does not imply a 'two-stage' descent;[88] (5) parallels to Eph 4:8-10 such as John 3:13 and 17:5 did not suggest a reference to hell; and (6) a reference to the conquest of the underworld would be alien to the context of Eph 4:9. Thus Barth concluded that the descent of Christ mentioned in Eph 4:9 referred to his incarnation and most probably to his crucifix-

---

low) Schnackenburg rejected the idea that the author's emphasis in Eph 4:9-10 was directed against Moses.

[84] Although Schnackenburg did not cite a specific reference, this was probably an allusion to Eph 2:2 rather than 6:12.

[85] M. Barth, *Ephesians: Translation and Commentary on Chapters 4-6*, AB 34A (Garden City, NY: Doubleday, 1974) 432-34.

[86] Examples cited were Gen 44:29, Pss 62 (63):10 and 138 (139):15, and Ezek 32:18, 24.

[87] This is a valid point, but the question remains, why did the author feel it necessary to introduce reference to a descent at all? The victorious ascent was sufficiently affirmed in the quotation from Ps 68:19.

[88] However, neither does the text of Eph 4:8-10 specifically mention a descent to earth at the incarnation (which would be the first 'stage' of a 'two-stage' descent). Ephesians contains no other explicit reference to the incarnation or to the pre-incarnate Christ, although Barth (and others) who argued for a reference to the incarnation by rejecting a 'two-stage' descent appeared to assume that the author of Ephesians shared a concept of the pre-incarnate Christ similar to the Johannine concept of the pre-incarnate Λόγος found in John 1:1-18. Whether Ephesians was written by Paul or not, it is far from clear that such a concept of a pre-incarnate Christ is reflected here.

ion.[89] Elsewhere Barth suggested that the author of Ephesians was acquainted with *Targum* Psalms or other antecedents of the tradition later found in the Talmud and rabbinic literature, and in his exposition of Ps 68:19 in Eph 4:9-10 engaged in a correction of the contemporary exegesis of the psalm. According to Barth, what the author did could be called a midrash.[90]

J. Ernst (1974) also understood the descent in Eph 4:9-10 to refer to the incarnation. Ernst mentioned the later Jewish interpretation of Ps 68:19 as a reference to Moses' ascent of Mt. Sinai to receive the Law and give it to men.[91] The author of Ephesians altered this tradition by replacing Moses with Christ and interpreting the distribution of the gifts as the installation of the offices mentioned in Eph 4:11-16. Before this, however (in a midrashic exegesis from the first part of Ps 68:19), what Ernst described as "a cosmic exaltation-christology" ("eine kosmische Erhöhungschristologie") was developed, which interrupted the immediate context ("die zwar den unmittelbaren Zusammenhang unterbricht").[92] It is from the ascension that the necessity of a previous descent was inferred. Ernst then stated that although the Moses-typology still had a formal effect on this passage, the primary emphasis was on the christological dogma: the ascension took precedence over the incarnation. The concept of Christ's pre-existence was assumed throughout by the author of Ephesians. Ernst also mentioned the chiastic arrangement of the ascent and descent according to the formula AB—BA, although he thought it questionable whether the order of ascent—descent represented here could be traced back exclusively to the Moses-typology. More in the forefront was the imagery of the cosmic triumphal procession. Ernst was unwilling to rule out completely the possibility that the mythical concept of the ascent of the 'redeemed Redeemer' ("Urmensch-Erlöser") underlies the passage, but in the final analysis he acknowledged that the theological content of these verses remained without analogy.

R. Schnackenburg (1982) addressed again the problems of Eph 4:7-11. While his overall position regarding the descent as a reference to the

---

[89] M. Barth, *Ephesians: Translation and Commentary on Chapters 4-6*, 434.

[90] Barth, *Ephesians*, 476. Barth noted here that "even if a person other than Paul wrote Ephesians, it is probable that he not only had rabbinic schooling but also was so concerned with some of its tenets and influence that he placed a correction before his Gentile-born readers."

[91] J. Ernst, *Die Briefe an die Philipper, an Philemon, an die Kolosser, an die Epheser*, RNT (Regensburg: Friedrich Pustet, 1974) 351. In connection with this Moses-typology *Midr. Teh.* 68.11, *Tg.* Ps 68:19, and *Abot R. Nat.* 2 were mentioned.

[92] Ernst, *Die Briefe an die Philipper*, 351-52. By interpreting verses 9-10 as an 'interruption' in the context, Ernst was able to see the reference to the descent in 4:9f. as a virtual parenthesis in the author's argument.

incarnation remained unchanged, Schnackenburg refined his view in a number of ways. He acknowledged that the Jewish interpretation of Ps 68:19 as a reference to Moses and the Decalogue might well be pre-Christian, although an intentional departure from the Jewish tradition was not recognizable. The author's emphasis in Ephesians was not directed against Moses nor against God (as the original subject of ἀνέβη), but was to be understood only positively in terms of Christ. Schnackenburg also maintained that the perspective in Ephesians of a descent (at the incarnation) which preceded the ascent of Christ at his exaltation was identical to that of the Gospel of John, although he admitted that there was no direct connection between Ephesians and the text of the Fourth Gospel. It was rather the common theological concept of the way of the Redeemer ("vom Weg des Erlösers") which lay behind both writings and which was also expressed in somewhat different terminology in Phil 2:6-11. As in his 1973 essay Schnackenburg saw in the latter passage similarities to the ascent and descent of Eph 4:7-11.[93]

A. Lindemann (1985) also presented a similar view of the *descensus* in Eph 4:7-11. Lindemann understood verses 9-10 to constitute an interpretation of the first line of the quotation from Ps 68:19 in verse 8. The author of Ephesians assumed without question that the psalm applied to Christ; he gave no explanation for the introduction of such a christological meaning into the context of Eph 4:7-11. In other words, according to Lindemann, what the author expounded in 4:9-10 he did not get from the text of Psalm 68; it was rather assumed and afterwards connected with the OT quotation. The author of Ephesians thus implied by the statement of the ascent in Eph 4:8a a prior descent of Christ to the "lower parts of the earth" ("den «unteren Teilen der Erde»"). This phrase referred to the earth itself, which seen from heaven was 'lower' or 'below'. In any case, the author of Ephesians did not think of a journey of Christ to hell (cf. 1 Pet 3:19-20; 4:6) but rather (with respect to the descent and ascent of Christ) referred to the incarnation. Lindemann mentioned in this connection John 3:13 and Phil 2:6-11.[94]

3. *The Descent in Eph 4:7-11 as the Descent of the Spirit*

The other major alternative proposed for the meaning of the *descensus* in Eph 4:9-10 has found fewer adherents. This view, put forward by H. von Soden shortly before the end of the last century and endorsed soon afterwards by T. K. Abbott, sees the descent as subsequent to the ascent mentioned in Eph 4:8. The descent thus represents the return (i.e., de-

---

[93] R. Schnackenburg, *Der Brief an die Epheser*, EKKNT 10 (Zürich: Benziger Verlag; Neukirchen-Vluyn: Neukirchener Verlag, 1982) 180-82.

[94] A. Lindemann, *Der Epheserbrief*, ZBK (Zürich: Theologischer Verlag Zürich, 1985) 77.

scent) of the previously exalted Christ (in the person of the Spirit; according to some, at Pentecost) to bestow gifts (or gifted individuals) on his church.

H. von Soden (1893) stressed the connection between Eph 4:7 and 4:11 through the concept of the gifts bestowed by the ascended Christ. He concluded that the concept of the ascent mentioned in the quotation from Ps 68:19 would have had no meaning whatsoever for the author of Ephesians if it were not connected with a corresponding descent. This connection was indicated in the text of Ephesians by the καί which precedes κατέβη in 4:9. According to von Soden the word order of the text strongly suggested that καὶ κατέβη denoted an event that followed the ascent instead of preceding it. Furthermore, the identification of ὁ καταβάς in 4:10 with ὁ ἀναβάς would have been superfluous if the descent had preceded the ascent. And this one who descended, ὁ καταβάς, was clearly the one who was the subject of the verb ἔδωκεν in 4:11, as shown by the resumption of αὐτός from 4:10 as the subject of the verb in 4:11. Thus for von Soden the descent introduced in Eph 4:9-10 referred to the return of the ascended Christ to bestow on his followers the gifts mentioned in 4:11-16. The reference to Christ's purpose in Eph 4:10, ἵνα πληρώσῃ τὰ πάντα, did not necessitate a visit to Hades to 'fill' the underworld because the phrase referred instead to Christ's filling of the church, previously mentioned in Eph 1:23. Finally, the ascent took place from the earth itself, not from Hades, as would be the case if a *descensus ad inferos* were in view.[95]

T. K. Abbott (1897) argued for a similar interpretation of the passage. He rejected a descent to the underworld or simply to the grave for the following reasons: (1) τὰ κατώτερα was comparative in form, while a superlative would have been expected if the author had intended to say that Christ descended to a depth below which there was nothing deeper; (2) the OT passages which were adduced to explain the phrase τὰ κατώτερα μέρη τῆς γῆς in Eph 4:9 were poetic figures, and would have been understood as such by the author of Ephesians, who would not have used them to indicate a material locus for the place of departed spirits; and (3) the antithesis in Ephesians was between earth and heaven: since the ascent was from earth to heaven, the descent (by analogy) would be from heaven to earth.[96] Understanding the descent as a descent from heaven to earth suggested either a reference to the incarnation or a subsequent descent of Christ to distribute the gifts mentioned

95 H. von Soden, ed., *Die Briefe an die Kolosser, Epheser, Philemon; die Pastoralbriefe,* 2d ed. HKNT 3 (Freiburg and Leipzig: Mohr, 1893) 135-36.

96 T. K. Abbott, *A Critical and Exegetical Commentary on the Epistles to the Ephesians and to the Colossians,* ICC (Edinburgh: Clark, 1897) 115.

in 4:11-16. According to Abbott the latter view was preferable because (1) a reference to the incarnation was superfluous in the present context, involving the assumption of the heavenly pre-existence of Christ; (2) a reference to the incarnation did not explain the emphasis on the identity of the one who ascended with the one who descended in 4:10, since this would be obvious if the descent occurred at the incarnation; (3) the descent was immediately followed in 4:11 by a reference to the gifts, suggesting that the descent was contemporaneous with the giving; and (4) the phrase καὶ κατέβη in 4:9 suggested a descent subsequent to ἀνέβη.[97] One of the most significant points raised by Abbott was the necessity for the author to infer a reference to the descent at all, unless he wished to relate it somehow to his overall theme of unity (4:1-6) and the distribution of the gifts which were intended to promote that unity (4:11-16). It is also worth noting that the arguments put forward by both von Soden and Abbott were primarily contextual ones which concerned the logic of the passage and the coherency of the author's argument.

In the years which followed, the view of von Soden and Abbott won relatively few adherents. E. Graham (1928) noted that the context favored a descent subsequent to the ascent, and referred to the gifts bestowed on the church by the ascended Christ descending as the Spirit at Pentecost. Graham pointed out that in this case the phrase "the lower parts of the earth" equalled simply 'this world below'; verse 10 indicated it was the ascended Christ himself who, in spite of the heights to which he had ascended, still condescended to dwell in his church.[98] Another scholar who expressed apparent agreement with the concept of a subsequent descent in Eph 4:9-10, although his own view was not clearly articulated, was U. Simon (1958).[99]

J. J. Meuzelaar (1961) endorsed a subsequent descent in Eph 4:9-10 in which the ascended Christ returned to his church as the indwelling Spirit who distributed the gifts mentioned in Eph 4:11-16. The modifications to the text of Ps 68:19 as quoted in Eph 4:8 could be traced back to an ancient Jewish tradition associating Moses and his ascent of Mt. Sinai to receive the Torah with the words of the psalm; the 'gifts' were the tablets of the Law which Moses received on behalf of Israel. Meuzelaar noted that the author of Ephesians did not refer in 4:10 to "a filling of the universe" ("eine Erfüllung des Weltalls"), but to a filling of

---

[97] Abbott, *Epistles to the Ephesians and to the Colossians*, 115-16. Abbott noted that the final observation concerning καὶ κατέβη was also made by von Soden.

[98] E. Graham, "The Epistle to the Ephesians," *NCHS* (New York: Macmillan, 1928) 1.547.

[99] U. Simon, *Heaven in the Christian Tradition* (New York: Harper & Brothers, 1958) 185, n. 3.

the church, which was the point of the quotation from Ps 68:19. The descent in 4:9-10 was not a reference to the incarnation, since the author of Ephesians made no reference to the pre-existence of the Messiah. Nor was there any indication in the context of a reference to the death of the Messiah which would indicate a descent to the grave or to the underworld. What the author emphasized was the necessity of a descent by which the ascended one could give gifts to men.[100]

According to E. D. Roels (1962) Eph 4:8-10 dealt with the exaltation and ascension of Christ, which he understood to be the same as the exaltation mentioned in Eph 1:19-22. But the author's purpose in introducing a reference to the ascension in 4:8 was different from that of 1:19-22, and for that reason the author returned to the theme of the exaltation also. The emphasis in Ephesians 4 was not on the ascension itself, but on the giving of gifts (4:7, 8, 11) by the ascended one. Roels saw the descent as subsequent to the ascent and mentioned that this view was defended by von Soden and Abbott.[101] He understood the descent as a reference to Christ's distribution of gifts as exalted ruler, fulfiller of prophecy, and the one who filled all things. The question the author asked in 4:9 thus concerned the value of the fact that Christ ascended: of what value was his ascent, unless he also descended to the earth to provide gifts of leadership and grace for the church? Verses 9 and 10 were not, therefore, an interlude in the development of the author's thought or an incursion into his discourse, but should rather be seen as an essential part of its proper development. Roels observed that a subsequent descent was also suggested by the order in which the ascent and descent were mentioned in Ephesians 4, including the presence of the καί before κατέβη in 4:9.[102] Such an interpretation was more in harmony with the general cosmology of Ephesians, which appeared to involve a 'two-storied' universe. On the other hand, a reference to a *descensus ad infernum* was completely foreign to the context in Ephesians 4; mention of it here would add little, if anything, to the significance of the ascension.[103]

New arguments have recently been put forward in favor of a subsequent descent which go beyond the immediate context and involve the traditional interpretation of Psalm 68 in the first century CE and its connection with Pentecost and the giving of the Torah. A major contributor

---

[100] J. J. Meuzelaar, *Der Leib des Messias: Eine exegetische Studie über den Gedanken vom Leib Christi in den Paulusbriefen* (Assen: Van Gorcum, 1961; reprint ed., Kampen: Kok, 1979) 134-37.

[101] E. D. Roels, *God's Mission: The Epistle to the Ephesians in Mission Perspective* (Franeker: T. Wever, 1962) 161-63.

[102] Roels, *God's Mission*, 163, n. 18.

[103] *Descensus ad infernum* is Roels' term (162).

to this discussion was G. B. Caird (1964), who argued that neither the incarnation nor a descent to Hades could be inferred from Ps 68:19 as quoted in Eph 4:8. No satisfactory solution for the descent could be reached which did not explain why the author of Ephesians believed that in the psalm, the descent could logically be inferred from the ascent, and why the author wanted to emphasize the identity of ὁ καταβάς with ὁ ἀναβάς.[104] However, if the descent mentioned in Eph 4:9-10 were subsequent to the ascent of 4:8 it would have been necessary for the author to infer it from the psalm in order to explain the giving of the gifts (4:11-16). The Spirit at Pentecost was thus to be identified with the Christ who had previously ascended. This was possible for Paul because he did not always draw distinctions between the Spirit and the indwelling Christ. In this regard Caird mentioned Rom 8:9-10, 2 Cor 3:17, and 1 Cor 15:45, as well as the implication of Eph 2:17 which referred to "a coming of Christ which had taken place since the crucifixion," an interpretation in which Christ (or perhaps, Christ in the person of the Spirit) came and proclaimed peace to Gentiles who were far away as well as to Jews who were near.[105] The evidence in favor of a subsequent descent was drawn from two areas: (1) grammatical evidence and (2) what Caird called 'liturgical' evidence. Concerning the grammatical evidence, Caird identified τῆς γῆς as a genitive of apposition, mentioning that this was a fairly frequent usage in Ephesians.[106] The locus of the descent was therefore not the underworld, but the earth itself. Caird's 'liturgical' evidence consisted of an attempt to associate Psalm 68 with Pentecost. The psalm was one of the appointed readings for Pentecost, which around the time Ephesians was written had come to be cele-

---

[104] G. B. Caird, "The Descent of Christ in Ephesians 4, 7-11," *SE* 2 (= TU 87), ed. F. L. Cross (Berlin: Akademie, 1964) 535-45.

[105] Caird, "The Descent of Christ," 537. Eph 2:17 has long been recognized as difficult by commentators and is subject to a number of interpretations regarding when this 'coming' of Christ took place and how he made this proclamation of peace. A number of differing interpretations of the verse were given by M. Barth (*Ephesians: Introduction, Translation and Commentary on Chapters 1-3*, AB 34 [Garden City, NY: Doubleday, 1974] 294-95). Barth concluded, "It is fruitless to try and pin down the specific moment of the peace proclamation to one event or period of Jesus Christ's ministry before, during, or after his death. A too precise dating and placing of the proclamation might amount to a limitation of its time and place, which would contradict the universal character of the peace made..." (295). It must still be acknowledged that the interpretation suggested by Caird could be valid if he were right about the subsequent nature of the descent in Eph 4:9-10, although in 2:17 it seems more probable that the author of Ephesians is thinking of nothing more than a 'coming' of Christ in the person of his apostles who carried the gospel to the Gentiles and made this proclamation of peace on his behalf.

[106] Caird cited Winer's *Grammar of New Testament Greek* which listed Eph 4:9 as an example of a genitive of apposition ("The Descent of Christ in Ephesians 4, 7-11," 539). Other examples in Ephesians which Caird mentioned are 2:14 (φραγμοῦ), 2:15 (ἐντωλῶν), 2:20 (ἀποστόλων), and 4 instances in 6:14-17. The grammatical issues are discussed below in ch. 2, 46-54; the appositive genitive in particular is discussed on pp. 50-54.

brated as the feast of the giving of the Torah at Moses' ascent of Sinai.
Caird also mentioned a possible connection between *Tg.* Psalm 68 and
Eph 4:8, both of which contained a textual variant in Ps 68:19 not preserved in either the LXX or the later MT.[107] Caird acknowledged that
Targum Psalms was a late work, but argued that it preserved an ancient
exegetical tradition which antedated Ephesians. Finally, Caird argued
that Psalm 68 was no longer a Jewish pentecostal psalm recording
Moses' ascent of Mt. Sinai, but a Christian pentecostal psalm (as interpreted by the author of Ephesians) recording the victorious ascent of
Christ and his subsequent descent at Pentecost.[108] Most of this evidence
was later restated (more briefly) by Caird (1976), but here he emphasized the unity of the theme of Christ's gifts to his church as introduced
in Eph 4:7 and continued in 4:11. Caird insisted that the intervening material must be treated as an exposition, not an interruption, of this theme.
He also highlighted the difficulty of explaining the necessity to infer a
descent from Ps 68:19 if the descent was a descent to Hades or a reference to the incarnation. If this were the case it would also be difficult to
see why the author of Ephesians felt it necessary to affirm the identity
of the one who ascended with the one who descended, as he did in Eph
4:10. Caird concluded that the author had made use of a Jewish midrash
on Ps 68:19 by reapplying it to Christ, in a fashion similar to Paul's use
of midrash in 1 Cor 10:4. A different midrash on another verse of Psalm
68 lay behind the account of Pentecost in Acts 2.[109]

C. H. Porter (1966) also held that Eph 4:9-10 referred to a subsequent descent of Christ as the giver of gifts to his church. He argued,
like Caird, that any valid exegesis of the passage must explain why the
author believed that a descent could be inferred from the ascent of the
psalm quotation, and why (in 4:10) the author insisted on the identity of
the one who descended with the one who ascended. Porter considered
a descent to Hades unlikely in Ephesians because in the epistle Christ's
victory over the demonic powers was connected with his ascent and
because there was no threefold division of the cosmos in Ephesians. A
reference to the incarnation was equally unlikely because John 3:13, a
passage often cited in support of such a view, presumed the heavenly
origin of the Son of man, while in Ephesians the identity of the ascended Christ became the basis for establishing the identity of the other

---

[107] G. B. Caird, "The Descent of Christ in Ephesians 4, 7-11," 539-41. A full discussion of
the variations in the text of Ps 68:19 between the MT, the LXX, the NT text of Eph 4:8, and
Tg. Ps 68:19 may be found in ch. 3 of the present work; see pp. 96-104.

[108] Caird, "The Descent of Christ," 541.

[109] G. B. Caird, *Paul's Letters from Prison*, NClarB (Oxford: Oxford University Press,
1976) 73-75.

figure, the one who descended (4:9-10).[110] Porter mentioned the reading of Ps 68:19 found in *Tg*. Psalms; he regarded this as the preservation of an ancient traditional interpretation known to the author of Ephesians. The connection of Psalm 68 with Pentecost as a celebration of the giving of the Torah at Mt. Sinai was also noted, although Porter introduced no new evidence to support this association.[111]

J. C. Kirby (1968) also endorsed the idea of a subsequent descent in Eph 4:9-10. He noted that the reason for the quotation of Ps 68:19 in Eph 4:8 was that the ascension of Christ and the gift of the Spirit were in the author's mind; the author of Ephesians took over the rabbinic association of Psalm 68 with Pentecost while polemically replacing Moses by Christ. Kirby found "strong support" for Abbott's position in Caird's 1964 article and cited a number of "reminiscences" of Psalm 68 throughout the entire Epistle to the Ephesians.[112]

J. L. Houlden (1970) cited with approval the interpretation of Eph 4:9-10 as a subsequent descent of Christ. He too mentioned Caird's 1964 article, noting that Caird had "convincingly argued that associations with that festival [i.e., Pentecost] were carried over into Christian use."[113] Houlden noted the similarity of such a presentation of Christ's ascension and the bestowal of the gifts of the Spirit to that found in Luke-Acts; the author of the latter was in fact the only other NT writer to portray the ascension and the gift of the Spirit as separate from the resurrection. In the unquestioned Pauline epistles such distinctions were not made, at least in terms of successive temporal events.

Another adherent of this interpretation, R. P. Martin (1971), related the descent mentioned in Eph 4:9-10 to the impartation of the Spirit following the enthronement of Christ, which brought with it all the gifts of Christ to the church to prepare it for life and witness. Martin found

---

[110] C. H. Porter, "The Descent of Christ: An Exegetical Study of Ephesians 4:7-11," in *One Faith: Its Biblical, Historical, and Ecumenical Dimensions*, ed. R. L. Simpson (Enid, OK: Phillips University Press, 1966) 45-55.

[111] Cf. Porter, "The Descent of Christ" 54, n. 26, with G. B. Caird, "The Descent of Christ in Ephesians 4, 7-11," 539-41.

[112] J. C. Kirby, *Ephesians, Baptism and Pentecost* (Montreal: McGill University Press, 1968) 145-46; Caird's article and the allusions to Psalm 68 in Ephesians were mentioned on p. 187, n. 51. The allusions are Ps 68:16 with Eph 2:22 and 3:17; Ps 68:9 with Eph 1:18; Ps 68:10 with Eph 2:7; Ps 68:4, 32 with Eph 5:19; and Ps 68:28, 35 with Eph 3:16 and 6:10. These were from W. Lock, *The Epistle to the Ephesians*, WC (London: Methuen, 1929) 11ff. Lock's theory that Psalm 68 lay behind all of Ephesians was discussed at length by P. D. Overfield, "The Ascension, Pleroma and Ecclesia Concepts in Ephesians" (Ph.D. thesis, University of St. Andrews, 1976) 99-103. While acknowledging that no individual parallel listed by Lock was convincing, Overfield was inclined to agree that some general similarities between Psalm 68 and Ephesians did exist.

[113] J. L. Houlden, *Paul's Letters from Prison: Philippians, Colossians, Philemon, and Ephesians*, PNTC (Harmondsworth: Penguin, 1970) 310-11. I have supplied the bracketed note.

confirmation of this interpretation in the translation of Eph 4:11 with its
emphatic pronoun αὐτός: "And it was he [Gk. *autos*, as an emphatic
pronoun—the One who fulfilled the prediction of Psalm 68] who
gave."[114]

One of the strongest advocates of a subsequent descent of Christ in
Eph 4:9-10 has been A. T. Lincoln, who first stated the view in *Paradise
Now and Not Yet* (1981), repeated it in an article on OT quotations in
Ephesians (1982), and discussed it again in his commentary (1990).[115] To
Caird's arguments Lincoln added the following: (1) it may be possible to
establish the association of Psalm 68 with Pentecost in pre-Christian
Jewish tradition by references to the *Book of Jubilees*, the annual covenant renewal ceremony of the Qumran community, and the early Jewish
synagogue liturgy; (2) the ἵνα-clause which concluded Eph 4:10 was
connected only to the immediately preceding statement about Christ's
ascent, so that a descent to Hades was not required in order for Christ to
"fill all things" (as the parallel with Eph 1:22-23 made clear); (3) the
cosmology encountered elsewhere in Ephesians was 'two-storied'
(heaven and earth) rather than 'three-storied' (heaven, earth, and underworld), and this fitted better with an understanding of the phrase
κατώτερα [μέρη] τῆς γῆς in Eph 4:9 as an appositive genitive rather
than a comparative or partitive genitive; (4) Philo in *Quaes. Gen.* 4.29
made the descent of Moses from Mt. Sinai following his ascent the basis
for his argument concerning the necessity of a subsequent descent in
conjunction with the ascent of a mystical experience. This last point is
particularly important because of the traditional association of Moses
with Ps 68:19 found in *Tg.* Ps 68:19 (which bears other similarities to
Eph 4:8) and the classical rabbinic literature.[116]

4. Conclusions on the History of Interpretation of the Passage

The doctrine of the *descensus ad inferos* was well established in the
early church. However, recent commentators have not reached a consensus as to whether the doctrine of the *descensus* lies behind Eph 4:7-
11 or not. Most modern interpretations agree with regard to the meaning
of verses 7-8. Verse 7 introduces the section 4:7-16, which consists pri-

---

114 R. P. Martin, "Ephesians," in *BBC* 11: *2 Corinthians—Philemon* (Nashville: Broadman, 1971) 155-56. Bracketed material is that of Martin in the original source.

115 A. T. Lincoln, *Paradise Now and Not Yet: Studies in the Role of the Heavenly Dimension in Paul's Thought with Special Reference to his Eschatology*, SNTSMS 43 (Cambridge:
Cambridge University Press, 1981) 155-63; "The Use of the OT in Ephesians," *JSNT* 14
(1982) 16-57; and *Ephesians*, WBC 42 (Dallas: Word, 1990) 242-48.

116 The Moses-traditions associated with Ps 68:19, as well as the relationship between *Tg.*
Ps 68:19 and Eph 4:8, are discussed at considerable length in ch. 3 below. The arguments put
forward by Lincoln may be found in *Paradise Now and Not Yet*, 157-61; they were reiterated
in "The Use of the OT in Ephesians," *JSNT* 14 (1982) 18-25.

marily of the well-known enumeration of spiritual gifts (or more accurately, gifted individuals) intended to facilitate the growth of the church
to maturity. The giving of gifts is substantiated by the quotation in verse
8 of Ps 68:19 LXX (68:18 English versions). Virtually all interpreters
would agree that verse 8 is here intended to refer to the victorious ascent of Christ following his death and resurrection (a topic previously
mentioned in Eph 1:20-23). This event was accompanied (or followed)
by the distribution to the church of the gifts described in 4:11-16.

The meaning of verses 9-10, a midrash on the quotation from Psalm
68, has created the major exegetical difficulty in the entire section.[117]
Two questions, if they can be answered, will point to a resolution of the
problem: (1) to where did Christ descend?, and (2) when did this descent take place in relation to the ascent mentioned in verse 8? As we
have seen, almost all recent interpreters have held with respect to the
first question that the descent was either from earth to the grave (i.e.,
Sheol, the place of the dead)[118] or from heaven to earth (i.e., the incarnation or a descent subsequent to the ascent of verse 8 to distribute the
gifts mentioned in 4:11-16). With respect to the second question, most
would agree that the descent introduced by the writer in the midrash
found in Eph 4:9-10 preceded the ascent of verse 8. However, the remainder of this book will argue that the descent introduced in Eph 4:9-
10 is actually subsequent to the ascent and represents the return to
earth of the ascended Christ as the Spirit to distribute gifts to his church
(4:11-16).

Several of the points raised by Caird and Lincoln will be discussed at
length in later chapters. Among these are the problem of the genitive τῆς

---

[117] In assigning the label 'midrash' to the Pauline exegesis of Ps 68:19 found in Eph 4:8,
it is recognized that as a method of rabbinic exegesis the term midrash itself has been subject to
a variety of definitions. In general the term is used in the present work to refer to an interpretive method which takes as its point of departure the biblical text itself and seeks to explain
the hidden meanings contained therein by following agreed upon hermeneutical rules in order
to arrive at a relevant contemporary application for the audience. One of the most thorough
modern attempts to define midrash as a literary genre is that of R. Bloch ("Note méthodologique pour l'étude de la littérature rabbinique," *RSR* 43 [1955] 194-227). P. Benoit identified the passage under discussion, Eph 4:9-10, as "une exégèse midrashique" ("Corps, tête et
plérôme dans les Épîtres de la captivité," *RB* 63 [1956] 41), as did R. N. Longenecker
(*Biblical Exegesis in the Apostolic Period* [Grand Rapids: Eerdmans, 1975] 124-26). A. T.
Lincoln identified the interpretation of Ps 68:19 found in Eph 4:9-10 as midrash pesher (*Paradise Now and Not Yet*, 156).

[118] As we have already seen, the modern view that Christ descended from the earth to Sheol
is more or less equivalent to the ancient interpretation that involved a *descensus ad inferos*,
except that no activity (such as preaching to imprisoned spirits) is posited of Christ during the
triduum. The descent of Christ into the grave simply affirms the reality of his death, and is
juxtaposed as such to his resurrection and victorious ascent. A similar affirmation of the death
and the resurrection of Christ is found in 1 Cor 15:3-8, although in this context the ascent as a
separate event is not emphasized.

γῆς in Eph 4:9, the relationship between Eph 4:8 and *Tg*. Ps 68:19, the tradition of Moses' ascent to heaven, and the associations of the imagery behind Eph 4:7-11 with the feast of Pentecost. Before these issues are discussed, however, the textual problems in Eph 4:9 and their influence on the interpretation of Eph 4:7-11 must be addressed.

C. TEXTUAL PROBLEMS IN EPH 4:9 AND THEIR EFFECT ON THE INTERPRETATION OF 4:7-11

Two textual variants in Eph 4: 9-10 have played a significant role throughout the history of the passage's interpretation. The first (and more important) is the omission or inclusion of πρῶτον following κατέβη in 4:9. Including πρῶτον after κατέβη would significantly alter the interpretive options with regard to the descent mentioned in the verse, because it would necessitate a descent prior to the ascent. This would effectively eliminate any possibility of a subsequent descent as proposed by von Soden, Abbott, Caird, and Lincoln.[119] The second textual problem, the inclusion or omission of μέρη before the genitive τῆς γῆς in the final clause of 4:9, is less significant; Abbott said the insertion or omission of μέρη made no difference in the sense.[120] This is perhaps somewhat overstated, because if μέρη is included as part of the original text it affects the interpretation of the genitive phrase τῆς γῆς which follows and which (together with κατώτερα) specifies the locus of the descent.[121] We shall examine both of these problems in turn and attempt to assess whether the words in question belong in the original text of Eph 4:9.

1. *The Omission of Πρῶτον Following Κατέβη in Eph 4:9*

Determining whether πρῶτον should be regarded as part of the original text of Ephesians is a fairly complex task. First, the evidence from extant manuscripts must be surveyed to determine the extent of support for the omission or inclusion of πρῶτον. Next, the manuscript evidence must be evaluated in three areas: (1) the date and quality of the manuscripts supporting both positions, (2) the geographical distribution of the readings with and without the word in question, and (3) the genealogi-

---

119 This view was discussed in the preceding section, 23-30.

120 Abbott, *Epistles to the Ephesians and to the Colossians*, 114.

121 E.g., J. D. G. Dunn stated that a genitive following μέρη would be partitive rather than appositive (*Christology in the Making: A New Testament Inquiry into the Origins of the Doctrine of the Incarnation* [London: SCM, 1980] 186-87). For discussion of the grammatical and syntactical issues surrounding the genitive phrase τῆς γῆς in 4:9, see ch. 2, 46-54.

cal relationship of texts and families of witnesses.[122] Finally, an examination of the transcriptional factors surrounding the inclusion or omission of πρῶτον will assess the probability that the text was lengthened or shortened in the course of its transmission.

1.1. *The Evidence From the Manuscript Tradition*

The longer reading, κατέβη πρῶτον εἰς τὰ κατώτερα μέρη τῆς γῆς, is supported by a significant amount of manuscript evidence. The Alexandrian uncial B (03 [Vaticanus], 4th century), as well as the corrected texts of both א (01 [Sinaiticus], 4th century)[123] and C (04 [Ephraemi Rescriptus], 5th century)[124] contain the longer reading. The Byzantine uncials K (018 in the epistles, 9th century) and L (020 in the epistles, 9th century) and the Alexandrian uncials P (025 in the epistles, also 9th century) and Ψ (044, 8th/9th century) also include πρῶτον, as do the later uncials 075 (10th century) and 0150 (9th century).

A number of minuscule manuscripts support the inclusion of πρῶτον after κατέβη. The most important of these is 104, a minuscule of Alexandrian text type from the 11th century. The majority of Byzantine minuscule manuscripts predictably include πρῶτον in keeping with that text type's tendency to follow the longer reading. A number of minuscules containing a mixed text also include πρῶτον (256, 263, 365, 424, 436, 459, 1175, 1319, 1573, 1852, 1912, 2127, 2200, and 2464).

The Byzantine lectionaries are unanimous in their support of the longer reading. The reading which included πρῶτον also found its way into a significant number of the early versions, including the Harclean Syriac and the Peshitta, all but one of the Sahidic Coptic manuscripts, and one manuscript of the Itala (Old Latin). The Latin Vulgate (more Alexandrian than Western in text type) supports the inclusion of πρῶτον in most of its manuscripts, as do the Armenian and Slavonic versions. A few Fathers also demonstrated knowledge of the longer reading: Eusebius of Caesarea (339 CE), Didymus, although the reading is doubtful (398 CE), Chrysostom (407 CE), Theodore of Mopsuestia, in the Latin text (428 CE), and Theodoret (ca. 466 CE).[125] Manuscripts which support the inclusion of πρῶτον are displayed in *Chart* 1.1 on the following page to provide a convenient overview of the external evidence.

---

[122] The procedure is outlined briefly by B. M. Metzger in *The Text of the New Testament: Its Corruption, Transmission, and Restoration*, 3rd ed. (New York and Oxford: Oxford University Press, 1992) 209.

[123] The insertion of πρῶτον was done by the second corrector of א according to NA27. The corrections are of a later date than the manuscript itself.

[124] The third corrector of C, according to NA27. Again, the corrections are later.

[125] The dates given in parentheses represent, in most cases, the date of death (often approximate).

Chart 1.1: Witnesses which include πρῶτον in Eph 4:9

Alexandrian	Byzantine	Western	Mixed, Other
B P Ψ	K L		ℵ² C³ 075 0150
104	*Byz Minuscule Manuscripts*		256. 263. 365. 424*. 436. 459. 1175. 1319. 1573. 1852. 1912. 2127. 2200. 2464
	Byz Lectionaries		
Sahidic Coptic Vulgate (most mss)	Harclean Syriac Peshitta Armenian, Slavonic	itala ᵒ	
	Chrysostom Theodoret	Theodore ˡᵃᵗ	Eusebius Didymus ᵈᵘᵇ

Despite this widespread evidence, there are significant early manuscripts of both Alexandrian and Western text type which omit πρῶτον. The earliest and most important of these is 𝔓⁴⁶ (ca. 200 CE), which is characterized as a somewhat free rendition of the Greek text by K. and B. Aland.[126] The uncorrected versions of the Alexandrian uncials ℵ (01, 4th century) and C (04, 5th century) also support the omission, as do A (02, 5th century), I (016, fifth century),[127] and 082 (6th century). The omission of πρῶτον is supported by the Western uncials D (06 [Claromontanus], 6th century), F (010 [Augiensis], 9th century), and G (012 [Boernerianus], 9th century). The shorter reading is also found in several minuscules of Alexandrian text type, 6 (13th century), 33 (9th century), 81 (1044 CE), 1241 (12th century), and 1739 (10th century), as well as the corrected manuscript 424 (11th century) and 1881, a 14th century manuscript of mixed text type. Among the early versions supporting the omission of πρῶτον are the Ethiopic and Bohairic Coptic, along with one manuscript of the Sahidic Coptic and several manuscripts of the Vulgate. A number of the individual manuscripts of the Itala (Old Latin) also lack the Latin equivalent of πρῶτον. A large number of Fathers quote a shorter form of the text without πρῶτον: Irenaeus (ca. 202 CE;

---

126 K. Aland and B. Aland, *The Text of the New Testament*, trans. E. F. Rhodes (Grand Rapids: Eerdmans, 1987) 99. The only other papyrus known to be extant for Ephesians is 𝔓⁴⁹, which covers only Eph 4:16-29 and 4:31-5:13.

127 For I (016) this is an apparent reading.

the Latin translation is dated from the third or fourth century), Clement of Alexandria (prior to 215 CE, quoting from Theodotus, a second century Gnostic), Tertullian (ca. 220 CE), Origen (253/254 CE; the shorter reading is found in both Greek and Latin manuscripts), Victorinus of Rome (362 CE), Ambrosiaster (366-84 CE),[128] Hilary (367 CE), Lucifer (370/371 CE), Jerome (420 CE), Pelagius (ca. 423-29 CE), and Augustine (430 CE). The manuscript evidence for the omission of πρῶτον is displayed in *Chart* 1.2.

Chart 1.2: Witnesses which omit πρῶτον in Eph 4:9

Alexandrian	Byzantine	Western	Mixed, Other
$\mathfrak{P}^{46}$			
ℵ* A C* I[vid] 082		D F G	
6. 33. 81. 1241. 1739			424[c]. 1881
	l 1439		
Sahidic Coptic (1 ms) Bohairic Coptic Vulgate (some mss)	Ethiopic	itala [ar, b, d, g, mon]	
Cyril		Irenaeus [lat] Tertullian Victorinus-Rome Ambrosiaster Hilary, Lucifer Jerome, Pelagius Augustine	Clement [(ex Thd)] Origen [gk, lat]

To evaluate the evidence from the manuscript tradition we must consider briefly the date and quality of the manuscripts supporting each reading as well as the geographical distribution of the variant readings themselves.[129] One assumes that the variant reading which achieves wide and early distribution throughout the major geographical regions has a higher probability of being the original than a variant which is localized or limited to a single region, or which achieves widespread distribution at a date considerably later than another variant.

---

128 For Ambrosiaster the dates given are those of Pope Damasus, during whose time the works are thought to have been written.

129 Another factor which is sometimes considered is the genealogical solidarity of a reading (see B. M. Metzger, *The Text of the New Testament*, 209). This is regarded as good when evidence within a given text type is solidly in favor of a single reading, and poor when the evidence is divided more or less equally between two or more readings. Genealogical solidarity will not be considered in this particular instance because it is indecisive. The Byzantine tradition is almost always allied in favor of a single reading (in part due to the character of the Byzantine text itself), and in the present case, both the Alexandrian and Western text types divide over the inclusion or omission of πρῶτον; this has the effect of neutralizing the evidence as far as genealogical solidarity is concerned.

1.2. *Date and Quality of the Manuscripts*

Of all the manuscripts considered, 𝔓⁴⁶ (the only extant papyrus for this section of Ephesians) is the earliest and most important, and it supports the omission of πρῶτον. In addition to 𝔓⁴⁶, K. Aland categorizes four of the uncial and minuscule manuscripts which favor the omission as category I manuscripts (manuscripts of a very special quality which should always be considered in the determination of a textual reading): ℵ, A, 33, and 1739.[130] The omission of πρῶτον is also supported by five category II manuscripts (manuscripts of a special quality, but distinguished from category I manuscripts by the presence of outside influences, particularly from the Byzantine text), C, D, I, 81, and 1881, and five category III manuscripts (manuscripts of a distinctive character with an independent text, usually important for establishing the original text), 082, F, G, 6, and 1241. Of the uncial manuscripts one (ℵ) is 4th century, three (A, C, and I) are 5th century, and two (082 and D) are 6th century.

In comparison to this, the longer reading is supported by only one category I manuscript, B, whose textual quality is considered inferior in the Pauline corpus.[131] Only three category II manuscripts (1175, 2127) support the inclusion of πρῶτον. Twenty category III manuscripts favor the inclusion (P, Ψ, 075, 0150, 104, 256, 263, 365, 424, 436, 459, 1175, 1319, 1573, 1852, 1912, 1962, 2127, 2200, and 2464). The Byzantine uncials K and L are classified by Aland as category V (manuscripts having a purely or predominantly Byzantine text, of much less value in establishing the original text), along with the majority of Byzantine minuscules, all of which support the inclusion of πρῶτον.

In view of the early date and importance of 𝔓⁴⁶, as well as the number of additional category I (four) and category II (five) manuscripts allied with it, the shorter reading which omits πρῶτον is clearly preferred based on the date and quality of the manuscript evidence.

1.3. *Geographical Distribution of the Variant Readings*

At first glance, a survey of the geographical distribution of the variants might seem to favor the longer reading, because it is well represented in all three of the major text types in comparison to the shorter reading, which lacks substantial Byzantine support. Both the Byzantine and Western support for the inclusion of πρῶτον is somewhat later in date, however. The corresponding Western manuscripts which support the shorter reading are relatively earlier, with D (06) dating from the 6th century, and one of the Itala manuscripts, d (75 in the Beuron Cata-

---

[130] K. Aland and B. Aland, *The Text of the New Testament*, 105-35. Descriptions of the five categories employed to classify the manuscripts are found on 105-106; the uncial manuscripts are classified according to these categories on 106-25, and the minuscules on 128-35.

[131] K. and B. Aland, *The Text of the New Testament*, 14.

logue) dating from the 5th or 6th century. To compare with this the longer reading has no support at all in the Western tradition except for the Latin text of Theodore of Mopsuestia before the 15th century, when one Latin manuscript (itala⁰, which for the Pauline corpus gives the readings from Pelagius manuscript B [Oxford, Balliol College 157]) supports the longer reading.

Likewise, although the Alexandrian tradition is divided between the two readings, there is earlier Alexandrian support ($\mathfrak{P}^{46}$, ca. 200 CE) and much better support in the 4th and 5th centuries (א, A, C, I) for the shorter reading. Thus the longer reading does not really have the advantage that it might at first appear to have. It is true that the shorter reading is not as widely represented, appearing only in the Alexandrian and Western text types, but the shorter reading makes its appearance in both these text types somewhat earlier than the longer reading. On the other hand, the reading which includes πρῶτον is also represented in two major text types (Alexandrian and Byzantine) but somewhat later (the evidence for the longer reading in the Western text type is insignificant).

1.4. *Conclusions Based on the Manuscript Evidence*

The manuscript evidence favors the omission of πρῶτον in Eph 4:9. The earlier date of the shorter reading, indicated by $\mathfrak{P}^{46}$, is a major factor favoring the omission. When the quality of the manuscripts which support the shorter reading is also considered, we may conclude that the evidence from the manuscripts themselves suggests that the omission of πρῶτον from the original text of Eph 4:9 is much more probable.

1.5. *Transcriptional Factors*

A consideration of transcriptional probabilities confirms and strengthens conclusions based on the manuscript evidence itself. One of the established 'canons' of textual criticism is that of *brevior lectio* (or more fully stated, *brevior lectio praeferenda est*), i.e., preference is to be given to the shorter reading.[132] In and of itself this would favor the omission of

---

[132] This rule of thumb for the evaluation of variants dates back at least to J. J. Griesbach (1745-1812), who listed it as the first of fifteen canons of textual criticism. Griesbach stated his first canon as follows: "The shorter reading (unless it lacks entirely the authority of the ancient and weighty witnesses) is to be preferred to the more verbose, for scribes were much more prone to add than to omit. They scarcely ever deliberately omitted anything, but they added many things; certainly they omitted some things by accident, but likewise not a few things have been added to the text by scribes through errors of the eye, ear, memory, imagination, and judgment. Particularly the shorter reading is to be preferred, even though according to the authority of the witnesses it may appear to be inferior to the other,—(a) if at the same time it is more difficult, more obscure, ambiguous, elliptical, hebraizing, or solecistic; (b) if the same thing is expressed with different phrases in various manuscripts; (c) if the order of words varies; (d) at the beginning of pericopes; (e) if the longer reading savours of a gloss or interpretation, or agrees with the wording of parallel passages, or seems to have come from lectionaries"

πρῶτον. Beyond this, however, it is difficult to imagine how (if the longer reading with πρῶτον represents the original) the word came to be omitted from the text by a copyist. The normal transcriptional factors resulting in accidental omission (e.g., homoioteleuton and homoioarcton) do not apply in this case, since there are no words in the immediate context with similar endings or beginnings. Neither can the omission of πρῶτον be explained by an error of hearing such as itacism (if copying were being done from dictation, or if a solitary copyist were pronouncing the text aloud to himself).

It is possible that πρῶτον was accidentally incorporated into the text of Eph 4:9, however. If the word were originally added to the margin of a manuscript as an interpretive gloss intended to explain the meaning of the passage by clarifying the time of the descent, it may well have been assimilated accidentally into the text of Ephesians by a later copyist who mistook it for a correction. We know that such accidental inclusions did occasionally occur; since the margins of ancient manuscripts were used for glosses as well as corrections it fell to the judgment of the scribe to discern between the two, and the simplest resolution was to incorporate the marginal note into the text being copied.[133] A scribe who found the word πρῶτον as a marginal comment in the manuscript he was copying would probably have felt little reluctance to incorporate it into the text itself as long as it agreed with his own understanding of the time and nature of the descent mentioned in Eph 4:9-10.

Although it is highly probable that the inclusion of πρῶτον was an accident by a copyist, there is still a possibility that someone wishing to promote or deny a particular interpretation of the passage on theological grounds made a deliberate alteration. In considering this possibility it is important to note, however, that a deliberate omission of πρῶτον by a copyist wishing to affirm a descent of Christ subsequent to his ascent results only in an inconclusive reading. Indeed, a number of the earlier Fathers, although they are known to hold to a prior descent (e.g., Ire-

---

(cited by B. M. Metzger, *The Text of the New Testament*, 120). Metzger himself held that the rule of *brevior lectio* was quite sound when applied by responsible NT textual critics, as he argued in "Trends in the Textual Criticism of the Iliad and the Mahabharata," in *Chapters in the History of New Testament Textual Criticism*, NTTS 4 (Grand Rapids: Eerdmans, 1963) 151.

[133] B. M. Metzger, in *The Text of the New Testament: Its Corruption, Transmission, and Restoration*, 194-95, cited a number of instances where such an accidental inclusion of marginal glosses into the text itself probably occurred. This may explain how John 5:7, originally a marginal comment explaining the moving of the water in the pool of Bethesda, came to be assimilated into the text of 5:3b-4; another example would be found in Rom 8:1. Lectionary formulas sometimes were incorporated in similar fashion (e.g., Matt 25:31 and Luke 7:31). J. A. Bengel (cited by Metzger, 194) even mentioned the almost incredible example of a scribe who included the words ἐν πολλοῖς τῶν ἀντιγράφων οὕτως εὕρηται directly in the text of 2 Cor 8:4!

naeus and Tertullian), nevertheless seem quite content to maintain the shorter reading; they show no tendency to expand the text to support their interpretation. On the other hand, it is quite easy to see how πρῶτον came to be added to the text as an explanatory gloss. This would be especially true if the doctrine of a descent of Christ to the underworld (which in Eph 4:9 would necessarily take place prior to his ascent) had already gained relatively wide acceptance. If, as J. N. D. Kelly suggests, the incorporation of such a doctrine of the *descensus* into early credal formulations represented an attempt to refute Docetism, then the desire to refute such heresy would provide even further impetus to the tendency to include πρῶτον in the text of Eph 4:9.[134]

With regard to the transcriptional probabilities, therefore, it appears much easier to explain how πρῶτον came to be added to the text (probably accidentally, possibly deliberately) than to explain its accidental or deliberate omission. This concurs with the manuscript evidence in suggesting that the shorter reading which omits πρῶτον should be regarded as original.

1.6. *Conclusions on the Omission of Πρῶτον in Eph 4:9*
We have examined both the evidence from the manuscript tradition behind Eph 4:9 itself and the transcriptional probabilities related to the inclusion or omission of πρῶτον in terms of scribal tendencies. Both lines of evidence agree in strongly supporting as original the reading which lacks πρῶτον. It thus appears overwhelmingly probable that the original text of Eph 4:9 did not contain πρῶτον. This agrees with the judgment of C. von Tischendorf, who in his eighth edition omitted πρῶτον from the text, relegating it to a place in the apparatus.[135] B. F. Westcott and F. J. A. Hort also rejected the longer reading in their 1881 edition.[136] H. von Soden likewise considered the longer reading to be dubious, enclosing it in brackets in his 1913 edition.[137] The shorter reading is currently endorsed by both *UBSGNT* 4th edition and NA 27th edition.

We may therefore proceed with the exegesis of the passage without bias concerning the time of the descent with respect to the ascent. Nevertheless (as G. B. Caird has observed), the very existence of this textual

---

134 J. N. D. Kelly, *Early Christian Creeds*, 382. This is, in fact, how Tertullian apparently used the doctrine of Christ's descent to the underworld; for him, it demonstrated the participation of Christ in the full extent of human experience and thus implied his true humanity (*De anima* 55.2).

135 C. von Tischendorf, *Novum Testamentum Graece, editio octava critica maior* (Leipzig: Giesecke & Devrient, 1872; reprint ed., Graz: Akademische Druck- u. Verlagsanstalt, 1965) 683.

136 B. F. Westcott and F. J. A. Hort, *The New Testament in the Original Greek* (London: Macmillan, 1881; reprint ed., New York: Macmillan, 1946) 2.433.

137 H. *Frhr.* von Soden, *Die Schriften des Neuen Testaments in ihrer ältesten erreichbaren Textgestalt hergestellt auf Grund ihrer Textgeschichte*, 2: *Text mit Apparat* (Göttingen: Vandenhoeck u. Ruprecht, 1913) 766.

variant undoubtedly influenced many interpreters, even though they may have accepted the shorter reading as representing the original text.[138]

2. The Inclusion of Μέρη Before Τῆς Γῆς in Eph 4:9

A second textual problem in Eph 4:9 also warrants brief attention. A number of manuscripts, some of them significant witnesses to the original text of Ephesians, omit μέρη after κατώτερα. Because this may affect the interpretation of the genitive phrase τῆς γῆς which together with κατώτερα specifies the locus of Christ's descent, the decision to include or omit μέρη could affect the exegesis of the entire passage. Again, as with the previous problem, the evidence from the manuscript tradition as well as transcriptional factors which may have affected the transmission of the text will be examined.

2.1. The Evidence From the Manuscript Tradition

The shorter reading, which omits μέρη, is supported by 𝔓[46] (ca. 200 CE), an important early witness of the Alexandrian text type. In addition the omission of μέρη occurs in several Western uncials: the original hand of D (06 [Claromontanus], 6th century), F (010 [Augiensis], 9th century), and G (012 [Boernerianus], 9th century). There is no minuscule support for the omission, but a single lectionary (l 921) has the shorter reading. Among the early versions the Sahidic Coptic and Ethiopic omit μέρη, as do all but a single manuscript of the Itala (Old Latin). A few Fathers also appear to quote a version of the text which reflects the omission of μέρη: Irenaeus (ca. 202 CE, in the Latin manuscripts; the Latin translation of Irenaeus' works dates from the third or fourth century), Clement of Alexandria (prior to 215 CE, quoting from Theodotus, a second century Gnostic), Tertullian (ca. 220 CE), Origen (253/254 CE; the shorter reading is found in the Latin text), Eusebius (339 CE), Victorinus of Rome (362 CE), Ambrosiaster (366-84 CE),[139] Hilary (367 CE), Lucifer (370/371 CE), and Jerome (420 CE). There is no support for the shorter reading from the Byzantine text type except for l 921 and the Ethiopic version; both the lectionary and the version are relatively late and therefore do not play a significant role in the decision to omit or include the word. Manuscripts which support the omission of μέρη are displayed in Chart 2.1 on the following page. These are considerably fewer in number than the manuscripts supporting the word's inclusion.

---

[138] G. B. Caird, "The Descent of Christ in Ephesians 4, 7-11," 538.

[139] Again, dates given in parentheses normally represent the approximate date of death. For Ambrosiaster, the dates given are those of Pope Damasus during whose reign the works are thought to have been written.

Chart 2.1: Witnesses which omit μέρη in Eph 4:9

Alexandrian	Byzantine	Western	Mixed, Other
𝔓⁴⁶			
		D* F G	
	l 921		
Sahidic Coptic	Ethiopic	itala (all but f)	
		Irenaeus ˡᵃᵗ Tertullian Victorinus-Rome Ambrosiaster Hilary, Lucifer Jerome	Clement ⁽ᵉˣ ᵀʰᵈ⁾ Origen ˡᵃᵗ Eusebius

On the other hand, most of the remaining textual witnesses extant for Ephesians support the longer reading which includes μέρη. Among these the following are significant: the Alexandrian uncials ℵ (01 [Sinaiticus], 4th century), A (02, 5th century), B (03 [Vaticanus], 4th century), C (04 [Ephraemi Rescriptus], 5th century), I (016, 5th century), P (025 in the epistles, 9th century), and Ψ (044, 8th/9th century). Also supporting the inclusion of μέρη are the Byzantine uncials K (018 in the epistles, 9th century) and L (020 in the epistles, also 9th century), the corrected Western text of D (06 [Claromontanus], 6th century),[140] and the uncials 075 (10th century) and 0150 (9th century). A large number of minuscule manuscripts also support the longer reading: the Alexandrian minuscules 6, 33, 81, 104, 1175, and 1739; all of the Byzantine minuscule manuscripts (without exception); and a number of minuscule manuscripts of mixed text type, including 256, 263, 365, 424, 436, 459, 1241, 1319, 1573, 1852, 1881, 1912, 1962, 2127, 2200, and 2464. Among the early versions, all manuscripts of the Vulgate support the inclusion of μέρη, as does a single manuscript of the Itala (Old Latin), f (78 in the Beuron Catalogue), along with the evidence from the Bohairic Coptic, Harclean Syriac, Armenian, and Slavonic versions. Some Fathers also include μέρη: Eustathias of Antioch (prior to 337 CE), Chrysostom (407 CE), Theodore of Mopsuestia, in the Latin (428 CE), Pelagius (ca. 423-29 CE), Augustine (430 CE), Cyril of Alexandria (444 CE), and Theodoret (ca. 466 CE). The evidence for the inclusion of μέρη is displayed in *Chart* 2.2 on the following page.

---

[140] The insertion of μέρη was done by the second corrector of D according to NA27 and is of a later date than the manuscript itself.

Chart 2.2: Witnesses which include μέρη in Eph 4:9

Alexandrian	Byzantine	Western	Mixed, Other
ℵ A B C I P Ψ	K L		D² 075 0150
6. 33. 81. 104. 1175. 1739	*Byz Minuscule Manuscripts*		256. 263. 365. 424. 436. 459. 1241. 1319. 1573. 1852. 1881. 1912. 1962. 2127. 2200. 2464
	Byz Lectionaries		
Bohairic Coptic Vulgate	Harclean Syriac Armenian, Slavonic	itala ᶠ	
Cyril	Chrysostom Theodoret	Theodore ˡᵃᵗ Pelgius Augustine	Eustathias

2.2. *Date and Quality of the Manuscripts*

Once again we shall consider first the evidence for the omission of μέρη. This reading is supported by 𝔓⁴⁶, the earliest and most important of the witnesses, which is classified by K. Aland as a category I manuscript.[141] One category II manuscript, D, and two category III manuscripts, F and G, also support the shorter reading.

In comparison to this, the inclusion of μέρη is supported by five category I manuscripts (ℵ, A, B, 33, and 1739). Seven category II manuscripts also support the longer reading (C, I, 81, 1175, 1881, 2127, and 2464), as do six category III manuscripts (P, Ψ, 075, 0150, 104, 256, 263, 365, 459, 1241, 1319, 1573, 1852, 1912, 1962, and 2200). All category V manuscripts, including the Byzantine uncials K and L and the Byzantine minuscules, support the inclusion of μέρη. Thus the weight of the manuscript evidence favors the inclusion of μέρη. Although 𝔓⁴⁶ is an early and important witness (perhaps the single most important witness) to the original text of Ephesians, it alone of the most important manuscripts (category I according to Aland's classification) supports the omission of μέρη. In addition, the shorter reading lacks significant secondary support (only one category II manuscript, D, favors it) and has no minuscule support at all. The evidence for the omission of μέρη is primarily confined to the Western text type, including most of the Itala

---

[141] K. and B. Aland, *The Text of the New Testament*, 99. For a description of the categories used in classifying the manuscripts, see *The Text of the New Testament*, 105-106, and p. 36 of the present work.

(Old Latin) manuscripts and a number of the Western Fathers.

2.3. *Geographical Distribution of the Variant Readings*

A superficial glance at the geographical distribution of the variant readings seems to favor the longer reading, since it is present in all three of the major text types, while the shorter reading is not. The shorter reading appears only in the Western and Alexandrian text types, and support in the latter consists of a single witness. The support for the omission of μέρη based on geographical distribution is better than it may at first appear, however. The Alexandrian witness which favors it is very early ($\mathfrak{P}^{46}$, ca. 200 CE), indicating the shorter reading was present at an early date in the Alexandrian tradition. In the Western text the shorter reading is well supported from a relatively early period, since although the earliest Itala manuscript dates from the fourth or fifth century (k, or 1 in the Beuron Catalogue), it represents a text whose Greek *Vorlage* is thought by some to be traceable to the second century.[142]

Nevertheless, evidence from the geographical distribution of the variants still favors the longer reading. The inclusion of μέρη is well represented in two of the major text types (Alexandrian and Byzantine) at a reasonably early date, and the agreement of so many major witnesses within each of these text types points to the existence of the reading itself at a time prior to the earliest surviving witness in each text type.[143] The shorter reading, on the other hand, is basically limited to the Western text type, with $\mathfrak{P}^{46}$ as the only exception.

2.4. *Conclusions Based on the Manuscript Evidence*

On the whole, the manuscript evidence favors the inclusion of μέρη. The early date for the shorter reading is not enough to outweigh the preponderance of evidence in favor of the inclusion of μέρη. The widespread geographical distribution of the longer reading confirms this. On the basis of the manuscript evidence it appears that while the shorter reading represents an ancient and significant tradition, it was primarily limited to the Western text and is not representative of the original text of Eph 4:9.

2.5. *Transcriptional Factors*

Transcriptional factors in this case favor the shorter reading which omits

---

[142] K. and B. Aland, *The Text of the New Testament*, 183.

[143] This is implied by the extent to which the reading has established itself in the Alexandrian and Byzantine text types. The assumption is that some time (one or two centuries, perhaps) would be necessary for a reading to have become so widespread and well-established within a given text type. Thus while the earliest Alexandrian manuscripts which contains the longer reading date from the 4th century (‭א‬ and B), the reading was probably present in the Alexandrian text some time in the second or third century.

μέρη in Eph 4:9. If the word were present in the original text but omitted in the process of transmission, the omission would almost certainly
have to be accidental, since there is no significant theological point to
be made by either the inclusion or the omission of μέρη. The normal
causes of accidental omission such as homoioteleuton or homoioarcton
(in the case of a copyist working individually from an exemplar) or itacism (if copying were being done from dictation, or if a solitary copyist
were pronouncing the text aloud to himself) do not seem to be present
here. There are no words or syllables in the immediate context which
resemble μέρη sufficiently to result in accidental confusion. It is perhaps
possible to suggest an unintentional harmonization with Ps 62:9 LXX or
Ps 138:15 LXX, where in both cases the phrase τὰ κατώτατα τῆς γῆς occurs. This possibility is remote, however, because neither passage in the
LXX has any further connection with the context of Ephesians 4 beyond this individual phrase. In addition there is no manuscript evidence
for a corresponding change from κατώτερα to κατώτατα in Eph 4:9
which would point to harmonization with the LXX at this point.

On the other hand, it is easier to see how a copyist who encountered
a version of the text which read εἰς τὰ κατώτερα τῆς γῆς would be inclined to add μέρη as an explanatory gloss to clarify the wording in order to reflect his own understanding of the passage. This is in keeping
with the standard guideline in textual criticism that the shorter reading
more often than not represents the original (the rule of *brevior lectio*).[144]
This may have taken place in the form of an accidental inclusion of a
marginal gloss by a copyist who mistook it for a correction.

Thus, with regard to the transcriptional probabilities, the shorter reading which omits μέρη is more difficult to explain and could probably
have given rise to the reading which includes μέρη without much difficulty. On the basis of transcriptional factors the omission of μέρη is to
be preferred.

2.6. *Conclusions on the Inclusion of Μέρη in Eph 4:9*
Although the transcriptional factors favor the shorter reading, in our
judgment the preponderance of the manuscript evidence (which favors
the inclusion of μέρη in the text of Eph 4:9) outweighs transcriptional
probabilities in this instance. The shorter reading is evidently ancient, as
indicated by 𝔓46, yet aside from this important witness it is confined to
manuscripts of the Western text type. This suggests that it represents an
accidental omission which, although early, did not find its way into
manuscripts of the other major text types (with the sole exception of

---

[144] For explanation and discussion of this rule or 'canon' of textual criticism, see n. 132
above.

𝔓⁴⁶). Therefore, we may proceed in our investigation of the grammatical and syntactical possibilities for the genitive phrase τῆς γῆς in Eph 4:9 on the assumption that μέρη was part of the original text.

CHAPTER TWO

TO WHERE DID HE DESCEND?
THE MEANING OF ΤΑ ΚΑΤΩΤΕΡΑ ΜΕΡΗ ΤΗΣ ΓΗΣ

A. THE SYNTAX AND SIGNIFICANCE OF THE GENITIVE PHRASE ΤΗΣ ΓΗΣ IN EPH 4:9

To answer the question "To where did Christ descend?" in Eph 4:7-11 we must investigate the syntactical force of the phrase τῆς γῆς in Eph 4:9. The prepositional phrase εἰς τὰ κατώτερα μέρη τῆς γῆς evidently specifies the locus of Christ's descent, thus answering the question posed above. However, the syntax of the final genitive phrase τῆς γῆς can be interpreted a number of different ways, all of which can have a significant effect upon the nature, time, and place of Christ's descent in Eph 4:9-10.

According to N. Turner, there are three possibilities for the syntactical relationship expressed by τῆς γῆς: (1) a partitive genitive ("the lowest parts of the earth itself"), (2) a comparative genitive ("the regions below the earth"), or (3) an appositive genitive ("the lower regions, namely, the earth").[1] Although recent interpreters have tended to prefer one of the last two options, support can still be found for a partitive genitive as the simplest explanation for a genitive following μέρη.[2] All three possibilities will now be evaluated in an attempt to determine the advantages and disadvantages of each.

1. Τῆς Γῆς as Partitive Genitive

In classical Greek the partitive genitive designated a given category or whole, a part or fraction of which was designated by the noun it restricted. The partitive genitive normally stood before or after the noun denoting the part: τῶν Θρᾳκῶν πελτασταί (Thucydides 7.27), οἱ ἄποροι τῶν πολιτῶν (Demosthenes 18.104). Rarely a partitive genitive would even stand between the restricted noun and its article: οἱ τῶν ἀδίκων ἀφικνούμενοι (Plato, *Gorgias* 525c). While the restricted noun normally indicated a part or portion of the whole, as in μέρος τι τῶν βαρβάρων (Thucydides 1.1), in some instances all could be included so

---

[1] N. Turner, *Syntax*, MHT 3 (Edinburgh: Clark, 1963) 215. Paraphrases of the phrase τὰ κατώτερα μέρη τῆς γῆς have been supplied by the present writer.

[2] F. Büchsel, s.v. "κατώτερος," *TDNT* 3.641. J. D. G. Dunn also argues that a genitive following μέρη would most likely be partitive (*Christology in the Making: A New Testament Inquiry into the Origins of the Doctrine of the Incarnation* [London: SCM, 1980] 186-87).

that there was no partition: τὸ πᾶν πλῆθος τῶν ὁπλιτῶν (Thucydides 8.93). The idea of division was not always clearly stated, and in some instances the governing noun which denoted the part could be omitted entirely: Ἀρχίας τῶν Ἡρακλειδῶν (Thucydides 6.3).[3] Some grammarians would also place in the category of partitive genitive the use of the genitive to denote the district or country in which a city or locality is found, e.g., τῆς Ἀττικῆς ἐς Οἰνόην (Thucydides 2.18) and τῆς Ἰταλίας Λοκροί (Thucydides 3.86).[4]

In the Koiné period the partitive use of the pure genitive was being replaced by the use of the prepositions ἐκ and, less frequently, ἀπό or ἐν.[5] Partitive genitives were frequently used following verbs in a sense overlapping with that of an accusative direct object.[6] Although some of these could be more appropriately labelled direct objects (e.g., Acts 9:7, ἀκούοντες μὲν τῆς φωνῆς), there are some more obviously partitive uses after nouns (referred to by J. Humbert as "adnominal" genitives).[7] These occur after words denoting a part or fraction of a whole, such as εἷς, τίς, ἕκαστος, οἱ λοιποί, etc., or after words referring to a group or subdivision (e.g., Rom 15:26, τοὺς πτωχοὺς τῶν ἁγίων, "the poor among the saints").[8] The phrase τὰ κατώτερα μέρη τῆς γῆς in Eph 4:9 would obviously fall into this category if (as concluded in the previous chapter) μέρη is regarded as part of the original text.[9] F. Büchsel conceded that a partitive genitive was "essentially simpler, for a gen. [sic] with μέρη most naturally denotes the whole to which the parts belong, esp. if this whole has not yet been named."[10] Büchsel himself apparently considered τῆς γῆς in Eph 4:9 a partitive genitive, since his comment in a corresponding footnote seemed to rule out a comparative genitive as unlikely.[11] There is still some ambiguity concerning Büchsel's view,

---

[3] H. W. Smyth, *Greek Grammar*, rev. G. M. Messing (Cambridge, MA: Harvard University Press, 1956; orig. pub. as *A Greek Grammar for Colleges*, 1920) 315-16.

[4] J. Humbert, *Syntaxe Grecque*, 3rd ed. (Paris: Klincksieck, 1960) 270.

[5] BDF, 90. Essentially the same observation is made by L. Radermacher (*Neutestamentliche Grammatik*, 2d ed. [Tübingen: Mohr, 1925] 139) and A. T. Robertson (*A Grammar of the Greek New Testament in the Light of Historical Research*, 4th ed. [Nashville: Broadman, 1934] 502).

[6] C. F. D. Moule, *An Idiom Book of New Testament Greek*, 2d ed. (Cambridge: Cambridge University Press, 1959) 36.

[7] J. Humbert, *Syntaxe Grecque*, 271.

[8] C. F. D. Moule, *An Idiom Book of New Testament Greek*, 43.

[9] Even if one were to conclude that μέρη should not be included as part of the original text of Eph 4:9, it might still be possible to consider τῆς γῆς a partitive genitive, since in classical Greek the governing noun with the partitive genitive was occasionally omitted. Note the example Ἀρχίας τῶν Ἡρακλειδῶν (Thucydides 6.3) mentioned in the discussion of the partitive genitive in classical Greek above.

[10] F. Büchsel, s.v. "κατώτερος," *TDNT* 3.641.

[11] Büchsel, n. 10, 641. Büchsel in this note argued against the earlier view that the form κατώτερος itself is comparative rather than superlative in degree. A comparative idea might be

however, because the most recent English edition of BDF (1961) states that Büchsel considered the genitive τῆς γῆς in Eph 4:9 to be comparative. Both partitive and appositive genitive are rejected without further explanation.[12] In any event, Büchsel's statement in *TDNT* 3 that a partitive genitive following μέρη would be the simplest way of understanding τῆς γῆς is probably correct. There is (as discussed in chapter one) some uncertainty over the authenticity of μέρη because a number of manuscripts of the Western text, along with 𝔓[46], omit it and read simply εἰς τὰ κατώτερα τῆς γῆς in Eph 4:9.[13] The shorter reading, in general, is preferred as the reading most likely to give rise to the other variants. But we concluded on the basis of strong manuscript evidence that μέρη should be regarded as a genuine part of the original text, and this would suggest that a partitive genitive is still a possibility for τῆς γῆς here.

With regard to the meaning of the phrase, a view that takes τῆς γῆς as strictly partitive (i.e., "the lowest parts of the earth itself") would probably imply that the locus of the descent is the grave, 'Sheol', which would be viewed as the lowest part of the lower 'story' in a 'two-storied' cosmology. This agrees more closely with the cosmology of Ephesians than a strictly comparative sense, which implies the existence of a third and lower 'story' below the earth itself. Aside from this it is difficult to see much difference in nuance between a partitive and comparative use of the genitive τῆς γῆς in Eph 4:9; this appears to be more a difference of terminology than of sense.

2. *Τῆς Γῆς as Comparative Genitive*

The genitive case used to express comparison was common in classical Greek, and occurs in the NT in similar constructions.[14] In such a construction κατώτερος in Eph 4:9 would be understood as a comparative adjective followed by μέρη and a genitive, τῆς γῆς, which specifies the thing with which the comparison is being made. The force of the entire construction would then be "the regions lower than the earth." BDF portrays such a meaning as representative of F. Büchsel's view. Although BDF does not explicitly label τῆς γῆς a comparative genitive, it is clear from the translation offered ("the regions under the earth") and from their rejection of the other options (partitive and appositive) that

associated with the genitive τῆς γῆς rather than κατώτερα, but Büchsel dismissed this as "unlikely."

12 BDF, 92. This is a translation and revision of the 9th-10th German edition.

13 The authenticity of μέρη as part of the original text of Eph 4:9 is discussed in ch. 1, 40-45.

14 BDF, 99; A. T. Robertson, *A Grammar of the Greek New Testament in the Light of Historical Research*, 666-67.

the phrase is understood as comparative.[15]

Also at issue in this discussion is a related but separate point, the nature of the comparison expressed by κατώτερος. Strictly speaking the adjective κατώτερος is comparative in degree. But degrees of comparison with adjectives were not always rigidly maintained in Koiné Greek. A. T. Robertson, for example, stated that no clear distinction could be made in the NT between the comparative and superlative degrees of adjectives, and that τὰ κατώτερα μέρη in Eph 4:9 is an example of a comparative form used in a superlative sense.[16] Likewise, J. H. Moulton argued that the true superlative form was disappearing in the Koiné papyri and was being replaced by the comparative.[17] On this point BDF agrees, stating that a simplification of degrees of comparison in the vernacular led to the virtual disappearance of the superlative (which, when retained in the NT, has mostly elative force) and its replacement by the comparative form.[18] Such substitution of forms (comparative for superlative) has also been observed in the secular papyri by E. Mayser.[19] On the other hand, however, L. Radermacher argued that the comparative form κατώτερος in Eph 4:9 was used as a positive rather than a superlative in degree.[20] Thus it appears legitimate from a purely grammatical standpoint to consider the comparative form κατώτερα in Eph 4:9 positive, comparative, or superlative in force, depending upon how one understands the context.

A view that takes the genitive τῆς γῆς as comparative (i.e., "the regions lower than the earth itself") suggests a locus for the descent in the underworld, with this as the third and lowest 'story' of a 'three-storied' cosmology. This is more consistent with the traditional interpretation of Eph 4:9-10 (involving a *descensus ad inferos*) than the other

---

[15] BDF, 92; compare F. Büchsel, s.v. "κατώτερος," *TDNT* 3.641, n. 10 (discussed in n. 11 above), which appears to contradict BDF's description of Büchsel's position.

[16] A. T. Robertson, *A Grammar of the Greek New Testament in the Light of Historical Research*, 668.

[17] J. H. Moulton, *Prolegomena*, 3rd ed., MHT 1 (Edinburgh: Clark, 1908) 78.

[18] BDF, 32.

[19] E. Mayser, *Grammatik der griechischen Papyri aus der Ptolemäerzeit*, 2: *Satzlehre*, part 1 (Berlin and Leipzig: Walter de Gruyter, 1934; reprint ed., 1970) 49-51.

[20] L. Radermacher, *Neutestamentliche Grammatik*, 2d ed. (Tübingen: Mohr, 1925) 69-70, 225. Κατώτερος is mentioned on pp. 69-70, but the only specific reference to Eph 4:9 occurs on p. 225 in a list of additions and corrections. These were not done by Radermacher himself; the note including Eph 4:9 was added by R. Hoffmann. No discussion of the context was offered, but only the remark that κατώτερος is to be understood as positive in degree (rather than comparative, as the form would indicate). Radermacher was cited by H.-J. Klauck in support of the possibility that κατώτερος may be understood as positive in degree ("Das Amt in der Kirche nach Eph 4, 1-16," *WiWeis* 36 [1973] 94, n. 68). Radermacher was also cited by M. Barth as supporting the meaning "the earth down here" for the phrase τὰ κατώτερα μέρη τῆς γῆς in Eph 4:9 (*Ephesians: Translation and Commentary on Chapters 4-6*, AB 34A [Garden City, NY: Doubleday, 1974] 434), but see n. 36 below.

interpretive options put forward for the genitive τῆς γῆς, although none of the ancient authorities who held such a view articulated the force of the genitive phrase in 4:9 in precisely this way. As we have already pointed out, such a three-storied cosmology is less in keeping with the cosmology of Ephesians, which elsewhere reflects only two stories, the earth below and the heavens above.

3. Τῆς Γῆς as Appositive Genitive

The genitive used in the sense of an appositive, that is, of an explicit word in the genitive case used to explain a more general word, is found in classical Greek primarily in poetic literature. G. B. Winer believed it to be infrequent in Greek and confined mostly to geographical expressions corresponding to *urbs Romae* or *fluvius Euphratis* in Latin.[21] H. W. Smyth cited a few poetic examples of this sort, such as Ἰλίου πόλις (Homer, *Iliad*, 5.642), but also some non-geographical expressions like ἄελλαι παντοίων ἀνέμων (Homer, *Odyssey*, 5.292). In addition there are some examples of the construction in prose, e.g., ὑὸς μέγα χρῆμα, " a great affair of a boar" (Herodotus, 1.36) and τὸ ὄρος τῆς Ἰστώνης, "Mount Istone" (Thucydides, 4.46).[22] From the Koiné period E. Mayser cited as an example of an appositive genitive an official letter containing topographical directions which include the phrase κατὰ πόλιν Μέμφεως.[23]

In the NT the use of the appositive genitive conforms to classical usage: one clear example of a geographical reference with πόλις is found in 2 Pet 2:6, πόλεις Σοδόμων καὶ Γομόρρας. BDF lists as a non-geographical use of an appositive genitive the phrase τὸν ἀρραβῶνα τοῦ πνεύματος in 2 Cor 5:5.[24] N. Turner described the appositive genitive (which he parenthetically labelled both *genitivus materiae* and *genitivus epexegeticus*) as conforming in the NT to both classical and Koiné usage, but incidentally Hebraic.[25] J. H. Moulton himself held that the appositive genitive was a well-known idiom in Homer (cf. the examples above) and needed no appeal to Semitic usage for justification; rather, the vernacular had merely preserved the poetic idiom.[26] C. F. D. Moule regarded the appositive genitive as a specialized use of the more

---

21 G. B. Winer, *Grammatik des neutestamentlichen Sprachidioms als sichere Grundlage der neutestamentlichen Exegese*, 3rd ed. (Leipzig: F. C. W. Vogel, 1830) 301-302.

22 H. W. Smyth, *Greek Grammar*, 317.

23 E. Mayser, *Grammatik der griechischen Papyri aus der Ptolemäerzeit*, 2: *Satzlehre*, 117.

24 BDF, 92.

25 N. Turner, *Syntax*, MHT 3.214. It would probably be more accurate to regard the genitive of material as a separate but related usage. M. Zerwick also refers to the appositive genitive (*genitivus appositivus*) as *genitivus epexegeticus* or «epexegetic» genitive (see below, n. 28).

26 J. H. Moulton, *Prolegomena*, 3rd ed., MHT 1, 73-74.

general category he referred to as the defining genitive. Moule cited as an example Rom 4:11, σημεῖον ἔλαβεν περιτομῆς, which he regarded as "exactly equivalent to the English idiom 'the city of Manchester' (= 'the city Manchester')."[27] M. Zerwick defined the appositive genitive as a construction "in which the substantive added in the genitive is in reality an apposition denoting the same person or thing as the substantive to which the genitive is attached," and listed a number of (what he considers to be) NT examples, among them τῆς γῆς in Eph 4:9.[28]

A view of Eph 4:9-10 that understands τῆς γῆς as an appositive genitive (i.e., "the lower regions, namely, the earth") would require as the locus of the descent the earth itself. As with a partitive genitive, this would imply a 'two-storied' cosmology and would thus be consistent with the cosmology found elsewhere in Ephesians. Specification of the earth itself as the locus of the descent would be compatible with two different interpretations of Eph 4:7-11: (1) one which refers the descent of Christ in 4:9-10 to the incarnation, or (2) one which considers the descent to describe the subsequent descent of Christ as the Spirit to distribute the spiritual gifts described in Eph 4:11-16. A large number of modern interpreters have endorsed one or the other of these views, as we have seen in our brief look at the history of interpretation of the passage in chapter one. Many of these interpreters have also commented on the use of the genitive τῆς γῆς in Eph 4:9, and we shall now examine briefly some of the more significant observations that have been made.

G. B. Winer, in his *Grammatik des neutestamentlichen Sprachidioms als sichere Grundlage der neutestamentlichen Exegese* (original ed. 1822), was among the first of the modern grammarians and interpreters to place τῆς γῆς in Eph 4:9 in the category of appositive genitive. He compared it to Isa 37:14 [38:14] LXX, εἰς τὸ ὕψος τοῦ οὐρανοῦ, and Acts 2:19, ἐν τῷ οὐρανῷ ἄνω…ἐπὶ τῆς γῆς κάτω, which reflects a 'two-storied' cosmology similar to that in Ephesians. Winer (who interpreted the descent in Eph 4:9 as a reference to the incarnation) believed that the earth, described in Eph 4:9 as a lower region, was being contrasted to ὕψος (i.e., heaven) in the quotation in 4:8.[29] This is similar to H. von Soden's understanding of the genitive phrase τῆς γῆς in Eph 4:9. Although von Soden understood the descent to be subsequent to the ascent introduced by the quotation in 4:8, he identified τὰ κατώτερα μέρη in 4:9 with the lower regions of the universe, to which τῆς γῆς as geni-

27 C. F. D. Moule, *An Idiom Book of New Testament Greek*, 38.
28 M. Zerwick, *Biblical Greek Illustrated by Examples* (Rome: Pontifical Biblical Institute, 1963) 16-17.
29 G. B. Winer, *Grammatik des neutestamentlichen Sprachidioms*, 3rd ed., 301.

tive stood in apposition.[30]

Like von Soden, T. K. Abbott in his 1897 commentary on Ephesians held that the descent in Eph 4:9 was subsequent to the ascent of 4:8 and referred to the descent of Christ to his church. Abbott, although he acknowledged that the genitive phrase in question could be either partitive or appositive, believed an appositive genitive to be the most probable in the context, describing the earth itself as the 'lower regions'. Since the ascent mentioned in 4:8 was from earth to heaven, the descent would most probably be from heaven to earth.[31]

One of the most thorough studies of the interpretive possibilities for Eph 4:9-10 is found in E. Haupt's *Die Gefangenschaftsbriefe* (1902). In his opinion the descent referred to Christ's descent from heaven to earth at the incarnation. If the author had intended to refer to a descent to the underworld as the lowest 'story' of a three-storied cosmology, a superlative form (κατώτατος) would have been more logical. Haupt acknowledged that (as we have already seen) a comparative form could have superlative meaning, but argued against such a possibility in Eph 4:9 because the author would surely have recalled the OT use of the superlative κατώτατος (Pss 62:9 and 138:15 LXX). This would leave an appositive genitive, by which the earth itself is viewed as the 'lower regions' of the universe under heaven, as the most probable use of the genitive τῆς γῆς.[32]

The majority of recent interpreters have continued to understand τῆς γῆς as an appositive genitive. H. Schlier, in his 1957 commentary on Ephesians, stated that τῆς γῆς must be understood as an appositive genitive because this agreed with the location of the evil 'powers' in Ephesians in the heavens rather than under the earth.[33] F. W. Grosheide in his commentary also understood τῆς γῆς as a genitive of apposition, citing additional examples of this usage in 2 Cor 5:5, Rom 4:11 and Rom 8:23.[34] M. Zerwick in his discussion of the "epexegetic" genitive considered τῆς γῆς in Eph 4:9 to be an appositive which referred not to

---

[30] H. von Soden, ed., *Die Briefe an die Kolosser, Epheser, Philemon; die Pastoralbriefe*, HKNT 3 (Freiburg and Leipzig: Mohr, 1893) 136.

[31] T. K. Abbott, *A Critical and Exegetical Commentary on the Epistles to the Ephesians and to the Colossians*, ICC (Edinburgh: Clark, 1897) 114-15.

[32] E. Haupt classified interpretations of Eph 4:9-10 into four major categories, because he distinguished between the view that saw the descent as Christ's descent into the grave at death and the view that held to a descent of Christ to the underworld (*ad inferos*) during the *triduum* (*Die Gefangenschaftsbriefe* [Göttingen: Vandenhoeck u. Ruprecht, 1902] 139). It seems more reasonable, however, to see the view that Christ simply descended into the grave as a development of the traditional view that held to a descent to the underworld, and this is the arrangement followed here.

[33] H. Schlier, *Der Brief an die Epheser*, 2d ed. (Düsseldorf: Patmos-Verlag, 1958) 192.

[34] F. W. Grosheide, *De Brief van Paulus aan de Efeziërs*, CNT(K) (Kampen: Kok, 1960) 65.

Christ's descent to the underworld, but to "His coming into the world itself, called τὰ κατώτερα μέρη with respect to heaven."[35] In his 1974 commentary M. Barth concluded that the phrase "the lower parts of the earth" was probably equivalent to "the low region of the earth" or "the earth down here," and although he did not specifically use the term "appositive genitive" in connection with the view, it is clear that Barth understood the phrase as such.[36] Another who argued for the interpretation of τῆς γῆς as an appositive genitive is A. T. Lincoln. In a 1982 article he cited the frequency of appositive genitives elsewhere in Ephesians in support of the view. Further examples of this use of the genitive in Ephesians mentioned by Lincoln were 2:14, 2:15, 2:20, 6:14, 6:16, and 6:17.[37] Finally, F. F. Bruce in his 1984 commentary described the genitive τῆς γῆς as "epexegetic after τὰ κατώτερα," following the terminology of M. Zerwick. It is clear from the context that Bruce understood the phrase as an appositive genitive because he stated that "'the lower parts of the earth' should be understood as meaning 'the earth below'."[38]

By now it should be clear that one's understanding of the syntactical force of the genitive τῆς γῆς in Eph 4:9 will be based upon one's understanding of the entire context of Eph 4:7-11. Each of the three possibilities we have considered can provide an acceptable explanation for the use of the genitive τῆς γῆς in Eph 4:9. Each of these possibilities has found adherents, although the tendency in the present century by grammarians and interpreters alike has been to prefer an appositive genitive as the most probable explanation for the author's use of τῆς γῆς in 4:9.

There is one additional factor which lends further support to the understanding of τῆς γῆς as an appositive genitive and thus warrants our consideration: the frequency of appositive genitives as a stylistic feature of Ephesians. This has been noted by A. T. Lincoln in his 1982 article mentioned above. He identified six other constructions in Ephesians as appositive genitives. Apart from τῆς γῆς in 4:9, these may be mentioned briefly. There are three in chapter two: τὸ μεσότοιχον τοῦ φραγμοῦ

---

35 M. Zerwick, *Biblical Greek Illustrated by Examples*, 17.

36 M. Barth, *Ephesians: Translation and Commentary on Chapters 4-6*, AB 34A (Garden City, NY: Doubleday, 1974) 434. Barth referred in n. 49 to L. Radermacher's *Neutestamentliche Grammatik* (2d ed. [Tübingen: Mohr, 1925] 69-70 and 225). While Radermacher discussed the interchangeability of comparative and superlative forms of adjectives in the NT, he did not discuss the appositive genitive at all. The only specific reference to Eph 4:9 is found on p. 225, and this is an addendum by R. Hoffmann. Radermacher did not discuss the genitive phrase τῆς γῆς or his own interpretation of the descent at all in *Neutestamentliche Grammatik*.

37 A. T. Lincoln, "The Use of the OT in Ephesians," *JSNT* 14 (1982) 22.

38 F. F. Bruce, *The Epistles to the Colossians, to Philemon, and to the Ephesians*, NICNT (Grand Rapids: Eerdmans, 1984) 343, n. 55.

(2:14), "the intervening wall, namely, the barrier," which describes the wall of enmity which formerly divided Jew and Gentile; τὸν νόμον τῶν ἐντολῶν (2:15), "the law consisting of commandments," which describes the totality of the Mosaic law as made up of individual commandments; and τῷ θεμελίῳ τῶν ἀποστόλων καὶ προφητῶν (2:20), "the foundation of the apostles and prophets," which (although alternative explanations are possible) is best understood as describing the apostles and prophets themselves as the foundation upon which the church is being built. In chapter six Lincoln noted three more appositive genitives: τὸν θώρακα τῆς δικαιοσύνης (6:14), "the breastplate of righteousness," τὸν θυρεὸν τῆς πίστεως (6:16), "the shield of faith," and τὴν περικεφαλαίαν τοῦ σωτηρίου (6:17), "the helmet of salvation." All of these describe pieces of the 'spiritual' armour which Christians are instructed to appropriate for their own defence against evil spiritual forces (cf. 6:12). In addition to the appositive genitives identified by Lincoln in Ephesians, εἰρήνης in the phrase ἐν τῷ συνδέσμῳ τῆς εἰρήνης in Eph 4:3 should probably be considered a genitive of apposition, since the bond (σύνδεσμος) which believers are to maintain consists of peace itself; W. Bauer labelled this an 'epexegetic' genitive, which as we have already seen is an alternative term for an appositive genitive.[39]

4. *Conclusions Regarding the Use of the Genitive Τῆς Γῆς in Eph 4:9*

Of course, the presence of other appositive genitives in Ephesians, no matter how frequent, cannot prove that τῆς γῆς in 4:9 should be understood in the same way. Nevertheless, there are sufficient instances of the appositive genitive in Ephesians to warrant the observation that its use is characteristic of the author's style, as E. Percy in his stylistic analysis of Colossians and Ephesians concluded.[40] As a stylistic technique of the author of Ephesians, an appositive genitive in a passage like 4:9 certainly represents a plausible explanation for the use of the genitive if other contextual factors are in agreement. Before we turn to the contextual factors relevant to this issue, however, we shall examine several other significant issues: (1) in the remainder of this chapter, the descent imagery in Eph 4:7-11 as it relates to Jonah in particular; (2) in Chapter Three, the relationship of Moses-traditions about a heavenly ascent at Sinai to Ps 68:19 (as quoted in Eph 4:8) in the rabbinic literature and other extra-biblical sources; (3) in Chapter Four, traditions about an ascent to heaven by Moses not related to Ps 68:19; and (4) in Chapter Five, the relationship between Eph 4:7-11 and Pentecost.

---

[39] BAGD, s.v. σύνδεσμος, 785.
[40] E. Percy, *Die Probleme der Kolosser- und Epheserbriefe* (Lund: Gleerup, 1946) 186.

B. DESCENT IMAGERY IN THE NT AND OTHER EARLY SOURCES

In a work published in 1980 A. T. Hanson examined the background of the NT doctrine of the *descensus ad inferos* with particular attention to the passage which is usually understood to support the doctrine, 1 Pet 3:18-4:6.[41] In the course of this study Hanson also examined a number of other NT passages, including Eph 4:7-10 and Rom 10:6-8, which are frequently understood as reflecting a *descensus ad inferos*. In evaluating the NT material Hanson turned to rabbinic accounts of the descent made by the prophet Jonah in the belly of the fish, some of which are quite elaborate in their descriptions of what Jonah did during his underwater sojourn.[42] Because of the potential relevance of both these areas (possible NT parallels and early Jewish descent imagery) to the understanding of the phrase τὰ κατώτερα μέρη τῆς γῆς (which specifies the locus of the descent in Eph 4:9), we shall examine each in turn and attempt to assess its relevance for the interpretation of Eph 4:9-10.

1. *NT Descent Imagery*

Two other NT passages also involve descent imagery and have sometimes been suggested as parallels to the passage in Eph 4:9-10. We will examine these briefly to see if they may indeed be related to the passage in Ephesians which is our primary concern.

1.1. *1 Pet 3:18-4:6*

This passage is a well-known *crux interpretum* and an attempt to solve its problems lies well beyond the scope of the present work. It is important to note, however, that beyond similarities in language or imagery which might provide interpretive clues to the *descensus* terminology in Eph 4:9-10, the interpretation of 1 Pet 3:18-4:6 is not determinative for the meaning of Eph 4:7-11; the author of Ephesians may or may not have intended a reference to a *descensus* in 4:9-10 regardless of what the author of 1 Peter meant in 3:18-4:6.

Major studies of 1 Pet 3:18-4:6 have been done by B. Reicke (1946), W. Bieder (1949), and W. J. Dalton (1965).[43] A majority of scholars have

---

[41] A. T. Hanson, *The New Testament Interpretation of Scripture* (London: SPCK, 1980) 122-56.

[42] E.g., *Midrash Tehillim* 26.9, b. *'Erubin* 19a, *Pirqe de Rabbi Eliezer* 10, etc.

[43] B. Reicke, *The Disobedient Spirits and Christian Baptism* (Copenhagen: Ejnar Munksgaard, 1946); W. Bieder, *Die Vorstellung von der Höllenfahrt Jesu Christi*, ATANT 19 (Zürich: Zwingli, 1949), and W. J. Dalton, *Christ's Proclamation to the Spirits: A Study of 1 Peter 3:18-4:6*, AnBib 23 (Rome: Pontifical Biblical Institute, 1965). Less lengthy examinations of the passage include those by E. Schweizer, "I Petrus 4.6," *TZ* 8 (1952) 152-54, and C. E. B. Cranfield, "The Interpretation of I Peter iii.19 and iv.6," *ExpTim* 69 (1957-58) 369-72.

believed 1 Pet 3:18-4:6 refers to some sort of *descensus*, although Dalton argued that the proclamation to the "spirits in prison" took place after Christ's resurrection in the realm of the air, where the disobedient spirits were confined.[44] Arguing against Dalton's view that the message proclaimed by Christ in 1 Pet 3:19 was solely a message of condemnation to rebellious angelic beings in captivity, A. T. Hanson contended that because in 1 Peter 3 we are dealing with a Christian text, the all-important redeeming mission of Christ must have been the content of Christ's message to the spirits.[45] But Hanson's objection must surely be questionable, since it involved an assumption about what the author of 1 Peter believed the mission of Christ to be, and whether or not a message of judgment to rebellious angelic beings might or might not legitimately comprise a part of that mission.

In any event, the terminology used in 1 Pet 3:18-4:6 does not resemble that in Eph 4:9-10 closely enough to suggest clear parallels; no phrase in 1 Pet 3:18-4:6 specifically corresponds to εἰς τὰ κατώτερα μέρη τῆς γῆς in Eph 4:9. If in fact a *descensus* is involved in 1 Pet 3:18-4:6, it provides (as far as the interpretation of Eph 4:9-10 is concerned) proof that such a concept was within the range of possibilities for a NT writer. But the immediate context of Ephesians 4 will have to provide evidence for such a *descensus ad inferos* before it would be valid to conclude that both passages were referring to the same (or a similar) event. As we have already seen from our discussion of the grammatical possibilities for the meaning of the phrase τῆς γῆς in Eph 4:9, a descent to the underworld is only one of several options available to the interpreter of Eph 4:7-11; unless one approaches the text with the presupposition that the passage must speak of a *descensus ad inferos*, it is far from clear that such a concept is in view.

1.2. Rom 10:6-8

Another NT passage often understood to allude to a *descensus ad inferos* is Rom 10:6-8. Such a reference would establish the *descensus* as a Pauline doctrine, and this would strengthen the possibility that such an interpretation could also be valid for Eph 4:9-10.[46] In Rom 10:6-8

---

44 W. J. Dalton, *Christ's Proclamation to the Spirits*, 165ff. It is worthwhile to note that Dalton's view is consistent with Eph 4:8, where ἠχμαλώτευσεν αἰχμαλωσίαν describes an activity contemporaneous with that described by the participle ἀναβάς. As H. Schlier points out, the author of Ephesians located the demonic powers in the air (ἐν τοῖς ἐπουρανίοις, Eph 6:12), and thus to overcome them Christ did not need to make a descent to the underworld; they were vanquished as part of his victorious ascent (*Christus und die Kirche im Epheserbrief* [Tübingen: Mohr, 1930] 3-5).

45 A. T. Hanson, *The New Testament Interpretation of Scripture*, 132.

46 Pauline authorship of Ephesians must of course be considered a factor here, but the presence of a descensus in Rom 10:6-8 would still strengthen the case for such an interpretation of Eph 4:9-10 even if Ephesians is considered non-Pauline as long as its dependence upon (or

Paul alluded to Deut 30:12-13, but in a form closer to the Palestinian Targum than to the MT or the LXX of Deut 30:13. *Tg.* Deut 30:12-13 reads:

> The law is not in the heavens, that thou shouldst say, O that we had one like Mosheh the prophet to ascend into heaven, and bring it to us, and make us hear its commands, that we may do them! Neither is the law beyond the great sea, that thou shouldst say, O that we had one like Jonah the prophet, who could descend into the depth of the sea, and bring it to us, and make us hear its commands, that we may do them. For the word is very nigh you, in your mouth....[47]

Both the association of Moses with the ascent to heaven and the association of Jonah with the descent into the depth of the sea may be significant in terms of the contrast developed by Paul in Rom 10:6-8. It is clear that Paul, if he was familiar with the targumic interpretation of Deut 30:12-13, has modified somewhat the statement dealing with the descent, changing "into the depth of the sea" to "into the abyss" (εἰς τὴν ἄβυσσον). R. LeDéaut and M. McNamara (both of whom have studied the Palestinian targum to the Pentateuch) have concluded that Paul was, in fact, familiar with the targumic rendition of Deut 30:12-13 at the time he wrote Rom 10:6-8.[48] McNamara explained Paul's use of ἄβυσσος in Rom 10:7 by suggesting that "the great sea" in *Tg.* Deut 30:13 was a reference to Jonah 2:6, where Jonah says that תהום (MT) has surrounded him, because the LXX translated this as ἄβυσσος. McNamara stated: "The conclusion that seems to flow from the facts of the case is that Paul knew of this paraphrase of the text of Dt and adapted it for his own purpose."[49] A somewhat different possibility has been raised by A. M. Goldberg, who suggested that Paul was acquainted with the traditional interpretation behind *Tg.* Deut 30:12-13 rather than with the text of the targum itself.[50] In light of the acknowledged difficulties involved in the dating of targumic materials, the more conservative stance taken by Goldberg is probably to be preferred.[51]

---

relationship to) genuine Pauline material is acknowledged.

[47] The text of *Tg.* Deut 30:12-13 is quoted from J. W. Etheridge (*The Targums of Onkelos and Jonathan ben Uzziel on the Pentateuch* [n.p., 1862; reprint ed., New York: Ktav, 1968] 654-55).

[48] R. LeDéaut, *Liturgie juive et Nouveau Testament* (Rome: Pontifical Biblical Institute, 1965) 45, and M. McNamara, *The New Testament and the Palestinian Targum to the Pentateuch* (Rome: Pontifical Biblical Institute, 1966) 75-77.

[49] M. McNamara, *The New Testament and the Palestinian Targum to the Pentateuch*, 77.

[50] A. M. Goldberg, "Torah aus der Unterwelt?," *BZ* 14 (1970) 127-31. A similar proposal for the relationship between Eph 4:8 and *Tg.* Ps 68:19 has been made by R. Rubinkiewicz ("Ps LXVIII 19 [= Eph IV 8] Another Textual Tradition or Targum?," *NovT* 17 [1975] 219-24). Rubinkiewicz's proposal is discussed at greater length in ch. 3, 105-109.

[51] For more extensive discussion of the difficulties in dating targumic literature, see ch. 3, 66-75.

We may conclude, therefore, that there is a good possibility that Paul was aware of an interpretation similar to that found in *Tg*. Deut 30:12-13 when he wrote Rom 10:6-8. The Moses and Jonah imagery may well be in the background of Rom 10:6-8, as McNamara and LeDéaut have argued. This would almost certainly establish such imagery as Pauline (since Pauline authorship of Romans is generally acknowledged). It is equally clear that in the case of Rom 10:6-8 the ascent imagery associated with Moses and the descent imagery associated with Jonah has been applied by the author of Romans to Christ. This does not constitute conclusive proof, however, that such imagery must be in the background of Eph 4:9-10, because the association of Moses' ascent to heaven with Ps 68:19, the OT text quoted in Eph 4:8, appears to be independent of any corresponding associations with Jonah.[52] There may well be allusions to both Moses and Jonah in Rom 10:6-8, but they are not specifically named in the context; only Christ is explicitly mentioned. It is true that the person doing the ascending and descending is not Christ himself, but someone going to bring him back, although in the context of Rom 10:6-8 (which consists of a pair of rhetorical questions) the point is that no one needs to ascend to heaven or to descend to the abyss to bring Christ back, since Christ himself has already made the descent and the ascent, and is now near at hand. Likewise in Eph 4:7-11 Moses is not specifically mentioned at all with respect to the ascent, and the context makes it absolutely clear that Ps 68:19 is understood as a reference to the triumphal ascension of Christ.[53] If Moses-traditions were in the background of Eph 4:7-11 (as we believe), the connection existed independently of Deut 30:12-13 and its targumic interpretation. As long as we do not conclude prematurely that the descent described in Rom 10:6-8 and that mentioned in Eph 4:9-10 must be identified as the same event,[54] the relationship between *Tg*. Deut 30:12-13 and Rom 10:6-8 is instructive, because it suggests that the later traditions describing Moses' ascent to heaven to bring down the Torah may, in fact, have had their basis in a tradition concerning Moses' ascent to heaven which predated Ephesians.[55] Of even more importance is the stress in Rom 10:8 on the present proximity of the "word" [τὸ ῥῆμά] which is the content of the apostolic preaching. The implication from the previ-

---

[52] See the present chapter, 59-63, and ch. 5, 144-52.

[53] In the case of Christ in Eph 4:7-11 this almost certainly presupposes his prior resurrection, but the resurrection is not explicitly mentioned in the context of Eph 4:7-11 either.

[54] Note the crucial difference in terminology: Rom 10:7 has εἰς τὴν ἄβυσσον, while Eph 4:9 has εἰς τὰ κατώτερα μέρη τῆς γῆς.

[55] The significance of the 'ascent' imagery with regard to Moses will be discussed in ch. 3, which examines the ascent imagery behind Ps 68:19 and Eph 4:8, and ch. 4, which discusses the ascent imagery surrounding Moses himself in (or prior to) the first century CE. See below, 91-95, 121-22, and ch. 4, 141-42.

ous verses is that one did not need to descend into the abyss or ascend into heaven in search of the Messiah, because he was near at hand as a result of the apostolic message presented to the readers. In other words, Christ was present 'spiritually' through the apostolic preaching rather than being remote and inaccessible either in the underworld or in the heights of heaven.[56]

2. Jonah and His Descent in Rabbinic Literature and Other Sources

In our examination of the descent imagery in the background of Rom 10:6-8 we have already encountered the suggestion that Paul was familiar with the targumic interpretation of Deut 30:12-13 at the time he wrote Rom 10:6-8, and that *Tg.* Deut 30:12-13 links the descent "into the abyss" (εἰς τὴν ἄβυσσον, Rom 10:7) with the figure of Jonah the prophet, who according to the targum descended "into the depth of the sea."[57] The imagery of Jonah and his descent was discussed in relation to Eph 4:9-10 by A. T. Hanson, who saw Jonah in the background of the *descensus* imagery in Ephesians 4, and also connected to what some consider to be baptismal imagery in Ephesians 5.[58] At this point we need not pursue any further the question of baptismal imagery in Ephesians 5, except to note that Hanson's attempt to link the use of ῥῆμα in Eph 5:26, which he referred to Christian baptism, with the use of the same word in Rom 10:8, where it refers to the apostolic *kerygma*, was tenuous at best.[59]

At the heart of Hanson's attempt to connect Jonah and the related *descensus* imagery to the descent described by the author of Ephesians in 4:9-10 lie the rabbinic accounts of Jonah's voyage in the belly of the fish. It is recorded in *b. 'Erubin* 19a (without elaboration) that Jonah

---

[56] The concept of the descent of Christ as the Spirit at Pentecost (the position of the present study with regard to the descent mentioned in Eph 4:9-10) would make a similar point in terms of the way in which the Christian in the present age has first-hand experience of the resurrected and exalted Christ. Christ, although exalted "above all the heavens," is not so distant as to be inaccessible to his people, thanks to the descent of the Spirit to the church at the first Christian Pentecost. This concept and its implications are discussed more fully in ch. 6 of the present study, 182-92.

[57] The suggestion was made by R. LeDéaut (*Liturgie juive et Nouveau Testament*, 45) and M. McNamara (*The New Testament and the Palestinian Targum to the Pentateuch*, 75-77); see n. 48 above.

[58] A. T. Hanson, *The New Testament Interpretation of Scripture*, 141-50. Hanson attempts to relate Eph 5:14 to Jonah 1:5-6 on the basis of similarities in terminology, although such a connection is not made by B. Noack in his attempt to trace the OT backgrounds of the quotation in Eph 5:14 ("Das Zitat in Ephes. 5,14," *ST* 5 [1951] 52-64). Hanson's suggestions regarding Eph 5:14 are interesting but inconclusive. Strangely, he does not mention at all one of the most suggestive links between Eph 5:14 and 4:8: both quotations are introduced by the unusual formula διὸ λέγει, which occurs as the introduction to an OT quotation nowhere else in the Pauline corpus.

[59] A. T. Hanson, *The New Testament Interpretation of Scripture*, 146.

visited the place of the dead (Sheol), where he exclaimed, in the words of Jonah 2:3, "Out of the belly of the nether world cried I...."[60] *Midr. Teh.* 26.9 adds that Jonah was the son of the widow of Zarephath, who died and was raised to life again by Elijah.[61] This would imply that Jonah was believed to have visited the place of the dead once before, prior to his descent in the fish. *Midr. Teh.* 26.9 also records that Jonah entered into Eden during his life by reason of his merit.[62]

By far the longest and most detailed account of Jonah's activities in the belly of the fish is found in *Pirqe de Rabbi Eliezer* 10.[63] Here we find Jonah, standing inside the mouth of the fish "just as a man enters the great synagogue," with the two eyes of the fish like windows of glass giving light to Jonah. He was also illuminated by a great pearl which hung inside the fish like the sun, showing all that was in the depths of the sea. During this time Jonah was supposedly in regular conversation with the fish. The fish was afraid of being swallowed by Leviathan, so when Leviathan appeared before them, Jonah showed him the seal of Abraham (i.e., circumcision). Leviathan then swam two days' journey away from Jonah and the fish and did not disturb them further. Jonah then asked the fish to show him all that was in the sea and in the depths. The fish, grateful for his rescue from Leviathan, obliged Jonah and took him on a veritable tour of the underworld. The sights included the great river of the waters of the Ocean,[64] the Reed Sea crossed by the Israelites in their escape from Egypt, the pillars of the earth and their foundations, the lowest Sheol[65] and Gehinnom[66] (the

---

[60] *The Babylonian Talmud: Seder Mo'ed*, ed. I. Epstein, *'Erubin*, trans. I. W. Slotki (London: Soncino, 1938) 130.

[61] *The Midrash on Psalms*, trans. W. G. Braude, YJS 13 (New Haven: Yale University Press, 1959) 1.363.

[62] Since Jonah is not numbered among the nine persons who, in rabbinic tradition, entered into paradise while still alive, H. L. Strack and P. Billerbeck understand *Midr. Teh.* 26.9 to mean that Jonah *saw* Eden (paradise) from the fish (*Kommentar zum Neuen Testament aus Talmud und Midrasch* [Munich: Beck'sche, n.d.; reprint ed., 1969] 1.646), just as *Pirqe de Rabbi Eliezer* 10 states that from the fish, Jonah looked upon Gehenna (Gehinnom). Nevertheless, the text of *Midr. Teh.* 26.9 does seem to state that Jonah not only saw Eden from afar, but entered there.

[63] *Pirkê de Rabbi Eliezer*, trans. and annotated by G. Friedlander (London: n.p., 1916; reprint ed., New York: Sepher-Hermon, 1981) 69-73.

[64] This is apparently a reference to the waters which were thought to surround the entire earth according to rabbinic cosmology.

[65] The Venice edition of *Pirqe R. El.*, printed in Hebrew in 1544 (the second printed edition; the first is the Constantinople edition of 1514), reads "Gehinnom" in place of "the lowest Sheol." Midrash Kônen likewise states, "there is one gate to Gehinnom in the sea of Tarshish."

[66] The first printed editions (Constantinople, 1514; Venice, 1544; and Sabbioneta, 1567) read "the lowest Sheol" (see the previous note). Only the order of the two terms ("the lowest Sheol" and "Gehinnom") is in dispute in the earliest printed editions, not their inclusion or omission.

lowest region of Gehenna), and the temple of God which stood on the seven mountains of Jerusalem.[67] Also included in Jonah's tour was a visit to the *Eben Shethiyah* (the foundation stone on which the entire earth stood). After this Jonah asked the fish to be still while he prayed, and immediately the fish spat Jonah out onto the dry land.

In evaluating the significance of these accounts of Jonah and his 'descent' in the belly of the fish, we must remember that all of the rabbinic accounts appear to be considerably later than the first century CE. Thus their usefulness in determining how Jonah as a prophetic figure was viewed during the period when the NT documents were being composed is extremely limited. It would not be valid to infer from the later rabbinic accounts that Jonah would probably have been understood by a NT author to have made a *descensus ad inferos*. Some of the material in the rabbinic writings undoubtedly reflects traditional interpretations of an earlier period, but this must be confirmed from contemporary non-rabbinic sources; it cannot merely be assumed.[68] A. T. Hanson did acknowledge the problem of dating the sources, but still continued to argue that such imagery lies behind Matt 12:40, thus proving that the tradition of Jonah's descent to the underworld antedates the composition of Matthew's gospel.[69] We need not involve ourselves in a discussion of the authenticity of Matt 12:40, which has been described by some scholars as an interpolation.[70] We may simply note that it is possible to understand the statement about Jonah in Matt 12:40 in a symbolic or typological sense, without insisting that at this time Jonah was literally thought to have descended to Sheol (which to be completely consistent would probably have necessitated his death and resurrection). Thus it is highly questionable whether the mention of Jonah in Matt 12:38-41 does indeed confirm, as Hanson asserted, that by the time of Matthew's composition Jonah was understood as making a *descensus ad inferos*. Such an inference is possible but by no means

---

67 According to *Pirqe R. El.*, the temple stood on all the seven hills (mountains) at the same time. Rabbinic exegesis designated the names of these seven mountains according to names found in the OT: Mount Zion, Mount Moriah, the Holy Mount, the Mount of My Holy Beauty, the Mount of the House of the Lord, the Mount of the Lord of Hosts, and the Lofty Mount of the Mountains. Of course in the original contexts in which these names occurred, they did not necessarily designate the temple mount in Jerusalem.

68 For a fuller discussion of the problems involved in attempting to date the rabbinic literature and traditions behind it, see ch. 3, 75-77.

69 A. T. Hanson, *The New Testament Interpretation of Scripture*, 149-50.

70 Among those who view Matt 12:40 as a later interpolation into the gospel are L. Cope ("Matthew 12:40 and the Synoptic Source Question," *JBL* 92 [1973] 115); K. Stendahl (*The School of St. Matthew and Its Use of the Old Testament*, 2d ed. [Uppsala: Almqvist & Wiksells, 1954] 132-33); A. H. McNeile (*The Gospel according to St. Matthew*, 2d ed. [London: Macmillan, 1915; reprint ed., 1961] 181-82); and H. J. Holtzmann (ed., *Die Synoptiker. —Die Apostelgeschichte*, HKNT 1 [Freiburg: Mohr-Siebeck, 1889] 141).

necessary from the evidence at hand.

While we are examining the possibility that Jonah was believed to have made a *descensus ad inferos* at least as early as the composition of Ephesians, we should look briefly at the LXX text of Jonah 1 and 2. If it appears likely that a *descensus* on the part of Jonah could have been inferred from the text of the LXX this might have some significance for the interpretation of Eph 4:9-10, because (as A. T. Lincoln has demonstrated) the OT quotations in Ephesians are primarily based on the LXX and suggest a familiarity on the part of the author with the Greek translation of the OT.[71]

In the prayer of Jonah from the belly of the fish in Jonah 2:7 LXX the prophet stated, "I descended into the earth... (κατέβην εἰς γῆν)."[72] This is close to (but not identical with) the text of Eph 4:9, which reads καὶ κατέβη εἰς τὰ κατώτερα μέρη τῆς γῆς.[73] A similar phrase also occurs in Jonah 1:3 LXX (καὶ κατέβη εἰς Ἰοππην) with respect to Jonah ("and he went down to Joppa"), and again in Jonah 1:5 LXX (Ἰωνας δὲ κατέβη εἰς τὴν κοίλην τοῦ πλοίου, "but Jonah went down into the belly of the ship"). In both these latter instances the phrases form part of the overall 'descent' motif connected with Jonah in the first two chapters of the book, but do not in context directly speak of a *descensus ad inferos*.

The first example (from Jonah 2:7), however, may well have been associated with such a *descensus* by a reader of the book in Greek, because in the immediately preceding context of Jonah's prayer there are at least two additional references which might call to mind a *descensus ad inferos*. In Jonah 2:3 LXX the prophet (in his prayer to Yahweh from the belly of the fish) said, «ἐκ κοιλίας ᾅδου κραυγῆς μου ἤκουσας φωνῆς μου», where the MT reads קולי שׁמעת שׁועתי שׁאול מבטן. Although this was probably intended to be understood as hyperbole in the poetic context of the original, a reader of the LXX could certainly have concluded from the Greek translation that Jonah had made the *descensus*.[74] Such a conclusion would probably have been reinforced by Jonah 2:6 LXX, ἄβυσσος ἐκύκλωσέ με ἐσχάτη, where the prophet said he was engulfed by the 'abyss'. As we have already seen in our discussion of Rom 10:6-8, M. McNamara believed that this reference to the 'abyss'

---

[71] A. T. Lincoln, "The Use of the OT in Ephesians," *JSNT* 14 (1982) 16-57.

[72] The LXX text of Jonah quoted here and throughout this section is from *Septuaginta: Vetus Testamentum Graecum auctoritate Societatis Litterarum Gottingensis editum* 13, *Duodecim Prophetae*, ed. J. Ziegler, 2d ed. (Göttingen: Vandenhoeck u. Ruprecht, 1967).

[73] The similarity between Jonah 2:7 LXX and Eph 4:9 would be even greater if μέρη were omitted from the text of Eph 4:9. For a discussion of this textual problem (in which we concluded that μέρη probably was part of the original text) see ch. 1, 40-45.

[74] It is also possible that the (later) rabbinic traditions arose from a similar literal interpretation of שׁאול in the Hebrew text of Jonah 2:3; this would certainly be in line with known rabbinic exegetical techniques.

(ἄβυσσος) in Jonah 2:6 provided the conceptual link between the tradition in *Tg.* Deut 30:12-13 and Rom 10:7 for the apostle Paul.[75] In summary, we may conclude that a reader of the LXX text of Jonah might indeed have come away from chapter 2 with the impression that Jonah accomplished a *descensus ad inferos*.

3. *Conclusions: Descent Imagery in the NT and Other Sources*

Since almost everyone would concede that the LXX translation of Jonah antedated the composition of Ephesians, it does appear possible (although certainly not conclusive) that the author of Ephesians might have written 4:9-10 with the *descensus*-imagery of Jonah 2 LXX in mind. If this were the case, it might further suggest that a reading of Eph 4:9-10 which associates the descent with a descent of Christ to Sheol, or the underworld, would be the most natural reading of the passage. Although we regard A. T. Hanson's attempt to relate the rabbinic accounts of Jonah's descent and the interpretation of Matt 12:40 to a *descensus* in Eph 4:9-10 as inconclusive, it does appear that the author of Ephesians could, without much difficulty, have arrived at similar conclusions for himself if he were familiar with the LXX text of Jonah. Since the OT quotations in Ephesians do suggest strongly a familiarity with (and dependence upon) the LXX by the author, we may consider it possible that our author was aware of the *descensus* imagery in Jonah 2 when he wrote Eph 4:9-10. Whether this awareness influenced him in his own reference to a descent beyond the level of similar (but not identical) terminology is a matter that must be decided on the basis of considerations in the immediate context of Eph 4:9-10.[76] Before turning to these, however, we must first examine in considerable detail the ascent-imagery surrounding Moses in light of the (later) rabbinic interpretation of Ps 68:19. In the following chapters we shall attempt to assess the development of this imagery linking Moses with Ps 68:19 and/or a heavenly ascent at Mt. Sinai and its implications for the ascent-descent motif in Eph 4:7-11.

---

[75] See above, 56-58.

[76] Contextual considerations affecting the interpretation of the descent mentioned in Eph 4:9-10 will be examined in ch. 6 of the present study.

CHAPTER THREE

THE ASSOCIATION OF MOSES WITH PSALM 68:19
AS BACKGROUND TO EPHESIANS 4

Now we must consider the significance of Moses' association with Ps 68:19 as background to Eph 4:8-10. Various associations of this imagery with other religious figures in Jewish or Gnostic literature who made ascents to heaven (or the heavenly realm) have been suggested. We shall examine a number of these other accounts and evaluate their possible influence on the writer of Ephesians in the composition of Eph 4:8-10. The primary set of associations we shall consider—the one most often suggested to be in the background of Eph 4:8-10—involves Moses and his legendary ascent to heaven as reflected in *Tg.* Psalms, the (later) rabbinic literature, and other early non-canonical sources. The Moses-traditions associated with Ps 68:19 are extremely important in determining the sequence of Christ's descent in Eph 4:9-10 with respect to the ascent mentioned in the psalm. If the author of Ephesians knew of the traditions associating Psalm 68 with Moses, these would probably have influenced his inclusion of a reference to the descent of Christ in the passage. A descent per se is not mentioned in the psalm quotation but is inferred from the psalm by the author of Ephesians in 4:9-10. If the Moses-traditions we are about to investigate were available in some form to the author of Ephesians, this would have provided him a basis for inferring a subsequent descent of Christ in Eph 4:9-10 corresponding to the ascent mentioned in Ps 68:19 itself, since Moses (following his ascent of Mt. Sinai to receive the Torah) descended to distribute it as 'gifts' to men. The 'giving of gifts' attributed to Moses in Ps 68:19 is therefore implicitly connected with a descent, and it would not have taken a great deal of imaginative creativity for the author of Ephesians to see in this implicit descent a descent of Christ as the Spirit, distributing gifts to his church.

But we must exercise extreme caution when appealing to rabbinic interpretations of Psalm 68 to validate any interpretation of the descent in Eph 4:9-10. The extant written sources are in many cases indisputably later than the composition of Ephesians, and vague appeals to 'prior oral tradition' must be backed up with sufficient evidence to establish a reasonable degree of certainty regarding the antiquity of these traditions. With this in mind we shall investigate thoroughly any possible allusions to Moses-traditions regarding a heavenly ascent connected with Sinai and the giving of the Torah in all the extant literature, rabbinic and otherwise, at our disposal. We shall attempt to determine what may or may not be said with any degree of certainty concerning the use of these Moses-traditions in the first century CE in general and by the author of Ephesians in 4:7-11 in particular.

A. MOSES' ASCENT TO HEAVEN IN PS 68:19: THE TRADITION AND ITS RELATIONSHIP TO EPH 4:8

Recent attempts to interpret Eph 4:7-11 have referred to *Tg. Psalms*, which applies Ps 68:19 to Moses when he ascended Mt. Sinai. In the words of *Tg.* Ps 68:19, "You ascended to the firmament, Prophet Moses; you led captive captivity; you learned the words of Torah; you gave them as gifts to the sons of men."[1] H. St J. Thackeray initially observed around the turn of the century that the text of Eph 4:8 was similar to that found in *Tg.* Psalm 68, while both differed from the Hebrew text and the LXX at a number of points.[2] Since Thackeray's remark, it has become increasingly common to find references to *Tg.* Psalm 68 in commentaries and other discussions of Eph 4:7-11.[3] But the antiquity of the tradition behind *Tg.* Ps 68:19 has not yet been definitively proven, and thus (before attempting to analyse the possible ways in which the writer of Ephesians might have made use of *Tg.* Psalms' application of Psalm 68 to Moses) we must investigate more fully *Tg.* Psalms and the tradition it reflects at 68:19. We must also attempt to evaluate whether the interpretation of Ps 68:19 with reference to Moses and his ascent of Mt. Sinai to receive the Torah[4] could indeed have been available to the writer of Ephesians in a form approaching that found in *Tg.* Psalms and the later rabbinic literature.[5]

---

[1] My translation from the Aramaic text of *Tg.* Ps 68:19 in *Hagiographa Chaldaice*, ed. P. A. de Lagarde (Leipzig: B. G. Teubneri, 1873). For the Aramaic text see below, 97.

[2] H. St J. Thackeray, *The Relation of St Paul to Contemporary Jewish Thought* (London: Oxford University Press, 1900) 182. For a detailed comparison of Ps 68:19 in the MT, LXX, Eph 4:8, and *Tg.* Psalms, see below, 96-104.

[3] E.g., E. E. Ellis, *Paul's Use of the Old Testament* (Edinburgh: Oliver & Boyd, 1957) 144; J. Cambier, "La signification christologique d'Éph. IV.7-10," *NTS* 9 (1963) 262-75; G. B. Caird, "The Descent of Christ in Ephesians 4, 7-11," *SE* 2 (= TU 87), ed. F. L. Cross (Berlin: Akademie, 1964) 535-45; J. C. Kirby, *Ephesians, Baptism, and Pentecost* (Montreal: McGill University Press, 1968) 146; J. Gnilka, *Der Epheserbrief*, HTKNT (Freiburg: Herder, 1971) 208; and A. T. Lincoln, "The Use of the OT in Ephesians," *JSNT* 14 (1982) 16-57.

[4] Based on the account given in Exod 19:3–20:21 and parallels.

[5] H. L. Strack and P. Billerbeck listed a number of parallels from rabbinic literature, but their list was by no means exhaustive (*Kommentar zum Neuen Testament aus Talmud und Midrasch* [Munich: Beck'sche, n.d.; reprint ed. 1969] 3.596-98). Similar lists of rabbinic parallels to *Tg.* Ps 68:19 are found in W. A. Meeks (*The Prophet-King: Moses Traditions and the Johannine Christology* [Leiden: Brill, 1967] 206 note) and D. C. Smith ("The Ephesian Heresy and the Origin of the Epistle to the Ephesians," *OJRS* 5 [1977] 94, n. 32).

1. Targum *Psalms*

The difficulty of dating the material found in the targums is a major
problem for their use in the interpretation of the NT, and the tradition
behind *Tg*. Ps 68:19 is no exception. Nevertheless, because of the importance of the interpretation of Ps 68:19 found in *Tg*. Psalms for the interpretation of the descent of Christ in Eph 4:9-10 (including the change
from 'received' to 'gave' shared by Eph 4:8 and *Tg*. Ps 68:19) we must
examine briefly the evidence from *Tg*. Psalms itself which points to a
later date for the extant document.

It is almost certain that *Tg*. Psalms in the form in which it now exists
is a relatively late work, although the time of final composition—or final
redaction[6]—cannot at present be determined with any degree of accuracy beyond the fourth to ninth century of the Christian era.[7] There are

---

[6] In light of the uncertainties surrounding the origin of *Tg*. Psalms in its present form, it is
difficult to know whether it should be viewed as an essentially early work which has been sub-
jected to one or more subsequent redactions, or whether it is for the most part a later composition drawing on a number of early traditions. B. J. Roberts, for example, proposed that
variation in the extent of paraphrase found throughout the present composition (ranging from
strict literalness on the one hand to extreme paraphrase on the other) suggested that *Tg*. Psalms
as it now exists may have been assembled from a number of earlier targumim (*The Old Testament Text and Versions* [Cardiff: University of Wales Press, 1951] 209). Yet Roberts also
proposed a later redaction intended to bring *Tg*. Psalms into agreement with the MT, based on
evidence of conflate readings such as that found in Ps 97:11 (see below, 71, also note 24). The
problems in dating the earliest *written* targums are extensive; in spite of the often-quoted prohibition of written targumim by R. Samuel in the Palestinian (Jerusalem) Talmud (*p. Meg.*
4.1), there is evidence that written targumim were in use during the Tannaitic period and even
earlier. According to R. Jose, a written *Tg*. Job was known to R. Gamaliel—although he did
not approve of it and had it buried in a wall (*b. Shab.* 115a; a parallel account with minor
variations is found in *Sof.* 5.15). There are also the fragmentary targums found at Qumran,
11QtgJob (see *Le Targum de Job de la Grotte XI de Qumrân*, ed. and trans. J. P. M. van der
Ploeg and A. S. van der Woude [Leiden: Brill, 1971], and A. S. van der Woude, "Das Hiobtargum aus Qumran Höhle XI," VTSup 9 [1963] 322-31) and 4QtgLeviticus (see R. Le Déaut,
Introduction à la Littérature Targumique, première partie [Rome: Pontifical Biblical Institute,
1966] 64-65). A. D. York gave details and an evaluation of the conflict among the rabbis over
the use of written targumim: according to R. Samuel (see above) the targum was by implication
a part of the oral law (hence the prohibition against writing it down) ("The Targum in the
Synagogue and in the School," *JSJ* 10 [1979] 75-79). Given the present state of targumic studies in general (and of *Tg*. Psalms in particular), attempts to apply source criticism and redaction criticism to *Tg*. Psalms make efforts to deal with the synoptic gospels using similar
methods appear simpler by comparison. For further examples of difficulties (and disagreement)
in dating *Tg*. Psalms, see W. Bacher (s.v. "Targum," *Jewish Encyclopedia*, ed. I. Singer [New
York and London: Funk & Wagnalls, 1906] 12.62); L. Zunz (*Die gottesdienstlichen Vorträge
der Juden*, 2d ed. [Frankfurt/Main: Kauffmann, 1892] 67-68, 84); R. Le Déaut (*Introduction à
la Littérature Targumique*, 131-35); and n. 7 of the present chapter (which follows).

[7] W. Bacher insisted on a date of final composition for *Tg*. Psalms prior to the fall of Rome
in 476 CE (s.v. "Targum," in *Jewish Encyclopedia*, 12.62; see below, 71), but this was con-
tested by G. H. Dalman who argued for a later date for the Palestinian targums on a linguistic
basis (*Grammatik des jüdisch-palästinischen Aramäisch*, 2d ed. [Leipzig: J. C. Hinrichs, 1905;
reprint ed. with *Aramäisch Dialektproben*, Darmstadt: Wissenschaftliche Buchgesellschaft,
1960] 32-33). This represented a reversal of Dalman's previous position, since he had indicated
in the first edition of *Grammatik* (1894) that the Palestinian targums might include sections of

indications of a later date (for the final redaction at least) to be found in a number of places in *Tg.* Psalms. Greek words occur fairly regularly throughout: in Ps 1:2, the Hebrew text has תורה twice (בתורת and ובתורתו); in the first instance *Tg.* Psalms translates this as בנמוסא (Greek νόμος), while the second is rendered by אוריתא (ובאוריתיה), almost as a stylistic variation. Elsewhere in *Tg.* Psalms (as is generally the case in the targmim) אוריתא is consistently used to translate תורה.[8] In a number of contexts אנגלי (Greek ἄγγελος) occurs: in Ps 50:6 the Hebrew text ויגידו שמים צדקו "and the heavens declare his righteousness" becomes ויתנון אנגלי מרומא "and the angels of heaven...," removing the metonymy found in the Hebrew. Concerning the presence of transliterated Greek words in the Palestinian Targum to the Pentateuch, G. J. Cowling has proposed that the Aramaic translation was actually made not from the Hebrew text, but from a Greek version, probably a revision of the LXX similar to the version associated with Theodotion.[9] If Cowling's evaluation of the evidence is correct, the Palestinian Targum should be dated considerably later than the NT period. In any case, many of the arguments adduced by Cowling apply to *Tg.* Psalms as well as to the Palestinian Targum to the Pentateuch.

There are other indications in *Tg.* Psalms which point to a fairly late date. A tendency to rephrase difficult or uncertain readings can be seen in Ps 68:18:[10] the Hebrew text contains the phrase אלפי שנאן "thousands

---

very early, possibly even pre-Christian, material. But he discarded this view in his later works, and it is largely due to their influence that Dalman's (revised) opinions—that the Palestinian targums were much later works, no earlier than 7th century CE—became the consensus view of scholars in the first half of this century. These historical developments were discussed by M. McNamara (*The New Testament and the Palestinian Targum to the Pentateuch*, AnBib 27 [Rome: Pontifical Biblical Institute, 1966] 19 ff).

[8] I.e., Ps 78:10; 94:12; 119:1, 18, 29, 51, 53, 85, 150, and 165. The MT quoted throughout the present work is taken from *BHS* (7th ed., ed. R. Kittel [Stuttgart: Württembergische Bibelanstalt, 1937]); the Aramaic text of *Tg.* Psalms employed throughout is that of *Hagiographa Chaldaice* (ed. P. A. de Lagarde [Leipzig: B. G. Teubneri, 1873]).

[9] G. J. Cowling, "New Light on the New Testament? The significance of the Palestinian Targum," *TSFBul* 51 (1968) 11-12. The main points cited by Cowling in favor of a Greek original behind the Palestinian Targum were as follows: (a) the complete absence of the pronominal object affixed to a finite verb (whereas the object was affixed to the verb in every other form of Aramaic; cf. להון יהבא in *Tg.* Ps 68:19); (b) in the translation of the text the relative pronoun followed Greek usage, while in interpolated or supplementary material it followed normal Aramaic usage; (c) Greek words were used in the translation which were not integrated into the language (cf. the examples from *Tg.* Psalms mentioned earlier in this chapter); (d) there were numerous agreements with Greek versions; and (e) the best manuscripts of the Palestinian Targum differentiated between the words 'bread' and 'food', following Greek usage, rather than using the word 'bread' for food in general, as both Hebrew and Aramaic did. It should be remembered that, while Cowling's suggestions regarding the dating of the Palestinian Targum run counter to much current scholarly opinion, almost all of these same authorities would agree that the targums to the Hagiographa (including *Tg.* Psalms) are relatively late compositions.

[10] The verse immediately prior to 68:19, the primary subject of this discussion.

of repetition (?),"[11] which the targumist (either because of his own uncertainty concerning the meaning or out of concern for the comprehen-
sion of his audience) simplifies as אלפין דאנגליא "thousands of angels."
A desire to guard the holiness or transcendence of God probably lies
behind the paraphrase of Ps 82:6, which in the Hebrew text reads אני־
אמרתי אלהים אתם ובני עליון כלכם "I said, 'You are gods, and sons of the
most High, all of you'," but is translated in *Tg.* Psalms as אנא אמריתהיך
כמלאכיא אתון חשיבין והיך אנגלי מרומא "I said, 'you are regarded (חשיבין) as
angels (כמלאכיא), and as angels of heaven (אנגלי מרומא), all of you.'" In
John 10:34 this verse is quoted by Jesus in defense of his self-appella-
tion 'Son of God', and it is possible that *Tg.* Psalms shows evidence at
this point of the growing rabbinic tendency in the early centuries of the
Christian era to reinterpret anything in the Jewish scriptures which
might be of use to Christian apologists.[12] In *Shem. Rab.* 29.5, for example, R. Abbahu, an Amora of the second generation (prior to 300 CE), is
said to have explained the verse "I am the Lord your God" (Exod 20:2)
with the following comment:

> A human king may rule, but he has a father and brother; but God said: 'I am
> not thus; I am the first, for I have no father, and I am the last for I have no
> brother, and besides Me there is no God, for I have no son.'[13]

It seems virtually certain that this is in response to Christian proclamation of Jesus as 'Son of God'. The rabbis were willing to go to considerable lengths to eliminate any basis for Christian claims concerning the
deity of Jesus, as illustrated in *b. Sanh.* 38b:

> R. Johanan said: In all the passages which the *Minim* have taken [as grounds]
> for their heresy, their refutation is found near at hand. Thus: *Let us make
> man in our image,* —*And God created* [sing.] *man in His own image; Come,
> let us go down and there confound their language,* —*And the Lord came
> down* [sing.] *to see the city and the tower; Because there were revealed
> [plur.] to him God,* —*Unto God who answereth* [sing.] *me in the day of my
> distress; For what great nation is there that hath God so nigh* [plur.] *unto it,
> as the Lord our God is [unto us] whensoever we call upon* Him [sing.]; *And
> what one nation in the earth is like thy people, [like] Israel, whom God went
> [plur.] to redeem for a people unto* himself [sing.], *Till thrones were placed
> and one that was ancient did sit.*

---

11 According to BDB (s.v. שוא [III.], 1041) the meaning of שאון is uncertain.

12 This point is not dependent on the authenticity of the account in John 10:31-39, which
reflected in any case the understanding and usage of the material by the early church at the time
of the Fourth Gospel's composition.

13 *Midrash Rabbah*, ed. H. Freedman and M. Simon, *Exodus*, trans. S. M. Lehrman
(London: Soncino, 1939) 339-40; punctuation follows the edition cited. The idea expressed in
Shem. Rab. 29.5, that God has no son, is echoed in *p. (j.) Shab.* 8, *Midr. Sam.* 5.7, and *Ag.
Ber.* 31; the last (admittedly late) is a collection of homilies, probably compiled in the 10th
century.

Why were these necessary? —To teach R. Joḥanan's dictum; viz.: The Holy One, blessed be He, does nothing without consulting His heavenly Court (פמלי׳א), for it is written, *The matter is by the decree of the watchers, and the sentence by the word of the Holy* Ones.[14]

The מינים to whom R. Johanan refers are, in this case, almost certainly Christians[15] who have appealed to the plural forms in the OT passages cited as evidence for their claims about Jesus and his relationship to God. The rabbinic response in such instances is equally clear—and for the most part typical.[16]

While it is possible that *Tg.* Ps 82:6 represents a rabbinic reinterpretation of a passage done purposely to refute Christian apologists, it is equally possible that the paraphrase of Ps 82:6 found in the Targum

---

14 *The Babylonian Talmud: Seder Nezikin*, ed. I. Epstein, *Sanhedrin*, trans. J. Shachter (London: Soncino, 1935) 1.244-45. Quotations, punctuation, and bracketed notes (with the exception of the Heb. פמלי׳א, inserted parenthetically from 245, n. 4) are in the form given in the translation.

15 Albeit probably Jewish Christians. The precise scope of the term מינים is difficult to determine; it usually refers to sectarians or infidels, and is often applied to Jewish Christians, according to M. Jastrow (ed., *A Dictionary of the Targumim, the Talmud Babli and Yerushalmi, and the Midrashic Literature* [n.p., n.d.; reprint ed., Brooklyn, NY: P. Shalom, 1967], s.v. מין [III.], 776). The claim of H. J. Schoeps that מינים was "invariably applied only to Jewish heretics" does not seem warranted (*The Jewish-Christian Argument: A History of Theologies in Conflict*, trans. D. E. Green [London: Faber & Faber, 1963] 14-15). He cited *b. Ḥullin* 13b, "There are no *minim* among the gentiles"; but this is represented in the context of *b. Ḥul.* 13b only as the opinion of R. Naḥman (in the name of Rabbah b. Abbuha). The tractate went on to add: "But we see that there are! Say: The majority of gentiles are not *minim*." Whether Jews or gentiles, it is clear from the context of R. Joḥanan's remark in *b. Sanh.* 38b that the מינים to whom he referred were Christians, since the discussion of plural forms in the OT appears to be related to disputes with Christians. It looks as if the people to whom R. Johanan referred were attempting to prove their point by arguing that the OT passages which involved plurals foreshadowed or implied the Christian doctrine of the trinity.

16 C.f., e.g., the 'stock' response of Justin's opponent in *Dialogus cum Tryphone Judaeo* 38: βλάσφημα γὰρ πολλὰ λέγεις, τὸν σταυρωθέντα τοῦτον ἀξιῶν πείθειν ἡμᾶς γεγενῆσθαι μετὰ Μωυσέως καὶ Ἀαρὼν, καὶ λελαληκέναι αὐτοῖς ἐν στύλῳ νεφέλης· εἶτα ἄνθρωπον γενόμενον, σταυρωθῆναι, καὶ ἀναβεβηκέναι εἰς τὸν οὐρανόν, καὶ πάλιν παραγένεσθαι ἐπὶ τῆς γῆς, καὶ προσκυνητὸν εἶναι. And again, in 48 we find: παράδοξός τις γάρ ποτε καὶ μὴ δυνάμενος ὅλως ἀποδειχθῆναι δοκεῖ μοι εἶναι. Τὸ γὰρ λέγειν σε προυπάρχειν θεὸν ὄντα πρὸ αἰώνων τοῦτον τὸν Χριστόν, εἶτα καὶ γεννηθῆναι ἄνθρωπον γενόμενον ὑπομεῖναι, καὶ ὅτι οὐχ ἄνθρωπος ἐξ ἀνθρώπου, οὐ μόνον παράδοξον δοκεῖ μοι εἶναι, ἀλλὰ καὶ μωρόν. A further instance in which Christian doctrine might have influenced (later) rabbinic exegesis can be found in the emergence of the concept of the Aqedah at some point early in the second century; the rabbis saw in the sacrifice of Isaac not only a solution to the destruction of the Temple, but also an answer to the claims of the early Christians that Jesus' crucifixion represented the ultimate sacrifice and sole means of atonement. This was suggested by P. R. Davies and B. D. Chilton ("The Aqedah: A revised tradition history," *CBQ* 40 [1978] 514-46). Their dating of the Aqedah as post-Christian runs counter to the general scholarly consensus. Their view was defended further by B. D. Chilton, who examined the Poem of the Four Nights from *Tg.* Exod 12:42, which is often taken as evidence that Isaac was seen as an expiatory figure associated with Passover in pre-Christian Judaism ("Isaac and the Second Night: a Consideration," *Bib* 61 [1980] 78-88). Chilton's conclusion was that the material relating to Isaac was an addendum which was (in substance) Amoraic, and therefore did not substantiate the existence of a pre-Christian Aqedah.

could be merely the result of the general tendency in most of the targumic literature against anthropomorphisms or any other statements which might threaten the transcendence or majesty of Yahweh.[17] In light of the changes made in the other passages in the Psalms where אנגלי occurs, the latter explanation is more probable.[18] In Ps 86:8, באלהים "among the gods" becomes in the targumic rendition באנגלי מרומא "among the angels of heaven," and this is probably the result of a tendency similar to that which produced the change in 82:6: the suggestion that there might be other 'gods'—even if this were only a figurative reference to pagan deities—was one that could no longer be tolerated.[19]

A tendency toward expansion of the text (as well as subtle refinement) is suggested by Ps 96:1, where the Hebrew text reads simply שירו ליהוה כל־הארץ "Sing to Yahweh, all the earth," which in *Tg.* Psalms is amplified to שבחו אנגלי מרומא שבחו קדם יהוה כל צדיקי ארעא "Praise, angels of heaven, praise before Yahweh, all the righteous of the earth." Not only has the simple collective "all the earth" (meaning "all who dwell upon the earth") been restricted to 'the righteous', but also a second (and entirely new) category has been introduced into the context with the inclusion of 'all the angels of heaven'. The use of the preposition קדם in *Tg.* Ps 96:1 does not, however, represent an anti-anthropomorphism;[20] its frequent use throughout *Tg.* Ps 96 (11 times in

---

[17] Although the targums are not consistent in this regard, as is often assumed. Occasionally anthropomorphic expressions are perpetuated and even amplified in the targums, alongside the circumlocutions and paraphrases which avoid human forms. See for example M. L. Klein ("The Preposition קדם ['before']. A Pseudo-Anti-Anthropomorphism in the Targums," *JTS* 30 [new series, 1979] 503).

[18] *Tg.* Ps 82:6 may, of course, represent the work of a later redactor. But if he was concerned with Christian apologetic use of the Psalms, he was not very thorough (or perhaps was very nearsighted!), since he would have allowed a clearly messianic interpretation of Ps 45:3 to remain (see below, 72).

[19] Unfortunately this does not provide a great deal of help in dating the tradition. It could be argued that for post-Christian Judaism the perceived threat to strict monotheism came from Christianity. But this is not necessarily the case; during the early centuries of the Christian era the growth of apocalypticism and mysticism forced an expansion of such tensions within Judaism as well. [Cf., e.g., the speculation concerning Metatron (Enoch) in *3 Enoch* 3-16 as discussed by H. Odeberg (*3 Enoch or the Hebrew Book of Enoch* [Cambridge: Cambridge University Press, 1928; rpt. with prolegomenon by J. Greenfield, New York: KTAV, 1973] 79-146). Odeberg's dating of the main body of this work in the latter half of the 3rd century was, however, disputed by G. G. Scholem, who placed this part of the work several centuries later (*Die jüdische Mystik in ihren Hauptströmungen* [Zürich: Rhein-Verlag, 1957] 48-49).] Speculation concerning the existence of other divine powers in heaven within Judaism has been traced back as far as the time of Philo (who himself calls the λόγος a 'second God' in *Quaestiones et Solutiones in Genesin* 2.62) by A. F. Segal (*Two Powers in Heaven: Early Rabbinic Reports about Christianity and Gnosticism*, SJLA 25 [Leiden: Brill, 1977] 159-81). Segal also surveyed all the pertinent rabbinic literature on the subject (33-155).

[20] *Contra* É. Levine, who stated that מן קדם י was "the only characteristic targumic expression avoiding anthropomorphism and anthropopathism that is found regularly in Jewish Aramaic outside of targum texts" (*The Aramaic Version of Ruth*, AnBib 58 [Rome: Pontifical Biblical Institute, 1973] 90).

13 verses)[21] is simply an expression of respect or deference to high office which is not necessarily limited to Deity per se.[22] Ps 97:6, הגידו השמים צדקו "the heavens proclaim his righteousness," demonstrates the same tendency to avoid metonymy which was encountered in Ps 50:6, becoming יתניין אנגלי מרומא צדקתיה "the angels of heaven proclaim his righteousness." Finally, in Ps 148:1, הללוהו במרומים "praise him in the heights," is expanded in *Tg*. Psalms to שבחו יתיה לכ חילי אנגלי מרומא "praise him all the hosts of the angels of heaven."

The tendencies toward amplification, refinement, and removal of theologically objectionable ideas noted in the preceding examples (in many respects typical of targumic literature), are not the only evidence on which to base a suggested date for the final redaction of *Tg*. Psalms in its entirety.[23] There is at least one clear instance of conflation between the Hebrew text and the LXX: the Hebrew of Ps 97:11 has אור זרע לצדיק "Light is sown for the righteous," which is read by the LXX (as well as Jerome and the Peshitta) as אור זרח לצדיק "Light dawns for the righteous." *Tg*. Psalms combines both readings as נהור דנח ומיטמר לצדיקיא "Light dawns and is sown (scattered) for the righteous." B. J. Roberts sees this conflation as evidence that an early *Tg*. Psalms was later corrected to bring it into agreement with the Hebrew text.[24] Additional evidence supporting a later date is found in *Tg*. Ps 108:11, where mention is made of the "godless city of Rome" (כרכא דרומי רשיעא) and "Constantinople of Edom" (קושטנטינא דאדום).[25] W. Bacher has argued that this mention of both cities in connection with the Empire dates the composition of *Tg*. Psalms before the fall of Rome in 476 CE.[26] Such a conclusion is not certain, however: G. Dalman rejected Bacher's argument for an earlier date on the basis that both Rome and Constantinople could

---

[21] I. e., 96:1 (twice), 2, 6, 7 (twice), 8 (twice), 9 (twice; one of these with מן), and 13.

[22] M. L. Klein, "The Preposition קדם ('before'). A Pseudo-Anti-Anthropomorphism in the Targums," *JTS* 30 (new series, 1979) 502-7.

[23] For a discussion of the problem of 'final redaction' versus 'final composition', see notes 6 and 7 above.

[24] B. J. Roberts, *The Old Testament Text and Versions*, 209; see also note 6 above. The conflate reading was also mentioned by R. Le Déaut (*Introduction à la Littérature Targumique*, 135). Neither Roberts nor Le Déaut, however, offered any comments regarding the scope of this proposed redactional activity throughout *Tg*. Psalms (or why the conflate reading in Ps 97:11 could not represent merely the preservation, once again, of a tradition which antedated the composition of the targum—although this would be less likely the earlier *Tg*. Psalms is dated).

[25] 'Edom' is a metaphorical reference to the Roman Empire. See G. H. Dalman (*Aramäisch-neuhebräisches Handwörterbuch zu Targum, Talmud und Midrasch* [Göttingen: Vandenhoeck u. Ruprecht, 1938; reprint ed. Hildesheim: Georg Olms, 1967], s.v. אדום, 6).

[26] W. Bacher, s.v. "Targum," *Jewish Encyclopedia*, 12.62. The clause referring to Rome and Constantinople is apparently not present in all manuscripts of *Tg*. Psalms, however; according to R. Le Déaut, the simultaneous mention of the two cities is not found in the text of *Tg*. Psalms printed in the London Polyglot (*Introduction à la Littérature Targumique*, 132).

continue to be mentioned as 'types' of the power of Edom long after Rome had been destroyed. In my opinion, the value of these phrases for establishing the date of the entire *Tg*. Psalms is tenuous at best, since they may have been interpolated into the work at some later time in the process of transmission.[27]

Although much of the evidence discussed thus far is usually taken to indicate a later date for *Tg*. Psalms, there is some evidence pointing to an earlier date as well. Later Jewish sources such as Tanḥuma (39b) and Naḥmanides (כיתשא 73d on Ps 45:4 and שער הגמל 100d on Ps 73:20) quote *Tg*. Psalms and *Tg*. Job and refer to both as '*Targum Yerushalmi*';[28] this might point to a Palestinian origin for both targumim.[29] The version of Psalm 18 found in *Tg*. Psalms is parallel to the same psalm found in *Tg*. 2 Samuel 22,[30] but according to R. Le Déaut, there are fewer traces of Babylonian influence in *Tg*. Psalm 18 than in *Tg*. 2 Samuel 22, which may again indicate a Palestinian origin for *Tg*. Psalms.[31] This coincides with Bacher's observation that *Tg*. Psalms contains a large number of variants (more than fifty) from the Hebrew text in both pointing and in the consonantal text, yet in many of these variants *Tg*. Psalms agrees with both the LXX and the Peshitta against the Hebrew text.[32] Furthermore *Tg*. Ps 45:3, which reads שופרך מלכא משיחא מבני נשא ("Your beauty, King Messiah, is more excellent than the sons of men"), preserves a messianic intepretation, in spite of the fact that in the NT Heb 1:8-9 interprets Ps 45:7-8 (44:7-8 LXX) of Christ (πρὸς δὲ τὸν υἱόν, Heb 1:8). The interpretation found in *Tg*. Ps 45:3 is probably independent of the Christian exegesis of this passage. It seems likely that it is in fact very early, standing as it does in sharp contrast to the interpretation(s) of Psalm 45 found in *Midrash Tehillim* (45.6): 45:3 ("You are fairer than the sons of men") is referred to the sons of Korah, whose deeds were fairer than those of Korah and his company; 45:4-5 ("Gird your sword on your thigh, mighty warrior...in your majesty ride victori-

---

[27] I.e., some time after Rome was rebuilt and had regained some of its former prominence. The omission of the phrases from at least some of the manuscripts (see the previous note) suggests some uncertainty over their authenticity. Dalman's evaluation of Bacher's arguments regarding the dating of *Tg*. Psalms is found in his *Grammatik des jüdisch-palästinischen Aramäisch* (2d ed., 34, n. 2). See also n. 7 above.

[28] As does R. Samuel Zarza, מקור חיים 18b on Ps 110:7.

[29] In the opinion of R. Le Déaut (*Introduction à la Littérature Targumique*, 133).

[30] These are parallel recensions in the MT.

[31] R. Le Déaut, *Introduction à la Littérature Targumique*, 133.

[32] W. Bacher, s.v. "Targum," *Jewish Encyclopedia*, 12.62. This agreement between *Tg*. Psalms and the LXX may, in fact, point to the use of a Greek version of the Psalms (rather than the Hebrew text itself) as the basis for *Tg*. Psalms. If so, the case would parallel that put forward by G. J. Cowling with respect to the Palestinian Targum to the Pentateuch ("New Light on the New Testament? The significance of the Palestinian Targum," *TSFBul* 51 [1968] 6-14); see the discussion in n. 9 above.

ously, for the cause of truth and meekness and righteousness") refer to Moses, who was thought worthy of Torah, which is compared to a sword; Moses rode up to heaven on a cloud, and was also very meek. Verses 6-8a ("Your arrows are sharp...your throne...is forever and ever...you have loved righteousness") also refer to Moses, who fought against Amalek, Sihon, and Og with sharp arrows, who grasped hold of the throne of the LORD,[33] and who executed the righteousness of the LORD.[34] Verse 8b, however ("Therefore God, your God, has anointed you with the oil of gladness..."), is referred to Aaron, since it speaks of his anointing as high priest. All of these interpretations are given despite the fact that in *Midr. Tehillim* on Ps 45:2, the 'King' has been understood as God himself. The tendency in *Midr. Tehillim* is obviously to derive, without regard for internal consistency, all possible applications of the verses except the obvious messianic one. Whether or not this represents a reaction to Christian apologetic use of Psalm 45 in a christological sense, the simple and direct messianic interpretation of Psalm 45 by *Tg.* Psalms appears to be considerably earlier than that found in *Midr. Tehillim.* Yet this by no means demands a pre-Christian date for *Tg.* Psalms, since *Tg.* Ps 45:3 may simply have preserved a much older tradition with its messianic interpretation at this point. It is also possible, as Cowling suggests, that a revival of messianic interest in Judaism took place some time in the 4th century, and this would be reflected on occasion in *Tg.* Psalms (either as a result of interpolations or because *Tg.* Psalms in its entirety dates from this period).[35]

The examples cited thus far from *Tg.* Psalms are, of course, far too few to provide an adequate basis upon which to propose a date of composition (or final redaction) for the work as a whole. A detailed analysis of the form and content of *Tg.* Psalms in its entirety would be necessary before such conclusions could be drawn with any degree of validity.[36]

---

[33] Moses' grasping hold of the throne of Yahweh during his ascent to heaven (to save himself from the angels who wished to destroy him to prevent him taking the Torah from heaven) is a theme which appears in some of the rabbinic accounts (e.g., *b. Shab.* 88b and *Pesiq. R.* 20.4) discussed later in the present chapter. See below, 88-91.

[34] The verse quoted in *Midr. Teh.*, "he executed the righteousness of the LORD" (Deut 33:21), actually refers, in context, to the sons of Gad in Moses' final blessing of the tribes.

[35] G. J. Cowling suggested that in the 4th century Jewish-Christian conflict over the identity of the Messiah had become "pretty much a dead letter," yet messianism continued to flourish among the Jewish communities both in Babylon and northern Palestine (Galilee) ("New Light on the New Testament? The significance of the Palestinian Targum," *TSFBul* 51 [1968] 13). Cowling's theories regarding the date and origin of the Palestinian Targum to the Pentateuch may well be applicable, in large part, to *Tg.* Psalms as well, as mentioned in notes 9 and 32 above.

[36] See, e. g., P. Wernberg-Møller, in which he critiqued the validity of a selective approach in studies attempting to establish a date for a targum by comparisons with other text-forms in the MT and LXX (in this case referring to A. Díez Macho's arguments for the date of *Tg. Neofiti I*) (Wernberg-Møller, "An Inquiry into the validity of the text-critical argument for an

Such examples do, however, serve to illustrate the difficulties inherent in any attempt to establish a date for *Tg*. Psalms. It is reasonably safe to conclude, given the current state of studies on the origin and date of *Tg*. Psalms, that the targum as it now exists probably consists of an eclectic combination of a number of different targumim, which were collected either in oral or written form before being assembled into the present composition.[37] Whether or not this represents the work of a single redactor cannot at present be determined, although a modification of Cowling's theory of the origin of the Palestinian Targum to the Pentateuch appears very attractive. The targumist, working from a Greek version of the Psalms which was probably closer to the Greek version of 'Theodotion' than to what is presently known as the LXX, translated the Psalms from Greek to Palestinian Aramaic, adding supplementary comments (mostly parenthetical) which may often have reflected earlier traditions; the Hebrew text of Psalms was little used, if at all. If a date can be loosely assigned, the late 4th century would allow for the mention of both Rome and Constantinople in *Tg*. Ps 108:11 (agreeing with Bacher's suggestion) if the mention of the two capitals formed part of the original composition.[38] The conflate reading in *Tg*. Ps 97:11 might already have been present in the version of Psalms employed by the targumist.[39] The variants found in *Tg*. Psalms which agree with the LXX against the Hebrew text would add further support for such a thesis.[40] Appealing as this explanation is, however, the evidence cannot be regarded as conclusive.

Yet, even if there is much uncertainty over the final date and method of composition of *Tg*. Psalms as it now exists, it very probably reflects at some points ancient (and possibly even pre-Christian) traditions.[41] The presence of late words and phrases only suggests that the immediate

---

early dating of the recently discovered Palestinian Targum," *VT* 12 [1962] 312-30). Wernberg-Møller did not intend to imply that such arguments have no validity, but rather that they must involve a thorough study of the work in its entirety, with consideration given to all possible explanations for the forms and variants in the text under study, before conclusions can safely be drawn regarding the date of the entire composition. No such study has yet been done in the case of *Tg*. Psalms (as far as I can determine).

[37] Cf. the similar conclusion by B. J. Roberts (*The Old Testament Text and Versions*, 209) mentioned above in n. 6.

[38] The mention of Rome and Constantinople may, of course, result from a later interpolation. See above, 71-72.

[39] See above, 71. For that matter, the change in Ps 68:19 from לקחת (MT) and ἔλαβες (LXX) to יהבתא (*Tg*. Psalms) may have been present in the version used by the targumist as well, although at this point such a suggestion is purely speculative.

[40] See above, 72.

[41] That such is the case (to differing degrees) with almost all of the targums has been the increasing realization of those concerned with this area of study over the last several decades. This shift in the critical evaluation of targumic materials by recent scholarship was discussed at some length by M. McNamara ("Targumic Studies," *CBQ* 28 [1966] 1-19).

contexts in which they occur comprise more recent additions. Even this is not guaranteed, since the individual words and phrases may themselves represent interpolations. Likewise, the absence of earlier grammatical forms or other traces of Palestinian origin cannot disprove the inclusion of earlier traditions, since a later writer may have reformulated such older material using contemporary syntax and terminology. This is especially true in the case of the targums, whose very *raison d'être* consisted, to a large extent, of an attempt to render ancient texts—material which could no longer be understood by the average members of the community—intelligible and applicable to a contemporary audience.[42] Thus, in the case of *Tg.* Psalms, where a date for the final form of the entire work cannot yet be assigned (and which, in any case, would almost certainly turn out to be post-Christian), some of the traditions which are preserved in the targum may still prove relevant to the exegesis of specific NT texts.[43] But each of these traditions must be considered on a case-by-case basis. If *Tg.* Psalms as a whole cannot be reliably dated, we must employ an approach which will enable the tradition in question to be dated independently of the entire work.[44] We will now consider such an approach to the problems of dating the Moses-tradition behind *Tg.* Ps 68:19.

2. *An Approach to the Tradition Behind* Tg. *Ps 68:19*

Thus far we have seen that for the scholar who seeks to use material from the targums (like the Moses-tradition associated with Ps 68:19) in the interpretation of specific NT texts (like Eph 4:7-11), the central problem is the necessity of establishing the antiquity of the traditions involved. This difficulty is inherent in the use of any targumic material in so far as the final written form of all targumim would almost certainly be later than the NT documents themselves. The use of traditions from *Tg.* Psalms is (as we have seen in the previous section) particularly uncertain as a result of the special problems it presents, combined with the rela-

---

[42] According to A. D. York, the targums served an educational purpose in the synagogue schools as well ("The Targum in the Synagogue and in the School," *JSJ* 10 [1979] 83). This was an additional role which did nothing to change the primary purpose of the Aramaic translations, however. They were originally intended (in either oral or written form) to make the scriptures accessible to the majority of the people who no longer understood Hebrew. Cf. the remarks by A. Sperber; in his opinion the educational level of the audience for which the targums were intended was not very high (*The Bible in Aramaic*, 4B: *The Targum and the Hebrew Bible* [Leiden: Brill, 1973] 21). If Sperber was correct in his assessment that with the Hagiographa the targums were becoming less and less translations as such, and more and more tended to show characteristics of midrash, then the tendency to reformulate earlier traditions would, in these targums, be particularly influential (4A, *Hagiographa* [Leiden: Brill, 1968] viii).

[43] E.g., such as Eph 4:7-11.

[44] This approach would also need to be followed if the entire targum could be dated, but its date turned out to be post-NT (as in the case of *Tg.* Psalms it almost certainly would).

tively small amount of attention devoted thus far to the study of the targums to the Hagiographa. In each instance, the task must be to reconstruct (if possible) the history of the tradition in question, since one cannot assume the antiquity of the final form in which the tradition appears in the written targum.[45]

The difficulties surrounding the dating of traditions within the rabbinic literature are basically very similar, and therefore we will consider briefly the approach first suggested by R. Bloch. In order to classify and date traditions within the rabbinic literature, she proposed that analysis should proceed in two stages, external and internal comparison (in addition to the use of standard historical and philological criteria). External comparison consisted of setting alongside rabbinic writings containing undated traditions those non-rabbinic Jewish (and related) texts which could be dated (at least approximately). These external criteria could be found in Hellenistic Jewish works, apocrypha and pseudepigrapha, the works of Josephus, the ancient versions, glosses in the biblical text, the Qumran documents, the NT, early Christian literature (especially that related to Jewish sources), and the ancient Jewish liturgy. In contrast to this, internal comparison sought to reconstruct the development of a given tradition within the bounds of rabbinic literature itself, taking into account known rabbinic methods of exegesis and transmission.[46]

---

45 Thus the observation of G. R. Driver was particularly apt: "Although the Targums contain much ancient matter going far back into the period of the Second Commonwealth, no individual statement can be dated except by external evidence" (*The Judaean Scrolls* [Oxford: Basil Blackwell, 1965] 459).

46 The method suggested by R. Bloch was adopted by G. Vermes (*Scripture and Tradition in Judaism*, SPB 4 [Leiden: Brill, 1961] 7-9). In this study Vermes set out to subject Bloch's method to a rigorous test. Her original articles on a proposed method for the study of *Traditionsgeschichte* in rabbinic materials are (in chronological order): "Écriture et tradition dans le judaïsme—Aperçus sur l'origine du Midrash," CSion 8 (1954) 9-34; "Note méthodologique pour l'étude de la littérature rabbinique," RSR 43 (1955) 194-227; and "Note sur l'utilisation des fragments de la Geniza du Caire pour l'étude du Targum palestinien," REJ 114 (1955) 5-35. There are obviously some similarities in this method to *Traditionsgeschichte* as employed in the study of the literature of the NT, e.g., see D. Catchpole ("Tradition History," in *New Testament Interpretation*, ed. I. H. Marshall [Exeter: Paternoster, 1977] 168). J. Neusner was critical of Bloch's approach because he saw little of value in being able to state that a certain story or saying circulated prior to the formulation of an otherwise undated document; instead, he was interested in working with entire documents and not with individual accounts or stories, and thus Bloch's method appeared of little use to him (*Comparative Midrash: The Plan and Program of Genesis Rabbah and Leviticus Rabbah*, BJS 111 [Atlanta: Scholars Press, 1986] 187-93). He did acknowledge that what she discussed in the first phase of her approach (which she referred to as "external comparison") was tradition history (191). Neusner believed Bloch to be using the term "midrash" to mean something like "story" or "statement" (i.e., *haggadah*), so that what she was attempting was a new kind of *Traditionsgeschichte* or *Überlieferungsgeschichte*, with "midrash" understood merely as another word for "tradition." Neusner may well have been correct; Bloch's method (as we have already noted) bears similarities to *Traditionsgeschichte* as applied to the study of the NT. Neusner's criticisms, however valid, do not affect the usefulness of Bloch's method for the present study, since all that interests us is the comparison of the various rabbinic accounts concerning Moses' ascent to heaven, with a

This approach to the study of traditions within rabbinic literature is extremely valuable for targumic studies as well since it seeks to provide criteria by which the antiquity of a given tradition can be verified.[47] This is particularly useful in dealing with traditions found in *Tg*. Psalms, which (as discussed in the previous section) is of mixed character, making the material it contains especially difficult to date.

B. PSALM 68 AND MOSES' ASCENT TO HEAVEN IN RABBINIC LITERATURE

We shall now apply the method originally proposed by R. Bloch for the study of traditions in rabbinic literature to the tradition concerning Moses' ascent to heaven found in *Tg*. Ps 68:19. This will help to determine the approximate date of this tradition in relation to the composition of Eph 4:7-11. It will also help us to decide whether the author of Ephesians could have been familiar with such an ascent tradition concerning Moses and might thus have been influenced by it when he wrote Eph 4:8-10. Knowledge of such Moses-traditions associated with Psalm 68, if they were common and widespread, would have predisposed the author to infer from the psalm a subsequent descent of Christ in Eph 4:9-10 corresponding to the ascent mentioned in Ps 68:19 itself, since Moses after his ascent of Mt. Sinai to receive the Torah descended to distribute it as 'gifts' to Israel. We shall begin with a survey of the relevant rabbinic sources (the procedure called "internal comparison" by Bloch in her approach). Since there exists an enormous amount of material dealing with Moses and his activities related to the giving of Torah within rabbinic Judaism, only those texts which explicitly associate Ps 68:19 with Moses and his ascent to heaven can be examined here. Furthermore, as most of the rabbinic literature is by its very nature extremely difficult to date, our discussion will follow thematic lines, assuming (unless otherwise noted) that development generally took place from the simpler to the more complex form of the tradition (given the recognized rabbinic methods of explanation, quotation, and transmission).

1. Pesiqta Rabbati *47.4*

The shortest account of Moses' ascent which mentions Ps 68:19 occurs

---

view to determining their antiquity and possible relationship to Eph 4:8-10.

[47] R. Bloch herself saw the Palestinian Targum as standing at the base of the later haggadic tradition, as an expression of the transition between the Bible per se and the later rabbinic literature, representing the point of departure ("le point de départ") of what is properly called midrash, of which the targum contained all the structure and all the themes ("Note méthodologique pour l'étude de la littérature rabbinique," *RSR* 43 [1955] 212).

in *Pesiq. R.* 47.4, attributed to R. Phinehas:

> Another comment: The merit of Israel is implied, Israel to whom it was said
> *This (z' t) thy stature is like to a palm tree* (Song 7:8). R. Phinehas said: In-
> deed Moses, who ascended on high and took the Torah captive and brought
> it down, was able to do so not by virtue of his own strength, but by virtue of
> Israel's merit, as is said *Thou hast ascended on high, thou hast led captivity
> captive, thou hast received gifts by virtue of men* (Ps. 68:19)—that is, by vir-
> tue of Israel's merit, to whom it is said *And ye My sheep, the sheep of My
> pasture, are men* (Ezek. 34:31).[48]

The lack of elaboration concerning Moses' ascent demonstrated by this
account is probably best explained by the emphasis in the context on
Aaron rather than Moses. When Aaron entered the Holy of Holies on
the Day of Atonement, Satan would appear to make accusations against
the people of Israel, but was forced to flee from Aaron's presence on account of the merits which accompanied him. The passage quoted, from
section 4, is intended as a proof that the merit of Israel is included
among those merits which went with Aaron into the innermost sanctuary. Ps 68:19 is quoted only to show that it was on behalf of Israel's
merit that Moses was able to receive the Torah. This involves a rather
forced rendition of the ב-preposition at the end of the third clause of Ps
68:19 (באדם is interpreted to mean "by virtue of men"). The brevity of
the account in *Pesiq. R.* 47.4 is probably not indicative of an early
stage in the tradition surrounding Moses' ascent, but a natural result of
the secondary and supporting nature of the reference to Ps 68:19 within
the context. In fact the tradition could have been so widespread and
well known at this point that a passing mention was considered sufficient by the author to evoke the desired associations with Moses and
his ascent of Sinai.

2. Midrash Tehillim *68.11*

Next we consider the interpretation of Ps 68:19 found in *Midrash Tehillim* (*Midr. Teh.* 68.11). As might be expected, Ps 68:19 in the Midrash
on the Psalms is interpreted of Moses and his ascent to the presence of
God to receive the Torah:

> 11. *Thou hast gone up on high, thou hast led captivity captive; thou hast re-
> ceived gifts for men* (Ps. 68:19). These words are to be read in the light of
> what Scripture says elsewhere: *A wise man goeth up to the city of the mighty,
> and bringeth down the strength wherein it trusteth* (Prov. 21:22). This *wise
> man* is Moses, of whom it is said "And Moses went up unto God" (Ex.

---

48 *Pesikta Rabbati*, trans. W. G. Braude, YJS 18 (New Haven and London: Yale University
Press, 1968) 809. Scriptural quotations, parenthetical references, italics, and punctuation are
given in the form employed by the translator.

19:3); the words *thou hast received gifts for men* refer to the Torah which was bestowed upon Israel as a gift, at no cost. The words *The rebellious dwell but in a parched land* (Ps. 68:7) refer to the nations of the earth who were unwilling to accept the Torah; on the other hand, in the words *Yea, among the rebellious also, that the Lord God might dwell among them* (ibid. 68:19), *among the rebellious* refers to the children of Israel who had also been rebellious, but among whom, the presence of God came to dwell after they accepted the Torah.[49]

A number of significant points emerge: in typical rabbinic fashion, other scriptures are adduced to interpret Ps 68:19, in this case Prov 21:22 and Exod 19:3. No specific mention of heaven as the place to which Moses ascended occurs in *Midr. Teh.* 68.11, but this is probably assumed as implicit in the mention of the "city of the mighty" (Prov 21:22) and the statement that Moses went "up unto God" (Exod 19:3). Emphasis is placed on the fact that Torah was given to Israel as a gift, without cost (one might wonder about the possible relation of this emphasis on Torah as a gift to the substitution of the verb יהבת in *Tg.* Ps 68:19). Yet it is Moses who 'receives' these gifts on behalf of men in *Midr. Teh.* 68.11; the *Vorlage* is obviously לקחת as read by the Hebrew text. By the introduction of a previous verse from Psalm 68 (v. 7), reference is made to the rebellious nations of the earth who refused to accept the Torah.[50] The mention of 'the rebellious' in the latter part of Ps 68:19 must obviously refer (from the standpoint of rabbinic logic) to Israel rather than the nations, since the 'presence of God' had chosen to dwell in their midst (something which could never be said of the nations, who were without Torah).[51] Significant also in this account is what does not appear: there is no mention of any angelic opposition to Moses when he attempted to remove the Torah from heaven (indeed, there is no reference to angels whatsoever), no mention of any dialogue between Moses and God, and no mention of any 'gifts' given to Moses on behalf of men (other than the Torah itself). Although arguments from silence must be employed only with great caution (if at all!), nevertheless, the account of Moses' ascent to heaven in *Midr. Teh.* 68.11 shows a great deal of restraint in the relative simplicity of its exegesis and lack of embellishment in its description when compared with most of the other

[49] *The Midrash on Psalms*, trans. W. G. Braude, YJS 13 (New Haven: Yale University Press, 1959) 545. Again, the translator's form is employed in the inclusion of scriptural quotations, references, italics, and punctuation.

[50] Reflecting the rabbinic belief that the Torah was offered to all the 70 nations of the earth, but was accepted only by Israel. This belief may well be pre-Christian, in light of the writings of Philo of Alexandria. See ch. 5, 149-51.

[51] This interpretation may be at variance with *Tg.* Ps 68:19, which inserts the participle מתגיירין "becoming proselytes," probably to indicate that the rebellious in 68:19 are to be understood as Gentiles who repent.

rabbinic discussions of the giving of Torah. In this respect it is closer to
Tg. Ps 68:19 than many of the other rabbinic accounts.

3. Soferim *16.10 and* Midrash Tehillim *22.19*

Since these two accounts are essentially identical we shall consider
them together. The first, *Soferim* (one of the minor tractates of the Talmud), mentions Ps 68:19 and Moses' ascent to receive the Torah in
16.10 (41b). This account consists of a saying attributed to R. Joshua
ben Levi concerning written haggadah.[52] It needs to be examined in
some detail (and compared with the parallel account in *Midr. Teh.* 22.19
as well), since it contains an ambiguity which led to a significant misunderstanding on the part of R. Rubinkiewicz concerning the relationship between *Tg.* Ps 68:19 and the text of Eph 4:8.[53] Tractate *Sof.* 16.10
reads as follows:

> Rule 10. R. Joshua b. Levi said: I have never looked into a book of *'aggadta*
> [*sic*] except once when I looked and found written therein that the one hun-
> dred and seventy-five sections of the Torah, in which occurs any expression
> of speaking, saying or commanding, correspond to the number of years of
> our father Abraham; for it is written, *Thou hast ascended on high, Thou hast
> led captivity captive; Thou hast received gifts for the sake of the man,* and it
> is also written, *The greatest man among the Anakim.* On this account the
> Rabbis instituted one hundred and seventy-five orders in the Torah [to be
> read in public worship] every Sabbath [as regularly as the] continual burnt-
> offering.[54]

Rubinkiewicz, having just quoted from *b. Shab.* 89a (also attributed to
R. Joshua ben Levi) in which Ps 68:19 is interpreted as a reference to
Moses' ascent to heaven, then quoted the present text,[55] *Sof.* 16.10
(41b), in which he (mistakenly) understood Ps 68:19 to refer to Abraham, despite the editor's footnote to the contrary.[56] Rubinkiewicz then
drew the conclusion (incorrectly) that Ps 68:19 was not always interpreted consistently of Moses in rabbinic literature.[57] As far as I can determine, however, there is not a single instance in the extant rabbinic

---

[52] R. Joshua b. Levi is also mentioned in connection with the ascent of Moses and the quotation of Ps 68:19 in *Midr. Teh.* 22.19 (a parallel account of the same incident) and *b. Shab.*
88b, which is a far more elaborate treatment of Moses' journey to heaven to receive the Torah.

[53] R. Rubinkiewicz, "Ps LXVIII 19 (= Eph IV 8) Another Textual Tradition or Targum?,"
NovT 17 (1975) 219-24.

[54] *The Minor Tractates of the Talmud,* ed. A. Cohen (London: Soncino, 1965) 1.292.
Scriptural quotations, parenthetical notes, italics, and punctuation follow Cohen's edition.

[55] He differed, in the process, at no less than four points from the text of *The Minor Tractates of the Talmud* (ed. A. Cohen, 1.292), which he cited as reference; one of these variants
may have contributed to his misunderstanding of this text. See n. 59 below.

[56] I.e., n. 49, 292, in which the editor, Cohen, clearly stated that Ps 68:19 referred to Moses.

[57] R. Rubinkiewicz, "Ps LXVIII 19 (= Eph IV 8) Another Textual Tradition or Targum?,"
224.

literature where Ps 68:19 is quoted in which it is not referred to Moses and his ascent to heaven to receive the Torah. Furthermore, the same incident is recounted in *Midr. Teh.* 22.19, and had Rubinkiewicz examined this parallel account, it is unlikely that he could have misunderstood the text of *Sof.* 16.10 as he did, since in *Midr. Teh.* 22.19 Moses is explicitly mentioned, and the reference to Abraham thus becomes clear:

> R. Joshua ben Levi said: May evil befall me, if ever in my entire life I looked into a book of *'Aggadah*, except once, when coming upon such a book I read the following in it: The one hundred and seventy-five sections of the Pentateuch, in which the words "speech," "saying," and "command" occur, correspond in number to the one hundred and seventy-five years of Abraham. And the proof? What God said to Moses: *Thou hast ascended on high …thou hast received gifts because of a man* (Ps. 68:19). This *man* was Abraham, described as "the greatest man among the Anakim" (Josh. 14:15).[58]

Here it is obvious that Moses is the one who ascended to heaven (Ps 68:19), while it is on the merit of Abraham that the giving of Torah to Israel is based ("because of a man," reading באדם in Ps 68:19 as a particular individual, rather than as the collective singular, 'mankind').[59]

Turning now to consider the characteristics of the tradition associating Moses and his ascent to heaven with Ps 68:19 in these accounts, we find that neither *Sof.* 16.10 nor *Midr. Teh.* 22.19 have much to contribute, since the tradition is not highly developed in either context. This is not surprising, however, since neither context is particularly concerned with Moses and the giving of Torah directly. The main point in both is the correspondence between the 175 divisions of the Torah for public reading and the 175 years of Abraham's life. From a rabbinic point of view this correspondence required an explanation (as it obviously could not have been mere coincidence). Thus Ps 68:19 was conveniently invoked to explain the correspondence, since its third clause could (with a bit of stretching) be interpreted as a declaration that the Torah was, in fact, given because of the merit of Abraham. Therefore (as was also the case in *Pesiq. R.* 47.4) the tradition concerning Moses and his ascent to receive the Torah was not elaborated in great detail in either *Sof.* 16.10 or *Midr. Teh.* 22.19, because it was not the primary concern in the respective contexts. Thus it cannot be inferred that the degree of simplicity reflected in these parallel accounts is indicative of an early stage in the history of the tradition, any more than it could from

---

[58] *The Midrash on Psalms*, trans. W. G. Braude, 314. Scriptural quotations, italics, and punctuation follow Braude's translation.

[59] Perhaps one reason Rubinkiewicz misunderstood *Sof.* 16:10 as he did is that he misread "the man" as "the men," obscuring the reference to a single individual, Abraham. See R. Rubinkiewicz, "Ps LXVIII 19 (= Eph IV 8) Another Textual Tradition or Targum?," 224.

Pesiq. R. 47.4.[60]

4. Shir haShirim Rabbah *8.11.2 (viii.11.2)*

In *Shir. Rab.* 8.11.2 there is a brief discussion of the giving of Torah to Israel in which Ps 68:19 is quoted:

> So when the Holy One, blessed be He, sought to give the Torah to Israel, the ministering angels tried to thrust Israel away, and they thrust themselves before the Holy One, blessed be He, and said: 'Sovereign of the Universe, it is Thy happiness, Thy majesty, Thy honour that Thy law should be in the heaven.' He replied to them: 'You have no concern with it. It is written therein, *And if a woman have an issue of her blood many days* (Lev. xv, 25). Is there any woman among you? So you have no concern with it.' Further it is written therein, *When a man dieth in his tent* (Num. xix, 14). Is there death among you? So you have no concern with it. And so the Scripture praises him [Moses] with the words, *Thou hast ascended on high, thou hast taken thy captive* (Ps. lxviii, 19), on which R. Aḥa said: This refers to the rules which apply to human beings, such as those relating to men and women with an issue, unclean women, and women in childbirth. So 'you have no concern with it'.[61]

This is the first rabbinic text we have examined which makes any mention of angels at all in connection with the giving of Torah. It is significant that they are portrayed here as seeking to oppose it. Later in the same context (beyond the section quoted above) the angels' motives are explained: they feared that if the Torah were removed from heaven and given to men, sooner or later the Divine Presence would leave heaven to abide in the lower world as well. This brought forth divine reassurance that even if Torah were given to those who dwell on earth, the Holy One himself would continue to dwell with the celestial beings. Thus the angels were satisfied to allow Torah to pass to men. The text of *Shir. Rab.* 8.11.2 as quoted, however, does not present a completely consistent account of the action. It was Yahweh himself who entered into dialogue with the angels, quoting Lev 15:25 and Num 19:14 to prove to them that Torah was intended for men and not for angelic beings.[62] Yet Ps 68:19 was introduced in a way which implied that Moses

---

[60] In further support of this point, R. Joshua b. Levi, to whom both accounts are attributed (*Sof.* 16.10 and *Midr. Teh.* 22.19), was also associated with the account of Moses' visit to heaven in *b. Shab.* 88b-89a, which represents one of the most elaborate and highly developed forms of the tradition (see below, 88-90).

[61] *Midrash Rabbah*, ed. H. Freedman and M. Simon, *Song of Songs*, trans. M. Simon (London: Soncino, 1939) 320. Scriptural references, quotations, italics, and punctuation conform to the edition cited.

[62] It may be significant, as far as the dating of this version of the tradition is concerned, that both examples quoted are taken from the Pentateuch rather than from the Decalogue per se; elements from the Decalogue do appear in some rabbinic versions of this debate. But it is almost certain that long before any of these accounts existed in written form, the entire Penta-

ought to be given credit for successfully refuting the angels and 'capturing' Torah. This may reflect a certain amount of confusion with other versions of the story which do, in fact, present Moses as the one who dialogues with the angels and convinces them to relinquish Torah.[63] It should be noted as well that although Moses' name is not explicitly mentioned in *Shir. Rab.* 8.11.2 in connection with Ps 68:19,[64] the preceding context makes it clear that 'him' must refer to Moses.[65]

5. Pirqe de Rabbi Eliezer 46

A brief account of Moses' ascent to heaven to obtain the Torah is found in *Pirqe R. El.* 46:

> The ministering angels said to him: Moses! This Torah has been given only for our sakes. Moses replied to them: It is written in the Torah, "Honour thy father and thy mother." Have ye then father and mother? Again, it is written in the Torah, "When a man dieth in the tent." Does death happen among you? They were silent, and did not answer anything further.
>
> Hence (the sages) say: Moses went up to the heavenly regions with his wisdom, and brought down the might of the trust of the ministering angels, as it is said, "A wise man scaleth the city of the mighty, and bringeth down the strength of the confidence thereof." When the ministering angels saw that the Holy One, blessed be He, gave the Torah to Moses, they also arose and gave unto him presents and letters and tablets for healing the sons of men, as it is said, "Thou hast ascended on high, thou hast led thy captivity captive; thou hast received gifts among men."[66]

Here again the angels are portrayed as seeking to dissuade Moses from taking the Torah from heaven; this time, however, it was Moses himself who disputed with them, and there is no mention of any direct intervention by Yahweh except the note that the Holy One himself presented

---

teuch had come to be regarded as Torah.

[63] E.g., *Pirqe R. El.* 46, *b. Shab.* 88b-89a, and *Pesiq. R.* 20.4. But it is also possible that the apparent discontinuity in the account given in *Shir. Rab.* 8.11.2 is actually a result of extreme 'compression', i. e., some (crucial) details and transitions were omitted. Thus "*He* replied to them: 'You have no concern with it'" may, in fact, refer to Moses rather than to Yahweh; what was omitted from the account (perhaps because it was assumed to be understood) would be Yahweh's command to Moses to give a reply to the angels (cf. *b. Shab.* 88b and *Pesiq. R.* 20.4).

[64] The inclusion of his name in brackets is a note by M. Simon, the translator.

[65] Ps 68:13 is quoted twice in the immediately preceding context; the second time it is referred to Moses: "'*And the fair one in the house divideth the spoil*': O thou fairest in the house, thou dividest spoil below. 'The fairest in the house' is Moses, as it says, *He is trusted in all my house* (Num. xii, 7). Thou givest it to him, and he divides it as spoil among the dwellers on earth" (*Midrash Rabbah*, ed. H. Freedman and M. Simon, *Song of Songs*, trans. M. Simon, 320).

[66] *Pirkê de Rabbi Eliezer*, trans. and annotated by G. Friedlander (London: no publisher, 1916; reprinted New York: Sepher-Hermon, 1981) 361-62. Quotations, punctuation, and parenthetical notes are in the form given in Friedlander's translation.

the Torah to Moses. Only two citations from the Torah are mentioned in
the dialogue: the command to honor fathers and mothers (Exod 20:12,
also mentioned in *b. Shab.* 89a and *Pesiq. R.* 20.4) and the law regarding ritual uncleanness when a man died in his tent (Num 19:14, also mentioned in *Shir. Rab.* 8.11.2). Prov 21:22 is quoted and interpreted of
Moses, as it was in *Midr. Teh.* 68.11 (and *Shem. Rab.* 28.1). Ps 68:19 is
actually included in the account as final proof of the angels' response
when Moses was given the Torah: they "arose and gave unto him presents and letters and tablets for healing the sons of men." With this text
for the first time one encounters the tradition that Moses received other
gifts in heaven in addition to the Torah, and that these were bestowed
by the angels, who showed no sign of resentment at having lost the debate. While this account is brief, the actual specification of the gifts
(particularly the "tablets for healing the sons of men")[67] seems to indicate a later stage in the development of the tradition (even when
compared with the description of the angelic gifts in *b. Shab.* 89a).
What *Pirqe R. El.* 46 does not contain (at least in its present form) is
mention of Moses being given the secret of preserving life by the Angel
of Death, an element which does appear in some other versions of the
story.[68]

6. Abot de Rabbi Nathan 2.3 (18b)

This text is primarily an account of how Moses came to break the tablets
of the Decalogue when he came down Mount Sinai with them and
found the Israelites sinning with the golden calf. In the course of this
explanation there is one allusion to Ps 68:19 and one direct quote, as
follows:

> 'He broke the tablets.' How was this? It is related that when Moses ascended
> on high to receive the tablets which had been inscribed and were lying in
> readiness [to be revealed] since the six days of creation, as it is stated, *And
> the tables were the work of God, and the writing was the writing of God,
> graven [haruth] upon the tables* —read not *haruth* [graven] but *heruth*
> [freedom], for only he is truly free who occupies himself with the Torah—at
> that time the ministering angels arraigned Moses, saying, 'Lord of the uni-
> verse! *What is man, that Thou art mindful of him? And the son of man, that
> Thou thinkest of him?*... They were referring disparagingly to Moses, saying,
> 'What virtue is there in man born of woman that he has ascended on high, as
> it is stated, *Thou art ascended on high, thou hast led captivity captive, thou
> hast received gifts?*' Moses took the tablets and descended with them, re-

---

67 Apparently *Pittaḳin* (πιττάκιον) in the original, according to the translator; see *Pirkê de
Rabbi Eliezer*, 362, n. 4.
68 Cf. *b. Shab.* 89a and *Pesiq. R.* 20.4. The "tablets for healing the sons of men" mentioned in *Pirqe R. El.* 46 may be related, however.

joicing exceedingly. But as soon as he saw the depravity with which they had depraved themselves in the episode of the calf, he said to himself, 'How can I give them the tablets, thereby binding them to the performance of weighty commandments, and in consequence condemning them [if they disobeyed] to death before Heaven, for it is written therein, *Thou shalt have no other gods before Me?* He turned back, but when the seventy elders saw this they hurried after him. He seized one end of the tablets while they seized the other end, but the strength of Moses prevailed over theirs, as it is stated, *And in all the mighty hand, and in all the great terror, which Moses wrought in the sight of all Israel.* He glanced at the tablets and saw that the writing had flown from them; so he exclaimed, 'How can I give Israel these worthless tablets? I will grasp hold of them and break them,' as it is stated, *And I took hold of the two tables, and cast them out of my two hands, and broke them.*[69]

Here again, the angels sought to prevent Moses from taking the Torah—in this case the actual tablets of the Decalogue—from heaven. They did not, however, threaten to assault him, although they did speak of him disparagingly using the words of Psalm 8 (quoted in *Abot R. Nat.* 2.3 virtually in its entirety). No mention is made of any dialogue between Moses and the angels or Yahweh and the angels. In fact God himself is almost absent from the scene: the tablets are prepared beforehand (from the creation of the world, according to the text of *Abot R. Nat.* 2.3) and God is not even mentioned directly in the account aside from the fact that the angels' accusation against Moses was directed to him as 'Lord of the universe'. Much of this can be seen as a result of the primary interest in the context—to provide a justification for the breaking of the original tablets of the Decalogue by Moses. No doubt many of the missing elements in this account are simply assumed as understood (as is often the case in rabbinic exegesis). Of more significance for our present investigation is the allusion found in the initial words of the section: "It is related that *when Moses ascended on high to receive* the tablets." No further reference to Ps 68:19 occurs until Moses actually prepared to take the tablets and depart with them, but the wording (italicized in the above quotation) makes it clear that Ps 68:19 is in view. That such a passing reference to Moses' ascent to heaven could be phrased in terms so much like the text of Ps 68:19 suggests that by the time of this account Moses had come to be so closely identified with the interpretation of Ps 68:19 that the reference to the ascent taken from the psalm is almost assumed as a stock phrase. That Moses made the ascent to heaven from Sinai in order to receive the Torah, and that this ascent

---

[69] *The Minor Tractates of the Talmud*, ed. A. Cohen (London: Soncino, 1965) 1.20-21. The ellipsis indicated at the end of the quotation from Psalm 8 is mine; all other quotations, punctuation, italics, and bracketed notes are in the form given in the translation. The quotation from Psalm 8 has been shortened for the sake of brevity, since virtually the entire psalm is quoted in *Abot R. Nat.* 2.3.

was described by Ps 68:19, appear to be accepted facts by the time *Abot R. Nat.* 2.3 was committed to writing.

7. Shemoth Rabbah *28.1*

Shem. Rab. 28.1 is a midrashic exegesis of Exod 19:3, and as such it should not be surprising to find Ps 68:19 quoted at some point. As it turns out, however, practically the entire exegesis of Exod 19:3 is based on Ps 68:19. A number of familiar themes emerge along with several new ones:

> I. AND MOSES WENT UP UNTO GOD (xix, 3). It is written, *Thou hast ascended on high, Thou hast led captivity captive* (Ps. lxviii, 19). What is the meaning of '*Thou hast ascended*'?—Thou hast been exalted, because thou didst wrestle with angels on high. Another explanation of '*Thou hast ascended on high*': No creature on high has prevailed as Moses did. R. Berekiah said: The length of the Tablets was six handbreadths; two were—could we but speak thus!—in the hands of Him who called the world into being; two handbreadths were in the hands of Moses, and two handbreadths separated the two pairs of hands. Another explanation of '*Thou hast ascended on high, thou hast led captivity captive*': One who enters a city usually takes away something unnoticed and unprized by the inhabitants, but Moses ascended on high and took away the Torah on which all had their eyes—hence: '*thou hast ascended on high, thou hast led captivity captive*': Lest you think that because he captured it, he took it gratis, the Psalmist adds: *Thou hast received gifts among men* (ib.), that is, it was given to him for a price. Lest you think that he actually paid in money, the Psalmist assures us that it was '*gifts*', namely, that it was given to him as a gift. At that moment, the angels wished to attack Moses, but God made the features of Moses resemble those of Abraham and said to the angels: 'Are you not ashamed to touch this man to whom you descended from heaven and in whose house you ate?' God said to Moses: 'It is only for the sake of Abraham that the Torah is given to you,' as it says, '*Thou hast received gifts among men*' (be-adam). The word '*adam*' in this verse refers to Abraham, for it says, *Which Arba was the greatest man among the Anakim* (Josh. xiv, 15). Hence, AND MOSES WENT UP TO GOD.[70]

Whatever else may be said, it is difficult to see how the tradition associating Ps 68:19 with Moses could be more firmly established at this point, since it is in fact the primary text employed in the exegesis of Exod 19:3. The first explanation of 'Thou hast ascended'—that Moses 'wrestled' with angels on high—suggests by its wording the account of Jacob and the angel at Penuel (Gen 32:22-32), but it also recalls the angelic opposition to Moses which appeared in *Abot R. Nat.* 2.3, *Pirqe R. El.* 46, and *Shir. Rab.* 8.11.2 (although the opposition in all these instances was

---

[70] *Midrash Rabbah*, ed. H. Freedman and M. Simon, *Exodus*, trans. S. M. Lehrman (London: Soncino, 1939) 331-32. Quotations, italics, and punctuation conform to the edition cited.

only verbal). Later in the present text (and in *b. Shab.* 88b-89a and *Pesiq. R.* 20.4 as well) the angels actually threatened to attack Moses when he prepared to take the Torah down to Israel. Here in *Shem. Rab.* 28.1 God miraculously caused Moses to resemble Abraham (whom the angels visited, an allusion to Gen 18:1-21) in order to dissuade the angels from attacking.[71] The reference to Abraham, however, provides the basis for introducing mention of his merit in obtaining Torah for Israel. God informed Moses that it was only because of Abraham that Torah was given. The third clause of Ps 68:19, לקחת מתנות באדם, is interpreted as a reference to Abraham, and further support for this point is adduced by the quotation of Josh 14:15. This discussion of Abraham proceeds along lines very similar to the discussions in *Sof.* 16.10 and *Midr. Teh.* 22.19, both of which mention Josh 14:15 as well. The unique element in the case of *Shem. Rab.* 28.1 is the use of Abraham (or more specifically, the miraculous transformation of Moses to appear like Abraham) to explain how Moses was protected from the angels (in other accounts he was delivered from their attack by grasping hold of the throne of God and quoting to them—at God's direction—words from the Torah).[72] It is possible that the extended role of Abraham in the account of the giving of Torah in *Shem. Rab.* 28.1 developed out of Abraham's association with Ps 68:19 (באדם) and Josh 14:15 as seen in *Sof.* 16.10 and *Midr. Teh.* 22.19, and it may well be that the other version of Moses' deliverance from the hostile angels was also known at the time, with no attempt being made to reconcile the two accounts.[73]

In addition there are similarities to the account in *Midr. Teh.* 68.11, particularly in the use of Prov 21:22 (to which the present text alludes) and in the stress on Torah as a gift given at no cost (although *Shem. Rab.* is a bit difficult to follow on this point; nevertheless, it does clearly conclude that Torah was a 'gift'). Conspicuous by its absence is the account of the dialogue between Moses and the angels found elsewhere; in its place (presumably to explain why the angels allowed Moses to take the Torah) is the transformation of Moses to resemble Abraham. There is no mention of angelic gifts given to Moses following his acquisition of the Torah.

---

[71] The modern reader might wonder why God did not simply order the angels to refrain from attacking Moses. Perhaps such a seemingly logical solution was too straightforward to appeal to rabbinic exegetes! (But see the discussion in the text above concerning Abraham's role in *Shem. Rab.* 28.1).

[72] *B. Shab.* 88b and *Pesiq. R.* 20.4.

[73] Of course, it is also possible that the (more restricted) role of Abraham mentioned in *Sof.* 16.10 and *Midr. Teh.* 22.19 may have been influenced by the account as given in *Shem. Rab.* 28.1, but since these accounts are generally shorter and make no mention of angelic opposition to Moses, this is not as probable.

8. b. Shabbat *88b-89a*

One of the more detailed accounts of Moses' ascent to heaven is found
in *b. Shab*. 88b-89a where (as in the shorter accounts in *Sof*. 16.10 and
Midr. Teh. 22.19) most of the material is attributed to R. Joshua ben
Levi. The section is quoted at length because when compared with accounts examined previously it provides valuable insight into the way in
which the traditions surrounding Moses' receiving of Torah have been
expanded and developed.

> R. Joshua b. Levi also said: When Moses ascended on high, the ministering
> angels spoke before the Holy One, blessed be He, 'Sovereign of the Uni-
> verse! What business has one born of woman amongst us?' 'He has come to
> receive the Torah,' answered He to them. Said they to Him, 'That secret
> treasure, which has been hidden by Thee for nine hundred and seventy-four
> generations before the world was created, Thou desirest to give to flesh and
> blood! *What is man, that thou art mindful of him, And the son of man, that
> thou visitest him? O Lord our God, How excellent is thy name in all the
> earth! Who hast set thy glory [the Torah] upon the Heavens!*' 'Return them
> an answer,' bade the Holy One, blessed be He, to Moses. "Sovereign of the
> Universe' replied he, 'I fear lest they consume me with the [fiery] breath of
> their mouths.' 'Hold on to the Throne of Glory,' said He to him, 'and re-
> turn them an answer,' as it is said, *He maketh him to hold on to the face of
> his throne, And spreadeth* [PaRSHeZ] *his cloud over him*, whereon R.
> Naḥman observed: This teaches that the Almighty [SHaddai] spread [PiRash]
> the lustre [Ziw] of His Shechinah and cast it as a protection over him. He
> [then] spake before Him: 'Sovereign of the Universe! The Torah which
> Thou givest me, what is written therein? *I am the Lord thy God, which
> brought thee out of the land of Egypt.*' Said he to them [the angels], 'Did ye
> go down to Egypt; were ye enslaved to Pharaoh: why then should the Torah
> be yours? Again, what is written therein? *Thou shalt have no other gods*: do
> ye dwell among peoples that engage in idol worship? Again what is written
> therein? *Remember the Sabbath day, to keep it holy*: do ye then perform
> work, that ye need to rest? Again what is written therein? *Thou shalt not take*
> [tissa] [the name...in vain]: is there any business [massa] dealings among
> you? Again what is written therein? *Honour thy father and thy mother*; have
> ye fathers and mothers? Again what is written therein? *Thou shalt not mur-
> der. Thou shalt not commit adultery. Thou shalt not steal*; is there jealousy
> among you; is the Evil Tempter among you? Straightway they conceded
> [right] to the Holy One, blessed be He, for it is said, *O Lord, our Lord, How
> excellent is thy name*, etc. whereas '*Who hast set thy glory upon the heavens*'
> is not written. Immediately each one was moved to love him [Moses] and
> transmitted something to him, for it is said, *Thou hast ascended on high,
> thou hast taken spoils* [the Torah]; *Thou hast received gifts on account of
> man*: as a recompense for their calling thee man [adam] thou didst receive
> gifts. The Angel of Death too confided his secret to him, for it is said, *and he
> put on the incense, and made atonement for the people*; and it is said, *and he*

stood between the dead and the living, etc. Had he not told it to him, whence had he known it?[74]

The section begins with an allusion to Ps 68:19 in the phrase "when Moses ascended on high"; the phrase by this time has become virtually a title for any discussion of the giving of Torah when Moses' ascent of Mt. Sinai is mentioned.[75] The dialogue which follows involves Moses, the angels, and Yahweh himself. The angels are portrayed as protesting at first (quoting Psalm 8, as a disparaging reference to Moses)[76] and then as overtly hostile.[77] In the angels' protestation the Torah itself was spoken of not merely as preexistent, but "hidden...for nine hundred and seventy-four generations before the world was created."[78] Moses' deliverance from the angels' threat occurred when Yahweh commanded him to hold on to the divine throne and answer the angels from the words of the Torah.[79] As proof, Job 26:9 was cited: this latter verse was understood to mean that God spread the glory of his *shekinah* over Moses to protect him from the angels.[80]

The series of quotations from the Torah, addressed by Moses to the angels, is the longest in any of the rabbinic accounts. Six elements are included in the account, each followed by an appropriate rhetorical question[81] intended to demonstrate to the angels that Torah was not given for immortal celestial creatures such as they, but for human beings. Thus persuaded to relinquish the Torah, the angels responded with a refrain from Ps 8:10, and each was (rather suddenly) moved to 'love' Moses and bestow gifts upon him.[82] Ps 68:19 is actually quoted at this point as proof of the angelic gifts. Although באדם is taken as singular (not collective), no mention is made of Abraham in this version of the story as the man on whose account the Torah was given. Instead the angelic gifts were presented as recompense to Moses for the angels'

---

[74] *The Babylonian Talmud: Seder Mo'ed*, ed. I. Epstein, *Shabbath*, trans. H. Freedman (London: Soncino, 1938) 2.421-23. Quotations, bracketed notes, italics, and punctuation conform to the edition cited. *M. Sabb.* 9.3 (the corresponding section of the Mishna) contains no mention of any of this; it is all *gemara*.

[75] Cf. the rabbinic practice of using the first word of a section as its title, as in the five books of the Pentateuch (*Bereshith, Shemoth*, etc.) and the titles of the *sedarim*.

[76] As also in *Abot R. Nat.* 2.3.

[77] As implied in Moses' words, "I fear lest they consume me...."

[78] Again, cf. *Abot R. Nat.* 2.3.

[79] Cf. *Pesiq. R.* 20.4.

[80] Based on the exegesis of פרשז in the text of Job 26:9 (cf. *Pesiq. R.* 20.4). There is uncertainty over the rabbi to whom this observation should be attributed: in the present text it is R. Naḥman, but in *Pesiq. R.* 20.4 the same observation was attributed to R. Nahum, and in *b. Suk.* 5a (a related account which does not mention Ps 68:19, and thus is not considered further at this point) R. Tanḥum [Tanḥuma?] was credited with the observation. A corruption of the name in the process of transmission would appear to lie behind the confusion.

[81] Appropriate from a rabbinic standpoint!

[82] Cf. the accounts in *Pirqe R. El.* 46 and *Pesiq. R.* 20.4.

disparaging reference to him as 'man' (in their previous quotation of Ps
8:5). Specific mention of the Angel of Death and his gift to Moses appears for the first time in any of the accounts examined thus far.[83] This
leads in turn to the mention of Moses' intercession in the plague of Num
17:11-13.[84]

New elements present in the account of Moses' ascent in *b. Shab.*
88b-89a include the mention of the throne of Yahweh, the *shekinah*,
the Angel of Death, and the plague of Num 17:11-13. No mention is
made in this account of Moses being transformed into the appearance of
Abraham, nor of Abraham's merit before God as the reason that Torah is
given to Israel. The immediate context of *b. Shab.* 88b-89a contains
more embellishment and elaboration than any other rabbinic account of
the giving of Torah in which Ps 68:19 is mentioned.

9. Pesiqta Rabbati 20.4

The final rabbinic account to be examined which refers to Ps 68:19 is
Pesiq. R. 20.4. All the major elements included in this account of the
giving of the Torah to Moses are also found in *b. Shab.* 88b-89a. In fact
the two accounts are so similar that to quote *Pesiq. R.* 20.4 would be
superfluous. Ps 68:19 is employed in exactly the same way as in *b.
Shab.* 89a, to prove that Moses, having obtained the Torah, also received a gift from the Angel of Death.[85] Slightly less attention is given to
the 'dialogue' between Moses and the angels, when Moses quoted
from the Torah and asked rhetorical questions which proved that Torah
was intended for mankind rather than for celestial beings (only four
questions are mentioned in *Pesiq. R.* 20.4).[86]

What is most interesting in the account in *Pesiq. R.* 20.4 is the larger
context in which the events surrounding Moses' ascent to heaven and
the giving of Torah to Israel are placed. Section 4 of Pisqa 20 gives
elaborate details of Moses' journey to heaven when he went up to receive the Torah. Moses was carried up to the firmament by a cloud;
when he prepared to walk about on it, he was challenged by the angel
Kemuel, leader of twelve thousand destroying angels, whom Moses
struck with a single blow and made to perish out of the world. Then
Hadarniel, sixty myriads of *parasangs* taller than the next tallest angel,

---

[83] Cf., however, the reference to "tablets for healing the sons of men" found in *Pirqe R. El.*
46, a similarity which may suggest a relationship between the two accounts.

[84] Also mentioned in *Pesiq. R.* 20.4.

[85] The only difference in the two accounts is that in *b. Shab.* 89a Moses received gifts from
all the angels, while in *Pesiq. R.* 20.4 only the gift presented by the Angel of Death was explicitly mentioned.

[86] Compared to six questions in *b. Shab.* 88b-89a.

frightened Moses so badly that he almost fell from the cloud.[87] God was forced to intervene, reminding Hadarniel that when the angels had sought to prevent the creation of man, he [God] had burned companies of them in the fire. Then God had to station himself in front of the fires of Sandalphon to allow Moses to pass safely by. Later God intervened again to bring Moses past Rigyon, the river of fire whose coals consumed angels and men. God led Moses past Gallizur, whose task it was to proclaim the evil that was to come upon men. Then Moses was attacked by a troop of angels of destruction, who wished to burn him with the breath of their mouths for attempting to take the Torah from them. At this point God told Moses to hold on to his throne and answer the angels from the Torah. Moses did so, the angels were satisfied, and the Angel of Death even taught Moses the secret of preserving life.

The fantastic and mystical elements of the account of Moses' ascent to heaven in *Pesiq. R.* 20.4 can be seen even in this brief summary. Traces of *merkabah* mysticism are present as well as indications of gnostic speculation.[88] Yet when the fantastic element is discounted, the same basic elements found in a number of the other rabbinic accounts (particularly *b. Shab.* 88b-89a) remain. This account is basically similar to a number of other rabbinic accounts of Moses and Ps 68:19 aside from the degree of mystical embellishment it demonstrates.

10. *Conclusions: Rabbinic Texts Which Apply Ps 68:19 to Moses*

A number of significant observations emerge from our investigation of rabbinic texts which quoted Ps. 68:19. First, every time Ps 68:19 was mentioned in the rabbinic literature, it was (without exception) interpreted of Moses and his ascent to heaven to receive the Torah. All sources are in agreement that Ps 68:19 referred to Moses and his heavenly ascent; the 'captivity' he 'captured' referred to Torah.

Second, there is much more variation as far as other elements of Ps 68:19 are concerned. The third clause, לקחת מתנות באדם, was interpreted in at least four different ways: (a) Torah was given 'by virtue of men', i.e., Israelites, in *Pesiq. R.* 47.4; (b) Torah was given 'for the sake of the man', i.e., Abraham, according to *Sof.* 16.10, *Midr. Teh.* 22.19, and *Shem. Rab.* 28.1; (c) Torah was given as a recompense to Moses for being called 'man' (in a disparaging sense) by the angels, in *b. Shab.* 89a; and (d) Torah was given to Moses 'as a mere man' (i.e., Moses as a mere mortal was given the Torah) in *Pesiq. R.* 20.4. These interpretations,

---

[87] A *parasang* is a Persian mile, roughly 3.6 kilometres.
[88] Although not included in detail in the summary presented above. Note in relation to the presence of *merkabah* mysticism, however, the mention of the throne in both *Pesiq. R.* 20.4 and *b. Shab.* 88b.

usually related to a forced exegesis of the ב-preposition in the Hebrew text, were given without regard for their mutual inconsistency. Such a degree of diversity in the interpretation of this clause of Ps 68:19 becomes even more significant when viewed in relation to the relatively small number of rabbinic texts involved.

Third, the final clause of Ps 68:19 (ואף סוררים לשכן יה אלהים) was not included in most rabbinic citations of the verse. The only text which did in fact include it was *Midr. Teh.* 68.11 (on 68:19); in this case it was interpreted as a reference to rebellious Israel, among whom, nevertheless, the presence of God came to dwell.

Fourth, not all accounts make mention of the presence and intervention of the angels. Those which do so demonstrate a developing tendency to portray the angels as (a) disparaging of Moses, because he is a mere 'mortal'; (b) seeking to dissuade Moses from removing the Torah from their presence in heaven; and (c) openly hostile, seeking to attack and destroy Moses, whom God must intervene to protect. Although it is beyond our scope to speculate on how the role of the angels in the giving of Torah evolved in rabbinic literature, we may mention briefly two possibilities here. The phrase שבית שבי "you led captive captivity" (that is, Torah) in Ps 68:19 might have given rise to a natural question on the part of the rabbis, "From whom was Torah captured?" Not from God, certainly—thus it must have been captured from the angels. In addition, the previous verse, 68:18, contains a difficult reading, אלפי שנאן, which *Tg.* Psalms translates as אלפין דאנגליא ("thousands of angels"), probably reflecting what was by the time of the targum a traditional interpretation of the Hebrew text. However it came about, once the tradition associating the presence of angels with the giving of Torah was firmly established, it provided a point of departure for hellenistic and gnostic influences, culminating in fantastic accounts of Moses' journey to heaven such as *Pesiq. R.* 20.4.

In conclusion, it is reasonable to assume that the basic elements underlying the traditional rabbinic interpretation of Ps 68:19 consisted of two main points: (a) Moses ascended to heaven to receive the Torah,[89]

---

[89] Although some authorities insisted that Moses did not go 'up' to heaven; rather, heaven came 'down' to him. See, e.g., *b. Suk.* 5a (which does not mention Ps 68:19) and *Mek. Bahodesh* 4.54-58 (on Exod 20:20) which states: "Neither Moses nor Elijah ever went up to heaven (לא עלה משה ואליהו למעלה), nor did the Glory (הכבוד) ever come down to earth. Scripture merely teaches that God said to Moses: Behold, I am going to call you through the top of the mount (לך מראש ההר) and you will come up, as it is said: 'And the Lord called Moses to the top of the mount'" (*Mekilta de Rabbi Ishmael*, trans. J. Z. Lauterbach [Philadelphia: Jewish Publication Society of America, 1933] 2.224). This interpretation of Moses' 'ascent' may be particularly significant in light of the probability that the *Mekilta* is quite ancient. According to J. Bowker, it is one of the earliest midrashim to have survived, and although it has since been revised and expanded, it dates originally from the Tannaitic period (*The Targums and*

and (b) he there took Torah 'captive'. Later on it would be generally agreed that angels were present (whether or not they sought to attack Moses), and that Moses received gifts on behalf of men (whether or not this implied other things besides Torah itself). The variation evident in the rabbinic accounts makes it less likely that these elements of the tradition are as old as the first two. Finally, the last clause of Ps 68:19 was not usually included in rabbinic citations of the verse and played very little part in the traditions related to the giving of Torah.[90]

At this point we may reconsider briefly the question of the date of the tradition behind *Tg*. Ps 68:19. It is very significant that the two elements which appeared most consistently in the rabbinic accounts and which in fact seem to form the basis for those accounts—that Moses ascended to heaven to receive the Torah, and that he there took Torah 'captive'—are identical with the interpretation of Ps 68:19 found in *Tg*. Psalms. Until now we have not examined any external evidence by which these elements of the tradition might be (approximately) dated in relation to the time of composition of the NT (and of Ephesians in particular). Nevertheless, these elements appear to be quite ancient. It is certainly possible that the tradition interpreting Ps 68:19 as Moses' ascent to heaven to receive the Torah was already in existence at the time Ephesians was written. As noted already, awareness of such Moses-traditions associated with Ps 68:19 would have predisposed the author of Ephesians to deduce from the account of the ascent mentioned in Ps 68:19 itself (quoted in Eph 4:8) a corresponding subsequent descent of Christ in 4:9ff. to distribute gifts to his church, since Moses after his ascent of Mt. Sinai to 'take captive' the Torah descended to distribute it as 'gifts' to men.

Because at this point it appears possible that Moses-traditions associated with Ps 68:19 were available to the author of Ephesians, we should look briefly at conclusions made on the basis of the rabbinic literature by A. T. Hanson. He believed the interpretation of Ps 68:19 as a reference to Moses' ascent of Mt. Sinai to receive the Torah was known and accepted by the author of Ephesians:

> Rabbinic exegesis had already interpreted the psalm in terms of Moses re-

---

Rabbinic Literature [Cambridge: Cambridge University Press, 1969] 70). Thus, while the tradition that Moses ascended to heaven to receive the Torah is ancient, it appears that there were a few dissenting voices. Nevertheless, it should be noted that neither *Mek. Bah*. 4.54-58 nor *b. Suk*. 5a made any mention of Ps 68:19; all the rabbinic sources which did quote or allude to the psalm were unanimous in their interpretation that it referred to Moses' ascent to heaven to receive the Torah.

[90] Although it easily could have: it would seem (by standards of rabbinic exegesis) to be an excellent text to relate to the rebellion of Israel with the golden calf, which Moses discovered when he came down from the mountain with the tablets of the Decalogue.

ceiving the Torah on Mount Sinai and bringing it down as God's gift to Israel. Our author was well aware of this, and can accept the Moses typology
exactly as Paul accepts it in Romans 10:6-8.[91]

We would differ with Hanson as to whether the author of Ephesians
used the Moses typology "exactly" as it was used in Rom 10:6-8, since
the two contexts are not identical (as we have already noted in our discussion of Rom 10:6-8 in chapter 2).[92] Hanson did not acknowledge
that awareness of such Moses-traditions involving Ps 68:19 would have
influenced the author of Ephesians with regard to a subsequent descent
of Christ. In fact, he continued to hold to a *descensus ad inferos* as the
preferred interpretation of Eph 4:9-10. The problem of dating the tradition we shall discuss in relation to Hanson's next point. He went on to
mention the rabbinic emphasis on angelic opposition to Moses when he
sought to remove the Torah from heaven. In relation to the author of
Ephesians, he stated:

> ...we can also cite *Shabbath* 89a, where Satan encounters Moses. Even more
> emphatic is *Pesikta Rabbati*, where a troop of angels of destruction meet
> Moses and attempt to burn him with a breath of their mouths, and where he
> even overcomes the angel of death. This would confirm our author in the
> belief that the psalm refers to Christ's conquest of the powers.[93]

Several observations must be made with regard to these remarks: (1)
Hanson appealed to the rabbinic evidence without regard for the problems of dating it. The account he mentioned in Pesiqta Rabbati (20.4) is
especially late (this is evident when one compares it with other rabbinic
accounts of Moses' ascent to heaven). As we have seen from the preceding examination of rabbinic exegesis relating to Ps 68:19, it is not absolutely certain that Ps 68:19 was in fact interpreted as a reference to
Moses' ascent of Sinai any earlier than the second or third century of
the present era. Although I agree with Hanson's conclusions regarding
the antiquity of the tradition concerning Moses' ascent to heaven—it
does appear to be pre-Christian—the rabbinic literature alone offers insufficient evidence to support such a conclusion. The evidence from the
rabbinic literature (particularly in the case of what appear to be later accounts) is not so clearly in support of such a view as Hanson apparently
believed. One can always appeal to the argument that the tradition behind the written sources is undoubtedly more ancient than the written
form of the documents themselves, and such contentions cannot be easily disproven. But the antiquity of the tradition regarding Moses' ascent

---

91 A. T. Hanson, *The New Testament Interpretation of Scripture* (London: SPCK, 1980)
140. Hanson considered Ephesians to be deutero-Pauline (136).

92 The discussion of Rom 10:6-8 is found above in ch. 2, 56-59.

93 A. T. Hanson, *The New Testament Interpretation of Scripture*, 141.

of Sinai based solely on evidence from the later rabbinic literature is not the foregone conclusion that many scholars have tended to assume. If the antiquity of this particular tradition can be established with any certainty, it will be through examination of other non-rabbinic texts which can be (approximately) dated, not from assumptions made about the age of rabbinic interpretations based on the rabbinic texts themselves.[94] (2) I am unable to discover a reference to Satan encountering Moses in *b. Shab.* 89a as mentioned by Hanson: the angels who sought to prevent Moses from removing the Torah from heaven were all 'good'. Furthermore the only allusion to Satan appears in Moses' rebuke of the angels when he says to them, "is there jealousy among you; is the Evil Tempter among you?"[95] (3) Moses' 'overcoming' of the angel of death appears in both accounts mentioned by Hanson (*b. Shab.* 89a and *Pesiq. R.* 20.4), but not in the context of Moses overcoming his *own* death through resurrection from the dead. Rather, both accounts state that Moses was taught the secret of preserving life by the angel of death. This refers specifically to Moses' action in stopping the plague in Num 17:11-13: *b. Shab.* 89a actually quotes from Numbers 17 in this instance, so the reference is clear and unambiguous. (4) Hanson's concluding statement, "This would confirm our author in the belief that the psalm refers to Christ's conquest of the powers," assumed the point he was seeking to prove, i.e., that the author of Ephesians was indeed aware of some form of the tradition behind the rabbinic accounts of Moses' ascent to heaven based on Ps 68:19. It furthermore assumed that the elements of the later rabbinic tradition mentioned specifically by Hanson antedate Ephesians. As we saw in our examination of the rabbinic sources, however, it is precisely these elements of the tradition which appear to be later embellishments that do not go back as early as the first century CE. The two elements which we have found to be present in all the rabbinic accounts, and which are therefore most likely to be ancient, are (1) that Moses ascended to heaven to receive the Torah, and (2) that he there took Torah 'captive'. If any elements of the Moses-traditions concerning a heavenly ascent at Sinai are older than the NT writings it would almost certainly be these, and these elements would be the ones most likely to have influenced the author of Ephesians in his use of Ps 68:19 (Eph 4:8). To find confirmation of this, we must turn to sources external to *Tg.* Psalms and the classical rabbinic literature.

---

[94] This involves what R. Bloch referred to as a process of "external comparison." Her approach to the dating of rabbinic literature, which we have generally applied to the tradition of Moses' ascent to heaven in the rabbinic literature and *Tg.* Psalms, is discussed above, 75-76.

[95] *The Babylonian Talmud: Seder Mo'ed*, ed. I. Epstein, *Shabbath*, trans. H. Freedman (London: Soncino, 1938) 2.421ff.

C. PSALM 68:19 IN EARLY NON-RABBINIC SOURCES

After examining the use of Ps 68:19 in the rabbinic literature, it is apparent that the two elements of the tradition most likely to be ancient are the interpretation of the 'one who ascends' (in Ps 68:19) as Moses and the 'captivity led captive' as the words of Torah which Moses received from God and brought down to distribute as gifts to men. As noted already, these basic elements are found in *all* the interpretations of Ps 68:19 in the rabbinic literature in a form virtually identical with the interpretation of the psalm found in *Tg.* Ps 68:19. We have not yet demonstrated that they are as old as (or older than) the Epistle to the Ephesians, however, because none of the rabbinic sources we have so far examined are as old as Ephesians in their extant (written) forms. If we are to establish the antiquity of these elements of the tradition, we must examine all available sources outside the rabbinic literature and *Tg.* Psalms which make use of Ps 68:19 to see if there is any evidence that the interpretation of Psalm 68 as Moses' ascent of Sinai might antedate the composition of Ephesians. (This procedure was referred to as "external comparison" by R. Bloch in her groundbreaking approach to the study of rabbinic literature.)[96] But first we need to take a closer look at the text of Ps 68:19 itself as it appears in four of the major sources.

1. *Ps 68:19 in the Hebrew Text, the LXX, Eph 4:8, and* Tg. *Psalms*

A detailed comparison of *Tg.* Ps 68:19 with Eph 4:8 is a necessary preliminary to the examination of non-canonical sources which relate to the interpretation of the psalm found in the targum. At the same time, it is appropriate to include in the comparison the text of Ps 68:19 as found in the Hebrew text and the LXX, since Eph 4:8 bears the outward form, at least, of a quotation. The presence of common features among the various texts and versions could suggest points of contact between the traditions in question and their underlying sources.

The text of Ps 68:19 according to these four sources may be arranged in parallel to facilitate comparison. The interpretive comments (expansions) included in the text of in *Tg.* Psalms are placed in parentheses since they have no parallel in the other textual traditions. Nevertheless they provide a significant clue to the way in which the ascent passage in Ps 68:19 was understood by the author or editor of the final version of *Tg.* Psalms. *Chart* 3 on the following page presents a detailed comparison of the text of the passage in question (including major textual variants).

---

[96] Bloch's approach was discussed above, 75-76.

Chart 3: Ps 68:19 in the Hebrew MT, LXX, Eph 4:8 and *Tg.* Ps 68:19

68:19 (MT)[97]	67:19 (LXX)[98]	EPH 4:8[99]	68:19 (TG. PSS)[100]
עלית	ἀνέβης [B²,³ א²] ἀνέβη [א*] ἀναβὰς [B*]	ἀναβὰς	סליקתא
למרום	εἰς ὕψος	εἰς ὕψος	לרקיע (משה נבייא)
שבית	ᾐχμαλώτευσας [א² B] ᾐχμαλώτευσεν [א*]	ᾐχμαλώτευσεν	שביתא
שבי	αἰχμαλωσίαν	αἰχμαλωσίαν	שבייתא (אלפתא פיתגמי אוריתא)
לקחת	ἔλαβες	ἔδωκεν	יהבתא להון
מתנות	δόματα	δόματα	מתנן
באדם	ἐν ἀνθρώπῳ ἀνθρώποις [B² א]	τοῖς ἀνθρώποις ἐν ἀνθρώποις [F G pc]	לבני נשא
ואף	καὶ γὰρ	(end of quotation in Eph 4:8)	וברם
סוררים	ἀπειθοῦντες [B²,³ א*] ἀπιθοῦντες [B*] ἀπειθοῦντας [א²]		סרבניא
			(די מתניירין תייבין בתתובא)
לשכן	τοῦ κατασκηνῶσαι		שרת עליהון שכינת
יה	κύριος		יקרא דיהוה
אלהים	ὁ θεὸς		אלהים

Verse 19 begins in both the Hebrew text and *Tg.* Psalms with the verb in the second person singular (עלית and סליקתא). This was probably the original reading of the LXX as well (ἀνέβης, read by the two correctors of B and the second corrector of א), but there is some uncertainty over the LXX reading, since the original hand of א has the third singular (ἀνέβη) while the original hand of B supplies the participle ἀναβάς (as does Eph 4:8). Since א and B are both fourth century manuscripts, it is probable that the text of Ps 68:19 which they reflect has been influenced (either accidentally—i.e., unconsciously—or deliberately) by the

---

[97] The Hebrew MT is that of *BHS* (ed. R. Kittel, 7th ed. [Stuttgart: Württembergische Bibelanstalt, 1937]). Of course the MT may have differed at some points from the Hebrew text available to the author of Ephesians or the editor of *Tg.* Psalms.

[98] The Greek text is from *Septuaginta* (ed. A. Rahlfs, 5th ed. [Stuttgart: Württembergische Bibelanstalt, 1935]). The textual variants [bracketed] are found in *The Old Testament in Greek* (ed. H. B. Swete [Cambridge: Cambridge University Press, 1909]).

[99] The NT text is from NA27.

[100] The text of *Tg.* Psalms is that of *Hagiographa Chaldaice* (ed. P. A. de Lagarde [Leipzig: B. G. Teubneri, 1873]).

NT citation of the psalm in Eph 4:8.[101]

Next, the Hebrew text reads למרום, which both the LXX and Eph 4:8 translate as εἰς ὕψος; *Tg.* Psalms has לרקיע. This term may represent a later interpolation in the targum, of course, but *Tg.* Psalms does use מרומא elsewhere.[102] It seems more likely that רקיע occurs in Ps 68:19 because of its (admittedly later) association with the tradition of Moses' ascent of Mt. Sinai.[103] There are numerous discussions in the rabbinic literature which recount how Moses walked about on the firmament (רקיע), how thick the firmament was, how long it would take a man to journey across it, etc.[104]

Tg. Psalms follows the reference to the firmament (רקיע) with the first of three interpretive comments (we may regard them as parenthetical expansions) in verse 19: the words משה נבייא are added to specify who it was who ascended (and to whom the initial words of Ps 68:19 are addressed). No trace of this comment is to be found in the Hebrew text, the LXX, or Eph 4:8, of course, but the association of Moses with Ps 68:19 was a 'stock' interpretation in the rabbinic literature, as noted in the preceding section.

The verbs in the following clause in both Hebrew text and targum (שבית and שבית) are second person singular; this is probably the original reading of the LXX (ᾐχμαλώτευσας) as well, although the original hand of א substitutes third person singular (ᾐχμαλώτευσεν). Again, this may well represent a harmonization with the NT text (Eph 4:8) which reads the same.[105]

Following the reference to 'captivity' (שבייתא), *Tg.* Psalms makes the second of its interpretive expansions on Ps 68:19, אלפתא פיתגמי אוריתא,

---

[101] That this is, in fact, highly probable in the case of [the original hand of] א is demonstrated by the use of the third person singular in the case of the first two verbs (ἀνέβη and ᾐχμαλώτευσεν, the second agreeing with Eph 4:8), whereas the third verb abruptly (and inconsistently) becomes second person (ἔλαβες). The [second] corrector of א, probably because he noticed this inconsistency, changed the first two verbs, which were in the third person, to participles, producing agreement with B and removing the inconsistency (since the person of the Greek adverbial participle is ambiguous, being determined by that of the finite verb to which it is subordinate). Since both א and B are manuscripts which contain the NT as well as the OT and various apocryphal books, it is easy to see why there would be a tendency to harmonize the OT and NT citations of the psalm.

[102] I.e., in Pss 56:3, 71:19, 75:6, 93:4, 102:20, 144:7, and 148:1.

[103] Naturally, this is in line with previous conclusions regarding a relatively late date for the final form of *Tg.* Psalms. See the previous section of this chapter, "The Targum to the Psalms," 66-75.

[104] In *b. Pesah.* 94a, for example, the thickness of the firmament is given variously as 1,000 *parasangs* (a *parasang* is a Persian mile, roughly 3.6 kilometres), one tenth of a day's journey (!), and (in 94b) 500 years' journey; in Ber. R. 4.5 it was described (by R. Aḥa) as having the thickness of a metal plate, while R. Joshua b. R. Nehemiah said the firmament is about two fingers in thickness. See also *b. Ḥag.* 13a and *Midr. Teh.* 4.3.

[105] And again, the change may be either accidental or deliberate.

which explains the preceding phrase ("you led captive captivity") in terms of Moses' learning the words of Torah. Though not implied in the Hebrew text, the LXX, or Eph 4:8, this interpretation also is common in rabbinic literature, as noted previously.[106]

At this point the major divergence occurs between the Hebrew text and the LXX on one hand and Eph 4:8 and *Tg*. Ps 68:19 on the other. The two former sources state (as do all of the rabbinic sources which make use of Ps 68:19) that the one who ascended 'received' gifts (לקחת, ἔλαβες), whereas Eph 4:8 and *Tg*. Ps 68:19 read 'gave' (ἔδωκεν, יהבתא) with reference to the gifts. It is primarily because of this similarity that the use of *Tg*. Psalms (or the tradition behind it) by the writer of Ephesians has generally been proposed.[107] In addition, there are two less noticeable differences: first, in Eph 4:8 the verb occurs as third person rather than as second, while the Hebrew text, LXX, and targum all have second person verbs. Second, *Tg*. Ps 68:19 supplies the pronominal object (להון) following the verb, to specify that it was the words of Torah (אוריתא פיתגמי, from the preceding interpretive expansion) which were given as gifts. Yet *Tg*. Psalms maintains the use of second person verbs throughout the verse (following the Hebrew text); according to the interpretation of the targum these are consistently addressed to Moses.

In the Hebrew text, באדם specifies those who present the gifts; the phrase is best understood as a collective singular. This probably lies behind the original reading of B, ἐν ἀνθρώπῳ (followed also by one of B's correctors), which is preferred as the original LXX reading. The dative

---

[106] See the preceding section, "Psalm 68 and Moses' Ascent to Heaven in Rabbinic Literature," 77-95.

[107] This was first proposed by H. St J. Thackeray (*The Relation of St Paul to Contemporary Jewish Thought* [London: Oxford University Press, 1900] 182). However, the similarity between the texts of Eph 4:8 and *Tg*. Ps 68:19 could be merely coincidental, whether the modification of Ps 68:19 to read 'gave' rather than 'received' was made by the writer of Ephesians himself [so J. Bonsirven, who stated that it was "impossible" to explain the modification to the text of Psalm 68 by another Greek version, or a targum, or a metathesis of the Hebrew letters, although he gave absolutely no justification for his claim, (*Exégèse Rabbinique et Exégèse Paulinienne*, BTH [Paris: Beauchesne, 1939], 307-308), and A. M. Harmon ("Aspects of Paul's Use of the Psalms," *WTJ* 32 [1969] 6-7)] or was adopted from a pre-existing source other than *Tg*. Psalms (e.g., the text of Ps 68:19 may already have been modified by the early Christian community) [so B. Lindars (*New Testament Apologetic: The Doctrinal Significance of the Old Testament Quotations* [London: SCM, 1961] 52-56)]. The possibility that the targumist himself made use of a source (e.g. a Greek version of the Psalms) which had already changed the text of Ps 68:19 to ἔδωκεν was mentioned above, 72, n. 32, also 74, n. 39. Obviously, the writer of Ephesians may have been following the same Greek version in quoting 68:19, independently of *Tg*. Ps 68:19 or the tradition behind it. In contrast to the complexities of the foregoing discussion, H. P. Hamann asserted that "it is easier to accept that explanation that Paul was quoting from memory and was quoting inaccurately" ("Church and Ministry: An Exegesis of Ephesians 4:1-16," *LTJ* 16 [1982] 123). However, most of those who have investigated the problem find such a solution too simplistic in light of the similar modification of the text found in *Tg*. Psalms.

plural ἀνθρώποις (read by ℵ and the other corrector of B) is more likely
a harmonization (either accidental or deliberate) with Eph 4:8. The original text of Eph 4:8 itself almost certainly read τοῖς ἀνθρώποις, although
F, G, and a few other manuscripts contain ἐν ἀνθρώποις, resembling the
LXX text of Psalm 68 found in ℵ and followed by one corrector of B.
The omission of the preposition ἐν in favor of the simple dative τοῖς
ἀνθρώποις is more consistent with the interpretation of Ps 68:19 given
in Ephesians, where 'men' have become the recipients of the gifts mentioned in the psalm. *Tg.* Psalms, likewise, has replaced באדם with לבני
נשׁא; this change of prepositions is again consistent with the change in
the preceding verb. With *Tg.* Ps 68:19, as with Eph 4:8, the 'men/sons of
men' have become the recipients of the gifts rather than the donors.

At this point the quotation of Ps 68:19 in Eph 4:8 ends. However, to
compare the remainder of the verse as found in the targum with the Hebrew text and the LXX will prove helpful for the study of the tradition
behind *Tg.* Ps 68:19 in non-canonical sources. The Hebrew text begins
the final clause of Ps 68:19 with סוררים, which is translated by the LXX
with the participle ἀπειθοῦντες and by *Tg.* Psalms as סרבניא, the Aramaic equivalent for 'rebellious, wilful, stubborn'. Following this, in the
third of its interpretive expansions in verse 19, the targum adds a
lengthy qualification, די מתגיירין תייבין בתחובא. By the inclusion of the
participle מתגיירין *Tg.* Ps 68:19 seems at first glance to imply that the
'rebellious' (סרבניא) are to be understood as Gentiles rather than as Israelites, since they must (in addition to repenting) become proselytes before the *shekinah* of Yahweh will come to dwell with them. But there is
one highly suggestive exception to this 'obvious' understanding of the
reference to proselytes. In the section of the Talmud which deals with
the regulations regarding proselytes, *b. Yebam.* 46a-48a, the question of
whether a proselyte must undergo both circumcision and ritual ablution
before being considered a 'proper' proselyte is answered as follows:

> Our Rabbis taught: If a proselyte was circumcised but had not performed the
> prescribed ritual ablution, R. Eliezer said, 'Behold he is a proper proselyte;
> for so we find that our forefathers were circumcised and had not performed
> ritual ablution'. If he performed the prescribed ablution but had not been
> circumcised, R. Joshua said, 'Behold he is a proper proselyte; for so we find
> that the mothers had performed ritual ablution but had not been circum-
> cised'.[108]

The inference made by R. Eliezer and R. Joshua, that both rites need not

---

[108] *The Babylonian Talmud: Seder Nashim*, ed. I. Epstein, *Yebamoth*, trans. I. W. Slotki
(London: Soncino, 1936) 1.302-303. It is of no consequence, as far as the present observation
is concerned, that the debate over the validity of the conclusions reached by R. Eliezer and R.
Joshua continued at considerable length.

have been performed before the individual may be properly considered a full proselyte, is drawn from the experience of Israel in the wilderness, after the Exodus and just prior to the giving of Torah at Mt. Sinai.[109] The implication is that those who departed from Egypt as 'heathen' became 'proselytes' when they received the Torah and were, so to speak, 'converted' to Judaism. Thus, the conventional distinction between native Israelites and Gentile proselytes would not apply in this one instance. It seems possible that such an understanding lies behind the use of מתגיירין in Tg. Ps 68:19, especially since the Sinai-motif is already assumed in the targumic interpretation of the preceding clauses of verse 19. Furthermore, Sinai is explicitly mentioned in the Hebrew text of the preceding verse (Ps 68:18). Furthermore, such an understanding of the 'proselytes' in the targum agrees with one of the few rabbinic interpretations of Ps 68:19 to include the final clause.[110] Midr. Teh. 68.11 (on 68:19) clearly understands 'the rebellious' (Hebrew, סוררים) as the Israelites themselves, despite the fact that in a preceding verse (68:7, "only the rebellious dwell in a parched land") the same word (סוררים) is interpreted as the nations of the earth who were unwilling to accept the Torah.[111]

The remaining phrase of Ps 68:19 is translated literally from the Hebrew text by the LXX, and Tg. Psalms expands לשכן יה אלהים by rendering it as שרת עליהון שכינת יקרא דיהוה אלהים, incorporating a reference to both the shekinah and the 'glory' of Yahweh. This demonstrates the normal targumic tendency to avoid anthropomorphic expressions by the introduction of verbal 'buffers' which prevent God from appearing to come into close proximity with human and earthly affairs.[112]

---

109 See, e.g., Exod 19:3-6 and Deut 5:1-3.

110 However (as is common), such an understanding of סוררים in the final clause of Ps 68:19 is not unanimous in the rabbinic literature. Shem. Rab. 33.2, e.g., interpreted the 'rebellious' in v. 19 as the heathen, with whom, in spite of their idolatry, Yahweh continued to dwell.

111 See the preceding section, "Psalm 68 and Moses' Ascent to Heaven in Rabbinic Literature," 78-79, for the relevant text of Midr. Teh. 68.11 (on 68:19). Of course, it is possible that the participle מתגיירין represents a later interpolation in the existing text of Tg. Ps 68:19; this might be suspected since the interpretive comment made by the targum remains intelligible even if מתגיירין is omitted. Nevertheless, its presence tends to confirm conclusions reached in a previous section regarding a relatively late date for Tg. Psalms (see the section "The Targum to the Psalms," 66-75, for a discussion of the problems of dating the work). Furthermore, the interpretation provided by the participle מתגיירין in Tg. Ps 68:19 does coincide with the rabbinic interpretation of the verse in Midr. Teh. 68.11 (as discussed in the text above, 79). Finally, there is no evidence for the omission of the participle in any of the surviving mss. of Tg. Psalms.

112 G. F. Moore, "Intermediaries in Jewish Theology: Memra, Shekinah, Metatron," HTR 15 (1922) 41-85. It is important to note Moore's point that the targumists were not so much concerned with the elimination of anthropomorphic ideas which occurred in the Hebrew texts they translated, as with the avoidance of certain anthropomorphic expressions (44-45). But such instances were 'buffer-words', not ideas or hypostatizations (53). Concerning שכינה he stated that it "acquires what semblance of personality it has solely by being a circumlocution for God in contexts where personal states or actions are attributed to him" (59). R. D. Middle-

The main point of divergence between the four versions of Ps 68:19 included in the preceding analysis (Hebrew text, LXX, Eph 4:8, and *Tg. Ps* 68:19), as noted above, consists of the change from לקחת / ἔλαβες (Hebrew text, LXX) to ἔδωκεν / יהבתא (Eph 4:8, *Tg. Psalms*). While this does show agreement between Eph 4:8 and *Tg. Ps* 68:19 against the Hebrew text and LXX, it does not offer conclusive proof that the writer of Ephesians was personally aware of the targumic interpretation of Ps 68:19 (or the tradition behind it). Similarities do not prove borrowings, and even if they did it does not follow, in the case of two similar texts, that one 'borrowed' from the other.[113] Both may have borrowed independently from a pre-existing common source which accounted for their similarities. Thus, while we cannot say for certain that Eph 4:8 shows the direct influence of the tradition behind *Tg. Ps* 68:19,[114] there are other possibilities that must be considered, some of which represent interrelationships far more complex than simple literary dependence. For example, both Eph 4:8 and *Tg. Ps* 68:19 may independently reflect at this point a variant in the Hebrew *Vorlage* which differs from the Hebrew text as preserved in the MT, yet which has not been preserved in any extant Hebrew manuscript.[115] It is sometimes suggested that such a variant has been preserved in one of the early versions. The reading "gave" (*we-yahbhte*) for "received" in Ps 68:19 is also found in some manuscripts of the Syriac Peshitta, and this led W. E. Barnes to propose that these manuscripts preserved an ancient variant which was later harmonized with the LXX reading in part of the surviving Syriac manuscript tradition.[116] The possibility that such a variant was found in a

---

ton disagreed with Moore over the use of *memra* as a "buffer-word devoid of all theological content" ("Logos and Shekinah in the Fourth Gospel," *JQR* 29 [new series, 1938-39] 101-133,113). However, Middleton did agree with Moore that *shekinah* "does not indicate a Presence which takes the place of the Deity, but the Targums by the avoidance of the too frequent use of the divine name seek, in accordance with Jewish standards of thinking, a more reverent way of writing or speaking about God" ("Logos and Shekinah," 123; cf. Moore, 58).

113 See, e.g., A. D. York ("The Dating of Targumic Literature," *JSJ* 5 [1974] 56).

114 At this point the possibility that *Tg.* Psalms has been influenced by the interpretation of Ps 68:19 found in Eph 4:8 cannot be totally dismissed either, no matter how inherently improbable it may seem. After all, the final, written form of *Tg.* Psalms is almost certainly later than Ephesians (see the previous section, "The Targum to the Psalms," 66-75, for a discussion of the dating of *Tg.* Psalms).

115 Again, such a suggestion appears to have originated with H. St J. Thackeray (*The Relation of St Paul to Contemporary Jewish Thought* [London: Oxford University Press, 1900] 182).

116 W. E. Barnes printed *we-yahbhte* (agreeing with *Tg.* Psalms) in the text of Ps 68:19 and *wa-nesabhte* (agreeing with the MT and LXX) in the apparatus (*The Peshitta Psalter according to the West Syrian Text* [Cambridge: Cambridge University Press, 1904]). This arrangement was followed by the standard modern critical edition, *The Old Testament in Syriac according to the Peshitta Version* (part 2, fascicle 3, *The Book of Psalms*, ed. D. M. Walter [Leiden: Brill, 1980] 74). Barnes noted that all the texts of the Jacobite recension read *we-yahbhte*, agreeing with Eph 4:8 and *Tg.* Psalms, while those of the Nestorian recension read

Greek version known to both the writer of Ephesians and the targumist independently of one another may be even greater.[117] Or, however unlikely it may seem, it is possible that the writer of Ephesians and the targumist made the change from לקחת to ἔδωκεν / יהבת independently of one another and the agreement was coincidental.[118] It is also possible that the writer of Ephesians derived the version of Ps 68:19 which he quoted in 4:8 from a pre-existing liturgical source independent of *Tg. Psalms*; if so, the relationship of such an otherwise unknown source to *Tg.* Ps 68:19 would be impossible to reconstruct.[119] In the case of Ephesians it may be significant (with regard to the relationship between Eph 4:8 and the other three versions of Ps 68:19 involved in this discussion) that the writer of Ephesians employed a participle (ἀναβάς) followed by third person singular verbs (ᾐχμαλώτευσεν, ἔδωκεν) in the psalm citation, whereas the other three sources (including *Tg.* Psalms) consistently used second person singular verbs throughout, following the Hebrew *Vorlage*.[120] This change of person has often been dismissed as insignificant by those examining the texts in question, since it was frequently

---

wa-n^esabht^e, agreeing with the reading of the MT and LXX. The Jacobite manuscripts are older, and LXX influence can be demonstrated in other places, so Barnes concluded that the Jacobite reading *w^e-yahbht^e* was original, and the Nestorian *wa-n^esabht^e* representd a harmonization with the text of the LXX. If this is correct, it would provide an independent tradition which supports the change from "received" to "gave" in Ps 68:19. However, Barnes' conclusions have been challenged by B. Lindars, who thought it was *a priori* more probable that the original text was that of the MT and LXX, and that the change was made in the Jacobite recension (*New Testament Apologetic: The Doctrinal Significance of the Old Testament Quotations* [London: SCM, 1961] 52, n. 2). This was independent of influence from Eph 4:8 according to Lindars, because (1) the two words were very similar and could be easily confused in the Estrangela script, and (2) the following word for "gifts" was a cognate of the verb in Syriac and could easily have influenced a copyist. Regardless of whether Barnes or Lindars is right in the proposed reconstruction of the Peshitta text, we must agree with Lindars' ultimate conclusion: in light of the uncertain history of the variant in the Jacobite recension, it would be precarious to insist on its value as an independent witness to the variant reading found in Eph 4:8 and *Tg.* Ps 68:19.

[117] See above, 72, n. 32, also 74, n. 39 (preceding section) and below, n. 123, for further discussion of this possibility.

[118] So B. Lindars, *New Testament Apologetic*, 52-53.

[119] T. K. Abbott believed that Paul made use of the "Rabbinical interpretation" reflected in *Tg.* Psalms as suitable to his purpose, and this "renders needless a recourse to the supposition that the quotation is from a Christian hymn, which borrowed from the psalm" (*A Critical and Exegetical Commentary on the Epistles to the Ephesians and to the Colossians*, ICC [Edinburgh: Clark, 1897] 113). Others like J. R. Harris have proposed that Paul quoted from a collection of OT *testimonia*, quotations strung together with or without interpretive comment for use in religious instruction (*Testimonies* [Cambridge: Cambridge University Press, 1920] 2.39-42). Although the existence of such *testimonia* has now been confirmed not only by the patristic literature (to which Harris had appealed) but also by texts from Qumran such as 4QTestimonia and 4QFlorilegium, there is no extant text which reflects the variant found in *Tg.* Ps 68:19 and Eph 4:8, and the existence of such a document must remain hypothetical.

[120] There is some variation among the LXX mss. with regard to the form of the first verb (i.e., ἀνέβης / ἀνέβη / ἀναβάς), but the original LXX reading was most likely second person. See p. 97 above, and also n. 101.

assumed that such a change represented nothing more than a contextual adaptation by the writer of Ephesians.[121] However, it is not at all clear that this is the case, since the other OT quotations in Ephesians follow the text of the LXX quite closely.[122] The author of Ephesians could have incorporated Ps 68:19 using second person verbs (as all the rabbinic sources which refer to verse 19 do) without undue difficulty had he desired to do so. Therefore we must consider the possibility that the version of Ps 68:19 quoted in Eph 4:8 originated in a pre-existing source other than the Hebrew text, the LXX, or the tradition behind Tg. Ps 68:19. In the final analysis R. Rubinkiewicz was probably correct when he stated that the author of Ephesians was simply making use of a textual tradition which had come down to him rather than creating the change himself; it seems very unlikely that the textual tradition behind Tg. Psalms could be dependent on Ephesians.[123] In an attempt to confirm this we must continue our examination of Ps 68:19 as it is quoted in both canonical and non-canonical literature.

2. Ps 68:19 in the Testaments of the Twelve Patriarchs

We must now examine the citations of Ps 68:19 in the apocrypha and pseudepigrapha in order to determine whether interpretations similar to those found in Tg. Psalms and the classical rabbinic literature are present. If so, this will assist us in dating the tradition which associated Ps 68:19 with Moses and his ascent to heaven to receive the Torah. Awareness of such traditions associated with Ps 68:19 could explain how the author of Ephesians was able to deduce a descent in Eph 4:9-10 from the ascent mentioned in the psalm quotation. Knowledge of these Moses-traditions would have enabled the author to connect the ascent mentioned in Ps 68:19 with a corresponding descent of Christ to distribute gifts to his church, since by analogy Moses, following his ascent of Mt. Sinai to 'take captive' Torah, had descended to distribute it as 'gifts' to men. We begin our investigation of the extra-canonical cita-

---

121 Thus for example R. Rubinkiewicz stated: "The most important variant is ἔδωκεν because the others can be understood as a small adjustment of the text that does not change the main idea" ("Psalm LXVIII 19 [= Eph IV 8] Another Textual Tradition or Targum?," NovT 17 [1975] 220). Likewise, J. Dupont expressed a similar view: "Le fait que la construction passe de la deuxième à la troisième personne reste accessoire: l'adaptation au contexte peut justifier ce changement" ("Ascension du Christ et don de l'Esprit d'après Actes 2:33," in Christ and Spirit in the New Testament, ed. B. Lindars and S. S. Smalley [Cambridge: Cambridge University Press, 1973] 224-5).

122 As A. T. Lincoln has pointed out ("The Use of the OT in Ephesians," JSNT 14 [1982] 45).

123 R. Rubinkiewicz, "Psalm LXVIII 19 (= Eph IV 8) Another Textual Tradition or Targum?," NovT 17 (1975) 219-24. Rubinkiewicz's theory is examined at greater length in the section which follows, "Ps 68:19 in the Testaments of the Twelve Patriarchs."

tions of Ps 68:19 with the Testaments of the Twelve Patriarchs, since there are two possible allusions to Ps 68:19 found in the Greek text of this document as edited by M. de Jonge.[124]

2.1. Testament of Dan 5:11

We will consider Test. Dan 5:11 first since it is understood as a direct allusion to Ps 68:19 by R. Rubinkiewicz.[125] The Greek text of 5:10-13 reads:

Καὶ ἀνατελεῖ ὑμῖν ἐκ τῆς φυλῆς Ἰουδὰ καὶ Λευὶ τὸ σωτήριον κυρίου· καὶ αὐτὸς ποιήσει πρὸς τὸν Βελιὰρ πόλεμον, καὶ τὴν ἐκδίκησιν τοῦ νίκους δώσει πατράσιν ἡμῶν. καὶ τὴν αἰχμαλωσίαν λάβῃ ἀπὸ τοῦ Βελιάρ, ψυχὰς ἁγίων, καὶ ἐπιστρέψει καρδίας ἀπειθεῖς πρὸς κύριον, καὶ δώσει τοῖς ἐπικαλουμένοις αὐτὸν εἰρήνην αἰώνιον· καὶ ἀναπαύσονται ἐν Ἐδὲμ ἅγιοι, καὶ ἐπὶ τῆς νέας Ἰερουσαλὴμ εὐφρανθήσονται δίκαιοι, ἥτις ἔσται εἰς δόξασμα θεοῦ ἕως τοῦ αἰῶνος. καὶ οὐκέτι ὑπομένει Ἰερουσαλὴμ ἐρήμωσιν, οὐδὲ αἰχμαλωτίζεται Ἰσραήλ, ὅτι κύριος ἔσται ἐν μέσῳ αὐτῆς, τοῖς ἀνθρώποις συναναστρεφόμενος, καὶ ἅγιος Ἰσραὴλ βασιλεύων ἐπ᾿ αὐτοὺς ἐν ταπεινώσει καὶ ἐν πρωχείᾳ· καὶ ὁ πιστεύων ἐπ᾿ αὐτῷ βασιλεύσει ἐν ἀληθείᾳ ἐν τοῖς οὐρανοῖς.[126]

The Lord himself is clearly the subject of the verbs λάβῃ, ἐπιστρέψει, and δώσει (all in 5:11), picked up from the phrase τὸ σωτήριον κυρίου in 5:10 and referred to as αὐτός. This probably constitutes an eschatological or messianic allusion. One or more of the Christian copyists (or interpolators) of the Testaments obviously understood it as messianic, since the epexegetical phrase περὶ τοῦ χριστοῦ is found either in the margin or in the text itself (preceding verse 10) in a number of the principal manuscripts.[127] This person is the one who "will make war with Beliar" (10b), "give the vengeance of victory to our fathers" (10c), "receive the captivity from Beliar" (11a), "turn the hearts of the diso-

---

124 See n. 126 below.

125 Rubinkiewicz's statement is found in "Psalm LXVIII 19 (= Eph IV 8) Another Textual Tradition or Targum?," *NovT* 17 (1975) 222.

126 *The Testaments of the Twelve Patriarchs: A Critical Edition of the Greek Text*, ed. M. de Jonge (Leiden: Brill, 1978) 108-109.

127 The manuscripts which include the phrase as a marginal note are: Codex Graecus 731, ff. 97r.-166v., a 13th century ms. in the Biblioteca Apostolica Vaticana; Codex Graecus 1238, ff. 350r.-379v., a late 12th century ms., also in the Biblioteca Apostolica Vaticana; and Codex Graecus Z.494 (= 331), ff. 263r.-264v., a mid-13th century ms. in the Biblioteca Nazionale di S. Marco in Venice. The manuscripts which incorporate the phrase into the text itself are: Codex Graecus 547 (Gardthausen) [= 770 (Kamil)], ff. 1r.-70r., a 17th century ms.; Codex Graecus 2170 [= 608 (Kamil)], ff. 8r.-88r., an 18th century ms.; and an unnumbered ms., ff. 1r.-38r., not earlier than the 17th century, all in the Library of the Monastery of St. Catherine on Mt. Sinai. The relatively late dates of the manuscripts which actually incorporate the phrase into the text suggest that what may originally have been a marginal gloss was probably assimilated into the text itself during the process of transmission, either deliberately or through scribal error. The problem of later Christian interpolations in the Testaments is mentioned briefly below in n. 134.

bedient to the Lord" (11b), and "give to those who call upon him eternal peace" (11c).

Certainly the suggestion of Rubinkiewicz—that 5:11 constituted an allusion to Ps 68:19—seems at first plausible: τὴν αἰχμαλωσίαν in Test. Dan 5:11 appears similar to ἠχμαλώτευσας αἰχμαλωσίαν in Ps 68:19 (LXX); ἐπιστρέψει καρδίας ἀπειθεῖς πρὸς κύριον sounds very much like the final clause of Ps 68:19 (LXX), καὶ γὰρ ἀπειθοῦντες τοῦ κατασκηνῶσαι κύριος ὁ θεός; and δώσει τοῖς ἐπικαλουμένοις αὐτὸν εἰρήνην αἰώνιον parallels the reading found in both Eph 4:8 (ἔδωκεν δόματα τοῖς ἀνθρώποις) and Tg. Psalms (יהבתא להון מתנן לבני נשא), at least according to Rubinkiewicz.[128] If Rubinkiewicz was correct in his understanding of the parallelism, it would suggest that the interpretation of Ps 68:19 as a reference to Moses and his ascent to heaven to receive the Torah (which, as we have already seen, appears routine by the time of the classical rabbinic literature)[129] had not yet become established at the time the Testaments were written: the subject of Ps 68:19 (according to Test. Dan 5:10) is the Lord himself, as in the original psalm, rather than Moses. Thus—according to Rubinkiewicz—the targum tradition current at the time of the composition of Test. Dan 5 did *not* contain the references to Moses and the words of Torah found in the extant composition known as Tg. Psalms. Instead, this 'proto-targum' would have read almost exactly the same as the Hebrew text and LXX of Ps 68:19 as far as the allusion to Moses was concerned.[130]

But how plausible is such an attempt to reconstruct the tradition behind Tg. Ps 68:19 and Eph 4:8? Rubinkiewicz argued that the use of δώσει in Test. Dan 5:11 indicates that the targum tradition current at the time of composition of the Testaments had already incorporated the change from לקח (Hebrew text) and ἔλαβες (LXX) to ἔδωκεν as found in Eph 4:8. The obvious conclusion, for Rubinkiewicz, was that the reading represented by ἔδωκεν (more properly, ἔδωκες) in the text of Ps 68:19 "was known long before St Paul."[131] However, Rubinkiewicz overlooked the use of λαμβάνω in the opening clause of Test. Dan 5:11 (λήψεται, future tense, in the text he cited, though λάβῃ is the reading found in most of the manuscripts). According to the text of Test. Dan 5:11, the Lord himself (or the Messiah) receives the 'captivity' (αἰχμα-

---

128 "Psalm LXVIII 19 (= Eph IV 8) Another Textual Tradition or Targum?," *NovT* 17 (1975) 222.

129 See the conclusion to the earlier section, "Psalm 68 and Moses' Ascent to Heaven in Rabbinic Literature," 91-96 above.

130 Unlike the MT and LXX, however, the developing targum tradition would already have changed the לקח / ἔλαβες of Ps 68:19 to יהבו / ἔδωκεν as found in the present *Tg.* Ps 68:19 and Eph 4:8, according to Rubinkiewicz, *NovT* 17 (1975) 224.

131 "Psalm LXVIII 19 (= Eph IV 8) Another Textual Tradition or Targum?," 222.

λωσίαν) from Beliar (11a),[132] turns the hearts of the disobedient to the Lord (11b), and then gives (δώσει) to those who call on him eternal peace (11c).[133] Since both verbs—λαμβάνω and δίδωμι—occur in Test. Dan 5:11, it is impossible to say what the contemporary targum tradition would have been at this point, even if one is willing to grant that Test. Dan 5:11 constituted, in fact, an allusion to an interpretation (or translation) of Ps 68:19 earlier than Ephesians itself (*pace* Rubinkiewicz). What is found in Test. Dan 5:11 might represent the targum tradition behind Ps 68:19 actually in a state of flux—in transition from the לקחת and ἔλαβες of the Hebrew text and LXX to the יהבתא and ἔδωκεν of *Tg.* Ps 68:19 and Eph 4:8, since the ideas of *both* receiving and giving in connection with Ps 68:19 are combined in the text of Test. Dan 5:11 as it now stands. But it is equally possible that Test. Dan 5:11 was originally written (or redacted, with possible Christian interpolations) some time after the composition of Ephesians, and in fact the use of Ps 68:19 in Eph 4:8 had influenced the writer (or redactor) of the Testament of Dan at this point. As a result, we can say nothing with certainty about the change from לקחת (Hebrew text) to יהבתא (*Tg.* Psalms) in Ps 68:19 based on the text of Test. Dan 5:11 unless (1) the approximate date of composition for Test. Dan could be established with some degree of certainty, and (2) unless the extent of redactional activity present in Test. Dan 5:11 could be determined accurately. Unfortunately neither of these questions can be resolved at the present time. There is no complete consensus regarding a firm date for the composition of the Testaments or for the extent of Christian interpolation present within them. R. H. Charles and a number of others argued for an essentially Jewish work with a minimum of Christian interpolations and a date prior to the first century of the present era. These views have been challenged, however; the most well-known alternative theory is that of M. de Jonge, who maintained the Christian origin of the Testaments in the second century CE. Although de Jonge's theory has not gained wide acceptance, it does cast considerable doubt over the dating of the Testaments as far as our interest in them is concerned, and evidence from the Testaments can be

---

132 The following phrase, ψυχὰς ἁγίων, is highly suspect: it appears to be an interpretive gloss and, as such, suggests the work of a Christian interpolator. But the present argument is unaffected whether or not these words were found in the original text of Test. Dan 5.

133 It is possible that 5:11c (καὶ δώσει τοῖς ἐπικαλουμένοις αὐτὸν εἰρήνην αἰώνιον) was also the work of a Christian interpolator (although none of the editors of the Testaments have listed it as such). If the clause is an interpolation, Rubinkiewicz's argument would be seriously undermined. As a later interpolation the phrase would be extremely difficult to date, nor could it be said with any degree of certainty that the phrase itself was older than Ephesians. But in the latter instance, it is far more likely that the Christian interpolator of the Testaments was himself influenced by Eph 4:8, rather than that the writer of Ephesians was influenced by the (Christian) interpolator of the Testaments.

employed only with the greatest caution.[134]

Nevertheless, Test. Dan 5:11b (καὶ ἐπιστρέψει καρδίας ἀπειθεῖς πρὸς κύριον) does appear to contain an allusion to Ps 68:19c, the final part of the verse not quoted in Eph 4:8. The reference to the 'disobedient' (ἀπειθεῖς) again echoes the Hebrew text and LXX (סוררים, ἀπειθοῦντες,) as well as the סרבניא of the targum tradition. But the verb ἐπιστρέψει in Test. Dan 5:11 introduces the idea of repentance, an element included in the targum tradition (as found in the extant Tg. Ps 68:19) but not mentioned in the Hebrew text or LXX of Ps 68:19: די מתגיירין חייבין בתחובא, "who, becoming proselytes, repent in repentance," referring to the 'disobedient'. Thus here we are on more certain ground in attempting to establish a link between Test. Dan 5:11 and the tradition behind Tg. Ps 68:19, since no part of the clause is found in Eph 4:8. This eliminates the possibility that the author (or interpolator) of Test. Dan was influenced by the text of Eph 4:8. Yet Test. Dan 5:11ff. makes no mention of the 'disobedient' becoming 'proselytes' as does Tg. Ps 68:19. In fact, the previous context (Test. Dan 5:7) indicates quite

---

134 The theory that the Testaments of the XII Patriarchs are essentially a Jewish work which has been interpolated by Christian copyists was first advanced by F. Schnapp (*Die Testamente der zwölf Patriarchen untersucht* [Halle: Max Niemeyer, 1884] 5-88) and accepted by F. C. Conybeare ("On the Jewish Authorship of the Testaments of the Twelve Patriarchs," *JQR* 5 [1893] 375-98), W. Bousset ("Die Testamente der zwölf Patriarchen, I. Die Ausscheidung der christlichen Interpolationen," *ZNW* 1 [1900] 141-75), and R. H. Charles (see, e.g., Charles' discussion in *APOT* 2.282-83, 2.289-90). Charles tried to reduce the interpolations to a minimum and to find textual support for their removal, using primarily the Armenian version. His theory ultimately became the one commonly accepted. But objections have been raised: N. Messel argued convincingly that it is not possible to find a textual basis for the interpolation theories of Charles and Bousset either in the variants of the Armenian version or in those of the Greek manuscripts ("Über die textkritisch begründete Ausscheidung vermeintlicher christlicher Interpolationen in den Testamenten der zwölf Patriarchen," in *Wolf Wilhelm Grafen von Baudissin zum 26. September 1917*, BZAW 33 [Gießen: Alfred Töpelmann, 1918] 355-74). J. W. Hunkin successfully demonstrated that Charles had wrongly underestimated the value of Cambridge University Library Ms. Ff. I.24 (ff. 203r.-261v.) which (in Hunkin's view) was the best available manuscript ("The Testaments of the Twelve Patriarchs," *JTS* 16 [1915] 80-97). Finally, M. de Jonge made numerous attempts to show that the interpolation theory (in all its variations) could not be maintained (*The Testaments of the Twelve Patriarchs: A Study of Their Text, Composition, and Origin*, [Leiden: Brill], 1953; "The Testaments of the Twelve Patriarchs and the New Testament," *SE* 1 [= TU 73], ed. K. Aland et al. [Berlin: Akademie, 1959] 546-56; "Christian Influence in the Testaments of the Twelve Patriarchs," *NovT* 4 [1960] 182-235; "Once More: Christian Influence in the Testaments of the Twelve Patriarchs," *NovT* 5 [1962] 311-19). De Jonge himself held that the Testaments were basically the work of a Christian writing in the latter half of the second century ("The Testaments of the Twelve Patriarchs and the New Testament," *SE* 1 [= TU 73, Berlin: Akademie, 1959] 556). If he was correct, there would be no question of priority between Test. Dan 5:11 and Eph 4:8. On the other hand, H. C. Kee was not convinced by de Jonge's arguments for a Christian origin of the Testaments ("The Testaments of the Twelve Patriarchs," *OTP* 1.775-80). He favored instead a date in the mid-second century BCE during the Maccabean period, in what probably represents the current scholarly consensus. In any case, sufficient doubt has been cast over the date of composition of the Testaments and the amount of later interpolation (if any) to render their value as evidence for the textual tradition behind Eph 4:8 and *Tg*. Ps 68:19 highly suspect.

clearly that the 'disobedient' in 5:11, whose hearts the Messiah will turn back to the Lord, are in actuality the "sons of Dan," the "sons of Levi," and the "sons of Judah," who have rebelled and fallen into sin. Obviously, there would be no need for them to 'become proselytes'; they are already Israelites by descent from the patriarchs. If there is indeed a relationship between Test. Dan 5:11 and the tradition behind *Tg.* Ps 68:19, it appears that the targum at this stage in its development did not contain the participle מתגיירין, "becoming proselytes." It would be a very logical assumption that this word is in fact a later (and post-Christian) addition to the targum tradition. As such, it would provide an insistence that the Gentiles must not only repent (which Christianity likewise claimed) but must also become Jewish proselytes if the *shekinah* of Yahweh were to dwell with them.

Again we must emphasize that no link between Test. Dan 5:11 and *Tg.* Ps 68:19 can be conclusively demonstrated. Even the similarity between Test. Dan 5:11b and *Tg.* Ps 68:19c does not prove a relationship between the two. One cannot rule out the possibility that an interpretive translation of Psalm 68, or even a textual variant, was in circulation prior to the composition of Test. Dan, and this same version (or variant) also became the basis of the written *Tg.* Psalm 68. In light of the uncertainties surrounding the dating of both Test. Dan and *Tg.* Psalms, the most we can say with any certainty is that Test. Dan is probably prior to *Tg.* Psalm 68, at least in its written form.[135] Yet there is no indication in the context of Test. Dan 5 that the author was aware that Ps 68:19 was connected with a tradition of Moses' ascent to heaven to receive the Torah, as *Tg.* Ps 68:19 explicitly states; rather, in Test. Dan 5:10, it is the Lord himself who performs all the activities of deliverance and vindication for his people. There is no evidence, therefore, for establishing the prior existence of the tradition related in *Tg.* Ps 68:19 regarding Moses and a heavenly ascent based on Test. Dan 5:11. Furthermore, there is insufficient evidence to warrant the assumption that Test. Dan 5:11 constitutes an independent witness to a variant reading in the text of Ps 68:19 which has not been preserved in the Hebrew text or LXX, but appears elsewhere only in *Tg.* Ps 68:19, Eph 4:8, and the Peshitta.

2.2. Testament of Zebulun 4:8
The evidence that suggests a link between Test. Zeb. 4:8 and Ps 68:19 and/or *Tg.* Ps 68:19 is even less conclusive. Test. Zeb. 4:8 reads:

καὶ μετὰ ταῦτα ἀνατελεῖ ὑμῖν αὐτὸς ὁ κύριος, φῶς δικαιοσύνης, καὶ ἴασις καὶ εὐσπλαγχνία ἐπὶ ταῖς πτέρυξιν αὐτοῦ. αὐτὸς λυτρώσεται πᾶσαν αἰχ-

---

135 On the dating of *Tg.* Psalms see the preceding section, 66-75. Concerning problems involved with the dating of the Testaments of the Twelve Patriarchs, see n. 134 above.

μαλωσίαν υἱῶν ἀνθρώπων ἐκ τοῦ Βελιάρ, καὶ πᾶν πνεῦμα πλάνης πατη-
θήσεται· καὶ ἐπιστρέψει πάντα τὰ ἔθνη εἰς παραζήλωσιν αὐτοῦ, καὶ ὄψεσθε
θεὸν ἐν σχήματι ἀνθρώπου ἐν ναῷ, ὃν ἂν ἐκλέξηται κύριος...[136]

Possible allusions to Ps 68:19 may be found in the word αἰχμαλωσίαν
and the phrase ἐπιστρέψει πάντα τὰ ἔθνη εἰς παραζήλωσιν αὐτοῦ. But
in the case of Test. Zeb. 4:8, no mention of 'giving' or 'receiving' gifts
occurs, and the use of a word like λυτρόω (λυτρώσεται) to describe the
'redemption' of the 'sons of men' held captive by 'Beliar' strongly
suggests Christian influence (interpolation, if not outright composition).[137] Nor is there evidence for any connection with Tg. Ps 68:19:
here 'αἰχμαλωσίαν' is explained as 'men held captive by Beliar', while
in Tg. Psalms the phrase "you led captive captivity" is interpreted by
the following clause as Moses' learning the words of the Torah. It might
be possible to see in the phrase καὶ ἐπιστρέψει πάντα τὰ ἔθνη εἰς
παραζήλωσιν αὐτοῦ from Test. Zeb. 4:8 an allusion to the expanded
form of Ps 68:19c as found in the targum (וברם סרבניא די מתגיירין חייבין
בתחובא, "and even the rebellious, who, becoming proselytes, repent with
penance"), since the 'turning all the nations' of Test. Zeb. 4:8 might
suggest the 'proselytes' of Tg. Ps 68:19. But in the respective contexts,
the possibility of such a relationship seems remote. Once again, while
Test. Zeb. 4:8 might possibly contain an allusion to Ps 68:19, there is little evidence to suggest any connection with the interpretation of Ps
68:19 found in Tg. Psalms or the tradition behind the targum. The Testament of Zebulun contains no mention of Moses, his ascent to heaven,
or the Torah.

3. Ps 68:19 and the Book of Jubilees

At least one possible allusion to Ps 68:19 is found in the Book of Jubilees. In Jub. 24:31-32 we find the conclusion of Isaac's curse upon the
Philistines (which began in 24:28):

> Because if they go up to heaven, from there they will fall;
> and if they are set firm in the earth, from there they will be torn out;
> and if they are hidden among the nations, from there they will be uprooted;
> and if they go down to Sheol, even there their judgment will multiply,
> and also there will be no peace for them there.
> And if they go into captivity by the hand of those who seek their life,
> they will kill them along the way.
> And neither name nor seed will be left for them in all the earth,

---

136 The Testaments of the Twelve Patriarchs: A Critical Edition of the Greek Text, ed. M.
de Jonge, 100-101.

137 For a brief discussion of the problems involved in determining the extent of Christian
interpolations present in the Testaments of the Twelve Patriarchs, see n. 134 above.

because they shall walk in an eternal curse.[138]

In considering this passage and its similarities to Ps 68:19 several things must be noted: (1) in Ps 68:19 there is reference only to an ascent (the author of Ephesians found it necessary to deduce a descent after quoting Ps 68:19), while *Jub.* 24:31 refers explicitly to both ascent and descent; (2) in Ps 68:19 it is Yahweh who ascends, while in *Jub.* 24:31 it is the Philistine (collective singular); and (3) the contextual settings of the two passages are completely different. Ps 68:19 describes the triumphal ascent of Yahweh to his heavenly throne, while *Jub.* 24:31-32 recounts the curse Isaac placed upon the Philistines. In view of these significant differences we must conclude that *Jub.* 24:31-32 bears no relationship to Ps 68:19. It is far more likely that the OT passage behind *Jub.* 24:31-32 is Amos 9:2-4, which describes the Lord's coming judgment of unrighteous Israelites:

> Though they dig into Sheol,
> From there shall my hand take them;
> And though they ascend to heaven,
> From there will I bring them down.
> And though they hide on the summit of Carmel,
> I will search them out and take them from there;
> And though they conceal themselves from my sight on the floor of the sea,
> From there I will command the serpent and it will bite them.
> And though they go into captivity before their enemies,
> From there I will command the sword that it may slay them,
> And I will set my eyes against them for evil and not for good.[139]

In Amos 9:2-4 the context is one of judgment and is much the same as *Jub.* 24:31-32. Amos 9:4 also parallels *Jub.* 24:32 in its reference to prisoners who are slain as they are led forth into captivity. There are far more similarities between *Jub.* 24:31-32 and Amos 9:2-4 than between either of these passages and Ps 68:19. We may therefore conclude that there is neither direct reference nor allusion to Ps 68:19 (in particular) or to Moses' ascent of Mt. Sinai to receive the Torah (in general) present in *Jub.* 24:31-32. Other Moses stories are found in *Jubilees* 46-50, but none of these give any additional information about Moses' ascent of Sinai or his assumption to heaven.

---

[138] O. S. Wintermute, "Jubilees: A New Translation and Introduction," *OTP* 2.104. Wintermute dated *Jubilees* between 161-140 BCE (43-44). R. H. Charles dated the *Book of Jubilees* between 135-105 BCE, somewhat later than the date now suggested by Wintermute (*APOT* 2.1). For more extensive discussion of the dating of *Jubilees*, see ch. 5 of the present study, 147, 152-53, and especially 157, n. 53. Italics in the quotation from *Jubilees* are mine, added to facilitate comparison with Ps 68:19 and the text of Amos 9:2-4 which follows.

[139] Amos 9:2-4 is quoted from the NASB (La Habra, Calif.: Foundation, 1963). Italics in the quotation are mine.

4. Ps 68:19 in the Writings of Justin Martyr

Twice in his writings Justin Martyr (died ca. 165 CE) quoted from Ps 68:19 to substantiate his assertion that after the ascension Christ gave special gifts of the Holy Spirit to men. Both of these references occur in Justin's *Dialogus cum Tryphone Judaeo* and in context both appear to be related to Eph 4:7-16, since the giving of spiritual gifts is the subject under discussion both in Justin's text and in the context of Ephesians 4. Justin's words need to be examined in some detail, however, since his quotation of Ps 68:19 does not exactly parallel that of Eph 4:8 in one instance.

4.1. Dialogus cum Tryphone Judaeo 39.4-5

Justin's first use of Ps 68:19 appears in the context of an explanation of the spiritual gifts given by the ascended Christ, and may in fact be a quotation not from Psalm 68:19 directly, but from Eph 4:8. Justin had just explained to his Jewish acquaintance Trypho how God was currently withholding judgment on the Jewish people to enable more of them to become disciples of Christ. As they did this, they would "receive gifts, each one as they are worthy, when they become enlightened through this name of Christ" [39.2]. Justin then described to Trypho some of the various gifts: a spirit of understanding [συνέσεως], of counsel [βουλῆς], of strength [ἰσχύος], of healing [ἰάσεως], of foreknowledge [προγνώσεως], of teaching [διδασκαλίας], or of the fear of God [φόβου θεοῦ]. After Trypho expressed amazement, Justin explained that the giving of such gifts was predicted in the Jewish scriptures (the OT), and quoted Ps 68:19 as proof:

> ἀλλὰ μετὰ τὴν τοῦ Χριστοῦ εἰς τὸν οὐρανὸν ἀνέλευσιν προεφητεύθη αιχμαλωτεῦσαι αὐτὸν ἡμᾶς ἀπὸ τῆς πλάνης καὶ δοῦναι ἡμῖν δόματα. εἰσὶ δὲ οἱ λόγοι οὗτοι· «Ἀνέβη εἰς ὕψος, ᾐχμαλώτευσεν αἰχμαλωσίαν, ἔδωκε δόματα τοῖς ἀνθρώποις.» οἱ λαβόντες οὖν ἡμεῖς δόματα παρὰ τοῦ εἰς ὕψος ἀναβάντος ἡ ριστοῦ ὑμᾶς, «τοὺς σοφοὺς ἐν ἑαυτοῖς καὶ ἐνώπιον ἑαυτῶν ἐπιστήμονας,» ἀπὸ τῶν προφητικῶν λόγων ἀποδείκνυμεν ἀνοήτους καὶ χείλεσι μόνον τιμῶντας τὸν θεὸν καὶ τὸν Χριστὸν αὐτοῦ·[140]

It seems clear from the context that Justin was attempting to prove to Trypho the existence of spiritual gifts by quoting from the OT scriptures, since a quotation from the NT would carry no weight with a Jew.[141] Thus it is reasonable to assume that Justin was quoting (or intending to

---

140 *Dialogus cum Tryphone Judaeo* 39.4-5. The Greek text of Justin Martyr is from the Βιβλιοθηκη Ἑλληνων Πατερων και Ἐκκλησιαστικων Συγγραφεων, 3: Πολυκαρπος Σμυρνης—Ἑρμας—Παπιας—Κοδρατος—Ἀριστειδης—Ἰουστινος (Athens: Apostolic Diaconate of the Church of Greece, 1955) 243.

141 Even if Trypho was a contrived opponent, one could still assume that for the sake of realism Justin would not have consciously quoted from NT scriptures to convince a Jew.

quote) Ps 68:19 as it was found in the OT rather than Eph 4:8. However, this does not rule out the possibility that Justin's quotation of the text of Ps 68:19 had been influenced by his knowledge of Eph 4:8, either intentionally or unintentionally.[142] There does in fact seem to be some mixture in Justin's actual wording between the LXX of Ps 68:19 on the one hand and Eph 4:8 on the other. Justin's quotation begins with ἀνέβη, the third person singular verb read by the original hand of א in Ps 68:19 LXX, while Eph 4:8 reads the participle ἀναβάς. Yet with regard to the distribution of the gifts Justin agreed with Eph 4:8, reading ἔδω-κε[ν] against the ἔλαβες of Ps 68:19 LXX. Justin also agreed with Eph 4:8 in the inclusion of the article [τοῖς] before ἀνθρώποις, while the article was omitted by the LXX.

Based on the similarities and differences between the form of Ps 68:19 quoted by Justin in *Dialogus cum Tryphone Judaeo* 39.4-5 and the form of the psalm quoted by the author of Ephesians, it is not possible to establish the exact relationship between the two. But with respect to the substitution of ἔδωκε[ν] in Justin's text for the verb ἔλαβες found in both the Hebrew text and LXX at least two possibilities exist: either (1) both Justin and the author of Ephesians had access to a textual tradition in which the change from ἔλαβες to ἔδωκεν was already established, or (2) Justin has been influenced in his quotation of Ps 68:19 at this point by the text of Eph 4:8.[143]

Two further observations should now be noted which do not concern the relationship between the text of the *Dialogus* and Eph 4:8, but do reflect Justin's own understanding of the giving of the spiritual gifts: (1) it was *after* Christ's ascent to heaven that the spiritual gifts he described were distributed, and (2) the captivity mentioned in Ps 68:19 [αἰχμαλωσίαν] was understood to be the captivity of individuals to "error" [τῆς πλάνης].

4.2. *Dialogus cum Tryphone Judaeo* 87.5-6
The second text in which Justin quoted from Ps 68:19 is *Dialogus cum Tryphone Judueo* 87.5-6. Speaking again of the spiritual gifts given to believers, Justin said:

---

[142] Another possibility is that a later copyist of Justin's works, familiar with the quotation of Ps 68:19 in Ephesians, may have conformed the quotation to Eph 4:8 as well.

[143] Rubinkiewicz's argument ("Psalm LXVIII 19 [= Eph IV 8] Another Textual Tradition or Targum?," *NovT* 17 [1975] 219-24) was criticized by R. A. Taylor for not taking sufficient account of the possibility that patristic writers like Justin were influenced in their citation of Ps 68:19 by the text of Eph 4:8 ("The Use of Psalm 68:18 in Ephesians 4:8 in Light of the Ancient Versions," *BSac* 148 [1991] 335 n. 45). Such harmonization, either intentional or unintentional, is certainly possible. But as we shall see below, the text of Justin's *Dialogus* 87.6 reflects a reading *not* found in Eph 4:8 nor in the Hebrew or LXX text of Ps 68:19 but contained in *Tg.* Ps 68:19.

ἀνεπαύσατο οὖν, τοῦτ᾽ ἔστιν ἐπαύσατο, ἐλθόντος ἐκείνου, μεθ᾽ ὅν, τῆς οἰκονομίας ταύτης τῆς ἐν ἀνθρώποις αὐτοῦ γενομένης χρόνοις, παύσασθαι ἔδει αὐτὰ ἀφ᾽ ὑμῶν, καὶ ἐν τούτῳ ἀνάπαυσιν λαβόντα πάλιν, ὡς ἐπεπροφ-ήτευτο γενήσεσθαι δόματα, ἃ ἀπὸ τῆς χάριτος τῆς δυνάμεως τοῦ πνεύματος ἐκείνου τοῖς ἐπ᾽ αὐτὸν πιστεύουσι δίδωσιν, ὡς ἄξιον ἕκαστον ἐπίσταται. ὅτι ἐπεπροφήτευτο τοῦτο μέλλειν γίνεσθαι ὑπ᾽ αὐτοῦ μετὰ τὴν εἰς οὐρανὸν ἀνέλευσιν αὐτοῦ, εἶπον μὲν ἤδη καὶ πάλιν λέγω. εἶπεν οὖν· «Ἀνέβη εἰς ὕψος, ᾐχμαλώτευσεν αἰχμαλωσίαν, ἔδωκε δόματα τοῖς υἱοῖς τῶν ἀνθρώπων.» καὶ πάλιν ἐν ἑτέρᾳ προφητείᾳ εἴρηται· «Καὶ ἔσται μετὰ ταῦτα, ἐκχεῶ τὸ πνεῦμά μου ἐπὶ πᾶσαν σάρκα καὶ ἐπὶ τοὺς δούλους μου καὶ ἐπὶ τὰς δούλας μου, καὶ προφητεύσουσι.»[144]

Justin told Trypho that the Spirit "rested," that is, "ceased," when the Messiah [ἐκείνου] came, and thus the Spirit's activity among the Jewish people ceased at this time as well. But after the Messiah accomplished his "stewardship" among men, the gifts which had ceased among the Jewish people would be given again [λαβόντα πάλιν] to those who believed in him, as was prophesied beforehand. Justin said that he had mentioned before that the Messiah would give these spiritual gifts after he had departed into heaven (probably a reference to *Dialogus* 39.4, discussed above), and then quoted Ps 68:19 to prove his point. Next Justin quotes a second prophecy, this time from Joel 2:28-29, to show that spiritual gifts have been given to Christians after the ascension of Christ.

Two issues are of major importance here: (1) the determination (if possible) of the source Justin used for his quotation of Ps 68:19, and (2) the relationship Justin established between the giving of the gifts mentioned in Ps 68:19 and the first Christian Pentecost described in Acts 2 through his citation of Joel 2:28-29. As far as the source of the quotation is concerned (as with *Dialogus* 39.4), it is probable that Justin intended to quote Ps 68:19 and not Eph 4:8, since in the immediate context the other quotation (Joel 2:28-29) is also from the OT, and in a discussion with a Jewish opponent a NT citation would carry no weight.[145] This does not rule out the possibility of an unconscious assimilation of the quotation to Eph 4:8, as pointed out in the discussion of *Dialogus* 39.4-5 above.[146] Justin's quotation of Ps 68:19 here in *Dialogus* 87.6 is exactly the same as his quotation in *Dialogus* 39.4 in all respects but one: in the third clause of the quotation he expanded ἔδωκε δόματα τοῖς ἀνθρώποις to read ἔδωκε δόματα τοῖς υἱοῖς τῶν

---

[144] Again, the text of *Dialogus cum Tryphone Judaeo* 87.5-6 is from Βιβλιοθηκη Ἑλλη-νων Πατερων και Ἐκκλησιαστικων Συγγραφεων, 3.292.

[145] See n. 142 above.

[146] Nor does it rule out the possibility of assimilation to the text of Eph 4:8 by a later copyist; see n. 143 above.

ἀνθρώπων. The addition of the word υἱοῖς is important because it is not found in the text of Eph 4:8 nor in the text of Ps 68:19 as read by the Hebrew text or LXX, but is contained in the Aramaic text of *Tg*. Ps 68:19.[147] Would Justin have been familiar with the text of *Tg*. Psalms? Such a conclusion is highly unlikely, particularly in light of the indications of a far later date for *Tg*. Psalms as a written composition.[148] It is equally unlikely that Justin would have been familar with the Aramaic oral tradition behind *Tg*. Psalms. This led R. Rubinkiewicz to suggest that Justin's *Dialogus* serves as witness to an independent textual tradition which lay behind *Tg*. Psalms but survived in only four extant sources: *Tg*. Ps 68:19, Eph 4:8, the Peshitta psalter, and *Dialogus cum Tryphone Judaeo* 87.6.[149] This suggestion has some merit because the text of Ps 68:19 quoted by Justin does show a degree of divergence from all other known texts of Ps 68:19 except for *Tg*. Psalms and the Peshitta psalter in the inclusion of the word υἱοῖς. If there is a common textual tradition behind *Tg*. Ps 68:19, Eph 4:8, the Peshitta psalter, and *Dialogus* 87.6 then the other major divergence from the text of Ps 68:19 as found in the Hebrew text and LXX, the change from לקחת and ἔλαβες to ἔδωκεν and יהבתא as found in Eph 4:8 and *Tg*. Ps 68:19, could also have originated in the same independent textual tradition which was known to both the writer of Ephesians and the targumist, and which also lay behind the Peshitta translation of Ps 68:19.[150]

With regard to the second point mentioned above—Justin's quotation from Joel 2:28-29—it should be noted that the connection between the giving of the gifts mentioned in Ps 68:19 and the coming of the Holy Spirit at Pentecost (as described in Acts 2:1-47), while implicit in the text of Eph 4:7-16, is not directly asserted by the author of Ephesians. Yet this connection was made explicit in Justin's *Dialogus*, since his use of Joel 2:28-29 constituted a direct allusion to Peter's speech in Acts 2:14ff., where the same text from Joel was also quoted (Acts 2:17-21). As noted above, Justin was probably not discussing the text of Eph 4:7-16 directly in the *Dialogus*. Yet it appears probable that at this point Justin's argument is influenced by his knowledge of Eph 4:7-16 (if not derived almost totally from the argument of Ephesians itself) even if for polemic or apologetic reasons he has not explicitly quoted Ephesians 4.

---

[147] See the comparison of the texts of Eph 4:8 and Ps 68:19 in the MT, LXX, and *Tg*. Psalms, pp. 96-104 above.

[148] See the section on "The Targum to the Psalms," 66-75, for a discussion of the problem of dating *Tg*. Psalms and the indications of a later date for the written composition.

[149] R. Rubinkiewicz, "Psalm LXVIII 19 (= Eph IV 8) Another Textual Tradition or Targum?," *NovT* 17 (1975) 219-24.

[150] "The targumist" is used here as a designation either for the person responsible for the oral tradition or for the person who put *Tg*. Psalms in its final written form.

Thus we have in Justin's own use of Ps 68:19 in connection with Joel 2:28-29 evidence that the gifts mentioned in Ps 68:19 were understood by Christians at quite an early date to refer to the gifts of the Holy Spirit which began at Pentecost, and it is probable that Justin derived this insight from his understanding of the text of Eph 4:7-16 even though he did not cite it explicitly. We shall consider in the following chapter whether the connection between Psalm 68 and the feast of Pentecost could be even earlier than the time of Justin Martyr, and in fact antedated the first century CE (and thus might have influenced the author of Ephesians).

5. Ps 68:18-19 in the Writings of Irenaeus

Irenaeus, whose death is commonly put at around 202 CE at the time of renewed persecution under Septimius Severus, quoted Ps 68:18-19 once in his *Demonstratio apostolicae praedicationis*, a work written in Greek but surviving only in an Armenian version.[151] In *Dem.* 83 Irenaeus states:

> And that when raised from the dead He was to be taken up into heaven, David says as follows: *The chariot of God is myriadfold, thousands of charioteers; the Lord among them in Sina* [sic], *in the holy place, hath ascended on high, He hath led captivity captive. He hath taken, hath given gifts to men.* And "captivity" refers to the destruction of the dominion of the rebel angels. And he announced also the place whence He was to mount to heaven from earth; for *the Lord*, he says, *in Sion hath ascended on high.* For it was on the mountain which is called that of Olives, over against Jerusalem, after His resurrection from the dead, that, having assembled His disciples and having instructed them concerning the kingdom of heaven, He was lifted up in their sight, and they saw how the heavens opened and received Him.[152]

Irenaeus quotes not only Ps 68:19 but verse 18 as well. His quotation might therefore be independent of Eph 4:8, since in Eph 4:8 only verse 19 of the psalm is quoted. Irenaeus' interpretation of Ps 68:18-19 makes it clear that he understood it to refer to Christ's ascension. Thus we have clear evidence (in a tradition possibly independent from Ephesians) that as early as the end of the second century Psalm 68 was being interpreted christologically. There is a textual difficulty with Irenaeus'

---

151 This work, sometimes known by its English title, the *Proof of the Apostolic Preaching*, was mentioned by Eusebius but thought to have been lost until an Armenian manuscript was discovered in 1904.

152 *St. Irenaeus: Proof of the Apostolic Preaching*, trans. J. P. Smith, ACW 16 (Westminster, MD: Newman; London: Longmans, Green & Co., 1952) 99. Punctuation and italics are those of the translator in the edition cited. The English translation is cited because the Armenian text was not available; unlike the other extant works of Irenaeus the *Demonstratio* does not exist in Latin (see the previous note).

quotation of Ps 68:18, which in the Armenian version is read as *Sina*. In the interpretation which Irenaeus gave for this verse it is clear that he referred to Zion (*Sion*), that is, Mt. Zion in Jerusalem. On the basis of this L. M. Froidevaux (in the absence of any manuscript support) emended the text of the quotation from Ps 68:18 to read "Zion" instead of "Sinai."[153] It is possible that he was correct and *Sina* in the quotation from Ps 68:18 represented a scribal emendation to bring the text into conformity with the OT text of Psalm 68 known to the copyist. It is equally possible, however, that Irenaeus simply interpreted the reference to Mt. Sinai that he found in the text of Ps 68:18 as a reference to Mt. Zion in Jerusalem. Such word-plays were a common form of rabbinic interpretation in the period when Irenaeus wrote and would not be particularly unusual, even for a Christian writer.

Another interesting point about Irenaeus' quotation from Ps 68:19 is the conflation at the point of variance between the reading of the Hebrew text and LXX on the one hand and the reading preserved in Eph 4:8 and *Tg.* Ps 68:19 on the other. Irenaeus gave a conflate reading which combined the ideas of receiving and giving gifts: "He hath taken, hath given gifts to men." If we could be certain that Irenaeus' quotation of Ps 68:18-19 was independent of Eph 4:8, we would have evidence here that Irenaeus was familiar with the same textual tradition which lies behind Eph 4:8 and *Tg.* Ps 68:19, a variant not preserved in any manuscripts of the Hebrew text or LXX. But we cannot rule out the possibility that Irenaeus was familiar with Eph 4:8 and its use of the psalm, and was merely conflating the version of Ps 68:19 found in Ephesians with the OT text of the psalm as he knew it. It is also possible (although perhaps less likely) that the conflation is due to later scribal emendation. Thus it is difficult to be certain about just how much can be proven from Irenaeus' quotation of Ps 68:18-19 in *Dem.* 83. The most we can say with reasonable certainty is that by the end of the second century CE a Christian interpretation of Psalm 68 was in circulation, an interpretation which referred the ascent mentioned in Ps 68:19 to Christ's victorious ascent and conquest of the 'powers' following his resurrection. This sounds very much like the interpretation of Psalm 68 in Eph 4:7-10, however, and it is possible (even likely) that such a messianic interpretation of the psalm by patristic writers was derived from its use in Eph 4. We shall have to look further to find evidence that such an interpretation did not originate with the author of Ephesians but was older still.

---

153 L. M. Froidevaux, *Irénée de Lyon: Demonstration de la Prédication Apostolique* (Paris: Éditions du Cerf, 1959) 149 n. 2; 150 n. 4.

6. *Ps 68:19 in the Writings of Tertullian*

Tertullian (died ca. 220 CE) alluded to Ps 68:19 twice in the course of his works. The first allusion occurs in *Adversus Marcionem* 5.8.5 in a context where Tertullian connected the ascent of Christ with the giving of spiritual gifts:

> Accipe nunc, quomodo et a Christo in caelum recepto charismata obuentura pronuntiarit: ascendit in sublimitatem, id est in caelum; captiuam duxit captiuitatem, id est mortem uel humanam seruitutem; data dedit filiis hominum, is est donatiua, quae charismata dicimus. Eleganter 'filiis hominum' ait, non passim 'hominibus', nos ostendens filios hominum, id est uere hominum, apostolorum.[154]

As with Justin's quotations, it is not clear whether Tertullian was quoting from Ps 68:19 or Eph 4:8. In the immediate context he refers to other passages in 1 Corinthians and Galatians; this suggests he intended a reference to Eph 4:8 here.[155] Likewise, the assumed reference to Christ as the subject of the quoted material also suggests that Tertullian was quoting Eph 4:8 rather than Ps 68:19. Tertullian did, however, quote from Joel 2:28 in the next sentence after the material quoted above, so an OT allusion from Ps 68:19 cannot be ruled out completely. Tertullian's use of Joel 2:28 in this context assumed the same connection found in Justin Martyr between the giving of the spiritual gifts mentioned in Eph 4:8 [Ps 68:19] and the coming of the Holy Spirit at Pentecost. Joel 2:28 by its quotation in Acts 2:17-21 had become established in early Christian tradition with Pentecost and the coming of the Holy Spirit.[156]

In Tertullian's quotation from Eph 4:8 [Ps 68:19] he inserted phrases prefaced by "id est" which gave his explanation for the actions described by the quotation. The place to which Christ ascended ["in sublimitatum"] was interpreted as 'heaven' ["in caelum"]; the 'captivity led captive' were the dead ["mortem uel humanam seruitutem"], and the 'gifts' were the charismatic (spiritual) gifts distributed to Christians ["donatiua, quae charismata dicimus"]. Of special interest is Tertullian's digression on the phrase "filiis hominum," which he saw as an allusion to the sons of men, in particular the apostles ["nos ostendens filios hominum, id est uere hominum, apostolorum"]. Such a connection with the apostles would have seemed natural to Tertullian because 'apostles' were mentioned in Eph 4:11 as the first of a number of categories of spiritually gifted individuals, and also because of the apostles' connec-

---

154 *Tertulliani Opera*, CChr 1 (Turnhout: Brepols, 1954) 686-87.
155 E. g., 1 Cor 11:23-27, 29 in 5.8.3; Gal 4:19 in 5.8.6; Gal 4:4 and 1 Cor 7:29 in 5.8.7, etc.
156 See above, pp. 114-15.

tion with Pentecost (an idea also present in the context as indicated by Tertullian's quotation of Joel 2:28). It is important to note, however, that Tertullian's mention of the plural phrase "filiis hominum" to designate the recipients of the gifts indicated he was familiar with a textual variant not present in Eph 4:8. This is the same variant (found also in *Tg*. Ps 68:19 and the text of Ps 68:19 in the Peshitta psalter) quoted by Justin Martyr in *Dialogus cum Tryphone Judaeo* 87.6.[157] As in the previous instance, it is impossible to determine with certainty the source of Tertullian's quotation, but we must assume that Tertullian derived this reading from either *Tg*. Ps 68:19, Ps 68:19 in the Peshitta psalter, the writings of Justin Martyr, or an independent textual tradition also known by the preceding authors and/or copyists (but surviving today only in the four sources indicated).[158] On the whole, given the diversity of the four sources involved, the possibility of an independent textual tradition is the most probable, although the remaining possibilities cannot be completely ruled out. This further supports R. Rubinkiewicz's contention that an independent textual tradition lay behind *Tg*. Ps 68:19, the Peshitta psalter, and the quotations of Ps 68:19 in the writings of Justin Martyr.[159]

Tertullian made one further allusion to the text in question in *De Anima* 55.2:

> Quodsi Christus deus, quia et homo, mortuus secundum scripturas et sepultus secundum easdem, huic quoque legi satisfecit forma humanae mortis apud inferos functus, nec ante ascendit in sublimiora caelorum quam descendit in inferiora terrarum, ut illic patriarchas et prophetas compotes sui faceret...[160]

It is clear from the context that Tertullian is actually alluding to Eph 4:8-9 rather than the text of Ps 68:19, because he makes reference not only to the ascent of Christ to heaven ["ascendit in sublimiora caelorum"], but also to Christ's descent 'into the lower regions of the earth' ["in inferiora terrarum"]. This allusion to Eph 4:8-9 is important because it shows that Tertullian himself held the 'traditional' view of the *descensus*, that Christ descended to the underworld during the three days between his death and resurrection. Tertullian was one of the first to

---

[157] See above, p. 115.

[158] It is not likely that a later copyist of Tertullian's works managed to assimilate *Adv. Marcionem* 5.8.5 to *Tg*. Ps 68:19, the Peshitta psalter, the writings of Justin in *Dialogus cum Tryphone Judaeo* 87.6, or some other textual tradition, because of the nature of Tertullian's remarks, which are not a direct quotation but form an explanatory comment on the text of Eph 4:8 [Ps 68:19].

[159] R. Rubinkiewicz, "Psalm LXVIII 19 (= Eph IV 8) Another Textual Tradition or Targum?," *NovT* 17 (1975) 219-24. See the discussion of the quotations in Justin Martyr above, 112-16.

[160] *Tertulliani Opera*, CChr 2 (Turnhout: Brepols, 1954) 862.

articulate this view. He apparently saw no inconsistency between such an understanding of the descent of Christ in Eph 4:9 and the connection of the ascent in Eph 4:8 and the giving of gifted individuals to the Church in 4:11ff. with Pentecost, as indicated by his allusion to Joel 2:28 in *Adversus Marcionem* 5.8.6. However, Tertullian made no attempt (as far as we can tell from his surviving works) to relate the descent of Christ deduced by the author of Ephesians in Eph 4:9-10 to the ascent mentioned in the quotation from Ps 68:19. In this failure to relate Christ's descent to his ascent Tertullian has been followed by many later interpreters who have assumed the reference to the descent in Eph 4:9-10 to be extraneous to the argument of Ephesians 4.[161]

7. Origen, Ps. 68:19 and Pentecost

Origen (writing sometime after 234 CE)[162] alluded to Ps 68:19 (Eph 4:8) in a remarkable passage in his *Commentary on John* (6.37 [292]) which is part of a very long and complicated exposition of John 1:29 describing Jesus as "the Lamb of God who takes away the sin of the world." Origen went on to state,

'Αλλ' ἐπεὶ, ὡς προείπομεν, τὰ κατὰ τῶν ἀντικειμένων ἀνδραγαθήματα πεποιηκὼς, ἐδεῖτο τοῦ πλῦναι «ἐν οἴνῳ τὴν στολὴν αὐτοῦ, καὶ ἐν αἵματι σταφυλῆς τὴν περιβολὴν αὐτοῦ,» ἀνήει πρὸς τὸν γεωργὸν τῆς ἀληθινῆς ἀμπέλου Πατέρα, ἵν' ἐκεῖ ἀποπλυνάμενος, μετὰ τὸ ἀναβῆναι εἰς ὕψος, αἰχμαλωτεύσας τὴν αἰχμαλωσίαν, καταβῇ φέρων τὰ ποικίλα χαρίσματα, τάς διαμεμερισμένας τοῖς ἀποστόλοις γλώσσας ὡσεὶ πυρὸς, καὶ τοὺς παρεσομένους ἐν πάσῃ πράξει ἁγίους ἀγγέλους, καὶ ῥυσομένους αὐτούς. Πρὸ γὰρ τούτων τῶν οἰκονομιῶν, ἅτε μηδέπω κεκαθαρμένοι οὐκ ἐχώρουν ἀγγέλων παρ' αὐτοῖς ἐπιδημίαν, τάχα οὐδ' αὐτῶν βουλομένων πω τοῖς μὴ εὐτρεπισαμένοις καὶ κεκαθαρμένοις ὑπὸ τοῦ Ἰησοῦ παρεῖναι.[163]

But since, as we said previously, when he had performed heroic deeds against his opponents, it was necessary for him to wash his robe in wine, and his garment in the blood of grapes, he went up to the vinedresser of the true vine, the Father, so that having washed there, after he had ascended on high, having led captive captivity, he might descend bearing the various gifts, the

---

161 The relationship of the descent inferred by the author of Ephesians in 4:9-10 to the argument of 4:1-16 and the entire Epistle is discussed at length in chapter 6 below.

162 Origen said he dictated the commentary as far as Book 5 at Alexandria, and began Book 6 there. He then moved to Caesarea and resumed work on the commentary, but said he had to begin the sixth book over again because what he had dictated at Alexandria had not been brought along (Origen, *Commentariorum in Evangelium secundum Joannem* 6.1; *PG* 4, cols. 200-201). Since Origen's move to Caesarea probably occurred in 234 CE, this provides a fairly precise date for when he began working on Book 6 but not for when he finished it.

163 *Commentariorum in Evangelium secundum Joannem* 6.37. The Greek text of Origen is from the Βιβλιοθήκη Ἑλλήνων Πατέρων και Ἐκκλησιαστικῶν Συγγραφέων, 12: Ὠριγένης part 4 (Athens: Apostolic Diaconate of the Church of Greece, 1957) 62.

tongues as of fire distributed to the apostles, and the holy angels who will be present with them in their every deed and will deliver them. For before these dispensations, since they had not yet been cleansed, they could not receive the visitation of angels among them; perhaps the angels too did not wish to be present with those who had not yet been prepared and cleansed by Jesus.[164]

It is clear that in this passage Origen described a descent of Christ subsequent to his victorious ascent. The subsequent descent is related to Pentecost by the mention of tongues of fire, a clear allusion to Acts 2:3. Furthermore, and most important of all, Origen made the connection between the ascent and subsequent descent of Christ by quoting Ps. 68:19 (Eph. 4:8). Thus we have clear evidence that the interpretation of Eph. 4:7-10 proposed in modern times by T. K. Abbott and H. von Soden does indeed have early patristic support, a fact which has apparently gone unnoticed before now. Such an interpretation involving a subsequent descent may no longer be dismissed as merely recent innovation.

Of course, the fact that Origen provides third century evidence for such a view (and appears to hold it himself) do not necessarily prove that this was the understanding of the original author of Ephesians. One wonders where Origen came across such an understanding of Ps. 68:19 and Eph. 4:8. Since he mentions it naturally in the flow of the context in his commentary, we may presume that he did not originate it, but inherited the view from someone else. One particularly intriguing question is whether Origen brought this interpretation with him when he moved from Alexandria to Caesarea while writing the *Commentary on John*. It may well be that Origen was simply reflecting an accepted and established interpretation of Ps. 68:19 (and Eph. 4:8) based on a replacement motif where Christ as the "new Moses" makes a heavenly ascent followed by a distribution of gifts.

8. Conclusions: Use of Ps 68:19 in Early Non-Rabbinic Sources

We have now examined potential references to Ps 68:19 in early non-rabbinic sources, among them the Testaments of the Twelve Patriarchs, the *Book of Jubilees*, and the writings of Justin Martyr, Tertullian, and Origen. In the case of Test. Dan 5:11 we concluded (*pace* Rubinkiewicz) that no allusion to Ps 68:19 could be proven. Likewise, in Test. Zeb. 4:8 and *Jub.* 24:31-32 we concluded after detailed examination that Ps 68:19 was not in the background of these texts. In the writings of both Justin Martyr and Tertullian references to Ps 68:19 do

---

[164] My translation from the Greek text above.

exist. But in both of these cases it is difficult to be certain to what extent the author's knowledge of Eph 4:8 may have influenced his citation. In the case of Justin it does appear that he related the gifts mentioned in Ps 68:19 to the gifts of the Spirit given at Pentecost, because he linked the quotation of the passage to Joel 2:28-29, an OT passage clearly connected with the first Christian Pentecost by the account in Acts 2:17-21. Justin's use of Ps 68:19 also suggests he was familiar with a textual tradition independent of Eph 4:8 and closer to that found in *Tg.* Psalms. The form in which he cited the psalm in *Dialogus cum Tryphone Judaeo* 87.6 is closer to that surviving today in both *Tg.* Psalms and the Peshitta psalter than to the text of Eph 4:8. The same can be said for Tertullian's use of Ps 68:19 in *Adv. Marcionem* 5.8.5. Rubinkiewicz was probably correct in asserting that a textual tradition was in circulation at least as early as the beginning of the Christian era which differed in some respects from what we now find preserved in the Hebrew text and LXX of Ps 68:19. Hints of such a tradition survive in sources like *Tg.* Psalms, the Peshitta psalter, and the quotations of Ps 68:19 by Justin and Tertullian. Although this provides a plausible explanation for the change from לקחת (Hebrew text) and ἔλαβες (LXX) in Ps 68:19 to ἔδωκεν in Eph 4:8, it does not confirm the presence of Moses-imagery in the source employed by the author of Ephesians for his quotation of the psalm.

The situation with Origen's use of Ps 68:19 (Eph 4:8) in connection with Pentecost is somewhat different. In this case it is clear that Origen related the text in question both to a subsequent descent (explicitly stated in his commentary) and at the same time to a distribution of various gifts at Pentecost (his mention of the "tongues as of fire," a clear allusion to Acts 2:3, demonstrates this). Before we examine this linkage between Psalm 68 and Pentecost more closely, we first need to consider some other early sources which do not mention Ps 68:19 in any way, but which nevertheless involve an ascent of Moses to heaven.

CHAPTER FOUR

MOSES' ASCENT TO HEAVEN IN OTHER EARLY SOURCES NOT RELATED TO PSALM 68

There are a number of early sources which reflect an ascent of Moses to heaven but do not relate the ascent to Psalm 68 in any way. Most of these sources connect Moses' heavenly ascent with his ascent of Mt. Sinai to receive the Torah, although some accounts also involve an assumption to heaven at the end of Moses' life. If such traditions of Moses' heavenly ascent are as old as (or older than) the first century, then the author of Ephesians may well have known and used such a tradition in 4:7-11 whether or not it was explicitly connected with Ps 68:19 in his sources. Even if we cannot conclusively connect such Moses-traditions with Ps 68:19 prior to the composition of Ephesians, the circulation of widespread traditions concerning a heavenly ascent of Moses at Sinai could have influenced the author of Ephesians as he wrote 4:7-11 if he had other reasons to relate them to Ps 68:19 (e.g., because both the giving of the Torah and Psalm 68 were associated already with the feast of Pentecost by the first century CE, two possibilities which are investigated in Chapter Five below). Here we shall examine the early sources which contain such Moses-imagery and try to determine both how ancient and how widespread the tradition of Moses' heavenly ascent might be.

A. THE *EXAGOGE* OF EZEKIEL THE TRAGEDIAN

The *Exagoge* is a tragic drama from the hellenistic period, written in iambic trimeter, which describes the exodus of the Israelites from Egypt under the leadership of Moses. Its author, Ezekiel, was designated by Eusebius (quoting Alexander Polyhistor in *Praeparatio Evangelica* 9.28.1) "the poet of tragedies" (ὁ τῶν τραγῳδιῶν ποιητής).[1] The text of Ezekiel's work is extant only in fragments cited by Eusebius (who quoted from an earlier work, Alexander Polyhistor's Περὶ Ἰουδαίων), and in fragments cited by Clement of Alexandria and Pseudo-Eustathius.[2] The date of the *Exagoge* has been the subject of consider-

---

[1] *Eusebius Werke*, 8: *Die Praeparatio Evangelica*, part 1: *Einleitung, die Bücher I bis X*, ed. K. Mras, 2d ed. revised by É. des Places, GCS (Berlin: Akademie, 1982) 524.

[2] Extant portions of Ezekiel's drama, estimated to be about 20 to 25% of the original and consisting of 269 iambic trimeters, are to be found first in Eusebius' *Praeparatio Evangelica* 9.28-29 (see the previous note); second in Clement of Alexandria's *Stromata* 1.23.155-56

able discussion. The author demonstrated knowledge of the LXX, which argues for a date subsequent to its translation. Fragments of the *Exagoge* appear in Alexander Polyhistor's Περὶ Ἰουδαίων (written sometime in the first century BCE) indicating a date prior to the middle of the first century BCE for Ezekiel's drama. K. Kuiper (1903) argued for a date during or just after the time of Ptolemy Euergetes III (died 221 BCE), mainly on the basis of Ezekiel's mention of the legendary phoenix.[3] R. G. Robertson argued for a somewhat later date in the first half of the second century BCE based on the polemic against hellenistic Jewish poets using biblical material for their dramas in the *Epistle of Aristeas* (lines 312-16) and on the probability that Ezekiel's work employed a recension of the LXX text.[4] P. W. van der Horst suggested a date in the second quarter of the second century BCE citing affinities with Daniel 7 and *Jubilees* 47-49.[5] H. Jacobson in his major commentary *The* Exagoge *of Ezekiel* (1983) argued for a slightly later date in the second half of the second century BCE.[6] In any case there is a consensus that the *Exagoge* should be dated sometime in the second century BCE, making this work the earliest known source to allude to an ascent of Moses to heaven at the time he went up Mt. Sinai to receive the Torah.

One of the most curious passages in the extant portion of the *Exagoge* alludes to a tradition concerning Moses' heavenly ascent at the giving of the Torah. According to P. W. van der Horst this passage is one of the earliest extant examples of a *merkabah* vision, which also contains the earliest known instance of the idea of a viceregent or plenipotentiary of God (Moses).[7] It occurs in what is apparently the second act, when Moses had a dream which was interpreted by his father-in-law.[8] Moses' dream in the *Exagoge* has some similarities to those of Jo-

---

(*Clemens Alexandrinus*, 2: *Stromata Buch I-VI*, ed. O. Stählin; revised by L. Früchtel; 4th ed. with addenda by U. Treu, GCS [Berlin: Akademie, 1985]); and third in (Pseudo)-Eustathius' *Commentarius in Hexaëmeron*, PG 18, col. 729. It is important to note that Mras, in his edition of Eusebius' *Die Praeparatio Evangelica* (see the previous note) attempted to reconstruct Eusebius' text of Ezekiel. On the other hand B. Snell attempted to reconstruct the text of Ezekiel's work itself in *Tragicorum Graecorum Fragmenta* 1 (Göttingen: Vandenhoeck u. Ruprecht, 1971) 288-301.

[3] K. Kuiper, "Le Poète Juif Ezéchiel," *REJ* 46 (1903) 161-77.

[4] R. G. Robertson, "Ezekiel the Tragedian," in *OTP* 2.803-804.

[5] P. W. van der Horst, "Some Notes on the *Exagoge* of Ezekiel," in *Essays on the Jewish World of Early Christianity* (Freiburg [Schweiz]: Universitätsverlag; Göttingen: Vandenhoeck u. Ruprecht, 1990) 72-93, esp. 74-5. This article is a review of H. Jacobson's commentary on the *Exagoge* (see the following note).

[6] H. Jacobson, *The* Exagoge *of Ezekiel* (Cambridge: Cambridge University Press, 1983) 5-13.

[7] P. W. van der Horst, "Moses' Throne Vision in Ezekiel the Dramatist," in *Essays on the Jewish World of Early Christianity* (Freiburg [Schweiz]: Universitätsverlag; Göttingen: Vandenhoeck u. Ruprecht, 1990) 64.

[8] The use of the dream as a dramatic device is paralleled in the tragedies of Aeschylus and

seph (Gen 37:9) and Daniel (Dan 7:13-14), although as E. Starobinski-Safran observed, Ezekiel had departed entirely from the Exodus account at this point and engaged in a free creation.[9] The dream was related by Moses to his father-in-law (here called Raguel [= Reuel]) who then interpreted the dream.[10] The text of Moses' dream in the *Exagoge* is as follows:

Ἔ[δο]ξ᾽ ὄρους κατ᾽ ἄκρα Σιν[αί]ου θρόνον
μέγαν τιν᾽ εἶναι μέχρι᾽ς οὐρανοῦ πτύχας,
ἐν τῷ καθῆσθαι φῶτα γενναῖόν τινα
διάδημ᾽ ἔχοντα καὶ μέγα σκῆπτρον χερὶ
εὐωνύμῳ μάλιστα. δεξιᾷ δέ μοι
ἔνευσε, κἀγὼ πρόσθεν ἐστάθην θρόνου.
σκῆπτρον δέ μοι πάρδωκε καὶ εἰς θρόνον μέγαν
εἶπεν καθῆσθαι· βασιλικὸν δ᾽ ἔδωκέ μοι
διάδημα καὶ αὐτὸς ἐκ θρόνων χωρίζεται.
ἐγὼ δ᾽ ἐσεῖδον γῆν ἅπασαν ἔγκυκλον
καὶ ἔνερθε γαίας καὶ ἐξύπερθεν οὐρανοῦ,
καί μοί τι πλῆθος ἀστέρων πρὸς γούνατα
ἔπιπτ᾽, ἐγὼ δὲ πάντας ἠριθμησάμην,
κἀμοῦ παρῆγεν ὡς παρεμβολὴ βροτῶν.
εἶτ᾽ ἐμφοβηθεὶς ἐξανίσταμ᾽ ἐξ ὕπνου.[11]

In the dream Moses described his vision of a gigantic throne on the peak of Mt. Sinai, so large it appeared to touch the clouds of heaven. On the throne sat a man (φῶς)[12] with crown and scepter. This regal image may be related to the Danielic vision of the son of man and the 'Ancient of Days' (Dan 7:9-13); the scepter also played an important

---

other classical dramatists. See P. W. van der Horst, "Moses' Throne Vision in Ezekiel the Dramatist," 66.

[9] E. Starobinski-Safran, "Un poète judéo-hellénistique: Ezéchiel le tragique," *MH* 31 (1974) 216-24.

[10] Further discussion of the different traditions about the name of Moses' father-in-law may be found in W. F. Albright, "Jethro, Hobab, and Reuel in Early Hebrew Tradition," *CBQ* 25 (1963) 1-11.

[11] The Greek text of the *Exagoge* is from *Tragicorum Graecorum Fragmenta* 1, ed. B. Snell (Göttingen: Vandenhoeck u. Ruprecht, 1971) 292. A similar (but not identical) version of the passage is found in *Eusebius Werke*, 8: *Die Praeparatio Evangelica*, part 1: *Einleitung, die Bücher I bis X*, ed. K. Mras, 2d ed. revised by É. des Places, GCS (Berlin: Akademie, 1982) 529. The reading Σιν[αί]ου in the first line of the quotation is based on a conjecture originally made by Dübner in 1846 and accepted today by most editors, including Snell and Jacobson. Jacobson noted that a (medieval?) Hebrew translation of this scene (both the dream and Raguel's interpretation) exists which makes no mention of Sinai but has instead "on top of a high mountain" (Jacobson, *The* Exagoge *of Ezekiel*, 200, note 4). However, since the date and provenance of the Hebrew translation cannot at present be determined, it does not provide a basis for emendation of the Greek text. Whether Sinai is explicitly mentioned or not has little bearing on the overall significance of this text for our study, since (1) it clearly concerns Moses and (2) it precedes the account of the burning bush in the *Exagoge*, which suggests the dream refers to the Sinai ascent rather than an enthronement at Moses' death.

[12] This is a poetic term for man attested in Homer and the later poets.

role in Esth 5:1-2. When Moses approached the throne he was told to sit on it and take the crown and scepter. The imagery of the crown and scepter, as Jacobson noted, points to a transfer of regal authority and has a number of biblical and post-biblical parallels.[13] Most striking, however, is the summons to Moses to mount the divine throne. Jacobson suggested that the Jewish tradition here might be related to Ps 110:1, which continues (as does the *Exagoge*) with the transfer of the scepter and a prophecy of future dominion.[14] From the throne Moses looked on the whole earth all around (γῆν ἄπασαν ἔγκυκλον) and at things under the earth (ἔνερθε γαίας) and above the heavens (ἐξύπερθεν οὐρανοῦ). After this a multitude of stars fell at Moses' feet and he counted up their number (possibly referring to the imagery of Joseph's dream in Gen 37:9).[15] Finally Moses told how he awoke in terror from the dream. In the following section of the *Exagoge* the scepter, throne, and crown of the dream were interpreted by Moses' father-in-law as a reference to his accession as a ruler, while Moses' looking all around was related to his seeing of things present, past, and future (perhaps intended to refer to Moses' prophetic activity).

Van der Horst compared this passage in the *Exagoge* with other later *merkabah* literature, especially chapters 3-15 of the *Hebrew Book of Enoch* (referred to as *3 Enoch* by H. Odeberg).[16] Although this work is late (probably composed after the fourth century CE, much of its material is traditional and therefore considerably older.[17] The story told in *3 Enoch* 10:1-14:5 of Enoch (who is identified with the highest angel Metatron) shows a number of striking similarities with what is said of Moses in this passage of the *Exagoge*. God makes a throne for Enoch similar to the throne of glory, God's own throne (*3 Enoch* 10:1). Enoch is given a garment of glory and a royal crown (12:1-3). God makes Enoch ruler over all kingdoms and all heavenly beings (10:3). The angels of the sun, moon, stars and planets all fall prostrate when Enoch sits on his throne (14:1-5). God reveals to Enoch all the secrets and mysteries of heaven and earth so that Enoch knows the past, present and future (10:5; 11:1). God even calls Enoch "the little Yahweh" (*3 Enoch*

---

[13] The transfer of the scepter calls to mind Gen 49:10 and later extra-biblical parallels according to Jacobson, *The* Exagoge *of Ezekiel*, 91.

[14] Jacobson, *The* Exagoge *of Ezekiel*, 90; also note 6, 200.

[15] This may also be connected with Ps 147:4 where it is God who counts the number of stars.

[16] Odeberg's edition of the text of this work is *3 Enoch or the Hebrew Book of Enoch* (Cambridge: Cambridge University Press, 1928; rpt. with prolegomenon by J. Greenfield, New York: KTAV, 1973) A more modern translation is provided by P. Alexander in *OTP* 1.223-315 (which also refers to the work as *3 Enoch*).

[17] P. Alexander in *OTP* 1.225-9; see also P. S. Alexander, "The Historical Setting of the Hebrew Book of Enoch," *JJS* 28 (1977) 156-80.

12:5). As Horst noted, some of these elements also occur in the earlier *1 Enoch* and *2 Enoch*.[18] However, there is one striking difference between the throne vision of Moses in the *Exagoge* and the throne scene with Enoch in *3 Enoch* 10:1-14:5. In Moses' vision in the *Exagoge* there is only one throne, which is God's. Moses is told to be seated on it—not at God's side, but alone on God's throne. This scene appears to be unique in early Jewish literature and according to van der Horst "certainly implies a deification of Moses."[19] This tends to confirm the conclusions reached by W. A. Meeks that in some Jewish circles Moses was regarded as a divine being and that this was associated with a heavenly enthronement at the time of the Sinai theophany.[20]

Based on the imagery involved (regardless of debate over the status of Moses' deification) it seems clear that a tradition of Moses' heavenly ascent at Sinai is reflected in the *Exagoge* at this point. Although the sequence takes place in a dream and is not portrayed as a real occurrence, it does illustrate a connection between Moses as a historical figure (the way he is presented in the Pentateuch) and the literary development of Moses as a mystical or mythical figure that we have already encountered in the later rabbinic literature.[21] What we are seeing in the *Exagoge* of Ezekiel the Tragedian, as early as the first part of the second century BCE, are the beginning traces of a tradition which held that Moses, when he went up Sinai to receive the Torah, made a heavenly ascent and was enthroned there or perhaps even deified.[22] As Jacobson stated, "Here, in other words, we find evidence for a tradition of Moses' ascent of Sinai which included the divine throne."[23]

B. THE WRITINGS OF PHILO OF ALEXANDRIA

Moses is frequently mentioned in the works of Philo of Alexandria, who

---

[18] Horst, "Moses' Throne Vision in Ezekiel the Dramatist," 67.

[19] Horst, "Moses' Throne Vision in Ezekiel the Dramatist," 67, *contra* I. Gruenwald, *Apocalyptic and Merkavah Mysticism*, AGJU 14 (Leiden: Brill, 1980) 129 n. 8, and M. Hengel, who stated he was "no longer entirely convinced that the second sentence [referring to van der Horst's statement above] is correct," since this would involve an abdication of God (*Studies in Early Christology* [Edinburgh: Clark, 1995] 190-91).

[20] W. A. Meeks, "Moses as God and King," in *Religions in Antiquity: Essays in Memory of E. R. Goodenough*, SHR 14, ed. J. Neusner (Leiden: Brill, 1968) 354-71; see esp. 370-71. Meeks does not specifically discuss this passage in the *Exagoge* but his conclusions based on other texts would appear to be confirmed here.

[21] Along these lines see L. Cerfaux, "Influence des mystères sur le Judaisme alexandrine avant Philon," *Mus* 37 (1924) 36-48.

[22] *Pace* R. G. Robertson (see n. 4 above), who thought it was still sufficient to say that both the content and function of Moses' dream in the dramatic narrative may be adequately accounted for by the author's knowledge of the Greek tragedians and the content of the OT.

[23] Jacobson, *The* Exagoge *of Ezekiel*, 90.

wrote as an approximate contemporary of Jesus in the first half of the first century CE. A number of these references suggest that Philo may have known contemporary traditions about a heavenly ascent of Moses at the giving of Torah.

In *De Somniis* 1.36 Philo stated that while on Mt. Sinai Moses was in an incorporeal state as he listened to the divine music of the cosmos. The music created in him such longing that he neglected to eat for forty days and may have been the cause of his incorporeal experience, since after listening to it, Moses was said to have "become bodiless" (ἀσώμα-τον γενόμενον).[24] Philo in other places implied that Moses not only heard this celestial music, but became part of it himself, because on Mt. Sinai he came to "stand with" God, i.e., share God's immutability, participating in the divine nature. Philo mentioned this special relationship that Moses came to share with God on at least three occasions, each time in connection with an interpretive comment on the text of Deut 5:31: *De Posteritate Caini* 28-31, *De Confusione Linguarum* 30-32, and *De Sacrificiis Abelis et Caini* 8 (in the last-named work Deut 5:31 is applied to Moses' translation at death rather than to his ascent of Sinai to receive the law). A similar idea is also found in *Quaestiones et Solutiones in Exodum* 2.29 where Philo said that Moses, after he had left all mortal categories behind, was "changed into the divine" so that he might "become kin to God and truly divine."[25] The imagery of the celestial music appears again in *Quod Deus Immutabilis sit* 23-26, where it was said that the soul of Moses became like a lyre, in perfect tune with the virtues, producing the symphony of a life in which the ideal virtues were perfectly expressed in actions. In *Legum Allegoriae* 3.141-143 Moses' ability to live for forty days without material food, sustained by the divine communications he received from God as God gave his laws (χρησμῶν θεοῦ νομοθετοῦντος), was seen as a demonstration of his complete renunciation of the physical body.

Even more explicit references concerning Moses' heavenly ascent can also be found in Philo: according to *De Mutatione Nominum* 7 Moses, "the explorer of nature which lies beyond our vision," ascended "into the darkness" (εἰς γὰρ τὸν γνόφον), that is, into "the invisible and incorporeal existence" (τὴν ἀόρατον καὶ ἀσώματον οὐσίαν αἰνιτ-τόμενοι) in order to attempt to search "everywhere and into everything" (πάντα διὰ πάντων ἐρευνήσας). When Moses ascended Mt.

---

[24] The Greek text is from *Philonis Alexandrini, Opera quae supersunt*, ed. L. Cohn (Berlin: Georg Reimer, 1902; reprint ed., Walter de Gruyter, 1962) 3.212. All the following quotations from the Greek of Philo are from Cohn's edition unless otherwise noted.

[25] *Philo*, Supplement 2: *Questions and Answers on Exodus*, trans. R. Marcus, LCL (Cambridge, MA: Harvard University Press, 1953) 70. The Greek text of this work has not survived; the edition cited is a translation from the Armenian.

Sinai in *Quaestiones et Solutiones in Exodum* 2.27-52 he took with him
Aaron, Nadab, and Abihu, but these could not stand the glorious rays
from God's presence, which appeared as flame. Only Moses could go
onward toward the presence of God. The rays were not really flame, but
only appeared to be so (2.47). When Moses went up into this glory, he
went beyond the heaven into God himself, and there abided (2.40). The
clouds which the people saw, into which Moses disappeared, were only
a sign of the intelligibles, a mere figure to be used in teaching them
(2.52).

Finally, in *De Vita Mosis* 1.158 Philo may have employed a midrashic
tradition which had already interpreted Moses' ascent of Sinai as a
heavenly ascent.[26] Here Moses was said to have "entered into the darkness where God was" (εἴς τε τὸν γνόφον, ἔνθα ἦν ὁ θεός, εἰσελθεῖν
λέγεται), an allusion to Exod 20:21, which Philo then interpreted as entrance into the "unseen and invisible substance which is the immaterial
model of all things" (εἰς τὴν ἀειδῆ[27] καὶ ἀόρατον καὶ ἀσώματον τῶν
ὄντων παραδειγματικὴν οὐσίαν), that is (as in *Quaes. Ex.* 2.40), beyond
heaven and into the very presence of God himself.

Although some of the references to Moses' ascent of Sinai in Philo
probably represent no more than the assertion of a mystical (incorporeal) experience on the part of Moses, the last one mentioned, *De Vita
Mosis* 1.158, seems to go beyond this and affirm that Moses actually entered into the presence of God. Later when Philo described Moses'
translation (ascension) at death he used terminology strikingly similar to
that which he had used of Moses' ascent of Sinai.[28] In *Quaestiones et
Solutiones in Genesin* 1.86 Philo stated directly that three individuals,
Enoch (of whom he was speaking), the 'protoprophet' (ὁ πρωτοπρο-
φήτης, a reference to Moses), and Elijah, were all translated to heaven. In
the case of the latter, "it would be more proper and correct to say, he
ascended" (ἀνέβη).[29] In *De Sacrificiis Abelis et Caini* 8 Moses was

---

[26] W. A. Meeks stated: "The implication is that Philo is uniting the Hellenistic ideology of
kingship with an existing midrash which interpreted Moses' ascent of Sinai as a mystical
'ascension'" (*The Prophet-King: Moses Traditions and the Johannine Christology* [Leiden:
Brill, 1967] 111). A similar point was made by D. C. Smith ("The Ephesian Heresy and the
Origin of the Epistle to the Ephesians," *OJRS* 5 [1977] 95).

[27] E. R. Goodenough noted that all manuscripts and editors agreed on reading ἀειδῆ here,
which usually meant "formless" but here seemed to mean "unseen," parallel with the following
term ἀόρατον (*By Light, Light: The Mystic Gospel of Judaism* [New Haven: Yale University
Press, 1935; reprint ed. Amsterdam: Philo, 1969] 186 n. 33). Goodenough suggested the text
should be amended to read ἀιδῆ, although a passage in one manuscript of Plato's *Phaedo*
(79a) reads ἀειδῆ for ἀιδῆ as here. A scribal corruption is probably responsible for the variation.

[28] This observation was made by W. A. Meeks (*The Prophet-King: Moses Traditions and
the Johannine Christology*, 124-25).

[29] *Philo, Supplement 1: Questions and Answers on Genesis*, trans. R. Marcus, LCL (Cam-

said to have been "translated" (μετανίσταται) at his death. In *De Vita Mosis* 2.288 Philo stated that at the end of his life Moses had to make an "emigration (ἀποικίαν) from earth to heaven, abandoning this mortal life to be made immortal" (τὸν θνητὸν ἀπολιπὼν βίον ἀπαθανατίζεσθαι). The similarities in terminology between Philo's description of Moses' ascent of Sinai and his description of Moses' ascension to heaven at the end of his life strongly suggest that Philo was aware of traditions which associated Moses with a heavenly ascent. Furthermore (as far as Philo was concerned) these could be applied equally to either event in Moses' life. Thus the ascent of Sinai to receive the Torah could legitimately be viewed as an ascent to heaven, an ascent Moses made a second time at the end of his earthly life. The evidence from Philo's writings indicates that a tradition of Moses' ascent to heaven, both at the giving of the Torah at Sinai and later at the end of his life, was circulating at or before the time Philo wrote, prior to about 45 CE (the probable date of Philo's death). Of course this would also be prior to the composition of Ephesians.

Yet another passage in *Quaestiones et Solutiones in Genesin* mentions both an ascent and a descent in connection with Moses. *Quaes. Gen.* 4.29 reads:

> But it is necessary that the most pure and luminous mind should be mixed with the mortal (element) for necessary uses. This is what is indicated by the heavenly ladder, (where) not only an ascent but also a descent of the angels is mentioned. And this is what is said of the prophet, (namely) his descent and ascent reveal the swift turning and change of his thoughts.[30]

It is clear that "the prophet" here refers to Moses. Philo's reference was probably to the account of Moses' ascent of Mt. Sinai in Exod 19:17-25. Although heaven is not specifically named as the locus of the ascent, the previous sentence does speak of the ascent and descent of angels on the "heavenly ladder" (an allusion to Jacob's vision in Gen 28:12ff.). When taken together with the following reference to Moses, there are in these two sentences two references to ascent and descent, arranged in Philo's text in chiastic order: ascent—descent (referring to the angels) and descent—ascent (referring to Moses). This sequence of ascents and descents is particularly suggestive in light of the similar chiastic arrangement of ascents and descents found in Eph 4:8-10.[31] In ad-

---

bridge, MA: Harvard University Press, 1953) 54. This work, like *Quaestiones et Solutiones in Exodum*, is translated from an Armenian version since only a small portion of the original Greek text has survived.

[30] *Philo*, Supplement 1: *Questions and Answers on Genesis*, 304. Parentheses are those of the translator. See the previous note concerning the reason for citing an English translation of *Quaestiones et Solutiones in Genesin*.

[31] See the discussion of the chiastic structure of Eph 4:8-10 in ch. 6, 180.

dition to this chiastic arrangement of ascents and descents, Philo's use of such imagery in *Quaes. Gen.* 4.29 is important because (unlike his other references to a heavenly ascent by Moses) this one explicitly mentions a descent in conjunction with the ascent. It is also worth noting that in *Quaes. Gen.* 4.29 multiple ascents and descents of Moses must be in view, because the descent is mentioned first (which must be taken to imply a prior ascent).[32] There can be little doubt that Philo wrote this prior to the composition of Ephesians. Thus we may reasonably conclude that not only were traditions concerning Moses' heavenly ascent in circulation at the time, but also traditions which linked together references to both ascent and descent in connection with Moses.

C. THE *BIBLICAL ANTIQUITIES* OF PSEUDO-PHILO

Pseudo-Philo's *Biblical Antiquities* is generally dated between 135 BCE and 100 CE, with a date in the first half of the first century (around the time of Jesus) considered most likely by D. J. Harrington.[33] There are several passages which have been understood to refer to an ascent of Moses to heaven. We shall examine each of these in turn to see if a heavenly ascent is really implied. The first is *Bib. Ant.* 11:15: when the Lord spoke the Decalogue to Israel at Sinai, he called Moses to himself on the mountain. The text says that Moses "drew near the cloud, knowing that God was there," but does not explicitly state that Moses went up to heaven.[34] Moses was detained by God for forty days and forty nights, during which he was shown the tree of life.[35] One could understand the text to mean that Moses was shown a vision of the tree of life while on the mountain (later in the same paragraph the author stated that Moses was shown the likeness of the tabernacle and its contents). But with regard to the tree of life, the text goes on to note that Moses cut off a branch, which he kept with him and later threw into the waters of Marah to purify them.[36] Thus the author apparently intended to portray the tree of life as actually present, and this implies that Moses had made the ascent to paradise (heaven).

At the beginning of the next chapter (12:1) a similar claim was made concerning Moses' descent. Moses had been bathed with invisible light in the presence of God, and as he descended he "went down to the

---

[32] It is also possible to explain the order with regard to Moses as a result of the chiastic arrangement with the ascent and descent of the angels in the preceding sentence, however.

[33] D. J. Harrington, "Pseudo-Philo," in *OTP* 2.299.

[34] Harrington, *OTP* 2.319.

[35] Presumably the one planted in paradise, an allusion to Gen 2:9.

[36] An allusion to Exod 15:25.

place where the light of the sun and the moon are; and the light of his face surpassed the splendor of the sun and the moon."[37] It is clear that the author at this point portrayed Moses as being in heaven rather than just atop Mt. Sinai, since as he descended he passed "the place where the light of the sun and the moon are," probably a reference to the intermediate place between earth and heaven where the sun, moon, and stars were located.[38]

Another passage in *Biblical Antiquities* which is sometimes understood to imply that Moses made an ascent to heaven is 19:10-12. Unlike the two former passages, however, this one speaks not of Moses' ascent of Sinai to receive the Torah, but of his ascent of Mt. Nebo just prior to his death.[39] As in the account in Deut 34:1-8, the Lord showed Moses the land of Canaan from the mountain prior to his death. The account in *Bib. Ant.* 19:10 goes on to state other things shown to Moses, however: the place from which the clouds draw water to water the earth, the land of Egypt, the place from which only the holy land is watered, and the place from which manna was rained on the Israelites, "even unto the paths of paradise."[40] Although one could conclude from these statements that Moses had been taken up to heaven, they may also be understood to refer to events and places seen in a vision. This is probably preferable, since *Bib. Ant.* 19:12-16 records the death of Moses and his burial by God "with his own hands on a high place and in the light of all the world."[41] The sequence of the narrative argues against an ascension of Moses to heaven in *Bib. Ant.* 19:10 just *prior* to his death. The wording of the account, in any case, is sufficiently ambiguous to preclude certainty regarding a heavenly ascent.

In contrast to these statements, which affirm the reality of Moses' death and burial, one final passage in the *Biblical Antiquities* speaks of Moses' entrance into heaven. According to *Bib. Ant.* 32:9 Moses was shown various things prior to his death (as in 19:10-16), but then God said to him,"Let there be as a witness between me and you and my people the heaven that you are to enter and the earth on which you

---

[37] *Bib. Ant.* 12:1, in *OTP* 2.319.

[38] The cosmology of the author of the *Biblical Antiquities* was not clearly stated, but this seems to be a reasonable assumption based on what is known about contemporary beliefs.

[39] The name of the mountain Moses ascended in *Bib. Ant.* 19:10 is not clear; one variant is "Horeb," but the translator (D. J. Harrington) noted that this was "certainly wrong in the light of Deut. 32:49" (*OTP* 2.327, note j). Harrington supplied "Abarim" but noted that perhaps "Nebo" should be read (cf. Deut 32:49).

[40] *Bib. Ant.* 19:10, *OTP* 2.328.

[41] The last statement may imply that Moses' death and burial (although not the exact location) took place in public. Moses' death was also asserted in Josephus' *Jewish Antiquities* 4.8.48 (§326), and Testament of Moses (Assumption of Moses) 1:15 explicitly emphasized that Moses' death took place in public. All the aforementioned statements may indicate conscious opposition to the view that Moses did not really die, but was taken up to heaven.

walk until now.'"[42] It may be that this was in direct contradiction to
19:12, where Moses was told that he was to 'sleep' until God returned
to resurrect him; but it is also possible that 32:9 simply omitted reference
to the intervening period between Moses' death and his resurrection to
enter heaven at some later time. In any event, *Bib. Ant.* 32:9 is concerned with events at the end of Moses' life and not with his ascent of
Sinai to receive the Torah.

While these last two passages (*Bib. Ant.* 19:10-12 and 32:9) are concerned with events surrounding Moses' death, the two first-mentioned
passages (11:15 and 12:1) do apparently reflect a belief that Moses ascended to heaven when he went up Mt. Sinai to receive the Torah. Although the *Biblical Antiquities* cannot be dated precisely, the work
almost certainly belongs to the first century CE. Thus we have in *Bib.
Ant.* 11:15 and 12:1 some evidence that a tradition of a heavenly ascent
was associated with Moses' ascent of Mt. Sinai to receive the Torah at
least as early as the first century CE.

D. THE TESTAMENT OF MOSES (ASSUMPTION OF MOSES)

The surviving document known as the Testament of Moses or the Assumption of Moses is a Latin translation from an older Greek manuscript
which purports to be the farewell address given by Moses to his chosen
successor Joshua just prior to his death and the entry of the Israelites
into the land of Canaan. The work presents enormous difficulties for the
interpreter because of disputes over its date and identification and also
because the end of the document is obviously missing. We must consider these difficulties briefly before examining any of the extant passages relevant to Moses' heavenly ascent.

There is no current consensus concerning the date of the Testament
of Moses; opinions vary widely. They may be generally divided into
three categories: (1) those who would date the document in the first half
of the second century CE, probably just after the war of 132-135 CE (a
position argued by S. Zeitlin);[43] (2) those who would argue for a very
early date, sometime during the Maccabean war of 168-165 BCE
(supported by J. Licht and G. Nickelsburg);[44] and (3) those who would

---

[42] *Bib. Ant.* 32:9, *OTP* 2.346.

[43] S. Zeitlin, "The Assumption of Moses and the Bar Kokhba Revolt," *JQR* 38 (1947-48)
1-45.

[44] J. Licht, "Taxo, or the Apocalyptic Doctrine of Vengeance," *JJS* 12 (1961) 95-103. In
addition, G. W. E. Nickelsburg, Jr argued for a Maccabean date based on a form-critical analysis
of the document and the contents of chs. 8 and 9, which he believed to contain a description of
the persecutions under Antiochus Epiphanes (*Resurrection, Immortality, and Eternal Life in
Intertestamental Judaism*, HTS 26 [Cambridge, MA: Harvard University Press, 1972] 28-31;

place the composition of the document in the first century CE, before
the destruction of Jerusalem in 70 CE (R. H. Charles and J. Priest).[45] In
his recent critical edition of the Assumption of Moses J. Tromp favored a
date for the work in the early first century CE.[46] On the whole, a date in
the first century before 70 CE seems most probable, since in order to argue for a Maccabean date one must regard chapter 6 (at least) as a later
interpolation because Test. Moses 6:6 almost certainly refers to the reign
of Herod the Great. The number given for the years of this king's rule,
thirty-four, agrees exactly with the reign of Herod and no other, assuming no corruption of the text in the process of transmission.[47]

Another problem is the proper identification of the document itself.
Mention of apocryphal works associated with the name of Moses occurs frequently in early sources of both Jewish and Christian origin.[48]
Some lists of noncanonical books include both an Assumption of Moses
and a Testament of Moses, raising questions as to whether the surviving
document should be identified as one or the other.[49] Ever since A. Ceriani identified the existing document on the basis of a passage from the
Acts of the Council of Nicea that appears to cite 1:14 (and perhaps parts
of 1:6 and 1:9) as the Assumption of Moses, it has become common to
refer to the document presently under discussion as the Assumption of
Moses.[50] This is open to question, however, since the form of the extant
document is that of a farewell address or testament, a well-established
literary genre in its own right, and the document ends at 12:13 in the
middle of a sentence, so that it is impossible to know how Moses' death
was described. R. H. Charles proposed that there were originally two
separate works, a farewell address and an assumption account, that at an
early period were joined together and the combined document was subsequently known as the Assumption of Moses.[51] As attractive as this
theory may be, it cannot be proven, and we have followed J. Priest in

---

see esp. 43-45). Nickelsburg was forced to consider ch. 6 a later interpolation, however, since
there is virtually universal agreement that it referred to the reign and death of Herod the Great
and mentioned his three sons.

45 R. H. Charles, ed., *APOT* 2.411, and J. Priest, "The Testament of Moses," *OTP* 1.920-21.
Priest did not accept Charles' theory of a dislocation of the text in chs. 5-9, however, arguing
that contemporary canons of consistency need not apply to an apocalyptic author.

46 J. Tromp, *The Assumption of Moses: A Critical Edition with Commentary*, SVTP 10
(Leiden: Brill, 1993) 116.

47 Tromp, *The Assumption of Moses*, 202; also Priest, *OTP* 1.930. Both view the exact
number of years mentioned as decisive for a reference to Herod the Great.

48 A listing of these sources may be found in J. H. Charlesworth (*The Pseudepigrapha and
Modern Research*, SCS 7 [Missoula, MT: Scholars Press, 1976] 159-66).

49 A collection of these lists, with brief discussion, is found in D. S. Russell (*The Method
and Message of Jewish Apocalyptic* [Philadelphia: Westminster, 1964] 391-95).

50 A. M. Denis, *Fragmenta pseudepigraphorum quae supersunt graeca*, PVTG (Leiden:
Brill, 1970) 63-64.

51 R. H. Charles, ed., *APOT* 2.208.

referring to the existing document as the Testament of Moses on the basis of its predominant literary genre.[52]

There is no explicit reference in the surviving document to Moses' ascent of Mt. Sinai to receive the Torah or to his assumption to heaven at his death. In fact, the passages in the extant document which do refer to Moses' death appear to speak of a natural death and a burial of the body. The first of these is 1:15, spoken by Moses:

> ...the time of the years of my life is fulfilled, and I will go the the resting-place of my fathers, and before the entire people.[53]

This is so strongly worded that it may actually constitute a polemic against a tradition which asserted Moses' assumption to heaven, since it stresses the public nature of Moses' death as an event witnessed by the entire community.[54] This suggests that such an assumption tradition was in circulation at the time Test. Moses 1:15 was written, and the author of the Testament wished to discredit it. Another explicit reference to Moses' impending death is found in 10:11-12 and 14:

> But you, Joshua son of Nun, keep these words and this book. For from my death, my being taken away, until his advent, there will be 250 times that will happen... But I shall go the the resting-place of my fathers.[55]

The word *receptio*, translated "taken away" in 10:12, is sometimes rendered as "assumption" and understood as an interpolation attempting to relate the present document to an assumption of Moses. This is unlikely, however, since 10:14 stated explicitly that Moses would be "asleep with...[his] fathers," a clear reference in the same context to his death and burial, a state in which he would remain until the resurrection. An assumption immediately following his death would be very difficult to reconcile with such a statement. The word *receptio* does not necessarily have to refer to an assumption to heaven, however; as Tromp points out it may simple mean something like "be taken (to the realm of death)."[56] A final allusion to Moses' death occurs in Joshua's speech in 11:8:

---

[52] J. Priest, "The Testament of Moses," *OTP* 1.919-34. Tromp uses the name 'Assumption of Moses' which follows Ceriani and Charles and is probably more widely accepted.

[53] Test. Moses 1:15, Tromp, *Assumption of Moses*, 6-7. Priest's translation in *OTP* is similar: "The years of my life have come to an end and, in the presence of the entire community, I am going to sleep with my fathers" (*OTP* 1.927).

[54] See n. 41 above for a possible parallel in the *Biblical Antiquities* of Pseudo-Philo.

[55] Test. Moses 10:11-12, 14, Tromp, *Assumption of Moses*, 20-21. Priest translates the same passage: "But you, Joshua son of Nun, keep these words and this book, for from my death and burial until his coming there will pass 250 times... However, I shall be asleep with my fathers" (*OTP* 1.933).

[56] Tromp, *Assumption of Moses*, 239.

> For all who die when their time has come have a grave in the earth. But your grave extends from the East to the West, and from the North to the extreme South. The entire world is your grave.[57]

The reference to Moses' grave (*sepultura*) is somewhat obscure; it could perhaps be taken to mean that Moses' final resting place was not in the earth at all but that he was taken up to heaven. This is unlikely, however, since nothing else in the existing document refers explicitly to an assumption. It is far more probable that the writer is simply referring to the account of Moses' death in Deut 34:6 which stated that no one knew the location of Moses' grave. In connection with this is the thought of grandeur: if a monument could be built in keeping with Moses' glory, it would cover the entire earth.[58]

Because of the difficulties in dating the Testament and questions concerning its relation to another document known as the Assumption of Moses, we must be cautious in drawing inferences from it about traditions of Moses' heavenly ascent. It is clear that no mention is made in the surviving document of any ascent of Moses at Mt. Sinai to receive the Torah; any reference to a heavenly ascent which the document contains would refer to Moses' assumption to heaven at his death, not at the giving of the law. However, as we have seen in our examination of the relevant passages even a reference to Moses' assumption appears unlikely based on the extant form of the document. The most that can be said is that a tradition of Moses' assumption to heaven at death may have been in circulation at the time the Testament was written and the author may have been attempting to counter it by his assertion in 1:15. Such a conclusion gains additional support from similar assertions in other documents of approximately the same period such as the writings of Philo, Pseudo-Philo's *Bib. Ant.* 19:12, 16 and Josephus' *Ant.* 4.8.48 [§326].[59]

E. THE *JEWISH ANTIQUITIES* OF JOSEPHUS

The *magnum opus* of Flavius Josephus, *Antiquitates Judaicae*, contains several passages which concern the giving of the Torah at Sinai and the death of Moses. According to *Ant.* 20 [§267] (the concluding para-

---

[57] Test. Moses 11:8, Tromp, *Assumption of Moses,* 20-21. Priest's translation is similar (*OTP* 1.933).

[58] H. Rönsch pointed out a remarkable parallel to this idea in Thucydides' *Peloponnesian War* 2.43: Pericles praised the brave soldiers who died for their country as having obtained a most glorious grave—not the one in which they were buried, but "the entire world is the grave of excellent men, since their memory lives on throughout the world" ("Miscellen," *ZWT* 28 [1885] 102-4).

[59] See n. 41 above.

graph of the entire work) it was completed in the thirteenth year of Domitian's reign, i.e., 93-94 CE, although a second edition with additional material appears to have been produced some time after the death of Agrippa II around 100 CE. It is fairly certain in any case that the *Antiquities* dates from around the close of the first century CE.

The first reference to Moses' ascent is found in *Ant.* 3.5.3 [§88], when Moses appeared to the Israelites after his descent from Sinai and told them (among other things) that he had come to a sight of God and been a hearer of an immortal voice (τῷ θεῷ γὰρ εἰς ὄψιν ἐλθὼν ἀκροατὴς ἀφθάρτου φωνῆς ἐγενόμην·).[60] This passage does not explicitly assert that Moses had been taken up to heaven. Probably Josephus intended only to say that God had revealed himself to Moses atop Sinai. This is also true of a later passage, *Ant.* 3.5.8 [§99], where Moses described what happened to him during the forty days he was on the mountain with God. Nothing in Moses' description necessitates a heavenly ascent on his part. Josephus portrayed the scene in such a way that everything Moses described could have been revealed to him in the form of a vision. Unlike the passage we examined in Pseudo-Philo's *Biblical Antiquities* (11:15), Moses in this account performed no activity while in the presence of God that suggests he did not remain atop Mt. Sinai but was taken up to heaven itself.

One final passage in Josephus' *Antiquities* deserves attention because it contains elements of imagery which have been associated with a heavenly ascent. However, it is not connected with Moses' ascent of Sinai but with his death. *Ant.* 4.8.48 [§326] records the disappearance of Moses at the end of his life: while he was still speaking with Joshua and Eleazar who had accompanied him, a cloud suddenly descended upon him and he disappeared in a ravine (νέφους αἰφνίδιον ὑπὲρ αὐτὸν στάντος ἀφανίζεται κατά τινος φάραγγος). Josephus immediately went on to state, however, that in the holy books Moses wrote of himself that he died, lest it should be said of him that because of his virtue he had gone back to the Deity (δείσας μὴ δι᾽ ὑπερβολὴν τῆς περὶ αὐτὸν ἀρετῆς πρὸς τὸ θεῖον αὐτὸν ἀναχωρῆσαι τολμήσωσιν εἰπεῖν).[61] This latter statement by Josephus may be intended to counter a tradition that Moses did not die, but was taken up to heaven at the end of his life.[62] The mention of Moses being taken in a cloud is suggestive because such imagery was often connected with a heavenly ascent. But the

---

[60] *Josephus*, trans. H. St J. Thackeray, 4: *Jewish Antiquities, Books I-IV*, LCL (London: Heinemann, 1930) 358.

[61] *Josephus* 4.632. Josephus sided with the rabbis who considered the last eight verses of Deuteronomy to have been written by Moses himself rather than by Joshua.

[62] See also n. 41 above.

presence of such imagery proves little, because Josephus (although he included it in his own account) was quick to add that according to the OT record ("in the holy books") Moses really died. The most we can infer from this account is that the time Josephus wrote a tradition of Moses' assumption to heaven at the end of his life was circulating, and Josephus alluded indirectly to this tradition with the cloud imagery, but then deliberately refuted it by his statements about Moses' death. There is no evidence from Josephus' writings that Moses made the ascent to heaven when he went up Mt. Sinai to receive the Torah.

F. 2 BARUCH (SYRIAC APOCALYPSE OF BARUCH)

This pseudepigraphical work purports to have been written by Baruch, Jeremiah's assistant, shortly after the destruction of Jerusalem in 587 BCE. There is a general consensus today that it was written after the destruction of Jerusalem in 70 CE. E. Kautzsch placed the *terminus ad quem* around 96 CE because of the interrelationship between 2 Baruch and 4 Ezra.[63] A. F. J. Klijn thought that if 2 Baruch were dependent on 4 Ezra a date around 100 CE was most probable, but since dependence of both works on a common source seemed more likely, 2 Baruch was probably somewhat later because it showed a more advanced stage of theological development. Thus Klijn suggested a date for 2 Baruch in the first or second decade of the second century CE.[64]

There are two passages in 2 Baruch which relate to Moses' ascent of Sinai to receive the Torah and which may reflect a tradition of a heavenly ascent. 2 Bar. 4:2-7 contains a description of the heavenly, eternal Jerusalem which supposedly corresponded to the earthly city which was about to be destroyed. In 4:5 the Lord (the speaker) stated that he showed the heavenly city to Moses on Mt. Sinai when Moses was shown the likeness of the tabernacle and its utensils. There is no explicit statement that Moses visited heaven, however. In the context of 2 Baruch 4-5 (which contains a number of visions purportedly given to the author) it is more probable that the author of 2 Baruch merely intended to affirm that Moses was shown a vision of the heavenly Jerusalem.

The second passage which speaks of Moses' time atop Mt. Sinai is 2 Bar. 59:3-11. This section describes in much greater detail the things which were shown to Moses during his stay on the mountain in the presence of God. With typical embellishment (which recalls accounts of

---

[63] *Die Apokryphen und Pseudepigraphen des Alten Testaments*, trans. and ed. by E. Kautzsch, 2: *Die Pseudepigraphen des Alten Testaments* (Hildesheim and New York: Georg Olms, 1975) 407.

[64] A. F. J. Klijn, "2 (Syriac Apocalypse of) Baruch," *OTP* 1.616-17.

the visit of Jonah to the underworld in rabbinic literature)[65] the author
of 2 Baruch recounted what Moses saw:

> But he also showed him, at that time, the measures of fire, the depths of the
> abyss, the weight of the winds, the number of the raindrops, the suppression
> of wrath, the abundance of long-suffering, the truth of judgment, the root of
> wisdom, the richness of understanding, the fountain of knowledge, the height
> of the air, the greatness of Paradise, the end of the periods, the beginning of
> the day of judgment, the number of offerings, the worlds which have not yet
> come, the mouth of hell, the standing place of vengeance, the place of faith,
> the region of hope, the picture of the coming punishment, the multitude of
> the angels which cannot be counted, the powers of the flame, the splendor of
> lightnings, the voice of the thunders, the orders of the archangels, the treas-
> uries of the light, the changes of the times, and the inquiries into the Law.[66]

Again, nothing in the list of things shown to Moses explicitly states that
Moses made a heavenly ascent when he went up Sinai; all the things
seen by Moses could have been visionary. Yet 2 Baruch 59:3, introducing the account quoted above, stated that the heavens were torn asun-
der and those who stood next to the throne of the Almighty trembled
when he took Moses to himself. One could read the account in such a
way that God's taking Moses to himself in 59:3 is understood to mean
that God merely called Moses to himself atop Mt. Sinai. Given the description which follows, however (where the very powers of heaven are
shaken), it is much more probable that the author of 2 Baruch intended
his readers to understand that Moses was taken up into the very presence of God himself. Thus there is in 2 Bar. 59:3 evidence that Moses
was understood to have made a heavenly ascent when he went up Mt.
Sinai to receive the Torah. If assumptions about the dating of 2 Baruch
are correct, such a tradition was probably already in circulation around
100-120 CE.

G. THE *STROMATA* OF CLEMENT OF ALEXANDRIA

In *Stromata* 6.15 Clement (who died before 215 CE) recorded an illustration of how the words of the scriptures were subject to multiple interpretations and different readers perceived different things in them.
The illustration employed by Clement is generally thought to be taken
from the Assumption of Moses, although Clement never mentioned his
source by name. Recording how Joshua and Caleb witnessed the death
and assumption of Moses while caught up by the Spirit, Clement stated:

---

[65] See ch. 2, 59-63, for a description of these accounts.
[66] 2 Baruch 59:5-11, *OTP* 1.642.

εἰκότως ἄρα καὶ τὸν Μωυσέα ἀναλαμβανόμενον διττὸν εἶδεν Ἰησοῦς ὁ τοῦ
Ναυῆ, καὶ τὸν μὲν μετ᾽ ἀγγέλων, τὸν δὲ ἐπὶ τὰ ὄρη περὶ τὰς φάραγγας
κηδείας ἀξιούμενον. εἶδεν δὲ Ἰησοῦς τὴν θέαν ταύτην κάτω πνεύματι ἐπαρ-
θεὶς σὺν καὶ τῷ Χαλέβ, ἀλλ᾽ οὐχ ὁμοίως ἄμφω θεῶνται;δηλούσης, οἶμαι, τῆς
ἱστορίας μὴ πάντων εἶναι τὴν γνῶσιν...⁶⁷

This fragmentary account of Moses' ascent (or assumption) clearly relates to his death and burial, not to his ascent of Sinai to receive the Torah. It is interesting nonetheless, because it may contain a clue to the
manner in which the various ascent-legends connected with Moses re-
conciled his assumption to heaven with the explicit account of his burial
in Deut 34:6. Joshua and Caleb, who were both lifted up by the Spirit
(κάτω πνεύματι ἐπαρθείς), were witnesses of Moses' death, but they
saw him taken up double (τὸν Μωυσέα ἀναλαμβανόμενον διττὸν
εἶδεν): one Moses with the angels, who (it is implied) escorted him to
heaven, and another Moses on the mountains, honored with burial in
their ravines. Thus, while holding to the scriptural account of Moses'
death and burial, one could also claim for him at the same time an assumption to heaven. No mention of Caleb's presence occurs in the biblical account, and although Moses blessed Joshua in Deut 31:23 there is
no indication that he (or anyone else) accompanied Moses up the
mountain or witnessed his death. The extant document known as the
Testament of Moses (or Assumption of Moses) portrays Joshua in dialogue with Moses at the point where it breaks off.⁶⁸ Since the ending is
lost there is no way to determine whether or not Joshua was about to
witness Moses' departure. The idea encountered here in Clement—that
Joshua and Caleb were transported in the Spirit to witness the death of
Moses—may represent one attempt to explain how the account of
Moses' death in Deut 34:1-8 came to be written (since there was no one
present to witness these events).

The reference to Moses' assumption in *Stromata* 6.15 is of little help
in establishing the date of the tradition associating Moses' ascent of Sinai to receive the law with an ascent to heaven. First, it does not deal
with the ascent of Sinai at all, but with a legend of Moses' assumption
to heaven at death. Second, Clement did not mention the source he was
quoting, so we cannot know whether this does in fact represent a quotation from the lost ending of the extant work known as the Testament
of Moses (Assumption of Moses). Clement's own writings date from
some time in the final decades of the second century CE, and although
his source is undoubtedly older, there is no way to establish an inde-

---

⁶⁷ *Stromata* 6.15.132, 2-3, in *Clemens Alexandrinus, 2: Stromata Buch I-VI*, ed. O. Stählin;
revised by L. Früchtel; 4th ed. with addenda by U. Treu, GCS (Berlin: Akademie, 1985) 498.
⁶⁸ See the discussion of this document above, 133-36.

pendent date for it because this source is never specified, nor did Clement quote from it extensively enough to permit independent identification.

H. CONCLUSIONS: MOSES' ASCENT TO HEAVEN AND EPH 4:7-11

In examining the traditions concerning Moses' heavenly ascent at Sinai when he received the Torah, we have discovered a number of significant references which enable us to establish the approximate date of such traditions. The dream of Moses contained in the *Exagoge* of Ezekiel the Tragedian, although it contains no explicit reference to a heavenly ascent of Moses from Mt. Sinai, probably shows the influence of traditions concerning such an ascent by Moses. Thus it is likely that such traditions had their origins at least as early as the middle of the second century BCE, the approximate date of composition of the *Exagoge*. Furthermore, such traditions have almost certainly influenced Philo of Alexandria, writing before the middle of the first century CE. There are numerous references to Moses' ascent of Sinai in Philo's writings as well as several references to Moses' ascension at the end of his life. The similarities in the terminology Philo used to describe both these 'ascensions' suggest that he was indeed aware of traditions related to Moses' ascent to heaven at Sinai when the Torah was given. The *Biblical Antiquities* of Pseudo-Philo, written at about the same time, also indicates awareness of such Moses-traditions; several references imply that Moses made a heavenly ascent when he went up Mt. Sinai.

The surviving document known as the Testament of Moses or the Assumption of Moses also apparently alludes to traditions of an assumption to heaven at Moses' death, although this evidence is not conclusive because the end of the document is missing and it is difficult to date (it may be as late as the early second century CE). In the *Antiquities* of Josephus there may be a polemic against the tradition that Moses ascended to heaven when he died, since Josephus took pains to assert the biblical account of Moses' death and burial; this too points to traditions of a heavenly assumption circulating in the first century CE.

Somewhat later works like 2 Baruch (the Syriac Apocalypse of Baruch) also give evidence of traditions concerning Moses' ascent to heaven and suggest that such traditions were circulating at the beginning of the second century CE. Similar evidence can also be found in the writings of Clement of Alexandria dating from the end of the second century CE. Although it is often suggested that Clement was quoting from the document known as the Assumption of Moses, this cannot be proven, and Clement's account deals with Moses' assumption at death rather than a heavenly ascent at Sinai when the Torah was given.

The later evidence is of little overall value for establishing the earliest possible date for Moses-traditions concerning an ascent to heaven at Sinai and connected with the giving of the law. We have, however, found sufficient evidence in the earlier documents (from the first century CE or before) to warrant the conclusion that traditions concerning Moses' ascent to heaven go back at least as early as the beginning of the present era, and perhaps one or two centuries earlier. This is important for our study of the use of Ps 68:19 in Eph 4:8: while such ascent-traditions concerning Moses are not explicitly connected with the psalm, they appear to have been in general circulation and were probably fairly widespread. This suggests that such traditions of an ascent to heaven by Moses at Mt. Sinai when he received the Torah would have been known to the author of Ephesians, and in his interpretation of Ps 68:19 with reference to Christ's victorious ascent he built upon such Moses-traditions to suit his own purposes in the epistle. (Such references might even have been polemical in nature, but the absence of other disparaging allusions to Moses in Ephesians makes this difficult to prove.) Our case for such a reconstruction will be further strengthened if we can now go on to demonstrate a connection between traditions concerning Moses' ascent of Sinai and the Jewish feast of Pentecost (Weeks) as the celebration of the giving of the Torah. The next chapter will examine the evidence for such a connection in detail.

CHAPTER FIVE

EPH 4:7-11 AND THE GIVING OF THE SPIRIT

As we saw in chapter three, the major exegetical difficulty in Eph 4:8 is the use of ἔδωκεν in the quotation of Ps 68:19, since all extant versions of the LXX (following the Hebrew text) read ἔλαβες at this point. As we have also noted, *Tg*. Psalms reflects the same variation from the Hebrew text and LXX of Ps 68:19 found in Eph 4:8 (*Tg*. Ps 68:19 reads יהבתא where MT reads לקחת).[1] We have explored the possibility (first suggested by Thackeray in 1900) that the author of Ephesians was aware of the targumic interpretation of Ps 68:19 (that is, the oral tradition behind the written targum) and adapted it for his own purposes.[2] Use of such a tradition by the author of Ephesians is particularly significant for the interpretation of the descent mentioned in Eph 4:9-10. *Tg*. Psalms interpreted Ps 68:19 as a reference to Moses, who first ascended Mt. Sinai and 'captured' the words of Torah, which he then brought down and gave as gifts to 'the sons of men'. Since Moses' descent from Sinai to distribute to men the 'gifts' he had obtained there necessarily followed his ascent, use of this tradition by the author of Ephesians would explain why he found it necessary to deduce from the text of Ps 68:19 (as quoted in Eph 4:8) a descent not explicitly mentioned in the psalm, followed by the distribution of the gifts mentioned in Eph 4:11-16. Use of these Moses-traditions by the author of Ephesians would thus imply that the descent of Eph 4:9-10 is most naturally understood as subsequent to the ascent described in the psalm quotation.

Numerous difficulties associated with the dating of the tradition of Moses' ascent to receive the Torah as contained in *Tg*. Psalms were discussed at length in Chapter Three.[3] Our investigation discovered no conclusive evidence from the texts themselves which prove beyond any doubt that the author of Ephesians did in fact make use of the rabbinic interpretation of Ps 68:19 found in *Tg*. Psalms. Neither did we prove that such an interpretation of the psalm actually existed prior to the Christian era. However, while the evidence concerning Ps 68:19 examined thus far has been inconclusive, it still suggests an early date for the interpretation in question. The evidence is both ancient (although not neces-

---

[1] See the extended discussion and comparison of the texts of Ps 68:19 according to the MT, LXX, Eph 4:8, and *Tg*. Ps 68:19 in ch. 3 above, 96-104.

[2] H. St J. Thackeray, *The Relation of St Paul to Contemporary Jewish Thought* (London: Oxford University Press, 1900) 182.

[3] See ch. 3, especially 66-77.

sarily pre-Christian) and widespread. Wide geographical distribution of
the evidence in such a case requires sufficient time for such dissemina-
tion to occur, so that a given tradition would have to be older than any
single surviving written attestation. What we discovered in chapter four
is that traditions associated with Moses' ascent to heaven at Sinai when
he received the Torah (though not conclusively connected to Ps 68:19)
do appear to have circulated prior to the first century CE and thus were
available to the author of Ephesians when he wrote.

We now turn to another line of evidence which offers some promise
of demonstrating a connection between such Moses-traditions, Psalm
68, Pentecost, and Ephesians. Such a connection (in the context of the
spiritual gifts mentioned in Eph 4:11-16) would suggest that the author,
knowing of the interpretation of Ps 68:19 referring to Moses' ascent
and descent with the Torah, chose rather to see in it a reference to
Christ's ascension following his resurrection and the subsequent distribution of the gifts of the Spirit to his followers. Not finding in the quotation from Psalm 68 an explicit reference to the descent of Christ as the
Spirit, however, the author of Ephesians was obliged to deduce one.
The existing tradition of Moses' ascent and descent of Sinai at the giving of Torah had already prepared the way for our author to anticipate a
subsequent descent. This is what led him (in typical rabbinic fashion) to
write verses 9-10 which introduced into the context of Eph 4:7-11 a reference to the descent.

A. PSALM 68, THE EARLY JEWISH SYNAGOGUE
LITURGY, AND PENTECOST

G. B. Caird asserted that during the intertestamental period the feast of
Pentecost, in addition to its traditional role as a harvest festival, had also
come to be viewed as a celebration of the giving of the Torah to Moses
on Mt. Sinai.[4] According to Caird, since neither Philo nor Josephus happened to mention the commemoration of the giving of Torah in association with the feast of Pentecost, some have questioned whether such an
association can be regarded as pre-Christian. In an extended note Caird
attempted to answer such an objection by outlining five strands of evidence which (in spite of the silence of Philo and Josephus) still suggested that at some time before the Christian era Pentecost began to be

---

[4] G. B. Caird, "The Descent of Christ in Ephesians 4, 7-11," *SE* 2 (= TU 87), ed. F. L.
Cross (Berlin: Akademie, 1964) 539-40. Much of the same information is covered by C. H.
Porter ("The Descent of Christ: An Exegetical Study of Ephesians 4:7-11," in *One Faith: Its
Biblical, Historical, and Ecumenical Dimensions*, ed. R. L. Simpson [Enid, OK: Phillips Uni-
versity Press, 1966] 54, n. 26).

celebrated as the commemoration of the giving of the Torah to Moses at Sinai.[5] Caird's arguments and sources must be examined in some detail.

Caird began with the general assertion that the process of assigning historical associations to the old agricultural festivals of ancient Israel was already occurring in the priestly code within the Pentateuch, where both Tabernacles and Passover had become feasts commemorating historical events (Lev 23:42-43). Second, the rabbis had fixed the date of the giving of the Decalogue as 6 Sivan by calculating from the date given in Exod 19:1. This method of computation was so widely attested in the rabbinic writings that it is likely to be ancient. Caird did not state the actual rabbinic evidence for the dating of the giving of the Ten Commandments, but assumed that the widespread distribution of the calculation in the rabbinic accounts demonstrated its antiquity. This point may be granted; but what degree of antiquity is required Caird did not say. He referred to G. F. Moore's *Judaism in the First Centuries of the Christian Era*, suggesting that the computational method used by the later rabbis may even have been intended by the writer who introduced the date into Exod 19:1. As far as the rabbinic evidence is concerned, Moore mentioned only *b. Pesaḥim* 68b. By the time this part of the Talmud was written, the association of Pentecost with the giving of the Torah at Sinai was assumed as the generally accepted opinion.[6]

Caird's third point concerns the establishment of the triennial lectionary system (the so-called 'triennial cycle'). As soon as this system was established, Exodus 19 would have been the appointed reading for Pentcost in the second year of the cycle. Again Caird offered no substantiating evidence or sources for such a claim, and both the nature and date of the 'triennial cycle' have been disputed. The term 'triennial cycle' itself is usually applied to Palestinian sabbatical scripture readings thought to be employed on a three-year cycle in the synagogue as opposed to the annual cycle (a yearly cycle essentially similar to that still in use today). According to B. Wacholder, while one could perhaps argue that the custom of reciting the related Pentateuchal passages on festival days dated back to the time of Ezra, a great deal of diversity prevailed in the practice of regular sabbatical readings in talmudic and post-talmudic times, and the division between the so-called 'triennial cycle' and the annual cycle probably did not occur before the talmudic period (ca. 220-550 CE). This could be substantiated because Palestinian sources

---

[5] This evidence is contained in note 1 of Caird's article, 540. Caird did not point out (although he could have done so) that arguing against a pre-Christian celebration of Pentecost as the commemoration of the giving of Torah based on the omission of such a reference in Philo or Josephus is an argument from silence.

[6] G. F. Moore, *Judaism in the First Centuries of the Christian Era: The Age of the Tannaim* (Cambridge, MA: Harvard University Press, 1927; reprint ed., 1946) 2.48.

(including the Tosepta, halakic and haggadic midrashim) did not mention lectionary cycles at all. Furthermore, the term 'triennial cycle' itself was a misnomer, because the cycle did not work with the regularity of the shorter annual cycle, since it did not begin on the same day every time and probably took closer to four years than three to complete.[7] Therefore Caird's assertion that Exodus 19 was the reading appointed for Pentecost as soon as the triennial lectionary system had been established needs further substantiation, and the dating of the 'triennial cycle' itself is problematic, since it almost certainly post-dates the first century of the Christian era.

Caird's fourth point was taken from H. St J. Thackeray's *The Septuagint and Jewish Worship* (1921): Thackeray probably established that Habakkuk 3 was already one of the prophetic readings appointed for Pentecost before the LXX translation of the minor prophets was made. According to Thackeray it was chosen because the storm theophany it contained was seen as a commentary on (or parallel to) Exodus 19, although the harvest theme of Hab 3:17-18 would have been more appropriate to Tabernacles than Pentecost.[8] Thackeray gave some further information about the date of the association between Exodus 19, Psalm 68, and the feast of Pentecost which Caird did not mention (although it would have supported Caird's previous point concerning Exodus 19 as one of the appointed readings for Pentecost). The oldest authority, tractate *Megilla* in the Babylonian Talmud,[9] named the alternative readings for the feast of Pentecost: from the Law, Deut 16:9 or Exodus 19, and from the Prophets, 'Habbakuk' or 'the Chariot' (Ezekiel 1). Additionally, *b. Meg.* 31a stated that now that the festival lasted two days (presumably instead of one) all four of the lessons were used. Thackeray added that this statement dated from the first or second cen-

---

[7] B. Wacholder, Prolegomenon to *The Bible as Read and Preached in the Old Synagogue*, by J. Mann (New York: Ktav, 1971; original ed. without Prolegomenon, 1940) xv-xxii. Although Wacholder too resorted to an argument from silence when he suggested the division between the 'triennial cycle' and the annual cycle did not occur before the talmudic period because Palestinian sources did not mention cycles at all, nevertheless his major points were well taken and represented a considerable revision of Mann's original theories about the Palestinian triennial cycle which were originally published in 1940. Perhaps the most important point to note is the diversity which prevailed in the practice of sabbatical scripture readings during the first few centuries of the present era; this should cause one to be cautious in assertions about what specific passages would have been read on specific days. This *caveat* is only somewhat lessened in the case where one is dealing with a major festival like Pentecost.

[8] H. St J. Thackeray, *The Septuagint and Jewish Worship* (London: Oxford University Press, 1921) 47-54. Thackeray's evidence for his conclusions about Habakkuk 3 as an assigned reading for Pentecost is too lengthy to be repeated here.

[9] The reference is to *b. Meg.* 31a, although Thackeray did not give the specific page (folio) number. The specific page reference in the tractate was given by J. van Goudoever (*Biblical Calendars* [Leiden: Brill, 1959] 201) and A. T. Lincoln ("The Use of the OT in Ephesians," *JSNT* 14 [1982] 20).

tury of the Christian era, the age of the Tannaim.[10] This raised the question of when the feast was lengthened from one to two days. Thackeray suggested that the author of *Jubilees*, in describing the institution of Pentecost, placed such emphasis on its being confined to "one day in the year" (a statement repeated three times in *Jub.* 6:17-22) that he was actually engaged in a polemic against the innovation of adding a second day at the time he was writing.[11] Since R. H. Charles had suggested a date of "around 100 B.C." for *Jubilees*, this would indicate the assigned readings listed in *b. Megilla* were "certainly as old as A.D. 100, possibly as early as 100 B.C."[12] Of course, the assigned readings Thackeray mentioned up to this point did not include any from the Hagiographa. Yet the inclusion of Exodus 19 as one of the appointed readings for Pentecost strongly suggests that by this time the feast of Pentecost had somehow become associated with Moses' ascent of Sinai and the giving of the Torah. Thackeray did mention two psalms that were to be read on the feast of Pentecost, Psalm 29 (according to tractate *Soferim*) and Psalm 68 (according to unspecified rabbinic authorities). Thackeray proposed that the common theme which ran through all four of the passages from the Prophets and the Hagiographa (Habakkuk 3, Ezekiel 1, Psalm 29, and Psalm 68) was a theophany in a thunderstorm, and it was natural to infer that parallels with the terrors of Mt. Sinai were understood to make them particularly appropriate to the feast of Pentecost by those who selected them.[13] This assumed, of course (although Thackeray did not mention it), that the feast of Pentecost had already begun to be associated with the giving of the Torah at Sinai at some time before these readings were selected.

Thackeray did offer some specific evidence which he believed indicated a connection between Psalm 68 and Pentecost (again, this evidence was not mentioned by Caird). Because Psalm 68 was not mentioned by tractate *Soferim* along with Psalm 29 as an appointed reading for Pentecost, Thackeray held it to be more recent in this connection

---

[10] H. St J. Thackeray, *The Septuagint and Jewish Worship*, 46. Thackeray did not state how he arrived at the date given, however.

[11] J. Potin disagreed with Thackeray's hypothesis (*La Fête Juive de la Pentecôte: Étude des textes liturgiques*, LD 65 [Paris: Éditions du Cerf, 1971] 1.140, n. 30). Potin noted that the references in *Jubilees* with their insistence on "one day in the year" may simply have been reminders intended to recall the importance of the festival to those who had forgotten to celebrate it, or who did not accord it sufficient importance, without implying a polemic against the addition of a second day.

[12] Thackeray, *The Septuagint and Jewish Worship*, 46. For the date of *Jubilees* Thackeray referred to R. H. Charles. However, R. H. Charles gave the date of *Jubilees* as between 135 and 105 BCE (*APOT* 2.1). The same date was mentioned by A. T. Lincoln ("The Use of the OT in Ephesians," *JSNT* 14 [1982] 20). For further discussion of the problems involved in dating *Jubilees* see n. 31 and especially n. 53 of this chapter.

[13] Thackeray, *The Septuagint and Jewish Worship*, 47.

than Psalm 29. Thackeray understood the *Sitz im Leben* of Psalm 68 to be found in an incident recounted in 1 Macc 5:45-54 and 2 Macc 12:27-32 in which Judas Maccabaeus led an expedition into Gilead to rescue a number of his fellow-countrymen who were threatened with annihilation. This event became the basis, according to Thackeray, for the composition of the psalm; it was in celebration of the victory of the Maccabean forces in which no Israelite lives were lost. However, in 2 Macc 12:31-32 (which apparently referred to the same events), Judas Maccabaeus and his troops immediately afterward "went up to Jerusalem, as the feast of weeks was close at hand."[14] The feast of Pentecost (Weeks) would thus have coincided with the celebration of the victory, and (if Thackeray was correct in his belief that the psalm originated as a result of these historical events) it would have been natural for Psalm 68 to remain associated with the feast of Pentecost.[15] This could be an additional explanation (aside from the subject matter of the psalm itself) of how it eventually came to be one of the assigned readings for Pentecost. However, such a historical setting for Psalm 68 is far from clear, and Thackeray's proposal must be considered an unproven hypothesis.

We may now consider Caird's final point, that the association of Pentecost with the Torah seemed to be implied in Acts 2.[16] In support of this Caird referred to a note in A. Guilding's *The Fourth Gospel and Jewish Worship* (1960), so we begin by evaluating the evidence she offered for the association of Pentecost with the giving of the Torah based on Acts 2.[17] Guilding started with the observation that *b. Pesaḥ.* 68b preserved

---

[14] *The Apocrypha of the Old Testament*, Revised Standard Version, ed. B. M. Metzger (New York: Oxford University Press, 1957) 287.

[15] Thackeray's reconstruction of the historical setting of Psalm 68 was based on an article by C. J. Ball ("Psalm LXVIII *Exurgat Deus*," *JTS* 11 [1910] 415-32). The problems presented by Psalm 68 are extremely difficult and OT scholars have not been able to reach agreement concerning its background and setting. These problems have been discussed by S. Iwry ("Notes on Psalm 68," *JBL* 71 [1952] 161-65). A theory which has gained some recognition was proposed by W. F. Albright in the light of discoveries from the Ras Shamra tablets. He suggested that the psalm consisted of a collection of incipits (first lines of poems) from the Solomonic period, but later came to be understood (or perhaps better, misunderstood) as a unitary composition ("A Catalogue of Early Hebrew Lyric Poems [Psalm LXVIII]," *HUCA* 23 [1950-51] 1-39). More recently M. Dahood incorporated some elements of Albright's analysis, but argued for a much greater conceptual unity throughout the entire psalm than the earlier theory would have allowed. Dahood classified Psalm 68 as a triumphal hymn which, in mythopoeic language and mythological motifs that were sometimes historicized, celebrated the defeat of the Egyptians and the deliverance of the Israelites (68:2-7), the escape into the wilderness and the theophany at Sinai (2-9), and the settlement in Canaan (10-15), with the remainder of the psalm repeating variations on these themes. Within this framework he saw 68:16-19 as a reprise of the Sinai theophany theme (*Psalms II: 50-100*, AB 17 [Garden City, NY: Doubleday, 1968] 130-52, esp. 133). Whether or not one agrees completely with Dahood's analysis, it is easy to see why Psalm 68 became associated with the feast of Pentecost as soon as the feast itself began to be seen as a celebration of the giving of the Torah on Mt. Sinai.

[16] G. B. Caird, "The Descent of Christ in Ephesians 4, 7-11," 540, n. 1.

[17] A. Guilding, *The Fourth Gospel and Jewish Worship* (Oxford: Clarendon, 1960) 181 n.

a tradition that Pentecost was the day on which the Law was given.[18] Although no similar tradition had been discovered in Josephus or Philo, the similarities between the Lucan account of the giving of the Spirit at Pentecost and Philo's account of the giving of the Torah at Sinai had often been noted. Philo's statement in *De decalogo* 9 was of particular interest, because there he said that at the giving of the Law God commanded an invisible sound to be created which changed the air into flaming fire:

τὸν ἀέρα σχηματίσασα καὶ ἐπιτείνασα καὶ πρὸς πῦρ φλογοειδὲς μετα-
βαλοῦσα καθάπερ πνεῦμα διὰ σάλπιγγος φωνὴν τοσαύτην ἔναρθρον ἐξήχησεν.[19]

Although this parallel with Acts 2 was noted by Guilding in general terms, she did not mention an even more striking specific parallel with the giving of the Spirit in the NT: the occurrence in Philo's description of the giving of the Torah of the words πνεῦμα, φωνή, and ἐξήχησεν. Πνεῦμα used of the Spirit occurs throughout Acts 2; φωνή occurs in 2:6 as a description of the noise of those who began speaking with other tongues which caused a multi-national crowd to gather (presumably out of curiosity). Perhaps the most interesting word of the three, however, is ἐξήχησεν (from ἐξηχέω, "to sound forth"). This is similar enough to ἐξέχεεν (from ἐκχέω, "to pour out"), used in Acts 2:33 in reference to the outpouring of the Spirit, to have suggested itself as a sort of wordplay to a first century Christian reader, especially if one were already predisposed to associate the feast of Pentecost with the giving of the Torah.[20] Later in *De decalogo* 11 Philo adds,

φωνὴ δ' ἐκ μέσου τοῦ ῥυέντος ἀπ' οὐρανοῦ πυρὸς ἐξῄχει καταπληκτικω-
τάτη, τῆς φλογὸς εἰς διάλεκτον ἀρθρουμένης τὴν συνήθη τοῖς ἀκουομένοις, ᾗ
τὰ λεγόμενα οὕτως ἐναργῶς ἐτρανοῦτο, ὡς ὁρᾶν αὐτὰ μᾶλλον ἢ ἀκούειν
δοκεῖν.[21]

---

1. In a journal article Guilding also mentioned the use of Psalm 68 (along with Psalm 110) as a psalm for Pentecost in the synagogue liturgy ("Some Obscured Rubrics and Lectionary Allusions in the Psalter," *JTS* 3 [n.s., 1952] 54).

[18] Also mentioned by G. F. Moore (*Judaism in the First Centuries of the Christian Era*, 48 [see n. 6 above]).

[19] The Greek text of *De decalogo* is from *Philonis Alexandrini, Opera quae supersunt* (ed. L. Cohn [Berlin: Georg Reimer, 1902; reprint ed., Walter de Gruyter, 1962] 4.276).

[20] Of course, there is also the possibility that the suggested association of similar words was a deliberate attempt on the part of the author of Acts to model his account of the giving of the Spirit at Pentecost on Philo's account of the giving of the Torah at Sinai. Such may be the case, but it is almost impossible to establish such a relationship of literary dependence with certainty. Acts 2:33 and its relation to Psalm 68 and the giving of the Spirit will be discussed in the following section of the present chapter (see below, 159-69).

[21] Again, the Greek text is from *Philonis Alexandrini, Opera quae supersunt* (ed. L. Cohn [Berlin: Georg Reimer, 1902; reprint ed., Walter de Gruyter, 1962] 4.279).

...a voice sounded forth from the midst of the fire that streamed from heaven...for the flame became articulate speech in a language familiar to the hearers, and so clearly and distinctly did it express its words that the people seemed to see rather than hear them.[22]

Guilding saw this as an obvious parallel to Luke's account in Acts 2:5-13 that men "from every nation under heaven" (ἀπὸ παντὸς ἔθνους τῶν ὑπὸ τὸν οὐρανόν) were gathered in Jerusalem, and each heard the apostles speaking in his own language (καὶ πῶς ἡμεῖς ἀκούομεν ἕκαστος τῇ ἰδίᾳ διαλέκτῳ ἡμῶν). Guilding also mentioned two rabbinic accounts which showed similarity to the Lucan account in Acts 2: *Mek. Baḥodesh* (on Ex. 19:1), which stated that the Torah was given to all the nations of the earth, though only Israel accepted it, and *Tanḥuma* 26c, which recorded that the Decalogue went forth with a single sound which divided itself into seven voices and seventy tongues, so that all people received the Torah in their own language. Guilding suggested that although the account in Exodus 19 (one of the assigned readings for the feast of Pentecost)[23] mentioned fire and smoke atop Mt. Sinai, there was nothing that would correspond to the sevenfold voice of God described in the latter of the two rabbinic accounts, so another source had to be found for this idea. The source Guilding proposed was Psalm 29, assigned by *b. Soferim* 18.3 as a reading for Pentecost.[24] Seven times in the psalm the voice of Yahweh was mentioned (29:3, 4 [2x], 5, 7, 8, and 9), and verse 7 in particular stated, "the voice of Yahweh cleaves the flames of fire." These indications may have given rise to the rabbinic accounts mentioned above. Against this it must be noted, however (as Guilding herself pointed out), that the LXX superscription for Psalm 29 assigned it not to Pentecost but to the concluding ceremony of the feast of Tabernacles (ἐξοδίου σκηνῆς).

The evidence Guilding offered from the rabbinic sources is subject to the normal criticism of all classical rabbinic literature when used to explain NT material: it is unquestionably of later date than the NT itself. The strongest evidence offered is that from Philo's *De decalogo*, since his work was almost certainly completed prior to the writing of the NT documents. Philo's reference to the sevenfold voice of God and the seventy languages in which it was heard strongly suggests that (of the later rabbinic writings mentioned by Guilding) these elements (at least) had their origins in or before the first century CE. Whether the association of the feast of Pentecost with the giving of the Torah is implied by

---

[22] The English translation of this portion of *De decalogo* 11 is that given by A. Guilding (*The Fourth Gospel and Jewish Worship*, 181 n. 1).

[23] See above, 145-47.

[24] See above, 147-48.

Acts 2, however, has not yet been proven. Caird, in citing Guilding's evidence, appeared to assume that it suggested some sort of deliberate allusion to Philo's description (or at least of a tradition similar to that found in Philo) on the part of Luke, an allusion which indicated Luke's awareness of the association of the feast of Pentecost with the giving of the Law at Sinai. This is certainly possible, but much more evidence needs to be examined before we can concur with such a conclusion.

There is one additional piece of evidence surfaced in Caird's attempt to associate the feast of Pentecost with the giving of the Law that warrants brief discussion. Caird mentioned a rabbinic comment on Ps 68:11 found in *b. Sabb.* 88b:

> R. Jonathan said: What is meant by this verse, 'The Lord gives the word; they that publish the glad tidings are a great host'? Every single word that went forth from the Omnipotent was split up into seventy tongues.[25]

Caird concluded from this bit of rabbinic exegesis that behind the composition of Acts 2 (as well as Eph 4:7-11) there existed a Christian exegesis (or adaptation of a rabbinic exegesis) of Psalm 68. Again, references to the Babylonian Talmud (which as a written composition is certainly later than the NT) do not constitute definitive proof of either Christian or rabbinic doctrine in the first century CE. We may view the evidence as suggestive, however, because (1) there was certainly an oral tradition which preceded the written Talmud, although it cannot be precisely dated; and (2) the quotation from *b. Sabb.* 88b is similar to statements found in *Tanḥuma* 26c as mentioned by Guilding and discussed above. Repetition of evidence (multiple attestation) in rabbinic literature suggests it is considerably more ancient than the written sources in which it is found.[26]

Another recent study which argued for the association of the feast of Pentecost with the celebration of the giving of the Torah to Moses at Mt. Sinai was J. Potin's *La Fête Juive de la Pentecôte* (1971). Potin examined in detail the targums to Exodus 19 and 20 along with other related targums which deal with the theophany at Sinai and the giving of the Torah. He attempted to determine the religious significance of the feast of Pentecost with the aid of the targums read in the course of the synagogue liturgy. The major difficulty with such a study, as Potin himself pointed out, is to determine how and when the original feast of Weeks, an agricultural festival, became the celebration of God's covenant with Israel (according to Essene and priestly tradition) and of the

---

[25] G. B. Caird, "The Descent of Christ in Ephesians 4, 7-11," 543-44.
[26] See also the brief discussion of problems involved in dating the contents of rabbinic literature in ch. 3, 75-77.

giving of the Torah (according to rabbinic tradition).[27] Potin concluded
that in Essene tradition it was the renewal of the covenant which was
most significant, so that Pentecost was celebrated as an annual covenant renewal ceremony, with the old feast of Weeks becoming the most
important festival in the liturgical calendar. Such indications could be
found in *Jubilees*. This interpretation of Pentecost differed significantly
from the rabbinic tradition, however, where it was the theophany of Sinai and the giving of the Torah that were most important. Thus the two
traditions reflected significantly different theological emphases. Because
of the silence of Philo and Josephus regarding the feast of Pentecost as
a celebration of the giving of the law, Potin tended to date the assignment of such a significance to Pentecost at about the time of the destruction of the Temple, when the Pharisees were able to impose their
calendar and theological concepts on the remnants of Judaism.[28]

With regard to the use of Psalm 68 as a part of the synagogue liturgy
for the feast of Pentecost, Potin noted a number of themes in common
with other texts like *Tg.* Habakkuk 3 and *Tg.* Exodus 19, although he
did not propose a date for the association of the psalm with Pentecost.
Potin attributed the change in the text of *Tg.* Ps 68:19 to the targumist,
who had reversed the order of the consonants לקח to read חלק in order
to derive his interpretation of the verse as a reference to the ascent and
descent of Moses at Mt. Sinai. This interpretation appeared to have
been known and used by the author of Ephesians in 4:8, according to
Potin: "on peut donc dire que Paul a connu cette interprétation targumique."[29]

B. THE *BOOK OF JUBILEES*, ASCENSION, AND PENTECOST

Additional evidence indicating the association of the Jewish celebration
of Pentecost with the giving of the Torah at Mt. Sinai was mentioned by
A. T. Lincoln, who suggested this association existed from the mid-
second century BCE.[30] The *Book of Jubilees* made Pentecost the most
important of the annual festivals on the Jewish liturgical calendar. It was
associated with various covenants in Israel's history, but especially with
the covenant at Sinai (1:5, 6:11, 6:17, and 15:1-24). Since it is generally
accepted that *Jubilees* was written between 135 and 105 BCE, this

---

[27] J. Potin, *La Fête Juive de la Pentecôte: Étude des textes liturgiques*, LD 65 (Paris: Éditions du Cerf, 1971) 1.117-23.

[28] Potin, *La Fête Juive de la Pentecôte*, 137-39.

[29] Potin, *La Fête Juive de la Pentecôte*, 196-97.

[30] A. T. Lincoln, "The Use of the OT in Ephesians," *JSNT* 14 (1982) 20. Similar information is also found in his previous work *Paradise Now and and Not Yet* (SNTSMS 43
[Cambridge: Cambridge University Press, 1981] 157).

would point to the mid- to late second century BCE as the period in which the feast of Pentecost (Weeks) began to be regarded not just as a harvest festival but as a celebration of the giving of the Law at Sinai.[31] In addition to the evidence mentioned by Lincoln, there is an interesting correspondence between two notations in *Jub.* 1:1 and 15:1 which strengthens the argument that at the time it was composed *Jubilees* contained evidence for the celebration of the feast of Pentecost as the commemoration of the giving of the Torah to Moses. The date of Moses' ascent of Mt. Sinai to receive the Torah was noted in *Jub.* 1:1:

> [it was] ...in the first year of the exodus of the children of Israel out of Egypt, in the third month, on the sixteenth day of the month, that God spake to Moses, saying: 'Come up to Me on the Mount...'.[32]

In *Jub.* 15:1, Abraham was said to have celebrated the feast of Weeks (Pentecost) on the same day of the year:

> And in the fifth year of the fourth week of this jubilee, in the third month, in the middle of the month, Abram celebrated the feast of the first fruits of the grain harvest.[33]

Thus it is clear that the author of *Jubilees* believed (or wanted those for whom he was writing to believe) that the giving of the Torah to Moses and the celebration of the feast of Pentecost coincided. Whether the two events actually happened on the same date or not is insignificant. The point is that the author of *Jubilees* believed (or wanted others to believe) that they did. This is particularly understandable if, as Lincoln suggested, the traditional association between the feast of Pentecost and the celebration of the giving of the Law found in the later rabbinic literature is at least as old as *Jubilees*. Given the emphasis in *Jubilees* on Pentecost as the most important of the annual festivals (and given the special emphasis on its association with the covenant at Sinai) one of the probable reasons for writing the *Book of Jubilees* was to support the connection of the giving of the Law with the feast of Weeks (Pentecost). Such a conclusion is also suggested by the fact that the Qumran community followed the calendar of *Jubilees*. Their annual celebration of the renewal of the covenant was probably combined with the annual renewal of the vows made by each individual upon entrance into the community at Pentecost.[34] We shall return to examine further the rela-

---

[31] This is the date suggested for the composition of *Jubilees* by R. H. Charles (*APOT* 2.1, see n. 12 above). For further discussion concerning the date of *Jubilees*, see n. 53 below.

[32] R. H. Charles, *APOT* 2.11.

[33] Charles, *APOT* 2.34.

[34] A. T. Lincoln, "The Use of the OT in Ephesians," 20. Manual of Discipline [I QS] 1:7-2:19 was cited by Lincoln for comparison. Also mentioned in a note (p. 51 n. 25) was the calendrical work of J. van Goudoever (139-44, see note 9 above) and the comments of J. C. Kirby

tionship between *Jubilees* and the feast of Pentecost after we have investigated another approach that suggests connections between the
giving of the Torah to Moses at Sinai and the celebration of Pentecost.

So far we have seen strong indications that the feast of Weeks (Pentecost) became associated with the celebration of the giving of the Torah to Moses at Sinai some time prior to the first century CE. A similar
conclusion was also reached by G. Kretschmar in an article on the relationship between the ascension and Pentecost in early Christian tradition. He attempted to analyse traditions which attributed the celebration
of the ascension to the same day as Pentecost (i.e., fifty days after Easter
rather than the forty days indicated in the Lucan account in Acts 1:3).
Kretschmar believed that a variant tradition which celebrated the ascension and Pentecost on the same day could certainly be traced back as
early as the first century CE.[35] He began with a survey of the evidence
from the post-apostolic writings and the early Fathers: the *Doctrine of
Addai* appeared to place the ascension and the giving of the Spirit on
the same day, and as late as the first half of the fourth century CE Eusebius apparently celebrated the ascension fifty days after Easter.[36] Jerome
in his commentary on Matthew (on 9:15) mentioned that the Montanists
on the fiftieth day after Easter began another forty days of fasting like
the forty days before Easter.[37] Since Matt 9:15 (the text on which
Jerome commented) stated that the attendants of the bridegroom would
fast when the bridegroom was taken away from them, this would almost
certainly indicate that the Montanists understood the ascension to have
occurred on the fiftieth day after Easter.[38] Kretschmar saw in this evidence indications of a very old tradition independent from that recorded
in Acts and antedating the addition of that book to the canon. To trace
this tradition further back—into the first century—he then turned to
connections between the Christian celebration of the ascension and the
giving of the Spirit on the one hand and the Jewish feast of Weeks on
the other. The first of the NT passages which Kretschmar examined was
Acts 2:1-13, in which the ascension was closely connected with the
giving of the Spirit as Peter's speech in Acts 2:32-36 made clear. The

---

(*Ephesians, Baptism and Pentecost* [Montreal: McGill University Press, 1968] 61-69). A.
Jaubert discussed the relationship between *Jubilees* and the Qumran sectarians. Jaubert's hypothesis (which has not met with widespread scholarly acceptance) was that the calendar found in
Jubilees was preserved by the Essenes and was essentially the same as the one in use at Qumran in the first century ("Le Calendrier des Jubilés et de la Secte de Qumrân: Ses origines bibliques," *VT* 3 [1953] 250-64).

[35] G. Kretschmar, "Himmelfahrt und Pfingsten," *ZKG* 66 (1954-55) 209-53.
[36] *PG* 24, col. 700.
[37] *PL* 26, col. 58.
[38] Of course this assumes the accuracy of Jerome's information concerning the Montanists,
written some one and one-half centuries later.

second passage was Eph 4:7-12: here the gifted individuals named in 4:11 were clearly seen as gifts of the exalted Christ to the church (i.e., the gifts named in the quotation from Ps 68:19 in Eph 4:8). Thus Kretschmar thought Eph 4:7-12 spoke of the outpouring of the Spirit at Pentecost even though the specific word πνεῦμα was missing, since (1) the early church considered all the "offices" to be intimately connected with the Spirit, and (2) the connection of this passage with both Johannine and Lucan statements (John 15:26, 16:7, 20:17, and 20:22; Acts 2:1-13, 2:32-34) was so close.[39] Kretschmar argued based on the text-form of the quotation of Ps 68:19 in Eph 4:8 for a Palestinian origin for this layer of tradition. Here he mentioned the (later) rabbinic traditions which associated Ps 68:19 with Moses' ascent of Sinai to receive the Torah as 'gifts' to be distributed to men.[40] It appeared to Kretschmar that the author of Ephesians (or a still earlier tradition he employed) took a Jewish tradition concerning Moses and applied it to Christ. Kretschmar thought this tradition, involving Ps 68:19, could also be seen in the background of Acts 2:33-34.[41] He also claimed that the connection with Moses' ascent of Sinai could be established without doubt for Eph 4:7-11 and probably also for Acts 2:33.[42] For further support he pointed to several examples of early Christian art which appeared to link the Moses-typology with the ascension of Christ.[43] Kretschmar concluded that at this point there were so many similarities between the depiction of Christ's ascension in early Christian tradition and the giving of the Law to Moses in Jewish tradition that one must have been dependent on the other. While it is unimportant for his argument which was older, he did point out that it was inherently more probable that the Moses-typology was the older of the two.

Kretschmar then set out to establish the earliest possible date at which this Moses-typology could have become associated with the feast of Pentecost. It was clear that the feast of Weeks appeared in the OT as a harvest festival, yet in later rabbinic writings it had become the celebration of the giving of the Torah to Moses at Sinai.[44] The question for Kretschmar was, at what point did the significance of the feast of

---

[39] Kretschmar, "Himmelfahrt und Pfingsten," 214. The description of the gifts (or gifted individuals) given to the church in Eph 4:11ff. as "offices" is Kretschmar's terminology, not mine. He stated: "...für die frühe Kirche ist jedes Amt im Geist verwurzelt...."

[40] In the present work, these have been examined extensively in chapter 3. See above, 77-95.

[41] The relationship of Psalm 68 to Acts 2:33 and the giving of the Spirit will be discussed at greater length in the following section of this chapter. See below, 159-69.

[42] "Für Eph. 4 ließ diese Verbindung sich ja auch eindeutig aufzeigen, für Act. 2,33 wahrscheinlich machen," according to Kretschmar ("Himmelfahrt und Pfingsten," 218).

[43] Kretschmar, "Himmelfahrt und Pfingsten," 218-20.

[44] We have already examined many of the sources involved while evaluating G. B. Caird's article earlier in this section. See above, 144-51.

Pentecost shift from a harvest celebration to a celebration of the giving
of the Law? (At this point we may add the question whether such a
shift in significance was pre-Christian or not, for if it were older than the
composition of Ephesians it would mean that the Moses-typology—
involving Moses' ascent of Mt. Sinai to receive the Torah—would have
been available to the author. This would have predisposed him to think
in terms of a descent of Christ subsequent to the ascent mentioned in
the psalm quotation, since Moses' descent from Sinai with the 'gifts' of
the Torah naturally followed his ascent.) Kretschmar mentioned the assigned readings for Pentecost in the Jewish synagogue lectionary: according to the Mishna, Deut 16:9-12, and (in addition) from the Tosepta
and the Jerusalem Talmud, Exodus 19. Both of these were mentioned in
the Babylonian Talmud along with two additional prophetic readings,
Ezekiel 1 and Habbakuk 3. Later layers of tradition mentioned (as
readings from the Hagiographa) Psalms 68 and 29.[45] A liturgical poem
from the Egyptian diaspora found in the vicinity of Oxyrhynchos appeared to be a Pentecost-composition containing allusions to Exodus
19, Habbakuk 3, and Psalm 68, but a reliable date could not be assigned.[46] According to Kretschmar another provocative suggestion was
L. Finkelstein's hypothesis that the well-known controversy between
the Pharisees and the Sadducees over the dating of the feast of Weeks
fifty days after Passover had its origins in a difference of opinion concerning the nature of the feast of Weeks: the Pharisees considered the
feast a celebration of a historical event, the giving of the Law at Sinai,
and therefore required a fixed annual date; while the Sadducees auto-
matically counted fifty days after Passover, since for them the feast remained only a harvest festival.[47] If this could be proven, it would
strongly suggest that the shift in meaning for the feast of Weeks had already begun prior to the first century CE. However, Kretschmar in his
evaluation was forced to conclude that this remained a theory without
compelling proof.[48] There was no absolutely certain rabbinic evidence
for the observance of Pentecost as the celebration of the giving of the

---

[45] Kretschmar cited as his source for the assigned readings mentioned above I. Elbogen
(*Der jüdische Gottesdienst in seiner geschichtlichen Entwicklung*, 2d ed. [Frankfurt: Kauffmann, 1924] 138, 164). Elbogen listed Psalm 68 as the appointed reading for the feast of
Weeks (Pentecost) according to the Sephardic and Romanic ("der romanische, besser ru-
melische oder griechische") rituals (138). Both of these are later than the Palestinian and
Babylonian rituals. Of the two, the Romanic is older, although neither can be dated exactly,
since the first surviving editions are from Venice (1524) and Constantinople (1574).

[46] H. Loewe, "The Petrie-Hirschfeld Papyri," *JTS* 24 (1923) 126-41.

[47] L. Finkelstein, "The Book of Jubilees and the Rabbinic Halaka," *HTR* 16 (1923) 39-61;
the material on the calendar of *Jubilees* is found on pp. 40-45.

[48] "...hat diese Argumentation L. Finkelsteins manches für sich, aber sie bleibt doch reine
Hypothese ohne zwingende Beweiskraft" (Kretschmar, "Himmelfahrt und Pfingsten," 223).

Torah at Sinai before the second century CE.

From the rabbinic evidence, Kretschmar turned his attention to *Jubilees*.[49] Here he found evidence that the connection between the feast of Weeks and the giving of the Torah was older than the rabbinic traditions previously examined. One of the problems associated with *Jubilees* was its peculiar calendar, which was arranged so that a given date fell on the same weekday in every year. The feast of Weeks in particular occurred annually on the fifteenth day of the third month.[50]

As long ago as 1925 J. Morgenstern demonstrated that the calendar of *Jubilees* was older than that of the rabbis and in its essential elements contained ancient Israelite traditions.[51] More recently A. Jaubert proposed that this calendar originated at the same time as the priestly code ("le code sacerdotal") and the book of Ezekiel.[52] Since the *Book of Jubilees* was probably written in the Maccabean period (perhaps in the first quarter of the second century BCE) the older priestly calendar it contained probably had some influence on the Pharisees.[53] This calendar

---

[49] Some aspects of the relationship between the celebration of the feast of Weeks (Pentecost) and the *Book of Jubilees* have already been examined. See above, 147, 152-54.

[50] The details of the calendrical system can be found in *Jubilees* 6, which stated that a year was to contain 364 days (52 weeks) with 4 quarters of 91 days each. This can be interpreted in several different ways. If the calendar of *Jubilees* consisted of a solar calendar of 364 days with 12 months of 30 days each plus 4 commemorative days outside of the monthly reckoning, one at the beginning of each of the four seasons, it would have contained 52 weeks, and a given date would fall on the same day of the week in every year. Although Finkelstein argued for a calendar of 12 months of 28 days each with an intercalary week at the end of each quarter of the year (*HTR* 16 (1923) 42), O. S. Wintermute favored the former view, with months of 30 days and 4 annual commemorative days per year ("Jubilees: A New Translation and Introduction," in *The Old Testament Pseudepigrapha*, ed. J. H. Charlesworth [Garden City, NY: Doubleday, 1985] 2.35-142, esp. 39), and this appears to be the present consensus. Which of these reconstructions may be more accurate is beyond the scope of the present work. The important point to note is that with either system, a given date would fall on the same day of the week in every year, thus insuring absolute regularity for the celebration of the festivals.

[51] J. Morgenstern, "The Three Calendars of Ancient Israel," *HUCA* 1 (1925) 13-78; also "Supplementary Studies in the Calendars of Ancient Israel," *HUCA* 10 (1935) 1-148.

[52] A. Jaubert, "Le Calendrier des Jubilés et de la Secte de Qumrân: Ses origines bibliques," *VT* 3 (1953) 250-64, esp. 258-63. Kretschmar expressed some doubt over the validity of her thesis, at least in its entirety ("Himmelfahrt und Pfingsten," 225 n. 69). Caird, as we have seen, also mentioned that the process of assigning historical associations to the old agricultural festivals of ancient Israel was already occurring in the priestly code within the Pentateuch (see above, 145). Although he stated no source for his assertion, he may well have been aware of Jaubert's article.

[53] On the dating of *Jubilees* Kretschmar mentioned the work of H. H. Rowley and P. Kahle (H. H. Rowley, *The Relevance of Apocalyptic*, 2d ed. [London: Lutterworth, 1947; reprint ed., Greenwood, SC: Attic, 1980] 99-105; P. E. Kahle, *The Cairo Geniza* [London: British Academy, 1947; reprint ed., Munich: Kraus, 1980] 12, n. 3). An even earlier date for *Jubilees*, sometime in the post-exilic period prior to the time of the Maccabees, was proposed by S. Zeitlin ("The Book of Jubilees: Its Character and its Significance," *JQR* 30 [1939] 1-31). Zeitlin argued that the text of the Torah used by the author of *Jubilees* differed substantially from that known to us today, and that in the time when *Jubilees* was written several differing texts of the Torah may have been in circulation. This would suggest that *Jubilees* was older than the Mac-

also found its way into the astronomical book contained in the Ethiopic *Book of Enoch* (chs. 72-75) and in Slavonic *Enoch* (chs. 11-16).

But in *Jubilees* the feast of Weeks represented more than just an agricultural festival; it was the day on which the covenant God made with Israel at Sinai was to be celebrated. This took place on the fifteenth day of the third month, the day on which the Torah was given to Israel and the covenant between God and Israel was confirmed.[54] According to *Jubilees* 6:1-2 the feast of Weeks was instituted after the Noahic flood when God sealed the covenant with Noah. On the fifteenth day of the third month God made the covenant with Abraham, and he celebrated the feast of Weeks (14:10-11, 15:1). On the same date Isaac was born (16:13), and also on this date Jacob was blessed by Abraham (22:1-2), thus renewing the covenant (22:15). *Jub.* 6:19 seemed to Kretschmar to indicate that the celebration of the feast of Weeks was renewed at Sinai. In fact, it is likely that the author of *Jubilees* conceived of a single covenant of God made with Israel in the distant past and renewed throughout history on repeated occasions. It was as a commemoration of this covenant that the feast of Weeks was to be celebrated. Kretschmar thought it probable that such a significance for the feast of Weeks was connected to still earlier traditions and did not originate with *Jubilees* itself.[55] Hints of this could be found in 2 Chr 15:8-15 when King Asa gathered all Judah and Benjamin, along with many from the northern tribes, together at Jerusalem "in the third month" to renew the covenant between God and Israel. Thus Kretschmar concluded that the connection between the feast of Weeks and the giving of the Law at Sinai was pre-Christian, although the point of contact between the two

---

cabean period, before the present text of the Torah became established as the standard one. Zeitlin's theory, which placed great weight on the calendrical system of *Jubilees*, has not met with widespread acceptance (see also note 31 above). On the influence of the *Jubilees* calendar on the Pharisees, see S. Gandz, who gave a summary of the historical development as he had reconstructed it ("Studies in the Hebrew Calendar," *JQR* 40 [1949-50] 251-77, esp. 274-77). The most up-to-date survey of problems and theories concerning the dating of *Jubilees* is that of O. S. Wintermute ("Jubilees: A New Translation and Introduction," *The Old Testament Pseudepigrapha*, ed. J. H. Charlesworth [Garden City, NY: Doubleday, 1985] 2.35-142, esp. 43-44). Wintermute attempted to relate the discovery of fragments of *Jubilees* found at Qumran to the problem of dating the work. He concluded that *Jubilees* must have been written (1) before the date of the earliest fragment found at Qumran; (2) before the date of Qumran documents that depended on *Jubilees*; and (3) before the date of the split between the Maccabean establishment and the Qumran sect. This pointed to a date between 161-140 BCE, somewhat earlier than the previous consensus.

[54] This clearly appears to be an instance of covenant renewal as far as Jubilees was concerned. Moses ascended up to God on the 16th day of the 3rd month according to *Jub.* 1:1. The order of events of Moses' ascent appears to follow that of Exod 24:12. Thus the offering which ratified the covenant (described in Exod 24:3-8) would have taken place on the preceding day, the 15th day of the 3rd month. Probably, however, the entire giving of the Law recounted in Exod 19:16ff. would have also taken place prior to the ratification and offering of the 15th day.

[55] Kretschmar, "Himmelfahrt und Pfingsten," 226.

traditions was not the Law but the covenant. Later in Palestinian Christian circles the old Jewish feast of Pentecost continued to be celebrated, in which the previous content of the feast (Moses' ascension of Sinai to receive the Torah and the renewing of the covenant) was preserved as a type of the new salvation-history of the ascension and the founding of the church, in much the same way as the Jewish Passover carried over in the Christian celebration of Easter.[56] Kretschmar's reconstruction of the Jewish interpretation of Psalm 68 and its influence on early Christian tradition was cited with approval by both C. F. D. Moule and R. Le Déaut.[57] Le Déaut considered the connection between the ascension of Christ and Moses' ascent of Mt. Sinai to be well established. More recently conclusions similar to Kretschmar's have been advanced by J. Dupont who also regarded them as virtually certain.[58]

Thus it is likely that the feast of Weeks (Pentecost) became associated with the celebration of the giving of the Torah to Moses at Sinai some time prior to the first century CE, probably in the Maccabean period around the time the *Book of Jubilees* was written, if not sooner. This conclusion has important implications for our investigation, because it suggests that a tradition associating Moses' ascent of Sinai to receive the Torah was already associated with the feast of Pentecost (and probably with Psalm 68 as well) prior to the composition of Ephesians. Awareness of such traditions would explain why the author of Ephesians found it necessary to deduce a descent (in Eph 4:9-10) from the ascent mentioned in the quotation from Ps 68:19 (Eph 4:8), since Moses, following his ascent of Mt. Sinai to 'take captive' the words of Torah, descended to distribute them as 'gifts' to men. But just as for the author of Ephesians it was Christ who made the victorious ascent, so also it was Christ who descended (as the Spirit) to distribute gifts to his church. Before reaching any final conclusions, however, we turn now to the account of the first Christian Pentecost in Acts 2 to see if further corroborative evidence can be found there.

C. PSALM 68, ACTS 2:33, AND THE GIVING OF THE SPIRIT

It is highly probable that the feast of Pentecost in Jewish tradition had become associated with the celebration of the giving of the Torah to

---

[56] Kretschmar, "Himmelfahrt und Pfingsten," 229.

[57] C. F. D. Moule, "The Ascension—Acts i. 9," *ExpTim* 68 (1956-57) 206, n. 3; R. Le Déaut, "Pentecôte et tradition juive," *ASeign* 51 (1963) 32.

[58] J. Dupont, "Ascension du Christ et don de l'Esprit d'après Actes 2:33," in *Christ and Spirit in the New Testament*, ed. B. Lindars and S. S. Smalley (Cambridge: Cambridge University Press, 1973) 219-28. A list of Dupont's published works on the significance of Pentecost and the possible allusion to Ps 68:19 in Acts 2:33 is given in the article cited, 224 n. 20.

Moses some time prior to the first century CE. It is also possible that Psalm 68 had already become associated with this tradition as well because of its similarities to the description of the giving of the Law at Sinai in the accounts in the Pentateuch. In light of the Christian interpretation of Pentecost as the giving of the Spirit to the church found in Acts 2:1-47, it would not have taken a great deal of imagination for the author of Ephesians to relate Ps 68:19 (which in all probability he understood already as a reference to Moses' ascent of Sinai to receive the Torah for distribution as gifts to men on the basis of Jewish tradition) with the descent of the Spirit to distribute gifted individuals to the newly established church. Such a connection would have been even easier to make if the writer were familiar with a version of Ps 68:19 which contained ἔδωκεν, יהבת (as in *Tg*. Ps 68:19) or its equivalent in place of לקחת or ἔλαβες (as in the MT and LXX). Athough it is possible that the author of Ephesians could have made such an interpretive change in the text himself, it seems highly unlikely (given the existence of the same variant in *Tg*. Ps 68:19 and several other early sources we have already examined) that he found it necessary to do so.[59] According to R. A. Taylor, Paul was familiar with this textual variant and chose to follow it instead of the common text because it suited his theological purposes in Ephesians 4.[60]

Certainly the connection of Psalm 68 with Pentecost and the giving of the Spirit could have been original with the author of Ephesians. But if the psalm were already associated with Pentecost in early Christian as well as Jewish tradition, then it is much more probable that our author was merely adopting a use of Psalm 68 already familiar to him. We shall now attempt to trace the connection of Psalm 68 with Pentecost in early Christian tradition by showing that Psalm 68 also lies behind the account of the first Christian Pentecost in Acts 2:1-47.

Acts 2:33, toward the end of Peter's speech as recorded in Acts 2:14-36, has been a focus of attention for those who considered Psalm 68 to be in the background of the tradition concerning the first Christian Pentecost. The Greek text of Acts 2:32-33 reads:

τοῦτον τὸν Ἰησοῦν ἀνέστησεν ὁ θεός, οὗ πάντες ἡμεῖς ἐσμεν μάρτυρες· τῇ δεξιᾷ οὖν τοῦ θεοῦ ὑψωθείς, τήν τε ἐπαγγελίαν τοῦ πνεύματος τοῦ ἁγίου

---

[59] See ch. 3, 96-104, for a discussion of additional differences in the text of Ps 68:19 as found in the MT, LXX, *Tg*. Psalms, and the quotation in Eph 4:8. Among those who have held that the author of Ephesians himself was responsible for a deliberate alteration in the wording of Psalm 68 in order to achieve his interpretation was S. L. Edgar ("New Testament and Rabbinic Messianic Interpretation," *NTS* 5 [1958-59] 47-54).

[60] R. A. Taylor, "The Use of Psalm 68:18 in Ephesians 4:8 in Light of the Ancient Versions," *BSac* 148 (1991) 335.

λαβὼν παρὰ τοῦ πατρός, ἐξέχεεν τοῦτο ὃ ὑμεῖς καὶ βλέπετε καὶ ἀκούετε.[61]

It is clear that there is no direct quotation from Psalm 68 present in this text. However, considerable scholarly discussion has taken place concerning the possibility of an allusion to Ps 68:19 underlying the text of Acts 2 as we have it today.

The first modern interpreter to suggest that Ps 68:19 lay behind Acts 2:33 was F. H. Chase (1902).[62] He proposed that the connection between Christ's ascent to heaven and his exaltation to the right hand of God mentioned in the following verse (Acts 2:34) was best explained if the tradition behind 2:33 originally contained a citation of Ps 68:19 which had become virtually unrecognizable in the existing redaction. Chase suggested Psalm 68:19 as the source of the quotation in the underlying tradition not only because of the sequence of thought, but on the basis of the actual language of Acts 2:33-34, which used the words ὑψωθείς, ἀνέβη, and λαβών. Chase's suggestion was taken up by H. J. Cadbury (1933) in his study of the speeches in Acts, which was primarily concerned with the manner of presentation of the argument from scripture.[63] Cadbury saw in Acts 2:34, which began with οὐ γὰρ Δαυὶδ ἀνέβη εἰς τοὺς οὐρανούς, a reference to a psalm which spoke of an ascent to heaven. Beginning with οὐ γάρ the author (or speaker) of the source behind the present text of Acts affirmed—according to Cadbury—that the aforementioned ascent did not concern the presumed author of the psalm (the same explanatory use of γάρ could be seen in Acts 13:36).[64] Verse 34 contained a quotation from Ps 110:1, however, which corresponded only vaguely to the idea of an ascent to heaven, and did not appear sufficient to account for the entire statement in verse 33. Thus the reference to a heavenly ascent in 2:34 must have been inferred from something in 2:33; but the problem arose when one attempted to find in Acts 2:33 mention of a psalm which spoke of an ascent to heaven—no explicit quotation of such a psalm was to be found. What remained in 2:33 were traces of an allusion to Ps 68:19: the participle ὑψωθείς recalled the phrase ἀναβὰς εἰς ὕψος in Ps 68:19, and the phrase λαβὼν τὴν ἐπαγγελίαν suggested the phrase ἔλαβες δόματα (Ps 67:19 LXX).[65] Cadbury also noted that there were other instances

---

[61] According to NA27.

[62] F. H. Chase, *The Credibility of the Book of the Acts of the Apostles* (London: Macmillan, 1902) 151. This work constituted the Hulsean Lectures for 1900–1901.

[63] H. J. Cadbury, "Note XXXII. The Speeches in Acts," in *The Beginnings of Christianity*, part 1: *The Acts of the Apostles*, ed. F. J. Foakes Jackson and K. Lake, 5: *Additional Notes to the Commentary*, ed. K. Lake and H. J. Cadbury (London: Macmillan, 1933) 402-27. Cadbury's comments on Acts 2:33-34 are found on 408-9.

[64] This reference was incorrectly cited as Acts 13:37 by Cadbury, "Note XXXII," 409.

[65] See the comparison between the texts of Ps 68:19 found in the MT, LXX, Eph 4:8, and

where scriptures were implied but not actually quoted in Acts; this was clear from 13:15, where readings from the law and the prophets were mentioned, but not specified.

Cadbury's suggestion was repeated (with some expansion) by W. L. Knox (1948).[66] Knox also proposed that the argument of Acts 2:32-36 was much more easily understood if one supposed that the source used by Luke made allusion to Ps 68:19 at this point. According to Knox, "Luke was not well enough versed in rabbinical theology to appreciate an allusion which in his sources was probably made clearer."[67] Knox also mentioned that Psalm 68 is today one of the assigned readings for Pentecost in the modern Jewish prayer book. The rabbinic exegesis of the psalm applied it to Moses, who ascended Mt. Sinai to receive the law and bring it down to men. Knox went on to state:

> Luke's source was no doubt aware of the appropriateness of the Psalm in view of the rabbinical interpretation, and I suspect that we have in it evidence that the Psalm in question was already a Psalm for Pentecost in the Jewish liturgy.[68]

These assertions by Knox were criticized on two counts by J. Dupont: (1) they were based on later Jewish traditions, which Knox made no attempt to trace back as early as the first century CE; and (2) in positing that Luke's source quoted or alluded to Psalm 68, Knox made no attempt to find in the extant text of Acts 2:33 any remaining vestige of Ps 68:19.[69]

G. Kretschmar, whose 1955 article we have already discussed at some length in the preceding section, also saw the possibility that Acts 2:33 had been influenced by Ps 68:19.[70] He argued that the agreement between Eph 4:7-12, Acts 2:33, and the Johannine tradition concerning

---

Tg. Psalms in ch. 3 above, 96-104.

[66] W. L. Knox, *The Acts of the Apostles* (Cambridge: Cambridge University Press, 1948) 85-86.

[67] Knox, *The Acts of the Apostles*, 85-86.

[68] Knox, *The Acts of the Apostles*, 86. See ch. 3, 77-95, for a discussion of the rabbinic interpretations of Ps 68:19, and the preceding section of the present chapter, 144-59, for the evidence connecting Psalm 68 with the celebration of the giving of the law and the Jewish feast of Pentecost.

[69] J. Dupont, "Ascension du Christ et don de l'Esprit d'après Actes 2:33," 222. Although Dupont's criticisms of Knox's assertions were valid as such, much more work has been done on the antiquity of the Jewish traditions associating Psalm 68 with Moses' ascent of Sinai. See the discussions of this in ch. 3, 65-122, and the previous section of the present chapter, which deals with the tradition surrounding the Jewish feast of Pentecost and the celebration of the giving of the law at Sinai, 144-59. With regard to Dupont's second criticism, others before Knox had already shown such literary traces of Ps 68:19 in Acts 2:33-34 (see the discussion of the suggestions by F. H. Chase and H. J. Cadbury above).

[70] G. Kretschmar, "Himmelfahrt und Pfingsten," *ZKG* 66 (1954-55) 209-53. See the preceding section, 211ff.

the manner in which they associated the exaltation of Christ and the giving of the Spirit indicated an ancient tradition within Christianity. Kretschmar also established that by the time *Jubilees* and the related Qumran texts were written, the feast of Pentecost had already become associated with the celebration of the giving of the law at Sinai. Such a background suggested (if Ps 68:19 were understood in Jewish tradition at that time to refer to Moses' ascent of Sinai to receive the Torah) that the allusion to Ps 68:19 in Acts 2:33 implied a replacement of the then-current Moses-typology with that of Christ's ascent and the giving of the Spirit.

Not long after Kretschmar's article appeared, his suggestions were taken up by C. F. D. Moule (1957).[71] Moule noted that Ps 68:19, quoted in its "Rabbinical interpretation" in Eph 4:8, could also be alluded to in Acts 2:33.[72] In either case—according to Moule—the psalm was applied by Jewish interpreters to Moses, who ascended Mt. Sinai, received the Torah from God and gave it in turn to men, and Christians saw in Christ the new Moses. More recently R. Le Déaut (1961) also noted that Ps 68:19 probably influenced the redaction of Acts 2:33, although he did not elaborate as to how such influence originated or what the redaction history of the Acts passage might have been.[73]

In the same year that Le Déaut's article appeared (1961) B. Lindars put forward the theory that Ps 68:19 (alluded to in Acts 2:33) was behind the Christian concept of the giving of the Spirit. Lindars attempted through an approach based on tradition history to get behind the extant text of Acts 2 and to discover the redactional elements which could be attributed to Luke. He saw a relationship between Ps 68:19 and the texts explicitly cited in Acts 2:25-28 and 2:34b-35, Ps 16:8-11 and Ps 110:1. These quotations formed part of an argument intended to prove that Jesus was indeed the Messiah: Ps 16:10-11, in particular, demanded a messianic interpretation. Since it could not be true of David himself, it had to refer to the resurrection of Jesus, who was therefore the Christ. Following the repetition of Ps 16:10 in Acts 2:31 there were two comments on the final line of Psalm 16 (quoted in Acts 2:28). One concerned the place of the resurrected Messiah (exalted to God's right hand), preserved in Luke's composition in the quotation of Ps 110:1 (Acts 2:34b-35). The second comment concerned the Messiah's function: he received the Spirit (in order to dispense it to others) subsequent to his exaltation to the right hand of God (Acts 2:33). This, according to Lindars,

---

[71] C. F. D. Moule, "The Ascension—Acts i. 9," *ExpTim* 68 (1956-57) 205-209.

[72] Moule, "The Ascension—Acts i. 9," 206, n. 3.

[73] R. Le Déaut, "Pentecôte et tradition juive," *ASeign* 51 (1963) 33. This essay originally appeared in *Spiritus* 7 (1961) 127-44.

was probably derived from Ps 68:19. Although the quotation of Ps 68:19 did not survive intact in Luke's composition, the words λαβών and perhaps also ὑψωθείς in Acts 2:33 were probably derived from a reference to the psalm.[74]

Lindars then turned his attention to further instances where a similar use of Ps 68:19 could be found: Eph 4:8 and Acts 5:31. According to Lindars the former passage constituted a midrash pesher on the text of Ps 68:19. Although this text lay behind both Acts 2:33 and Acts 5:31, only in Eph 4:8 did the explicit quotation of the psalm survive in the present form of the text. In the quotation of Ps 68:19 in Eph 4:8 Lindars noted the changes in wording from the LXX, including the significant change from ἔλαβες to ἔδωκεν.[75] In his opinion this change did not result from the influence of *Tg*. Psalms (which reads יהבתא in place of לקחת in the MT) because he saw no other evidence that the interpretation of Ps 68:19 found in *Tg*. Psalms had influenced Eph 4:8.[76] It was possible that the author of *Tg*. Psalms and the author of Ephesians independently made use of a Hebrew textual tradition which read "gave" (חלקת) for "received" (לקחת).[77] Lindars thought it was unlikely, however, that such a variant would have yielded ἔδωκες in a Greek text and יהבתא in *Tg*. Psalms.[78] In Eph 4:8 the modification from "received" to "gave" was probably a case of midrash pesher which involved modification of the text. As such it seemed to have an interpretive motive, since the idea of giving dominated the immediate context in Ephesians, although it was probable that the author of Ephesians himself had not made the change, but was familiar with a form of the text of Ps 68:19 in which the change from "received" to "gave" had already been made.[79]

---

[74] B. Lindars, *New Testament Apologetic: The Doctrinal Significance of the Old Testament Quotations* (London: SCM, 1961) 42-45.

[75] Lindars, *New Testament Apologetic*, 52-53. Differences between the text of Ps 68:19 as found in the LXX and Eph 4:8 are discussed at length in ch. 3, 97-104.

[76] Again, see ch. 3, 97-104, for a comparison of the MT of Ps 68:19 with *Tg*. Ps 68:19, the LXX text, and Eph 4:8.

[77] This suggestion also originated with H. St J. Thackeray (*The Relation of St Paul to Contemporary Jewish Thought*, 182).

[78] The Greek text of Eph 4:8 reads ἔδωκεν; the second person singular verb of the Hebrew text has been modified to third person singular. A possibility that Lindars did not discuss, mentioned above in ch. 3, 99, n. 107, is that a variant which changed "received" to "gave" was already present in a Greek text of Ps 68:19 known to both the author of Ephesians and the targumist. Greek influence is clearly present in *Tg*. Psalms (see above, ch. 3, 66-75) and it is not inconceivable that the targumist was dependent on a Greek text to some extent for his translation.

[79] Lindars, *New Testament Apologetic*, 52-53. A theory similar to this, that Eph 4:8 and *Tg*. Ps 68:19 both witnessed to a form of the text in which the change from "received" to "gave" had already occurred, was advanced by R. Rubinkiewicz ("Psalm LXVIII 19 [= Eph IV 8] Another Textual Tradition or Targum?," *NovT* 17 [1975] 219-24). See ch. 3, 105-109 for a discussion of Rubinkiewicz's proposal.

Lindars specifically rejected any notion that the Moses-typology had affected the use of Ps 68:19 in Eph 4:8, since he did not see any influence of such a typology on the interpretation of the psalm found in the following verses of Ephesians.[80] We have seen already that the connection between Moses' ascent of Sinai to receive the Torah and the feast of Pentecost probably extended back much earlier than this, possibly as early as the second century BCE. Pentecost had already become associated with the celebration of the giving of the Torah long before the epistle to the Ephesians was written. Psalm 68 itself may or may not have become associated with the Jewish celebration of Pentecost at some time prior to the composition of Acts; if Chase, Cadbury, Knox, Kretschmar, Moule, Le Déaut, and others (including Lindars and myself) are correct in our assertion that the tradition behind Acts 2:33 in its present form has been influenced by Ps 68:19, then an association of Psalm 68 with Pentecost almost certainly antedates Ephesians in Christian tradition regardless of its associations in Jewish tradition. The one point that cannot be established with absolute certainty is the link between Moses and the interpretation of Ps 68:19 at such an early period. The influence that such Moses-typology had on the author of Ephesians need not have been a positive one, in the sense that Christ was presented as a new and greater Moses (as was the case in the Gospel of John if W. Meeks was correct in his interpretation of the influence of Moses-typology on the author of the Fourth Gospel).[81] The use of this typology in Ephesians appears more polemical in nature: it was not Moses who ascended to heaven and brought down the Torah as gifts for men, but Christ who ascended to heaven at his exaltation and subsequently descended as the Spirit to give spiritually gifted individuals to lead the church. If, as we have seen, the tradition of Moses' heavenly ascent appeared general and widespread at the time, the author of Ephesians would not necessarily have needed to make explicit mention of Moses in this context in order for the polemical nature of his use of Ps 68:19 to be evident.[82]

Lindars also observed that all three of the texts which appeared to be influenced by Ps 68:19 (Acts 2:33, 5:31, and Eph 4:8) were concerned with the concept of the giving of the Spirit. He suggested the possibility

---

[80] Lindars, *New Testament Apologetic*, 59, n. 1. Lindars did acknowledge in this note that such a typology might have been "a factor in the wider background of thought," however.

[81] W. A. Meeks, *The Prophet-King: Moses Traditions and the Johannine Christology*, NovTSup 14 (Leiden: Brill, 1967) 286-319.

[82] Although such mention of Moses elsewhere in Ephesians would obviously strengthen the case for such a polemical reference here. In the final analysis, the motivation of the author of Ephesians with regard to his use of the Moses-traditions associated with Ps 68:19 must remain the subject of speculation; a polemical interpretation, while possible, cannot be conclusively proven from the evidence at hand.

that ἐξέχεεν in Acts 2:33 could have been substituted for ἔδωκεν in the original quotation from Ps 68:19 under the influence of the quotation from Joel 2:28-32 in Acts 2:17.[83] If this were correct it would represent an intermediate stage in the modification of the text of Ps 68:19, where both the ideas of receiving and of giving were present.[84] This is a possible but not a necessary inference by Lindars and is not subject to verification. The quotation from Joel 2:28-32 is sufficient to explain the presence of ἐξέχεεν in Acts 2:33, so that the existence of a version of Ps 68:19 which contained such a conflate reading is not demanded. In spite of the speculative nature of this last point, Lindars was probably correct to relate the passages in question to the idea of the giving of the Spirit; certainly the following context in Eph 4:11-16 supports such a connection. Along these lines Lindars saw significance in another modification to the text of Ps 68:19 found in Eph 4:8: the words באדם and ἐν ἀνθρώπῳ of the MT and LXX[85] had become τοῖς ἀνθρώποις in the text of Eph 4:8.[86] This modification suggested to Lindars a shift (with the quotation of Ps 68:19 in Eph 4:8) to a concrete idea of the Spirit as gift 'to' men.[87] It is difficult to be sure whether this change carried such far-reaching significance as Lindars suggested, however, since it could be argued that it formed such a natural corollary to the change from ἔλαβες to ἔδωκεν in the quotation that it was almost unavoidable. Furthermore (to return to the question of whether the citation in Eph 4:8 has been influenced by a form of the text later attested in *Tg.* Ps 68:19), this same change appeared in *Tg.* Psalms (לבני נשא), a point Lindars neglected to mention. If this change was as significant as Lindars thought, it might argue more strongly for a relationship between the form of the text of Ps 68:19 found in Eph 4:8 and that found in *Tg.* Ps 68:19. However, as we have already noted, this is not conclusive, because the change of preposition (from the -ב of the MT to the -ל of *Tg.* Psalms, or from the ἐν of the LXX to the simple dative τοῖς ἀνθρώποις of Eph 4:8) followed so naturally from the change of the verbs in the respective texts from "received" to "gave" that it may not have carried a great deal of significance with the author. Lindars finally conceded that it was not possible to determine the exact point at which Ps 68:19 began to be associated with the giving of the Spirit by the exalted Christ. He did,

---

83 Lindars apparently misquoted this as Joel 3:1ff. (*New Testament Apologetic*, 54).

84 Lindars, *New Testament Apologetic*, 54.

85 The reading of א and the second corrector of B is ἀνθρώποις; however, this may represent a scribal attempt at harmonization with the text of Eph 4:8. See ch. 3, 96-104.

86 However, a few manuscripts of the so-called Western text (F, G, and a few others) read ἐν ἀνθρώποις in Eph 4:8, retaining the preposition ἐν from the text of the LXX, but modifying the singular ending of the LXX (ἀνθρώπῳ) to a plural.

87 Lindars, *New Testament Apologetic*, 57.

however, suggest that the idea of such a gift of the Spirit was probably a prior concept and that Ps 68:19 was subsequently adduced to support it.[88]

The arguments of Lindars (as well as those of Kretschmar and Cadbury) were examined by J. Dupont (1973).[89] Although each of these individuals had followed a different approach in suggesting an allusion to Ps 68:19 behind Acts 2:33, in Dupont's judgment these approaches were not mutually exclusive but complementary, and all tended to support the presence of such an allusion. In fact, Dupont himself went beyond the literary reconstructions of Lindars to suggest that Luke in Acts did make use of the Moses-typology by a comparison of the language of Acts 5:31 and 7:35. In Acts 5:31 the following terms described Jesus: τοῦτον ὁ θεὸς ἀρχηγὸν καὶ σωτῆρα ὕψωσεν τῇ δεξιᾷ αὐτοῦ; while Acts 7:35 described Moses: τοῦτον τὸν Μωυσῆν ὃν ἠρνήσαντο εἰπόντες· τίς σε κατέστησεν ἄρχοντα καὶ δικαστήν; τοῦτον ὁ θεὸς καὶ ἄρχοντα καὶ λυτρωτὴν ἀπέσταλκεν. Acts 7:25 also stated concerning Moses: ἐνόμιζεν δὲ συνιέναι τοὺς ἀδελφοὺς ὅτι ὁ θεὸς διὰ χειρὸς αὐτοῦ δίδωσιν σωτηρίαν αὐτοῖς. The description of Christ in Acts 5:31 corresponded so closely to that of Moses in 7:25 and 35 that Dupont suggested the Moses-typology was present even in Acts, and nothing would prevent us from supposing that it was also behind the interpretation which applied Ps 68:19 to the ascension of Christ and the giving of the Spirit.[90]

Not everyone has been convinced by the arguments of Cadbury, Lindars, and Dupont that an allusion to Ps 68:19 lay in the background of Acts 2:33. P. D. Overfield (1976) rejected Lindars' arguments for an allusion to Ps 68:19 behind Acts 2:33 because he believed Lindars' view necessitated a connection between verses 33 and 34a not only in the text of Acts itself but in the underlying tradition behind it.[91] Overfield acknowledged that the occurrence of ἀνέβη in Acts 2:34a suggested a connection to the text of Ps 68:19, and thus strengthened Lindars' case, but Lindars' arguments were primarily centered on the presence of ὑψωθείς and λαβών in 2:33. These pointed to a tradition behind Acts 2:33 which could be considered independently of 2:34-35, although it should be noted that even if the traditions behind 2:33 and 2:34f. differed, the general theme which they shared in common was

---

[88] Lindars, New Testament Apologetic, 58-59.

[89] J. Dupont, "Ascension du Christ et don de l'Esprit d'après Actes 2:33," in Christ and Spirit in the New Testament, ed. B. Lindars and S. S. Smalley (Cambridge: Cambridge University Press, 1973) 219-28.

[90] Dupont, "Ascension du Christ et don de l'Esprit d'après Actes 2:33," 226.

[91] P. D. Overfield, "The Ascension, Pleroma and Ecclesia Concepts in Ephesians" (Ph.D. thesis, University of St. Andrews, 1976) 97-98.

that of the exaltation of Jesus as the Messiah, and this may well have led
the compiler of Acts to juxtapose them as they now stand in the present
form of the text.

Another interpreter who was not persuaded that an allusion to Psalm
68 existed in Acts 2 was D. L. Bock (1987).[92] He found in the Lucan
material of Acts as a whole all of the terms and phrases suggested by
Lindars as parallels to Ps 68:19 except for the single participle λαβών.
This one word alone provided an insufficient basis for an allusion to
Psalm 68. Bock saw the absence of δόματα (as used in the psalm) from
Luke's material as further evidence that such an allusion to Ps 68:19 by
Luke was unlikely. Likewise, Dupont's attempt to relate Ps 68:19 and
Acts 2:33 through the Jewish traditions which associate the psalm with
Pentecost and Moses' ascent of Sinai to receive the law also failed to
persuade Bock that Ps 68:19 lay behind Acts 2:33. Bock failed to see
any mention of Moses or the law in Acts 2, an omission he regarded as
fatal for any theory that attempted to connect Moses and the tradition
that the law was given on the feast of Pentecost to an allusion to Psalm
68 at this point. He concluded that "for Luke, and probably also for the
tradition he communicates in Acts 2, Ps 68:19 played no significant
role."[93]

In response to this several observations are in order: (1) Bock did acknowledge in a note that Psalm 68 played a role in the earliest church
traditions about the gift of the Spirit, although Luke made no use of
these ideas in Acts 2.[94] Bock asserted that Luke could have mentioned
the Mosaic connection, however (as he does in chapters 3 and 7) if he
had wished to do so. Yet if the connection between Ps 68:19 and the
giving of the Spirit went back to the earliest church traditions, why must
it be ruled out that such traditions were behind the source of the account in Acts 2:33, especially as this purports to go back to Peter's
speech on the day of Pentecost? (2) Lindars went on to argue precisely
the point Bock conceded, that it was the early Christian concept of the
gift of the Spirit which was related to (or perhaps even deduced from)
the language of Ps 68:19 read in a christological sense. (3) Luke's failure in Acts 2:33 to develop the connection between Moses' ascent of
Sinai at the giving of the Torah and Pentecost does not disprove the
existence of such a connection in his sources; he simply did not make
use of it. Comparisons between Christ and Moses do appear in Acts
7:25 and 35 when read alongside Acts 5:31.

---

[92] D. L. Bock, *Proclamation from Prophecy and Pattern: Lucan Old Testament Christology*, JSNTSup 12 (Sheffield: JSOT, 1987).

[93] Bock, *Proclamation from Prophecy and Pattern*, 181-83.

[94] Bock, *Proclamation from Prophecy and Pattern*, 352, n. 92.

On the whole, in spite of the objections raised by Bock, it seems quite probable that an allusion to Ps 68:19 was present in the underlying tradition used by Luke in Acts 2. As we have seen, traces of the psalm appear to remain in the extant text of Acts 2:33, although there has not been a complete consensus on the exact words and phrases which should be attributed to Ps 68:19. In light of the obviously christological context of Acts 2 (especially the quotation from Ps 110:1 in the following verse, 2:34) it seems clear that Psalm 68 had assumed a christological interpretation at an early date. Ps 68:19 in particular was understood by the early church to refer to the gifts of the Spirit given by the exalted Christ.[95] Furthermore, it is probable that this association of Ps 68:19 with the distribution of spiritual gifts by the ascended Christ antedates the composition of Acts, since Luke did not develop this imagery in his reworking of the traditional source describing Peter's speech on the day of Pentecost. Although a specific date for such a Christian interpretation of Ps 68:19 cannot be assigned, we can assume that this interpretation was in circulation some time prior to the composition of Ephesians. This suggests that the christological interpretation of Ps 68:19 was not necessarily original with the author of Ephesians himself. Instead, he may have merely adopted an interpretation of the psalm already widely accepted in Christian circles at the time he was writing.

D. CONCLUSIONS: EPH 4:7-11 AND THE GIVING OF THE SPIRIT

So far we have examined a number of aspects of the relationship between Psalm 68, Pentecost, and Eph 4:7-11 with its emphasis on the distribution of gifts to the church. The association of the Jewish feast of Pentecost (Weeks) and the celebration of the giving of the Torah to Moses can be traced back as early as the *Book of Jubilees*, a work which should probably be dated in the second century BCE. The author

---

95 J. Potin concluded that Pentecost was considered a covenant celebration as early as the second (and perhaps the third) century BCE (*La Fête Juive de la Pentecôte: Étude des textes liturgiques*, LD 65 [Paris: Éditions du Cerf, 1971] 1.300-303). Although the rabbinic tradition associating Pentecost with the giving of the Torah could not be dated before 150 CE, it was certainly prior to this date. The actual assignment of the celebration of the giving of the Torah to the feast of Pentecost may have been carried out by the Pharisees in the years immediately following the destruction of the Temple. However, although the later synagogue liturgy was not totally elaborated at the time of the redaction of Acts (which Potin dated ca. 80 CE) the feast of Pentecost was already associated with the salvific event of Sinai in popular tradition by this time. Potin also suggested that texts of the Law, the Prophets, and the Psalms (including Psalm 68) were chosen for inclusion in the synagogue liturgy for Pentecost by the Pharisees after the destruction of the Temple because they had already been associated for some time with the covenant at Sinai as well. Thus the association of Pentecost with the giving of the Torah at Sinai may well have been known and used by Luke in the composition of Acts.

of *Jubilees* placed great emphasis on the idea that the date of the feast
of Weeks and the giving of the Torah to Moses coincided. In addition,
Psalm 68 was probably associated with Pentecost and the giving of the
Torah to Moses in pre-Christian (Jewish) tradition, although this cannot
be conclusively proven. It is almost certain, however, that the association of Psalm 68 with Pentecost antedated the composition of Ephesians
because of the christological interpretation of Ps 68:19 which existed in
early Christian tradition. Such an interpretation of Ps 68:19 probably lay
behind the present text of Acts 2:33. Thus it was used to refer to the
gift(s) of the Spirit in a layer of tradition which was almost certainly
older than the Epistle to the Ephesians. Therefore the author of Ephesians need not have been particularly innovative in his use of Ps 68:19
to refer to the ascension of Christ and his subsequent distribution of
gifts to the church. The innovation on the part of our author lay not in
the use of the psalm in a christological sense (an interpretation which he
probably inherited from prior Christian tradition) but in its explanation
in 4:9-10, where he identified the ascended Christ with the Spirit who
descended to distribute the gifts. We shall now proceed to examine the
context of Eph 4:7-11 closely to see if such an identification appears
likely as an explanation of the ascent and descent of Christ described in
4:8-10.

CHAPTER SIX

THE DESCENT OF CHRIST AS SPIRIT IN EPH 4:7-11

A. BACKGROUND

We have already seen (in Chapter Four) that there is substantial evidence for the existence of ascent-typology associated with Moses and the giving of the Torah at Sinai prior to the middle of the first century CE. It is highly probable that the author of Ephesians was aware of such traditions when he quoted Ps 68:19 with its reference to a heavenly ascent in Eph 4:8. Knowledge of these Moses-traditions would explain why the author found it necessary to deduce a descent of Christ in Eph 4:9-10 from the ascent explicitly mentioned in the quotation from Ps 68:19 (Eph 4:8): Moses, following his ascent of Mt. Sinai to 'capture' the words of Torah, descended to distribute them as 'gifts' to men. But for our author it was not Moses but Christ who made the ascent described in the psalm quotation, and thus it was Christ who descended (as the Spirit) to distribute gifts (i.e., gifted leaders) to his church. The likelihood that such traditions lie behind Eph 4:7-11 is even greater when we consider (as we have done in the preceding chapter) that the Jewish feast of Pentecost (Weeks) had almost certainly become associated with the giving of the Torah at Sinai as a celebration of the giving of the law to Moses some time prior to the first century CE. Furthermore, while we have not established with certainty that the association of Psalm 68 with the feast of Pentecost in later Jewish liturgy is as ancient as the first century of the Christian era, it does seem clear that Psalm 68 became associated at a very early date with the Christian celebration of the giving of the Spirit at Pentecost, as a way of expressing the gift of the Spirit by the ascended and exalted Christ. Such a use of Psalm 68 probably lies in the background of Acts 2:33 as well, although the psalm is not explicitly quoted in the existing text.

By the time the author of Ephesians wrote his epistle it is thus highly probable that all (or almost all) of the various elements were in place to enable him to represent the ascension of Christ in terms which were already commonly and widely used to describe Moses' ascent of Sinai to receive the Torah and distribute it as gifts to men. Such imagery had been used already in the tradition behind Acts 2:33 with its allusion to Ps 68:19 as a reference to the outpouring of the Spirit by the ascended and exalted Christ. Since the context of Eph 4:7 and 4:11-16 deals with the giving of spiritual gifts (or gifted individuals) to the church to equip it for ministry, the imagery of the gift of the Spirit (as reflected in the accounts of the first Christian Pentecost in Acts) would not be far removed. There is, in fact, only one remaining element in the proposed interpretation of Eph 4:9-10 as a subsequent descent of Christ as the Spirit which is truly unique to the author of Ephesians. This is the identification he made in 4:10 between "the one who descended" and "the one who ascended above all the heavens" (ὁ καταβὰς αὐτός ἐστιν καὶ ὁ ἀναβὰς ὑπεράνω πάντων τῶν οὐρανῶν), an identification which appears at first unnecessary. As we now proceed to examine the contextual argument in favor of a subsequent descent of Christ as the Spirit in Eph 4:9-10 in more detail, we shall attempt to show that such an identification is not as superfluous as it might initially appear.

B. THE CONTEXTUAL ARGUMENT FOR A SUBSEQUENT DESCENT

The strongest argument for a subsequent descent of Christ in Eph 4:9-10 can be found in the context of Ephesians 4 itself. After the exhortation to maintain "the unity of the Spirit" in Eph 4:3, the writer gave the basis for that unity in verses 4-6: using an asyndetic construction for added emphasis, he stated that everything about the Christian faith is characterized by unity.[1] There is one body of believers and one Spirit, one Lord, one faith, one baptism, and one God who is father of all.[2] Yet within this unified framework, there were found diversities of spiritual gifts, which the author introduced in verses 7-8 with the supporting quotation from Ps 68:19: the one who ascended on high gave gifts to men. The principal assertion is made in verse 7, followed by the quotation from Ps 68:19 and its subsequent explanation in verses 8-10. These verses appear to be offered as proof of the assertion in verse 7.[3] The qualifying phrase τῆς δωρεᾶς τοῦ Χριστοῦ in this verse makes clear that it was Christ who ascended and who distributed the gifts.[4] Following the psalm quotation in verse 8, the writer of Ephesians engaged in a midrashic exegesis of the word ἀναβάς from Ps 68:19 in which he deduced a descent from the stated ascent. Our author then went on to as-

---

[1] On the theme of unity in Eph 4:1-16, see S. Hanson (*The Unity of the Church in the New Testament: Colossians and Ephesians*, ASNU 14 [Uppsala: Almqvist & Wiksells, 1946]).

[2] Verses 4-6 have been understood by many to contain a confession or fragment of hymnic literature quoted by the author of Ephesians (e.g., M. Barth, *Ephesians: Translation and Commentary on Chapters 4-6*, AB 34A [Garden City, NY: Doubleday, 1974] 429). While this may well be true, the source of this material does not affect our present understanding of the place it has in the author's overall argument in its final form.

[3] As noted by J. Cambier (*Vie Chrétienne en Église: L'Épître aux Éphésiens lue aux chrétiens d'aujourd'hui* [Paris: Desclée, 1966] 126).

[4] J. D. G. Dunn took δωρεά here to refer to the gift of the Spirit, so that ἡ δωρεὰ τοῦ Χριστοῦ = τὸ πνεῦμα τοῦ Χριστοῦ ("A Note on δωρεά," *ExpTim* 81 [1969-70] 349-51).

sert in verse 10 that the one who descended was himself the one who ascended above all the heavens, in order that (ἵνα) he might fill all things.[5]

Up to this point it is clear that the one who both ascended and descended, the one who gave the gifts and filled the universe, is Christ (cf. v. 7). Furthermore (in keeping with the quotation from Psalm 68), it is apparently Christ (the referent of the pronoun αὐτός in the phrase καὶ αὐτὸς ἔδωκεν) who distributed the gifts (now described further as gifted individuals or offices) to the church at large (v. 11).[6] These gifted leaders were to equip the saints (i.e., the church at large) for the work of the ministry, for the edification of the body of believers, until collective maturity (on the part of the church as a whole) was finally achieved (vv. 12-16).[7] So far there is nothing new or particularly remarkable about our reconstruction of the context of 4:7-11. But such a reconstruction enables us to make a significant observation which has been overlooked by the majority of interpreters: if the writer's intention in quoting Ps 68:19 was to assert that Christ, upon his victorious ascent, gave gifts (or gifted individuals) to the church, there was no need whatsoever to in-

---

[5] Concerning the midrashic nature of the author's exegesis of Ps 68:19 in Eph 4:9-10, cf. the comment of M. Barth, who stated: "Without detriment to its substance and quality Paul's interpretation can be called a midrash" (*Ephesians: Translation and Commentary on Chapters 4-6*, 476; cf. also 432).

[6] These 'gifts' were described by J. Ernst as "verschiedenen Dienstämter" (*Die Briefe an die Philipper, an Philemon, an die Kolosser, an die Epheser*, RNT [Regensburg: Friedrich Pustet, 1974] 351).

[7] Two disparate interpretations of v. 12 are possible because of a dispute about the syntax of the three prepositions involved, πρός, εἰς, and εἰς, each of which introduces a distinct element concerning the giving of the gifts (or gifted individuals) in relation to the ministry of the church. The shift from πρός to εἰς has led some to see different purposes of the gifts in view, the first (πρὸς τὸν καταρτισμὸν τῶν ἁγίων) directed to the church at large, and the second (εἰς ἔργον διακονίας, εἰς οἰκοδομὴν τοῦ σώματος τοῦ Χριστοῦ) to specific leaders or specialized ministers who were to do the work of the ministry. This interpretation is usually indicated by the placement of a comma following the first element, πρὸς τὸν καταρτισμὸν τῶν ἁγίων, to indicate its separation from the following εἰς-phrases. The alternative interpretation sees the prepositional phrases as describing a single purpose for the gifts of v. 11, with some degree of progression from one prepositional phrase to the next: thus the gifts (gifted individuals) were given in order to equip the saints (themselves) to do the work of the ministry for the edification of the body of Christ. Since the earliest manuscripts contained no punctuation and either interpretation is syntactically possible, the choice must be made on the basis of contextual emphases and parallels. These seem to favor the second interpretation, since in 4:7 each member (ἑκάστῳ) of the church has been given "grace" (ἡ χάρις) and 4:16 speaks of the contribution of each individual member (ἐν μέτρῳ ἑνὸς ἑκάστου μέρους). Parallels in 1 Cor 12:7, 18 also stress that each member of the church is a recipient of "the manifestation of the Spirit for the common good" (ἑκάστῳ δὲ δίδοται ἡ φανέρωσις τοῦ πνεύματος πρὸς τὸ συμφέρον) and each one has been placed in the body just as God wished (ὁ θεὸς ἔθετο τὰ μέλη, ἓν ἕκαστον αὐτῶν ἐν τῷ σώματι καθὼς ἠθέλησεν). For further discussion of these difficulties see M. Barth (*Ephesians: Translation and Commentary on Chapters 4-6*, 477-84) and also R. Schnackenburg, (*Der Brief an die Epheser*, EKKNT 10 [Zürich: Benziger Verlag; Neukirchen-Vluyn: Neukirchener Verlag, 1982] 185-86).

troduce the midrash of 4:9-10 (which deduced a descent) because the psalm quotation itself asserted that gifts were given upon (or after) the ascent. Verses 9 and 10 are therefore relegated to the status of a parenthetical (and somewhat extraneous) comment.[8] This is, in fact, the way the editors of *UBSGNT* second and third editions punctuated the text.[9] As a parenthetical comment, however, the two verses make no contribution to the advancing argument; the most that can be said of them is that they constitute a rebuttal of some particular (and probably heretical) theological view, such as Docetism.[10]

The parenthetical nature of verses 9-10 has even been used on occasion to argue against a subsequent descent of Christ: F. Foulkes, for example, rejected the idea of a subsequent descent on the grounds that the giving of gifts to men was associated in the text with the ascent rather than the descent (thus demonstrating the superfluity of the reference to the descent in 4:9-10).[11] It may be true from a structural standpoint that the giving of gifts is connected to the ascent; but one must also consider why, within the given context, the author of Ephesians felt it necessary to introduce a reference to the descent in 4:9-10 at all. Since no descent was explicitly stated in Psalm 68 (although both the ascent and the giving of gifts were mentioned), the descent had to be deduced (i.e., inferred). Thus the juxtaposition of the ascent and the distribution of the gifts in these verses was necessitated by the order of the material in Ps 68:19 as quoted. The author's own introduction of a reference to the descent could hardly have been placed otherwise. Therefore, an associa-

---

[8] H. Chadwick asserted: "The parenthesis, a distracting digression, is intended to justify the forced exegesis of the Psalm-text by the Rabbinic (and typically Pauline) argument that an ascent implies a previous descent" ("Ephesians," *PCB* 980-84, esp. 984). F. W. Beare also acknowledged this problem in less forceful terms, but tried to get round it by attributing the apparently illogical inference in 4:9-10 to rabbinic methods of exegesis. Beare claims that the author "first adopts a form of text which was current among them [the rabbis], and then follows it by an arbitrary midrashic interpretation.... Strange and unconvincing as the argument appears to the modern reader, it is typical midrash" ("The Epistle to the Ephesians," *IB* 10 [New York: Abingdon, 1953] 688-89). To this the reply of G. B. Caird is sufficient: "we ought not to resort to unreason until we have exhausted the possibilities of reason" ("The Descent of Christ in Ephesians 4, 7-11," *SE* 2 [= TU 87], ed. F. L. Cross [Berlin: Akademie, 1964] 536). Caird went on to point out that it was hard to understand why, if verses 9-10 were only the product of irrational rabbinic exegesis, the author should have felt obliged in verse 10 to assert the identity of descender and ascender.

[9] Further information on how various major translations have punctuated verses 9-10 may be found in the punctuation apparatus of *UBSGNT*. It should also be noted, however, that neither the fourth edition of *UBSGNT* nor NA27 punctuates verses 9-10 as a parenthesis.

[10] It is worth pointing out that there are no other indications anywhere in Ephesians (as noted by G. B. Caird, "The Descent of Christ in Ephesians 4, 7-11," 536) that Docetic tendencies are at large and require refutation, although 1:19-23 might have provided a better place for such a refutation than 4:9-10 supposedly does.

[11] F. Foulkes, *The Epistle of Paul to the Ephesians: An Introduction and Commentary*, TNTC (London: Tyndale, 1963) 117.

tion of the giving of gifts with the descent rather than the ascent should not be rejected a priori, as Foulkes appears to have done.[12]

Another recent attempt to deal with the problems of Eph 4:8-10 is found in a doctoral thesis by P. D. Overfield (1976).[13] Overfield was concerned primarily with the identification and significance of the ascent mentioned in the passage rather than the descent. He dealt with the descent only in so far as it shed further light on the psalm quotation in 4:8. Overfield understood the descent as a reference to the incarnation based on the use of καταβαίνειν (the κατάβασις—ἀνάβασις motif) elsewhere in the Pauline corpus (only in Rom 10:6-8).[14] He examined Caird's proposals concerning a subsequent descent in Eph 4:9-10 and rejected them because in his opinion they placed the emphasis in 4:7-11 not on the ascension per se, but on the 'descent' of Christ, and this was not the primary focus of the passage.[15] While Overfield accepted Caird's grammatical analysis of the phrase τῆς γῆς in Eph 4:9 as an appositive genitive, he rejected the similarity between the ascension theme in Ephesians and the ascension theme in Acts which he believed Caird's view would necessitate. First, there was no evidence that in the early church Psalm 68 was part of the tradition concerning the gift of the Spirit. Sec-

---

[12] It should be noted with regard to the Greek text of Eph 4:8 that the aorist participle ἀναβάς may be understood to describe action either contemporaneous with or antecedent to the finite verbs ἠχμαλώτευσεν and ἔδωκεν (i.e., "when he ascended...he gave gifts" or "after he ascended...he gave gifts"). Both of the finite verbs in the quotation are also aorists, and since an aorist participle related to an aorist finite verb may indicate either contemporaneous or antecedent action, the ascension could very legitimately be understood as prior to the distribution of the gifts mentioned again in 4:11-12. E. D. Burton actually stated that an aorist participle normally indicated antecedent rather than contemporaneous action: "Among these various relations the case of action antecedent to that of the principal verb furnishes the largest number of instances. It is thus, numerically considered, the leading use of the Aorist Participle, and this fact has even to some extent reacted on the meaning of the tense, so that there is associated with the tense as a secondary, acquired, and wholly subordinate characteristic a certain suggestion of antecedence" (*Syntax of the Moods and Tenses in New Testament Greek*, 3rd ed. [Chicago: University of Chicago Press, 1900] 60). Burton's position was somewhat modified by BDF §339:"...the idea of relative past time became associated to a certain degree with the aorist participle....The notion of relative past time, however, is not at all necessarily inherent in the aorist participle...especially if its action is identical with that of an aorist finite verb" (BDF 174-75). Ultimately the question regarding the time of an action described by an aorist participle relative to the time of an action described by an aorist finite verb must be resolved contextually, as M. Zerwick pointed out (*Biblical Greek Illustrated by Examples* [Rome: Pontifical Biblical Institute, 1963] §262, p. 86). All of this merely indicates that an aorist participle may express action either simultaneous with or antecedent to that of an aorist verb. As far as Eph 4:8 is concerned, ἀναβάς could refer to an action either antecedent to or contemporaneous with the finite verbs ἠχμαλώτευσεν and ἔδωκεν which follow.

[13] P. D. Overfield, "The Ascension, Pleroma and Ecclesia Concepts in Ephesians" (Ph.D. thesis, University of St. Andrews, 1976).

[14] Overfield, "Ascension," 139, 162.

[15] Overfield, "Ascension," 110. The proposals of G. B. Caird to which Overfield made reference are found in "The Descent of Christ in Ephesians 4, 7-11," *SE* 2 (= TU 87), ed. F. L. Cross (Berlin: Akademie, 1964) 535-45.

ond, the ascension theme in Acts 1-2 was not a unified one; the tradition in Acts 2:14-36 differed from that in 1:9. The tradition in Acts 2:14-36 (a non-Lucan tradition according to Overfield) knew nothing of an ascension of Christ or outpouring of the Spirit as events separate from the resurrection. Overfield linked the tradition in Eph 1:20-23 to that in Acts 2:14-36 and concluded that this spoke decisively against Caird's view of a subsequent descent.[16]

With regard to Overfield's first point, we have argued in chapter 4 that Acts 2:33 does contain traces of the influence of Ps 68:19.[17] We have also shown, through our discussion of Kretschmar's work, that the early church did (in some instances, at least) associate the ascension with the outpouring of the Spirit, and that this tradition was associated with Pentecost, Moses, and the giving of the Torah.[18] It is difficult to see how such a view of the descent as von Soden, Caird, and others have proposed necessitates a unified ascension motif in Acts 1–2 as Overfield asserted. The author of Luke-Acts may or may not have been aware of conflicting traditions behind his sources, and he certainly did not develop or attempt to reconcile these motifs, but this does not eliminate the possibility that Eph 4:9-10 refers to a descent of Christ as the Spirit.

Finally, with regard to Overfield's point about the relative emphasis placed on the ascension versus the descent, it is hard to see how the theory of a subsequent descent contradicts Overfield's own analysis, which related the exaltation theology of Eph 1:20-23 to that of 4:8-10.[19] It seems obvious that the author of Ephesians quoted Ps 68:19 because it contained a reference to a victorious ascent followed by the distribution of gifts. If we understand the descent as a reference to Christ's descent as the Spirit to distribute spiritual gifts (or spiritually gifted individuals) to his church, the passage in question then serves as a transition linking the exaltation christology of Eph 1:20-23 (which depicted Christ exalted over all things and given as 'Head' to the church) with the emphasis on the activity of the Spirit in the life and conduct of the church described in Eph 5:15-6:9. In the final analysis what Overfield failed to explain adequately was why a parenthetical reference to the descent, which in his opinion contributed nothing to the argument, needed to be introduced by the author of Ephesians following the mention of the ascent which he found in the psalm quotation and obviously understood as referring to Christ.

---

16 Overfield, "Ascension," 158-62.
17 Overfield denied that Acts 2:33 contains any allusion to Ps 68:19 (97-98); his arguments are discussed in ch. 5, 167.
18 See ch. 5, 148-52.
19 Overfield, "Ascension," 170-71.

Thus the major contextual issue we are attempting to address at this point is why the author of Ephesians, if all he wanted to do was to assert that upon his victorious ascension Christ distributed spiritual gifts to the church, felt compelled to add verses 9 and 10 as a midrashic interpretation of Ps 68:19 (which he had quoted already in 4:8). The quotation from Ps 68:19 itself introduced the idea of gifts distributed to men at or subsequent to the ascent, and if all the author wanted to do was establish the giving of the gifts, the psalm quotation itself asserted that. The author could have proceeded with his argument in 4:11-16 without introducing the complicating factor of a reference to the descent at all, unless there was something about the nature or timing of the descent which he believed to be crucial to his argument. Yet if verses 9-10 are understood to refer either to the incarnation or to a descent into the underworld (or to Sheol or simply the grave), they do nothing whatsoever to advance the argument concerning the distribution of spiritual gifts.[20] On the contrary, they add an apparently superfluous note which gives the impression of theological pedantry.

But these two verses need not be relegated to a parenthesis; they can be explained perfectly well within the argument of Ephesians 4. If 4:9-10 are *not* understood as parenthetical, then a descent deduced by the writer from the victorious ascent of Psalm 68 would be understood most naturally as subsequent to the ascent from which it was derived.[21] Such an impression is further strengthened by the presence of the καί which precedes κατέβη in verse 9.[22] A subsequent descent is also per-

---

[20] The interpretive options mentioned here have been discussed in chapter 1 as part of the survey of the history of interpretation of Eph 4:7-11. Although there are disparate interpretations involved (incarnation vs. descent to the underworld, Sheol, or the grave), either approach produces the same result: the reference to the descent inferred by the author in 4:9-10 appears unnecessary and contributes nothing to the argument. This point was made emphatically by G. B. Caird, who noted the failure of interpretations involving a descent to the underworld or at the incarnation to explain *why* it was necessary for the author of Ephesians to infer a descent from the ascent stated in the quotation from Ps 68:19 and to affirm the identity of the one who ascended with the one who descended in 4:10 (*Paul's Letters from Prison*, NClarB [Oxford: Oxford University Press, 1976] 73-75).

[21] This much, at least, was conceded by C. L. Mitton although he viewed the descent as a reference to the incarnation (*Ephesians*, NCB [London: Oliphants, 1976] 148). The probability that a subsequent descent would be deduced (inferred) from the quotation from Ps 68:19 is even greater if the author of Ephesians was aware of the tradition behind the targumic interpretation of Ps 68:19, which referred the ascent mentioned in the Psalm to Moses and his ascent of Mt. Sinai to bring down the Torah. For an extensive examination of this possibility, and of the relationship of such Moses-typology to Ephesians, see chapter 3.

[22] This observation was originally made by H. von Soden when he first proposed the view that the descent was subsequent to the ascent: "Vielmehr lässt die Wortfolge vermuthen, dass das καί κατέβη als auf das ἀναβῆναι gefolgt gedacht sei" (ed., *Die Briefe an die Kolosser, Epheser, Philemon; die Pastoralbriefe*, 2d ed. HKNT 3 [Freiburg and Leipzig: Mohr, 1893] 136). It was repeated by E. D. Roels (*God's Mission: The Epistle to the Ephesians in Mission Perspective* [Franeker: T. Wever, 1962] 163 n. 18).

mitted (if not implied outright) by the sequence of tenses (aorist—aorist) represented by ἀνέβη—κατέβη (aorist—pluperfect, on the other hand, would be needed to determine conclusively a prior descent by tense sequence alone). Yet the same line of reasoning with regard to the most natural order of events cannot be applied to 4:10 in order to claim a prior descent for at least three reasons: (1) the switch from aorist finite verbs (ἀνέβη and κατέβη, verse 9) to aorist participles (ὁ καταβάς and ὁ ἀναβάς, verse 10) suggests that verse 10 is not intended to reflect the actual sequence of events, but rather to assert the identity of the one who descended with the one who ascended;[23] (2) the pronoun αὐτός, which follows καταβάς in verse 10, is repeated in verse 11, and since it carries emphatic (adjunctive) force in both instances, it suggests the connection of the *descent* (i.e., the one who descended, ὁ καταβάς) with the giving of the gifts mentioned in verse 11 (καὶ αὐτὸς ἔδωκεν κ.τ.λ.); and finally (3) there is a fairly complex chiastic structure present within the section. As it stands, the entire section under consideration (4:7-11) is bracketed by references to the giving of spiritual gifts (or gifted leaders) by the exalted Christ.[24] The section is introduced by the statement ἑκάστῳ ἡμῶν ἐδόθη ἡ χάρις in 4:7, a reference to the giftedness of each individual member of the church, and closed by the assertion καὶ αὐτὸς ἔδωκεν τοὺς μὲν ἀποστόλους... in 4:11, which refers to the gifts (or gifted leaders) given by Christ to the church as a corporate entity. Within this framework stands the quotation from Ps 68:19 (4:8), followed by the midrashic explanation (4:9-10) provided by the author. The midrash itself contains references to both ascent and descent, ar-

---

23 M. Barth contended that the phrase ὁ καταβὰς αὐτὸς ἐστιν καὶ ὁ ἀναβὰς κ.τ.λ. could not emphasize "exclusively personal identity" (as understood, e.g., by Aquinas et al.) because αὐτός, since it was anarthrous, could not be translated "he is the same as he who..." (*Ephesians: Translation and Commentary on Chapters 4-6*, AB 34A [Garden City, NY: Doubleday, 1974] 434 n. 51). It is true that αὐτός cannot be rendered "the same as" without the definite article in this context, but this observation alone does not negate an assertion of identity between "the one who descended" and "the one who ascended." This is implicit in the adjunctive use of καί in v. 10: "the one who descended [himself (αὐτός)] is *also* the one who ascended...." In context this amounts to an identification of the person who descended with the person who ascended, no matter how αὐτός is understood. In addition, other modern interpreters have affirmed the identity of ὁ καταβάς and ὁ ἀναβάς in 4:10, among them N. A. Dahl, who stated: "Aber in den V. 9-10 heißt es, daß Christus, der heruntergefahren ist, derselbe ist, der aufgefahren ist" (*Kurze Auslegung des Epheserbriefes* [Göttingen: Vandenhoeck & Ruprecht, 1965] 51), and A. Lindemann, who stated: "Jedenfalls betont V. 10, daß der Hinabgestiegene identisch ist mit dem Hinaufgestiegenen" (*Der Epheserbrief*, ZBK [Zürich: Theologischer Verlag, 1985] 77).

24 For a discussion of the nature of these gifts and a comparison with other passages in the Pauline corpus which describe similar gifts, see H. Schürmann (*Ursprung und Gestalt: Erörterungen und Besinnungen zum Neuen Testament* [Düsseldorf: Patmos-Verlag, 1970] 236-267). Concerning the assertion that the main point of Eph 4:7 and 4:11 is that gifts were given to the church by the exalted Christ, see S. D. Clark ("La Enseñanza Paulina sobre los Dones y los Ministerios: Un estudio exegético de Efesios 4,7-16," *RivB* 41 [1979] 141-53).

ranged in chiastic order (here represented by the key word in each phrase): ἀνέβη (4:9a), κατέβη (4:9b), ὁ καταβάς (4:10a), and ὁ ἀναβάς (4:10b). In verse 9 the order is ascent—descent, while in verse 10 it is descent—ascent. This appears at first to be completely non-prejudicial in terms of the actual order of events as understood by the author of Ephesians. In fact, however, since verse 9 constitutes a question regarding the implications of the term ἀναβάς in the quotation from Ps 68:19 (τὸ δὲ ἀνέβη, according to the midrashic formula employed by the author), the order of ascent—descent is necessitated, because it is the descent which is not explicitly mentioned in the quotation from Ps 68:19, but has to be deduced (i.e., inferred) by the author of Ephesians. In light of this, we might expect verse 10 to reflect, in the order of descent—ascent, the actual sequence of events involved (which would argue against a subsequent descent). But the point of the assertion made by the author in verse 10 is not the chronological order of events, but rather the identification of "the one who descended" as "the one who ascended." For emphasis ὁ καταβάς is placed at the beginning of the sentence, which produces a chiasm with the ascent and descent mentioned in verse 9.[25] It is probable, however, that the reference in verse 10a to "the one who descended" relates back not so much to verse 9b as to verse 8b, the giving of gifts mentioned in the quotation from Ps 68:19, since this is the point of departure from which the idea of a descent was originally deduced by the author of Ephesians. In this case, the final reference to the ascent (verse 10b) would parallel not verse 9a, but the quotation from Ps 68:19 in verse 8a instead. Thus the qualifying phrase in verse 10b, ὑπεράνω πάντων τῶν οὐρανῶν, would correspond to the phrase εἰς ὕψος in verse 8a (and possibly to ἠχμαλώτευσεν αἰχμαλωσίαν in the same verse as well, if an allusion to Christ's victory over the 'powers' is implied by the phrase ὑπεράνω...τῶν οὐρανῶν).[26] Final emphasis would then be returned to the de-

---

[25] According to BDF, "Any emphasis on an element in the sentence causes that element to be moved forward" (248).

[26] Whatever may be said about other NT writers and their placement of the evil spiritual 'powers' in the regions under the earth, the author of Ephesians made no explicit reference to such a locus for the powers. Instead, he repeatedly located the evil spiritual powers "in the heavenlies" (ἐν τοῖς ἐπουρανίοις) in 1:20, 3:10, and 6:12. What would therefore be required for Christ to achieve victory over the powers would not be a descent to the underworld, but a victorious ascent, and this is reflected in Eph 4:8 in the author's quotation of Ps 68:19. Although there may be a hint of Christ's victory over the powers in the phrase ἠχμαλώτευσεν αἰχμαλωσίαν quoted from Psalm 68, the writer drew no such direct inference from the psalm, and did not discuss the identity of the 'captives' further. Although the early church understood the 'captives' to refer either to redeemed saints who had been imprisoned in the underworld awaiting the salvation of Christ, or to condemned spirits awaiting punishment, the author of Ephesians demonstrated no further interest in such identifications, since no further mention was made of the 'captives'. See the history of the traditional interpretation of Eph 4:7-11 outlined

scent by verse 11a, καὶ αὐτὸς ἔδωκεν τοὺς μὲν ἀποστόλους, κ.τ.λ., which (as mentioned earlier) corresponds to verse 7, Ἑνὶ δὲ ἑκάστῳ ἡμῶν ἐδόθη ἡ χάρις κατὰ τὸ μέτρον τῆς δωρεᾶς τοῦ Χριστοῦ. Thus the references to the descent and the ascent throughout the section 4:7-11 appear as follows within the framework of the references to gifts mentioned in 4:7 and repeated in 4:11:

(gifts)	7	Ἑνὶ δὲ ἑκάστῳ ἡμῶν ἐδόθη ἡ χάρις
ascent	8a	διὸ λέγει· ἀναβὰς εἰς ὕψος
descent	8b	ἔδωκεν δόματα τοῖς ἀνθρώποις.
ascent	9a	τὸ δὲ ἀνέβη τί ἐστιν,
descent	9b	εἰ μὴ ὅτι καὶ κατέβη εἰς τὰ κατώτερα μέρη
descent	10a	ὁ καταβὰς αὐτός ἐστιν
ascent	10b	καὶ ὁ ἀναβὰς ὑπεράνω πάντων τῶν οὐρανῶν,
(gifts)	11a	καὶ αὐτὸς ἔδωκεν τοὺς μὲν ἀποστόλους

Seeing the gifts as given in conjunction with a descent of Christ as the Spirit would extend this pattern one step further, since the references in 4:7 and 4:11a would be implicitly related to the descent. Again we must emphasize that the part of the sequence represented in 4:9a-9b alone (i.e., ascent—descent) does not conclusively prove that a subsequent descent is in view, because mention of the descent would necessarily have followed the reference to the ascent due to its implicit nature (it was not explicitly mentioned in Ps 68:19 but deduced (inferred) by the writer from the ascent introduced in the quotation). In such a sequence, however, it is still more natural to understand the element which was inferred (in this case the descent) to follow the element which was explicitly mentioned (here the ascent). The close parallelism between the descent (10a) and the distribution of the gifts (8b) is also indicated by the complete sequence as illustrated above. This parallelism suggests that the distribution of the gifts was closely connected in the mind of the author with the descent.

Thus it was not sufficient for the author to quote Ps 68:19 with its reference only to an ascent; he had to deduce from this a corresponding descent, which for him represented the distribution of the gifts. If (as we have previously argued) the writer was aware of the Moses-traditions which associated Pentecost (and perhaps by this time Psalm 68 as well) with the celebration of the giving of the Torah at Sinai, he would have been predisposed to understand that the distribution of gifts took place following a subsequent descent, since Moses distributed the Torah as gifts to men following his descent from Mt. Sinai. Thus in all probability the author of Ephesians saw in Ps 68:19, connected as it was in early

in ch. 1, 3-14, and also R. Yates ("Principalities and Powers in Ephesians," *NBl* 58 [1977] 516-21).

Christian tradition with the victorious ascent of Christ, a reference to Christ's exaltation and distribution of gifts. But he could find in the psalm no corresponding reference to a descent at which those gifts were distributed, and thus was obliged to deduce one in his midrashic interpretation of Ps 68:19 contained in Eph 4:9-10.[27]

Such an understanding of the structure of Eph 4:7-11 suggests a similarity to at least one other passage in Ephesians. In 1:20-21 the ascent of the exalted Christ (καθίσας ἐν δεξιᾷ αὐτοῦ ἐν τοῖς ἐπουρανίοις ὑπεράνω πάσης ἀρχῆς καὶ ἐξουσίας καὶ δυνάμεως καὶ κυριότητος καὶ παντὸς ὀνόματος ὀνομαζομένου κ.τ.λ.) precedes his being given as 'head' over all things to the church which is his 'body' (καὶ πάντα ὑπέταξεν ὑπὸ τοὺς πόδας αὐτοῦ καὶ αὐτὸν ἔδωκεν κεφαλὴν ὑπὲρ πάντα τῇ ἐκκλησίᾳ ἥτις ἐστιν τὸ σῶμα αὐτοῦ) in 1:22-23.[28] In the case of the latter phrase, the 'giving' of Christ himself might be a particularly appropriate way of describing something that took place at Pentecost,

---

[27] R. Schnackenburg concluded that an allusion to the (Christian celebration of) Pentecost was unlikely in Eph 4:7-11, because while the quotation from Ps. 68:19 may be suitable to Pentecost, such a connection appeared improbable because the Spirit was not explicitly mentioned in Eph 4:9-10 ("Christus, Geist und Gemeinde [Eph. 4:1-16]," in *Christ and Spirit in the New Testament*, ed. B. Lindars and S. S. Smalley [Cambridge: Cambridge University Press, 1973] 287ff.). In reply it may be noted that while the Spirit was not explicitly mentioned in 4:9-10, in the immediate context (4:11-16) gifts similar to those attributed elsewhere by Paul to the Spirit were enumerated (cf. 1 Cor 12:7, 11), and the Spirit was mentioned in the preceding context in 4:3, 4 and frequently throughout Ephesians. Some of Schnackenburg's points regarding the passage lead to helpful and significant observations, however: (1) Whatever the background of the ascent-descent motif and Ps 68:19, it is clear that the author of Ephesians interpreted the quotation as a reference to Christ. We must then go on to decide if the writer could have referred to Christ and the Spirit in terms that were (functionally at least) interchangeable (see the following section of the present chapter). (2) It is possible that the author of Ephesians was aware of the Jewish exegetical tradition linking Moses to Ps 68:19, and was deliberately opposing it by applying Ps 68:19 instead to Christ. Such a polemical reinterpretation of the Moses-typology surrounding Psalm 68, while conceivable, is difficult to prove, especially in light of the absence of other references to Moses in Ephesians.

[28] Eph 1:20-23 with its references to τὸ πλήρωμα presents notoriously difficult lexical problems for the interpretation of Ephesians, most of which are beyond our scope here. Some have suggested that the concept of πλήρωμα demonstrated the presence of Gnostic thought within Ephesians, a suggestion which would have implications for the dating of the letter, given the current understanding of the development of Gnosticism. For a survey of the meaning of the term πλήρωμα in Nag Hammadi and other literatures, see in particular C. A. Evans ("The Meaning of πλήρωμα in Nag Hammadi," *Bib* 65 [1984] 259-65). The most comprehensive study of πλήρωμα in recent times is J. Ernst (*Pleroma und Pleroma Christi: Geschichte und Deutung eines Begriffs der paulinischen Antilegomena* [Regensburg: Friedrich Pustet, 1970]), although other significant contributions to the discussion (listed chronologically) have been made by S. Aalen ("Begrepet πλήρωμα i Kolosser- og Efeserbrevet," *TTK* 23 [1952] 49-67); P. Benoit ("Corps, tête et plérôme dans les Épîtres de la captivité," *RB* 63 [1956] 5-44); M. Bogdasavich ("The Idea of *Pleroma* in the Epistles to the Colossians and Ephesians," *DR* 83 [1965] 118-30); P. D. Overfield ("Pleroma: A Study in Content and Context," *NTS* 25 [1979] 384-96); and P. Benoit ("The 'plèrôma' in the Epistles to the Colossians and the Ephesians," *SEÅ* 49 [1984] 136-58). This is by no means a complete list of the literature on the subject.

when the ascended Christ was 'given' to his church in the person of the Spirit.[29] We may go on to ask what the significance of such an interpretation, which sees Eph 4:7-11 as a description of the exalted Christ's return to his church to distribute gifts, would have been for the readers of the letter. For them, it would have been a powerful argument that the one who had ascended and now ruled over all the universe from the right hand of the Father, Christ himself, had not abandoned his followers who were left behind on earth. Instead of observing their struggles and shortcomings from a distance, their exalted Lord had returned, in the person of the Spirit, to bestow gifts upon his church which would equip it for ministry and help it toward maturity. He ascended "above all the heavens in order that he might fill all things" (4:10); but part of what it meant for him to 'fill all things' was the distribution of the spiritual gifts which would bring his church to maturity and completion.[30]

C. THE ASCENDED CHRIST AS THE SPIRIT WHO DESCENDED AT PENTECOST

We must now examine some of the theological implications of an identification of Christ as "the one who ascended above all the heavens" (ὁ ἀναβὰς ὑπεράνω πάντων τῶν οὐρανῶν) in Eph 4:10 with the Spirit as the one who "descended to this lower earth" (κατέβη εἰς τὰ κατώτερα μέρη τῆς γῆς) in Eph 4:9. We have seen that the reference to "the gift of Christ" (τῆς δωρεᾶς τοῦ Χριστοῦ) in 4:7 and the resumptive statement "he gave some apostles, some prophets, etc." (καὶ αὐτὸς ἔδωκεν τοὺς μὲν ἀποστόλους, τοὺς δὲ προφήτας, κ.τ.λ.) in 4:11-16 makes it clear that the author of Ephesians viewed Christ as the giver of the gifts described in 4:11-12, which were designed to promote the growth of Christians from an immature state to a state of relative maturity (4:13). We have also seen that our author applied the quotation from Ps 68:19 (which was almost certainly understood in Jewish circles at the time as a

---

[29] Such a correspondence is suggestive since Pentecost is generally regarded as the point at which the NT church, as such, came into existence. A NT origin for the church is suggested by Eph 2:20, which describes the apostles and prophets as the foundation upon which the church is built, members of the "Gründergeneration." For further discussion, see F. Mußner ("Was ist die Kirche?," in *"Diener in Eurer Mitte" : Festschrift für Dr. Antonius Hofmann Bischof von Passau zum 75. Geburtstag,* ed. R. Beer et al., Schriften der Universität Passau: Reihe Katholische Theologie 5 [Passau: Passavia Universitätsverlag, 1984] 82-89). H. Schlier, in his discussion of the "mystery" described in Eph 3:6, also suggested that the church as described by the author of Ephesians was an entity that originated in the NT period (*Die Zeit der Kirche: Exegetische Aufsätze und Vorträge* [Freiburg: Herder, 1956] 159-60).

[30] For further discussion see D. E. Garland ("A Life Worthy of the Calling: Unity and Holiness, Ephesians 4:1-24," *RevExp* 76 [1979] 517-27, esp. 522-23).

reference to Moses and his ascent of Mt. Sinai to bring down the Torah) to the triumphal ascent of the victorious Christ. We have noted that an interpretation of Ps 68:19 in terms of Christ's victorious ascent probably antedated the writing of Ephesians.[31] Contextually there is good reason to believe (as we have shown in the preceding section) that the author's reference to a descent "to this lower earth" (εἰς τὸ κατώτερα μέρη τῆς γῆς) in 4:9 was not a superfluous theological assertion, but an attempt to relate the one who ascended victoriously (Christ) to the one who returned with power to distribute the gifts to the Church at Pentecost. At first this appears to be a somewhat radical theological assertion. We must now consider whether such a relationship between the exalted Christ and the Spirit of God lay within the range of possibilities open to the author of Ephesians by examining some of the other formulations of this relationship in the remaining literature of the NT.

Although the Pauline corpus might seem to be the logical starting-point, we should examine briefly a few non-Pauline passages first, notably in Luke-Acts and the Fourth Gospel. In these passages the exalted Christ is portrayed as the one who dispenses the Spirit. In Acts 2:33, for example, when Jesus was exalted to God's right hand (a theme which also occurs in Ephesians in 1:20-23 and 4:8-10) it was given to him to pour out the Spirit upon others.[32] Likewise in the Gospel of John the glorified Jesus is portrayed as the one from whom the Spirit would come (7:39), the one who would send the Paraclete (15:26), and the one who would bestow the Spirit (19:30, 20:22). At the same time in the Johannine material the Father is also said to be the one who would send the Spirit (14:17, 26), and even in 15:26 Jesus promised to send the Spirit from the Father. Yet Jesus' words to the disciples in 14:18 (οὐκ ἀφήσω ὑμᾶς ὀρφανούς, ἔρχομαι πρὸς ὑμᾶς) have often been understood by commentators as a reference to the coming of the Spirit, and this opens the door for an identification of the resurrected, exalted Jesus with the Johannine Paraclete.[33] Obviously the Lucan and Johannine formulations

---

[31] See ch. 5, 170.

[32] We should note, however, that at this point Jesus was in reality only the intermediary who sent the Spirit, receiving (λαβών) the promise of the Spirit "from the Father" (παρὰ τοῦ πατρός) and passing this along to the disciples. The problems concerning this passage and whether it contains an allusion to Ps 68:19 are discussed at considerable length in ch. 5, 159-69.

[33] This verse was generally understood by the Western [Latin] Fathers to refer to Jesus' return at the parousia. The Eastern Fathers limited it to the post-resurrection appearances of Jesus, although in Johannine circles it appears that the saying was not limited only to the post-resurrection appearances (which were of short duration), but was understood to refer to a more permanent presence of Jesus in the person of the Spirit. See R. Brown (*The Gospel According to John, xiii-xxi*, AB 29A [Garden City, NY: Doubleday, 1966] 645-46). The latter interpretation is also supported by E. Haenchen (*John 2: A Commentary on the Gospel of John Chapters 7-21*, trans. R. W. Funk [Philadelphia: Fortress, 1984] 126).

have no direct bearing on the relationship between Christ and the Spirit described in Ephesians. Yet they do demonstrate that the description of this relationship was not fixed or static, but was subject to a variety of expressions in the early church.[34]

Much more closely related to the exaltation of Christ and his descent as the Spirit in the Epistle to the Ephesians are the Pauline passages which deal with the relationship between Jesus and the Spirit.[35] A preliminary examination of the evidence from the Pauline corpus suggests that Paul was not only capable of an identification of the exalted Christ with the Spirit of God, but was predisposed to such a formulation. Paul's descriptions of the Spirit as the "Spirit of Christ" (Rom 8:9), the "Spirit of God's Son" (Gal 4:6), and the "Spirit of Jesus Christ" (Phil 1:19) are familiar to students of the NT.[36] Unlike the Lucan and Johannine authors Paul never actually described Christ as the one who bestowed the Spirit on others. For Paul, it was always God who dispensed the Spirit (1 Cor 2:12; 2 Cor 1:21-22, 5:5; Gal 3:5, 4:6; Eph 1:17; and 1 Thess 4:8). Although Luke and John were capable of attributing the gift of the Spirit equally to God or to the exalted Christ, Paul attributes the gift of the Spirit only to God.

Next we note the Pauline midrash on Exod 34:29-35 found in 2 Cor 3:7-18. The assertion in 2 Cor 3:17, ὁ δὲ κύριος τὸ πνεῦμά ἐστιν, has often been understood as Paul identifying the exalted Christ with the Spirit.[37] We should beware of an over-simplification, however, in understanding a simple assertion of identity between Christ and the Spirit here. A thoroughly researched attempt to argue for such an identity was put forward by I. Hermann (1961).[38] Hermann denied any personal understanding of the Spirit in Paul, and attempted to explain all the re-

---

[34] No attempt is being made to suggest any sort of literary dependence or other relationship between the Fourth Gospel and Ephesians. The problems of relative dating of the material alone are so complex as to render any attempt to relate the two purely hypothetical. The Johannine statements regarding Jesus' relationship to the Spirit are mentioned only to demonstrate the range of possibilities open to a NT writer.

[35] While I subscribe to Pauline authorship of Ephesians, such a view is not necessary in order for the following arguments to be valid. Those who deny Pauline authorship of Ephesians acknowledge it to be deutero-Pauline, that is, written by a disciple of the Apostle Paul or by someone within the Pauline school in deliberate imitation of Paul and with considerable dependence on Pauline theology. In such a case perspectives from genuine Pauline material would have almost certainly influenced the author of Ephesians had he been aware of their existence.

[36] See, for example, J. D. G. Dunn (*Christology in the Making: A New Testament Inquiry into the Origins of the Doctrine of the Incarnation* [London: SCM, 1980] 142-43).

[37] A comprehensive survey of the many interpretations given to this phrase can be found in E. B. Allo (*Saint Paul: Seconde Épître aux Corinthiens*, 2d ed. [Paris: Gabalda, 1956] 94-111).

[38] I. Hermann, *Kyrios und Pneuma: Studien zur Christologie der paulinischen Hauptbriefe*, SANT 2 (Munich: Kösel, 1961).

maining references to the Spirit in the Pauline *Hauptbriefe* in a non-personal sense. His approach to the problem of 2 Cor 3:17 has not been followed by all NT scholars, however. Many still believe, as C. K. Barrett and others have pointed out, that the definite article used with κύριος is best understood as anaphoric and pointed back to the previous verse.[39] Since this was virtually a direct quotation from the OT it appeared more likely that κύριος should be identified with Yahweh (rather than directly with the exalted Christ). Barrett and a number of other recent interpreters (e.g., R. P. Martin, V. P. Furnish, and J. D. G. Dunn) understood the assertion ὁ δὲ κύριος τὸ πνεῦμά ἐστιν in 2 Cor 3:17 to mean that, for Christians today, "the Lord" of the OT quotation (i.e., Yahweh) was represented by the Spirit.[40] In other words, for the readers of the epistle, that presence of Yahweh which Moses experienced in the account in Exod 34:29-35 was equivalent to the Spirit in their contemporary experience.

A different approach to 2 Cor 3:17 taken by some interpreters involved redefining the referent of τὸ πνεῦμα in this particular context (unlike Hermann, who redefined τὸ πνεῦμα in the entire Pauline corpus).[41] For example, P. E. Hughes (1962) held that there was no direct reference to the Spirit of God present in these verses.[42] He understood the assertion to be similar to that in 2 Cor 3:6, where the phrase "the spirit gives life" (τὸ δὲ πνεῦμα ζωοποιεῖ) was contrasted to "the letter kills" (τὸ γὰρ γράμμα ἀποκτέννει). In addition Hughes understood ὁ κύριος in 2 Cor 3:17 as a reference to Christ, with the resultant meaning, "the Lord (Christ) is the spirit" (i. e., of liberty), relating this to the second half of 3:17, οὗ δὲ τὸ πνεῦμα κυρίου, ἐλευθερία. Having said this, Hughes went on to state, however,

> Although...there is in our judgment no *direct* reference to the Holy Spirit here, yet there can be no doubt that the operation of the Holy Spirit is implicit in Paul's argument, especially in view of his plain teaching elsewhere that it is the Holy Spirit's office to apply the work of Christ to the believing heart.[43]

---

[39] C. K. Barrett, *A Commentary on the Second Epistle to the Corinthians*, BNTC (London: Adam & Charles Black, 1973) 122-23. The article used with κύριος in this verse was also considered anaphoric by N. Turner (*Grammatical Insights into the New Testament* [Edinburgh: Clark, 1965] 126-27).

[40] C. K. Barrett, *A Commentary on the Second Epistle to the Corinthians*, 123; R. P. Martin, *2 Corinthians*, WBC 40 (Waco, TX: Word, 1986) 73-74; V. P. Furnish, *II Corinthians: Translated with Introduction, Notes, and Commentary*, AB 32A (Garden City, NY: Doubleday, 1984) 236; and J. D. G. Dunn, *Christology in the Making*, 143-44.

[41] See n. 38 above.

[42] P. E. Hughes, *Paul's Second Epistle to the Corinthians*, NICNT (Grand Rapids: Eerdmans, 1962) 116.

[43] Hughes, *Corinthians*, 116.

Hughes apparently attempted to say two things at once in his interpretation of the assertion in 3:17: while τὸ πνεῦμα was not a direct reference to the Spirit of God, a reference to the Spirit working in the believer was nevertheless implicit here. This represents a minority opinion; it seems easier to see the reference to τὸ πνεῦμα in 2 Cor 3:17 as a direct reference to the Spirit, particularly in light of the phrase τὸ πνεῦμα κυρίου in 3:17b.

Yet another approach is that of J. Schildenberger (1963), who continued to argue that κύριος was used as a christological title in 2 Cor 3:17a, in spite of the OT associations related to its previous use in 3:16.[44] Schildenberger's approach was to redefine τὸ πνεῦμα in 3:17 so that it had a qualitative aspect (much as it does in reference to the Father in John 4:24). Thus the assertion Paul was making in 2 Cor 3:17, according to Schildenberger, was that Christ was 'spirit', i.e., now existed in a spiritual mode (similar to Paul's formulation in 1 Cor 15:45, where πνεῦμα is anarthrous). This, too, represented a minority opinion among modern interpreters, many of whom would identify the κύριος of 3:17a with Yahweh in the OT allusion in 3:16.

More recently there has been a return to the view that the occurrences of κύριος in 2 Cor 3:16-18 are best taken as referring to Christ, including the enigmatic one at the end of 3:18, καθάπερ ἀπὸ κυρίου πνεύματος. A. T. Hanson (1980) understood Paul to be asserting that when Moses went into the tabernacle to converse with God, he saw the glory of the pre-existent Christ and his face shone with the reflection of that glory. When Moses went out to convey the revelations he had received to the Israelites, he covered his face to hide the glory of the pre-existent Christ whom he had seen in the sanctuary. This was in contrast with what Paul and his companions were doing in proclaiming the glory of Christ (3:12-13). But when a Jew in Paul's day turned to Christ, the veil (now figurative) was lifted from his mind, and he too beheld the glory of Christ. Hanson observed (citing 1 Cor 15:45) that Christ was now known to us as the Spirit, and endorsed what he called an "economic" identity between Christ and the Spirit, an identity of experience but not of essence. According to Hanson all interpreters who understood ὁ δὲ κύριος in 3:17 to refer to Christ accepted such an "economic" identity of Christ and Spirit in some form or other.[45]

---

[44] J. Schildenberger, "2 Kor. 3,17a: «Der Herr aber ist der Geist» im Zusammenhang des Textes und der Theologie des hl. Paulus," in *Studiorium Paulinorum Congressus Internationalis Catholicus, 1961*, AnBib 17-18 (Rome: Pontifical Biblical Institute, 1963) 1.451-60.

[45] A. T. Hanson, "The Midrash in II Corinthians 3: A Reconsideration," *JSNT* 9 (1980) 2-28.

Another recent interpretation of 2 Cor 3:12-18 which saw in 3:17 a reference to Christ is that of M. D. Hooker (1981). Although she noted that Paul did not explain whether ὁ κύριος in verse 17 meant Yahweh (as in Exodus) or Christ (as is normal in Paul), she found a solution to the problem in the close parallelism of verses 14 and 16. While "the Lord" must have referred to Yahweh insofar as the words applied to Moses, Paul was applying the passage to the contemporary situation. In this case when the veil was taken away and a Jew turned to "the Lord" it had to refer to Christ, with whom the veil was abolished. Thus, while Hooker did not consider Moses to have seen the pre-existent Christ in the tabernacle, she nevertheless understood the contemporary application of the text to refer to Christ, in what amounted to an experiential identification of Christ and Spirit.[46]

In summary, we have seen that while the assertion made by Paul in 2 Cor 3:17 appears at first glance to identify the exalted Christ with the Spirit, there has been no consensus among interpreters that this was in fact what was being asserted in the context of 2 Corinthians 3. It may be, as some have proposed, that the author of 2 Corinthians was making no christological statement at all, particularly if κύριος could be understood as a reference to Yahweh, alluded to in 3:16. Such a connection, however probable, would not negate the observation that Paul in this case would still have viewed the Spirit as God's own power reaching out to interact with Christians and have its effect on them. Thus this became the means by which believers in the present age could have direct experience of God, just as Moses experienced the presence of Yahweh in the tabernacle.[47] However, it is more likely that Paul did intend a reference to Christ, at least in 3:17-18, and that this involved some sort of economic or experiential identification of Christ and Spirit.

Before we discuss this theme as it occurs in Ephesians, there are two other Pauline passages which contribute to our understanding of the relationship between the exalted Christ and the Spirit of God. These now need to be examined briefly. The first is a statement made by Paul in 1 Cor 6:17, "the one who is joined to the Lord is one S/spirit" (ὁ δὲ κολλώμενος τῷ κυρίῳ ἓν πνεῦμά ἐστιν).[48] Paul had been engaged in a debate with some in the Corinthian church who had argued that it was permissible for Christians to continue to engage in sexual relations with temple prostitutes.[49] Paul's reply to this position, beginning in verse 15,

---

[46] M. D. Hooker, "Beyond the Things That Are Written? St Paul's Use of Scripture," *NTS* 27 (1981) 295-309.

[47] See, e. g., J. D. G. Dunn (*Christology in the Making*, 144).

[48] The use of both upper and lower case [S/spirit] in the English translation indicates two interpretive options which will be explained in the following discussion.

[49] For a discussion of the development of Paul's argument within the context, as well as

attempted to show how unthinkable it was for the Christian, whose very 'members' were members of the body of Christ, to take away these members and make them members of a prostitute's body. In the parallel clause in 6:17, Paul contrasted this joining of one's members with a prostitute to the believer's union with the exalted Christ. The reference to πνεῦμα in 6:17 could be understood as a reference either to the believer's (human) spirit or as a direct reference to the Spirit of God. In either case, it is probable in light of the following statements in verses 18-19 that Paul was alluding to the work of the Spirit in 6:17, through which the believer's spirit had become one with Christ (or perhaps, one with Christ's Spirit).[50] Thus Paul represented the Spirit, in 1 Cor 6:17, as the medium through which the Christian was united to the exalted Christ.[51] An alternative explanation of 1 Cor 6:17 also exists, which would take πνεῦμα as the human spirit, contrasted with the physical body (which had been the subject of Paul's discussion up to this point). This interpretation, however, was refuted at some length by R. H. Gundry (1976).[52]

Another passage in the Pauline corpus which appears to present an unequivocal relationship between the exalted Christ and the Spirit is 1 Cor 15:45, "the last Adam [became] life-giving Spirit" (ὁ ἔσχατος Ἀδὰμ εἰς πνεῦμα ζῳοποιοῦν). Paul in his arguments for the resurrection in 1 Corinthians 15 had already asserted, "as in Adam all die, so also in Christ shall all be made alive" (15:21-22). In 15:45a, Adam was described as one who became a living ψυχή, while in 15:45b Christ likewise became a life-giving πνεῦμα. Since Paul in verse 44 had already contrasted two types of bodies, one ψυχικός and the other πνευματικός, it appears from the linguistic similarity of the terms ψυχικός and πνευματικός to ψυχή and πνεῦμα that he viewed the original bearers of each of these categories of bodies as Adam and Christ respectively.[53] With the additional term ζῳοποιοῦν predicated of Christ as the

---

particulars of the statement of Paul's position, see G. D. Fee (*The First Epistle to the Corinthians*, NICNT [Grand Rapids: Eerdmans, 1987] 250-66); W. F. Orr and J. A. Walther (*I Corinthians*, AB 32 [Garden City, NY: Doubleday, 1976] 201-203); C. K. Barrett (*A Commentary on the First Epistle to the Corinthians*, HNTC [New York: Harper & Row, 1968] 144-153); and H. Conzelmann (*1 Corinthians: A Commentary on the First Epistle to the Corinthians*, trans. J. W. Leitch, Hermeneia [Philadelphia: Fortress, 1975] 108-13).

[50] See, e. g., J. D. G. Dunn (*Baptism in the Holy Spirit: A Re-examination of the New Testament Teaching on the Gift of the Spirit in relation to Pentecostalism today* [Philadelphia: Westminster, 1970] 123-24).

[51] J. D. G. Dunn, *Christology in the Making*, 145-46.

[52] R. H. Gundry, *SOMA in Biblical Theology with emphasis on Pauline Anthropology*, SNTSMS 29 (Cambridge: Cambridge University Press, 1976) 65-69.

[53] See J. D. G. Dunn ("I Corinthians 15:45—last Adam, life-giving Spirit," in *Christ and Spirit in the New Testament*, ed. B. Lindars and S. S. Smalley [Cambridge: Cambridge University Press, 1973] 130).

last Adam, however, Paul emphasized not the mode of the resurrected Christ's existence so much as his function: the exalted Christ had now become the giver of life to all those who followed after.[54] This is the point of the statement in 15:45 as far as Paul's argument was concerned: he wished to demonstrate how it was that Christ's own resurrection became the basis for Christians receiving resurrection bodies, a point the Corinthians had apparently ignored or disputed. G. D. Fee was correct when he asserted that the concern of 1 Cor 15:45b was not christological (to assert the interchangeability of the terms 'Christ' and 'Spirit' for Paul), but soteriological and eschatological.[55] Thus it may be pressing Paul's language too far to say, as J. Ruef (1971) said, that Paul did not "draw any hard and fast line between the Spirit and Christ."[56] We must conclude that 1 Cor 15:45, while appearing to equate the exalted Christ with the Spirit (or perhaps to imply some transformation of the one into the other), did not really constitute, in Paul's argument, an identification of the two in essence, any more than 2 Cor 3:17 does. The most that can be said is that Paul was probably speaking here on an 'experiential' or 'economic' level (as we saw already in 2 Cor 3:17). There was a sense in which the believer's contemporary experience of the exalted Christ came through the Spirit: the activity of Christ in making others alive (at the resurrection, which was the point of Paul's argument in context) would be mediated through the Spirit.

At this point we may now turn to an examination of the Spirit as the mediator of God's power to the believer in Ephesians. Throughout the epistle there are significant indications that our author viewed the Spirit as the agency through which the power of God was to be mediated to the individual believer. In the initial blessing which constitutes the prologue (Eph 1:3-14) God was said to have blessed believers with "every spiritual blessing" (πάσῃ εὐλογίᾳ πνευματικῇ), a non-personal reference which nevertheless set the tone for the remainder of the letter. The blessings God wished to bestow were spiritual ones (that is, they were bound up with and mediated through the Spirit).[57] In view of the importance of the prologue in the structure of Ephesians—both J. T. Sanders and M. Barth saw it as a summary of the entire letter—such an allusion

---

54 Cf. A. T. Lincoln, *Paradise Now and Not Yet: Studies in the Role of the Heavenly Dimension in Paul's Thought with Special Reference to his Eschatology*, SNTSMS 43 (Cambridge: Cambridge University Press, 1981) 43-44.

55 G. D. Fee, *The First Epistle to the Corinthians*, 790.

56 J. Ruef, *Paul's First Letter to Corinth*, WPC (Philadelphia: Westminster, 1971) 173.

57 From a stylistic viewpoint the prologue (1:3-14) appears hymnic in character; almost all scholars would see some relationship to hymnic literature in these verses, whether or not they originated with or were adapted by the author of Ephesians. See G. Schille (*Frühchristliche Hymnen* [Berlin: Evangelische Verlagsanstalt, 1965] 22) and J. T. Sanders ("Hymnic Elements in Eph. 1-3," *ZNW* 56 [1965] 214-32).

must have been significant for the author's concept of the relationship of the Spirit to the believer as developed in the remainder of Ephesians.[58]

Twice in Ephesians (1:13 and 4:30) believers were said to be sealed with the Spirit; the second instance was a parenthetical reference which looked back to 1:13 where the concept was introduced in the letter. According to J. Adai, the sealing of the Spirit in 1:13, the climax of the entire prologue, constituted the direct application and actualization of the blessing (1:3-12) to the individual believer.[59] Since the sealing was carried out "in Christ" (ἐν τῷ Χριστῷ· ἐν ᾧ καὶ ὑμεῖς...ἐσφραγίσθητε), in 1:13 the inseparable relationship between Christ and Spirit is clearly visible; the Spirit had become accessible for the believer in and through Christ ("Der Geist ist in und durch Christus für die Gläubigen zugänglich geworden").[60] It might be equally accurate to say the opposite (although Adai did not do so), that the exalted Christ had become accessible to the believer in and through the Spirit as well.

Thus it is likely, since Paul's concept of the Spirit as the means by which God's own power interacted with believers in the present age— by which an individual Christian may directly experience the exalted Christ—is present elsewhere in the Pauline corpus, that the writer of Ephesians could have developed the implications of this concept somewhat further to include the distribution of the gifts (or gifted individuals) discussed in Eph 4:11-12 to the church. Ephesians does, in fact, contain a number of assertions regarding God's power at work in the life of the believer. This appeared as the ultimate object of the author's prayer in 1:16-23: that the recipients of the letter might know "the surpassing greatness of his [God's] power toward us who believe" (τί τὸ ὑπερβάλλον μέγεθος τῆς δυνάμεως αὐτοῦ εἰς ἡμᾶς τοὺς πιστεύοντας). The connection between the believer's experience of God's power in his or her personal experience is even more clearly expressed in the second prayer of the writer in 3:14-21. This section of the third chapter of Ephesians has often been thought to show traces of a liturgical form: the formalities expressed at the beginning of the prayer (3:14) and the benediction in 3:20-21 were considered to constitute elements of a more

---

[58] J. T. Sanders, "Hymnic Elements in Eph. 1-3," 214-15; M. Barth, *Ephesians: Introduction, Translation, and Commentary on Chapters 1-3*, AB 34 (Garden City, NY: Doubleday, 1974) 78. Concerning the connection between the Spirit and the phrase εὐλογίᾳ πνευματικῇ in 1:3, see J. Adai (*Der Heilige Geist als Gegenwart Gottes in den einzelnen Christen, in der Kirche, und in der Welt: Studien zur Pneumatologie des Epheserbriefes*, RSTh 31 [Frankfurt: Peter Lang, 1985] 53-60).

[59] J. Adai, *Der Heilige Geist als Gegenwart Gottes*, 62. The reference to 'sealing' is understood by many scholars to refer to Christian baptism, although this is a debated point.

[60] Adai, *Der Heilige Geist*, 76.

or less formal liturgical prayer by G. Schille and J. T. Sanders.[61] Whether these verses also contain hymnic elements is a related question which is not as easily answered. Sanders attempted to isolate parallels to what he considered the hymnic elements present in 3:14-21.[62] At this point we may speak of either liturgical or hymnic characteristics in the material, since it appears to reflect some qualities of both forms.

The content of this second prayer (understanding the ἵνα-clause of 3:16 to express the content of the prayer) was "that he [God] may grant you, according to the riches of his glory, to be strengthened with power by means of (διά) his Spirit in the inner man" (ἵνα δῷ ὑμῖν κατὰ τὸ πλοῦτος τῆς δόξης αὐτοῦ δυνάμει κραταιωθῆναι διὰ τοῦ πνεύματος αὐτοῦ εἰς τὸν ἔσω ἄνθρωπον). Here the writer explicitly stated that the Spirit was the means by which believers were to experience God's power in their own lives. Furthermore, since the author went on to state in v. 17 the result of this inner strengthening by the Spirit (using an infinitive, κατοικῆσαι, which is probably best seen as expressing the result of the preceding clause) in terms of Christ dwelling in the hearts of the readers through faith (κατοικῆσαι τὸν Χριστὸν διὰ τῆς πίστεως ἐν ταῖς καρδίαις ὑμῶν), a connection between the exalted Christ and the Spirit as they were both experienced by believers in the present age is implied. According to J. Adai, the relationship between δύναμις and πνεῦμα reflected in Eph 3:16 did not differ greatly from that found between the same two terms in Rom. 15:13-19: the 'power' at work here was the power of the Spirit; the Spirit appeared as the mediator of God's power to the believer.[63] This is completely consistent with the interpretation of Eph 4:7-11 we have proposed above, in which the descent introduced in 4:9-10 is understood as the descent of Christ as the Spirit at Pentecost, distributing spiritual gifts (that is, gifted individuals) to the church so that it might be equipped to grow to maturity.

But if it is the Spirit which had become operative in and for the believer as a result of the sealing which took place "in Christ" at the time of the believer's conversion (1:13), and was the means by which believers were to experience God's power in their own lives (3:16-17), it is also the Spirit that had become the means by which believers actually lived out the Christian life (5:18-6:9). Although it is beyond the scope of this study to investigate the numerous problems surrounding the mean-

---

[61] See, e. g., G. Schille (*Frühchristliche Hymnen*, 22) and J. T. Sanders ("Hymnic Elements in Eph. 1-3," 214).

[62] J. T. Sanders, "Hymnic Elements in Eph. 1-3," 216. He lists, among others, 3:15 with 1:10, 3:16 with 1:7, and 3:17 with 1:5.

[63] J. Adai, *Der Heilige Geist als Gegenwart Gottes*, 93-94. Adai considered Ephesians to be deutero-Pauline, while he considered Romans to be genuine Pauline material. This does not affect the validity of his observation on the similarities in terminology, however.

ing of the command in Eph 5:18 to "be filled with the Spirit" (πληροῦσθε ἐν πνεύματι) and its outworking in the remainder of the *Haustafel* (5:22-6:9), M. Barth suggested that the formula ἐν πνεύματι might correspond to the formula ἐν Χριστῷ which dominated the didactic section of the letter (chapters 1-3) and especially the prologue (1:3-14).[64] Such a correspondence would imply a functional relationship amounting to experiential identity (from the Christian's viewpoint) between the exalted Christ on the one hand and the Spirit by which he interacted with individual believers on the other. It should also be noted with regard to this passage that M. Barth raised the question whether the author of Eph 5:18 (with its reference to drunkenness as the alternative to the filling of the Spirit) was aware of the account of the first Christian Pentecost in Acts 2.[65]

D. SUMMARY AND FINAL CONCLUSIONS

We have now come to the end of our study. As we noted in our brief examination of the doctrine of the *descensus ad inferos,* the belief that Christ, in the three days between his burial and resurrection, descended to the underworld and participated in various activities there, was well established in the early church. It was natural—indeed almost inevitable—that the early Fathers understood Eph 4:7-11 in this light, particularly because it seemed to describe the same events discussed in 1 Pet 3:19-22, a passage which appeared to give an even more detailed account of the *descensus* than the present one. Thus it is not surprising that the early interpreters were almost unanimous in their understanding of the descent in Eph 4:9-10 (with the exception of Theodore of Mopsuestia, who held that the descent referred to Christ's incarnation rather than a descent to the underworld, and Origen, who apparently held the interpretation proposed here).

Modern interpreters who have attempted to address the question of the meaning of the descent of Christ in Eph 4:9-10 have not been nearly as unanimous in their conclusions, however. With regard to the locus of the descent most have seen it either as a descent from earth to the underworld (or to the grave) or as a descent from heaven to earth at the incarnation. However, we have argued that the explanation found in Origen's *Commentary on John,* proposed by H. von Soden and T. K. Abbott at the end of the nineteenth century, and espoused more recently by G. B. Caird, A. T. Lincoln, and others, is preferable. This inter-

---

[64] M. Barth, *Ephesians: Translation and Commentary on Chapters 4-6,* AB 34A (Garden City, NY: Doubleday, 1974) 582 n. 117.

[65] Barth, *Ephesians,* 582.

pretation held the descent occurred after the ascent and exaltation of Eph 4:8 and referred to the descent of Christ as the Spirit who distributed gifts (gifted leaders) to his church.

The major textual problem in Eph 4:9, the omission of πρῶτον following κατέβη, is of crucial importance for the proposed exegesis. If the word was original and should be included, it would rule out the possibility of a subsequent descent. This would limit the possibilities for meaning to a descent to the underworld or the grave (the traditional view) or to a descent from heaven to earth at the incarnation. Our examination of the manuscript evidence and the transcriptional probabilities has shown that the original text of Eph 4:9 almost certainly did not contain πρῶτον. It appears that a later copyist added the word, perhaps accidentally incorporating a marginal gloss (intended to elucidate the meaning of the descent) into the text itself. Most modern textual authorities endorse the shorter reading (without πρῶτον), and we have proceeded on the basis of the omission. The original text of Eph 4:9-10 gave no explicit indication of the time of the descent; this must be determined from the context and therefore cannot be separated from the question of the meaning of the descent itself.

A major grammatical problem in the passage is the use of the genitive construction τῆς γῆς in Eph 4:9. Various classifications for the phrase have been suggested; the most frequent proposals are partitive, comparative, or appositive genitive. An understanding of the genitive as partitive or comparative would support the traditional view of the descent in the passage as a descent of Christ from the earth to the underworld or to the grave. Both those who held that the descent referred to the incarnation and those who understood it as a reference to the subsequent descent of Christ as the Spirit have (*de necessitate*) preferred to see τῆς γῆς as a genitive of apposition (sometimes called an epexegetic genitive). This understanding is preferable, not only because of contextual factors which favor a subsequent descent, but because appositive genitives are characteristic of the style of Ephesians, as E. Percy in his stylistic analysis of Colossians and Ephesians concluded.[66] Certainly this stylistic feature alone does not prove the existence of a subsequent descent in the passage, but it does offer corroborative evidence for a descent from heaven to earth, either prior to the ascent (at Christ's incarnation) or subsequent to the ascent (at Pentecost).

Next we turned our attention to the use of descent imagery in the NT and the LXX. In particular we examined the possibility that the author of Ephesians was influenced by the *descensus* imagery of Jonah 2 LXX

---

[66] See ch. 2, 53-54. The contextual factors which favor a subsequent descent are discussed at some length in the first half of the present chapter.

and Matt 12:40. We concluded that such influence cannot be excluded absolutely, but similarities in terminology do not prove borrowing has occurred. In light of the ascent imagery associated with Psalm 68 and Moses found in a broad variety of contexts at about the same time as (or prior to) the composition of Ephesians, it is much more likely that any conceptual influence on Eph 4:7-11 would have come from this direction.

Thus we began our investigation of the ascent-descent imagery associating Ps 68:19 and Moses by examining *Tg.* Psalms and the later rabbinic literature. *Tg.* Ps 68:19 is an appropriate starting-point because it bears striking similarity to the quotation from Ps 68:19 in Eph 4:8—both *Tg.* Psalms and Ephesians read "gave gifts" in place of the phrase "received gifts" found in the MT and LXX. This has led to the frequent suggestion (or assumption) that the author of Ephesians was aware of the targumic interpretation of Ps 68:19 as a reference to Moses' ascent of Sinai to receive the Torah followed by his distribution of it as 'gifts' to men. These Moses-traditions associated with Ps 68:19 are extremely important to a proper understanding of the descent of Christ in Eph 4:9-10. If the author of Ephesians had at his disposal the traditions associating Psalm 68 with Moses, he was in all probability influenced by them in his inclusion of a reference to Christ's descent. No descent per se is mentioned in the psalm quotation (Eph 4:8), but a descent is nevertheless deduced by the author of Ephesians (4:9-10). Knowledge of Moses-traditions involving a heavenly ascent, especially one associated with Psalm 68:19, provides a reasonable explanation why the author of Ephesians thought it necessary to deduce a subsequent descent of Christ from the ascent mentioned in the psalm, since Moses' ascent of Mt. Sinai to receive the Torah was followed by a descent, implicit in Ps 68:19, to distribute it as 'gifts' to men. The 'giving of gifts' which is attributed to Moses in the ascent-tradition related to Ps 68:19 necessarily implies a corresponding descent, and if the author of Ephesians made use of this tradition his reference to a descent of Christ would naturally be subsequent to the ascent as well. Thus a considerable amount of attention has been given to these Moses-traditions as found in *Tg.* Psalms and other early non-rabbinic sources.

Tg. Psalms as a written composition is undoubtedly much later than Ephesians (probably third or fourth century CE), so that there can be no question of the literary dependence of Ephesians on a written *Tg.* Psalms. Nevertheless, as often noted, the tradition found in *Tg.* Ps 68:19 is surely much older than the written form of the targum, and probably reaches back into the first century CE or earlier. We have attempted to corroborate the dating of this tradition through an examination of rabbinic texts and other early literature (both canonical and non-canonical) which suggest or explicitly state an association of Moses, Psalm 68:19, and an ascent of Mt. Sinai to receive the Torah.

Although it is clear that the existing rabbinic literature which associates Moses' ascent of Sinai with Ps 68:19 is later than Ephesians, every time Ps 68:19 is mentioned in this literature it is *always* interpreted of Moses and his ascent to heaven to receive the Torah. As far as the other elements of Ps 68:19 are concerned, there is some variation. Thus I propose that the basic elements of the tradition, which are common to all rabbinic interpretations of Ps 68:19, are that (a) Moses ascended to heaven to receive the Torah, and (b) while there he took the words of Torah 'captive'. Later additions to the tradition introduced other elements involving angels, other gifts besides the Torah itself, and even elements of *merkabah* mysticism. The two basic elements common to all the rabbinic interpretations of Ps 68:19 are also found in *Tg.* Ps 68:19 and thus these elements of the tradition are almost certainly quite ancient.

However, it is still not clear whether the tradition of Moses' ascent to heaven to receive the Torah can be associated with Ps 68:19 as early as the first century CE. My attempts to verify such a connection by examining non-rabbinic sources such as the Testaments of the Twelve Patriarchs, the *Book of Jubilees*, and the writings of the early Fathers have proven inconclusive. This led me to turn to other early sources not related to Psalm 68 to see if the tradition of Moses' ascent to heaven to receive the Torah can be dated as early as the first century CE independently of Ps 68:19.

An examination of these sources revealed that the tradition of Moses' ascent to heaven to receive the Torah can be given an approximate date with a reasonable degree of certainty. In particular, the *Exagoge* of Ezekiel, which may be as old as the second century BCE, shows the influence of such traditions. Furthermore, such traditions have almost certainly influenced the writings of Philo of Alexandria. Philo uses similar terminology to describe Moses' ascent of Sinai to receive the Torah and his supposed ascension to heaven at the end of his life, suggesting that Philo himself was aware of Moses-traditions which related a heavenly ascent at Sinai when the Torah was given. This confirms the existence of such traditions prior to the middle of the first century CE, and thus they were available to the author of Ephesians. Given his awareness of such traditions, he would have been predisposed to think in terms of a subsequent descent of Christ to distribute gifts to his church.

Another document which also dates from approximately the same era, the *Biblical Antiquities* of Pseudo-Philo, also indicates that traditions concerning a heavenly ascent of Moses were circulating in the first century CE. Evidence from other early sources (such as the *Antiquities* of Josephus and the document known either as the Testament of Moses or the Assumption of Moses) does not apply to an ascent of Moses to receive the Torah at Sinai, but alludes to traditions concerning Moses' assumption to heaven at his death. The same is true of somewhat later evidence from 2 Baruch and the writings of Clement of Alexandria, both of which also refer to Moses' assumption to heaven and not to his ascent at Sinai.

While we have discovered sufficient evidence in the writings from the first century CE or earlier to conclude that Moses-traditions concerning a heavenly ascent at Sinai are early enough to have influenced the author of Ephesians to think in terms of a subsequent descent and widespread enough that he was probably aware of them, we have as yet related no specific evidence linking such traditions to the interpretation of Ps 68:19 earlier than *Tg.* Ps 68:19 and the rabbinic writings of the Amoraic and Tannaitic periods. Such a connection probably exists through the associations of Moses' ascent of Sinai to receive the Torah and the celebration of the Jewish feast of Pentecost (Weeks) on the one hand, and the Christian use of Psalm 68 in connection with the first Christian Pentecost (as described in Acts 2) on the other.

The association of the Jewish feast of Pentecost (Weeks) with the celebration of the giving of the Torah to Moses at Sinai can be found at least as early as the Book of Jubilees, which should probably be dated in the second century BCE. Psalm 68 may have been associated with Pentecost and the giving of the Torah to Moses in pre-Christian Jewish tradition as well, although conclusive evidence on this point is still lacking. Nevertheless, the association of Psalm 68 with Pentecost in Christian tradition almost certainly antedates the composition of Ephesians, because a christological interpretation of the psalm appears to lie behind the present text of Acts 2:33. This would indicate that Psalm 68 was already understood to refer to the victorious ascent of Christ and the gift(s) of the Spirit in a layer of tradition almost certainly older than Ephesians. Thus the innovation which the author of Ephesians brought to the use of Ps 68:19 in Eph 4:8 did not lie in the use of the psalm in a christological sense. This he probably inherited from established Christian tradition. Nor did the author's innovation lie in the introduction of a subsequent descent of Christ inferred from the ascent mentioned in Ps 68:19. If, as I have suggested, the Moses-traditions referring to a heavenly ascent at Sinai to receive the Torah have influenced the author of

Ephesians, he would already have been predisposed to think in terms of a subsequent descent, since Moses subsequently descended to distribute to men the 'gifts' of the Torah. The unique contribution made by the author of Ephesians lies in his identification of the ascended Christ as the Spirit who descended at Pentecost to distribute gifts (or gifted individuals) to his church. Such an understanding of the descent in Eph 4:9-10 fits the context of 4:1-16 well, because it establishes the connection between the gifts to individuals which are given through the grace of Christ (4:7) and the gifted leaders given to the church to equip it for ministry and assist its growth towards maturity (4:11-16). This understanding of the descent is also consistent with the Pauline concept of the Spirit as the means/medium/agency through which Christians presently experience God and, in this case especially, the resurrected and exalted Christ.

Admittedly my conclusion about the nature of the descent inferred by the author in Eph 4:9-10 cannot claim absolute certainty. But it does offer the best possible explanation at the present time of all available evidence linking Moses-traditions of a heavenly ascent at Sinai with Pentecost and Psalm 68. It is indeed remarkable that H. von Soden and T. K. Abbott argued—in the absence of almost all the evidence discussed in the present study except for the sequence of the argument in the context of Ephesians 4 itself—for a similar understanding of the passage nearly a century ago. Perhaps, as in their case, the final word has not been said, and more evidence remains to be discovered which will throw additional light on the descent in Eph 4:9-10. Every additional attempt to evaluate old evidence anew, or to uncover new evidence and new connections concerning this passage, brings us closer to the meaning of the text as understood by the author who wrote it. Nevertheless, at present, the evidence we have examined points to a subsequent descent of Christ connected with the giving of the Spirit and spiritual gifts (gifted leaders in Eph 4:11-16) at Pentecost as the preferred interpretation.

THE QUESTION OF AUTHORSHIP AND
ITS IMPACT ON THIS STUDY

Anyone who approaches the study of the Epistle to the Ephesians soon realizes that one of the major introductory problems which must be addressed is that of authorship. Although extremely well-attested in the early church, Pauline authorship of the letter has not gone unchallenged in the last two centuries. Questions were raised as early as 1519 by Erasmus, who found the style of Ephesians especially awkward because it differed greatly from that of the other Pauline epistles. This led him to doubt that the epistle was genuinely Pauline, but he remained convinced of its authenticity despite these doubts due to the spiritual content of the letter.[1] It was not until 1792 that the British Unitarian E. Evanson actually denied Pauline authorship of Ephesians. Only two years before (in 1790) W. Paley had affirmed the unanimity of scholarship regarding the authenticity of Ephesians. Paley firmly rejected the idea that either Ephesians or Colossians could be a forgery, one based upon the other. The relationship between Ephesians and Colossians continued to be a problem, however. In 1824 L. Usteri questioned the authenticity of Ephesians not on the basis of the imagery and style of the letter itself but because of the similarities it bore to Colossians. In the first half of the 19th century one of the most influential scholars to raise doubts concerning Pauline authorship of Ephesians was W. M. L. deWette, who objected to the traditional ascription of authorship on the basis of the close literary connection to Colossians and the style of Ephesians itself, which he described as rich in vocabulary but cumbersome due to the accumulation of relative clauses, participles, prepositional phrases, and genitives. Similar criticisms would continue to be made by F. C. Baur and others of the Tübingen school until the end of the 19th century.

In 1872 H. J. Holtzmann presented a complex theory of the interrelationship between Ephesians and Colossians which was to become widely influential.[2] According to Holtzmann Ephesians was not Pauline, but an imitation of Colossians, which in turn was a mixture of authentic Pauline and interpolated material. The author of Ephesians, who had

---

[1] Erasmus' objections were mentioned by A. van Roon (*The Authenticity of Ephesians*, NovTSup 39 [Leiden: Brill, 1974] 10).

[2] See H. J. Holtzmann (*Kritik der Epheser- und Kolosserbriefe* [Leipzig: Engelmann, 1872]).

produced an imitation of Colossians, later interpolated material from his own composition (Ephesians) back into Colossians. Thus both epistles as we now have them comprise a mixture of secondary material and authentic Pauline material. Although Holtzmann's analysis of the relationship between the two letters was widely respected at the time, his theory failed to win a large number of adherents. Later successors found it necessary to modify the theory to account for a greater degree of independence in Ephesians than Holtzmann himself had recognized.

The questions raised against the authenticity of Ephesians in the 19th century did not go unanswered, however. British and German scholars such as B. Weiss, F. J. A. Hort, and later T. K. Abbott, T. Zahn, and A. von Harnack continued to defend the authenticity of the epistle, responding to the arguments against Pauline authorship put forward by deWette, Baur, Holtzmann, and others. The next major turn in the debate came in 1933 with the publication of the American scholar E. J. Goodspeed's theory, which offered a reconstruction capable of explaining how Ephesians (if not genuinely Pauline) came to enjoy such early and widespread acceptance.[3] Goodspeed proposed that around 80-90 CE, long after the death of Paul, an Asian Christian put together a collection of Pauline epistles and wrote Ephesians as an introduction and summary intended to win acceptance for the nearly-forgotten work of the apostle he so admired. As he later developed the theory Goodspeed went so far as to identify the author and collector as Onesimus, bishop of Ephesus in the time of Ignatius (110-17 CE). Goodspeed's theory was refined further by J. Knox, one of his former students. Knox attempted to explain the obvious flaw in Goodspeed's hypothesis, namely, that no known list of the Pauline corpus places Ephesians at the beginning (where one would expect it if it were indeed composed as an introduction to all of the Pauline epistles).[4] The resulting theory gained worldwide recognition when it was taken up (with modifications) by the British scholar C. L. Mitton, first in one of a series of articles on unsolved NT problems in *ExpTim* (1948) and then with the publication of his commentary (1951).[5] Naturally Goodspeed's theory (as modified and expanded by Knox and Mitton) has not met with universal acceptance. It has been challenged on a number of points, especially with regard to the purpose it proposes for Ephesians (an introduction to the Pauline epistles) and

---

[3] E. J. Goodspeed, *The Meaning of Ephesians* (Chicago: University of Chicago Press, 1933).

[4] J. Knox, *Philemon Among the Letters of Paul* (Chicago: University of Chicago Press, 1935).

[5] C. L. Mitton, "Unsolved New Testament Problems: Goodspeed's Theory Regarding the Origin of Ephesians," *ExpTim* 59 (1948) 323-27, and *The Epistle to the Ephesians: Its Authorship, Origin and Purpose* (Oxford: Clarendon, 1951).

the position of the letter at the beginning of the original Pauline corpus. Knox's contributions to the theory in this regard have been questioned upon close examination by C. H. Buck, Jr. in a 1949 study.[6] The primary assumption on which the entire theory rests, however, is the non-authenticity of Ephesians. Two recent scholars who have continued to argue for the Pauline authorship of Ephesians are J. N. Sanders and D. Guthrie, both of whom pointed out the strength of the external evidence in favor of authenticity.[7] This was so strong as to warrant, in Sanders' opinion, a proof of non-authenticity amounting to demonstration. Guthrie, in particular, was not willing to accept Mitton's plea for cumulative consideration of the evidence against authenticity, and examined in some detail the case for pseudepigraphy (which he found unconvincing). Additional evidence in support of authenticity came from two scholars who conducted detailed investigations into the interrelationship of Ephesians and Colossians, E. Percy (1946) and A. van Roon (1974). While acknowledging the many difficulties associated with the position, both concluded that, on the whole, the probabilities still favored Pauline authorship of Ephesians.[8]

As we have seen, the debate over the authorship of Ephesians is a continuing one, a controversy that NT scholarship in general probably cannot resolve to the satisfaction of all concerned given the present state of our knowledge. At this point it is helpful to survey the range of scholarship which has divided over this question from the time the issue of authorship was first raised with regard to Ephesians at the end of the eighteenth century until the present day.

What follows is a list of scholars who have endorsed or rejected Pauline authorship of Ephesians in print during the last two centuries. It is arranged in chronological order from the earliest to the most recent, with those holding opposing views in juxtaposition. Dates given in parentheses are those of the commentary, NT introduction, book or essay in which the writer's position on the authorship of Ephesians was stated. This list is not intended to be exhaustive. It merely serves to illustrate the diversity of scholarly opinion regarding the authorship of Ephesians over the past two centuries. Clearly the debate over the authenticity of this letter and its sister epistle Colossians is not resolved (and probably cannot be, given the present state of our knowledge).

---

[6] C. H. Buck, Jr., "The Early Order of the Pauline Corpus," *JBL* 68 (1949) 351-57.

[7] J. N. Sanders, *Studies in Ephesians*, ed. F. L. Cross (London: A. R. Mowbray, 1956) 9-20, and D. Guthrie, *New Testament Introduction*, 2: *The Pauline Epistles* (London: Tyndale, 1961) 110-28. Guthrie responded in detail to many of Mitton's arguments.

[8] E. Percy, *Die Probleme der Kolosser- und Epheserbriefe* (Lund: Gleerup, 1946), and A. van Roon, *The Authenticity of Ephesians*, NovTSup 39 (Leiden: Brill, 1974).

AGAINST PAUL	UNCERTAIN	FOR PAUL
		W. Paley (1790)
E. Evanson (1792)		
		J. G. Eichhorn (1812)
L. Usteri (1824)		
W. M. L. deWette (1826, 43)		E. Mayerhoff (1838)[9]
F. C. Baur (1845)		
F. Schleiermacher (1845)[10]		
A. Schwegler (1846)[11]		
		B. Weiss (1855)
S. Davidson (1868)		
S. Hoekstra (1868)		
E. Renan (1869)		
F. Hitzig (1870)		
H. Ewald (1870)		
A. Hilgenfeld (1870, 75)		
H. J. Holtzmann (1872)		
W. Hönig (1872)		
O. Pfleiderer (1873, 90)		
		J. J. Koster (1877)
W. Seufert (1881)		
Hermann von Soden (1887)		
W. Brückner (1890, 1922)		
A. Klöpper (1891)		
C. Weizsäcker (1892)		G. Salmon (1892)
		F. J. A. Hort (1895)
		T. K. Abbott (1897)
	A. Jülicher (1899)	
		E. Haupt (1902)
E. von Dobschütz (1904)		J. A. Robinson (1904)
W. Soltau (1905)		
		B. F. Westcott (1906)
		T. Zahn (1906)
W. Wrede (1907)		
		A. von Harnack (1910)
Hans von Soden (1911)		
P. Wendland (1912)		
W. Bousset (1913)		
E. Norden (1913, 23)		
J. Weiss (1917)		
J. Moffatt (1918)		
R. Reitzenstein (1921)		
M. Goguel (1926, 35)[12]		
M. Dibelius (1927)		J. de Zwaan (1927)
H. Weinel (1928)		J. Schmid (1928)

[9] Mayerhoff accepted Ephesians as Pauline but rejected the authenticity of Colossians.

[10] Schleiermacher held that Ephesians was written by Tychicus (with Paul's consent) after the pattern of Colossians.

[11] Schwegler was a follower of F. C. Baur who dated both Ephesians and 1 Peter in the second century, although he thought 1 Peter to be the earlier of the two.

[12] M. Goguel at first completely rejected the Pauline authorship of Ephesians. Later he revised his position and considered portions of the epistle to be Pauline, with later interpolations bearing the influence of a Gnostic heavenly redeemer myth. In the genuine portions of Ephesians there was no evidence of gnosticism. Goguel's later position is articulated in "Esquisse d'une solution nouvelle du problème de l'épître aux Éphésiens" (*RHPR* 111 [1935] 254-85; 112 [1936] 73-99).

AGAINST PAUL	UNCERTAIN	FOR PAUL
		C. H. Dodd (1929)
		W. Lock (1929)
		R. Asting (1930)
		E. F. Scott (1930)
	H. Schlier (1930, 57)[13]	
E. Käsemann (1933)		O. Roller (1933)
E. J. Goodspeed (1933, 56)		
W. Ochel (1934)		
J. Knox (1935)		C. A. A. Scott (1935)
		P. Benoit (1937, 59)
W. L. Knox (1939)		
P. Schubert (1939)		
		F. C. Synge (1941)[14]
		L. Mowry (1944)
		W. Michaelis (1946)
		E. Percy (1946)
C. L. Mitton (1948, 51)		
		C. H. Buck, Jr. (1949)
		J. Dupont (1949)
R. Heard (1950)		P. N. Harrison (1950)[15]
R. Bultmann (1951, 55)		N. A. Dahl (1951)
C. Maurer (1952)		
H. F. D. Sparks (1952)		
F. W. Beare (1953)	A. H. McNeile (1953)[16]	
C. Masson (1953)	C. S. C. Williams (1953)	
D. E. Nineham (1956)		T. W. Manson (1956)
E. Schweizer (1956)		J. N. Sanders (1956)
S. G. F. Brandon (1957)		A. M. Hunter (1957)
		G. Schille (1957)
		H. J. Cadbury (1958)[17]
		A. Wikenhauser (1958)
J. A. Allan (1959)		M. Barth (1959, 74)
	H. Chadwick (1960)	
J. L. Price (1961)		D. Guthrie (1961)

---

13 Schlier had expressed doubts about the authenticity of Ephesians in his 1930 work *Christus und die Kirche im Epheserbrief* (BHT 6 [Tübingen: Mohr, 1930]). However, in later editions of his commentary *Der Brief an die Epheser* Schlier defended the view that, in spite of the use of gnostic language and emphasis on ecclesiology, the epistle was written by Paul (Düsseldorf: Patmos-Verlag, original ed. 1957; 3rd-6th ed. 1962-68). Finally, near the end of his life, Schlier's doubts concerning Pauline authorship were reiterated orally to R. Schnackenburg (*Der Brief an die Epheser*, EKKNT 10 [Zürich: Benziger Verlag; Neukirchen-Vluyn: Neukirchener Verlag, 1982] 21 n. 16).

14 Synge, like Mayerhoff, held that Ephesians was Pauline, but Colossians was not. See his brief commentary, *St. Paul's Epistle to the Ephesians* (London: SPCK, 1941).

15 Harrison believed Ephesians was written by a devoted Paulinist after the apostle's death, although he accepted most of Colossians (except for 1:15-25 and 2:4, 8-23) as genuine ("Onesimus and Philemon," *ATR* 32 [1950] 268-94).

16 Both A. H. McNeile and C. S. C. Williams thought the lack of conclusive evidence for or against Pauline authorship should cause one to refrain from a final decision (A. H. McNeile, *An Introduction to the Study of the New Testament*, 2d ed. rev. by C. S. C. Williams [Oxford: Clarendon, 1953] 165-75).

17 Cadbury acknowledged that the evidence for or against Pauline authorship was inconclusive, but seemed to prefer to regard the epistle as genuine Pauline ("The Dilemma of Ephesians," *NTS* 5 [1958-59] 91-102).

AGAINST PAUL	UNCERTAIN	FOR PAUL
H. Conzelmann (1962)		F. F. Bruce (1962, 84)[18]
G. Johnston (1962)		
R. Kasser (1962)		
W. Marxsen (1963)		R. M. Grant (1963)
W. G. Kümmel (1965)[19]		J. I. Cook (1965)
A. Q. Morton (1965)		A. Feuillet (1965)
P. Pokorný (1965)		J. Murphy-O'Connor (1965)[20]
		A. Robert (1965)
		E. Gaugler (1966)[21]
G. H. P. Thompson (1967)		A. F. L. Klijn (1967)
J. C. Kirby (1968)		
J. L. Houlden (1970)		
J. Gnilka (1971)		
R. P. Martin (1971)[22]		
J. Ernst (1974)		A. van Roon (1974)
N. Perrin (1974)		
		J. A. T. Robinson (1976)
H. Koester (1982)		
F. Mußner (1982)		
R. Schnackenburg (1982)		
A. T. Lincoln (1990)		

In my opinion Ephesians does represent the work of the Apostle Paul. The extent to which an assistant or amanuensis may have contributed to both the content and the form of the letter merits futher study. However, objections which have been raised against Pauline authorship, while presenting legitimate difficulties, do not appear sufficient (in my judgment) to overturn the early and widespread external evidence which favors authenticity. Thus in examining the descent of Christ in Eph 4:9-10 I have assumed that Paul was in fact responsible for the composition of Ephesians. Nevertheless I have attempted to examine the evidence in a non-prejudicial fashion with regard to authorship, and to point out in the notes places where one's assumptions about authorship may affect the interpretation of the data. Indeed, I have made a conscious effort to avoid direct reference to Paul in most instances and to refer instead to

---

18 Bruce maintained his opinion in favor of Pauline authorship in *The Epistles to the Colossians, to Philemon, and to the Ephesians* (NICNT [Grand Rapids: Eerdmans, 1984] 237-40).

19 *Einleitung in das Neue Testament*, 14th ed. (Heidelberg: Quelle & Meyer, 1965).

20 J. Murphy-O'Connor held that an amanuensis who was a former Essene wrote Ephesians under the direct supervision of Paul ("Who Wrote Ephesians?," *BiTod* 18 [1965] 1201-9).

21 Gaugler (*Der Epheserbrief*, ANS 6 [Zürich: EVZ, 1966]) was convinced by the work of E. Percy (*Die Probleme der Kolosser- und Epheserbriefe* [Lund: Gleerup, 1946]), that the question of authenticity needed to be re-examined. He thought Percy had by his study increased the probability of authenticity although he had not proven it. But Percy's work did convince Gaugler that one need not be an imprecise researcher simply because one argues for authenticity.

22 R. P. Martin held that the teaching of the epistle was Pauline, but that composition and style were entrusted by Paul to a colleague and amanuensis. Martin believed this colleague of Paul who composed Ephesians to be Luke ("Ephesians," ·in *BBC* 11: *2 Corinthians—Philemon* [Nashville: Broadman, 1971] 125-77).

"the author of Ephesians" so as not to distract the reader from the issues at hand. One could even argue that rejection of Pauline authorship would have made the defense of the preferred interpretation an easier task, since it would not have been necessary to take into account whether the imagery and concepts involved could have come from the same mind that produced the other Pauline epistles. As it stands, however, I am convinced that nothing in the interpretation of the descent defended here is inconsistent with Pauline authorship of Ephesians. In confirmation of this it is noteworthy that two of the earliest modern adherents of the proposed interpretation of Eph 4:7-11, H. von Soden and T. K. Abbott, held differing views on the authorship of the letter: Abbott endorsed Pauline authorship while von Soden rejected it. With this in mind the issues at hand, the locus of the descent and the identification of the one who ascended with the one who descended, may be considered without prejudice with regard to authorship.

BIBLIOGRAPHY

1. *Commentaries on Ephesians*

Abbott, T. K. *A Critical and Exegetical Commentary on the Epistles to the Ephesians and to the Colossians.* ICC. Edinburgh: Clark, 1897.

Allan, J. A. *The Epistle to the Ephesians: Introduction and Commentary.* TBC. London: SCM, 1959.

Barth, M. *Ephesians: Introduction, Translation and Commentary on Chapters 1-3.* AB 34. Garden City, NY: Doubleday, 1974.

—— *Ephesians: Translation and Commentary on Chapters 4-6.* AB 34A. Garden City, NY: Doubleday, 1974.

Beare, F. W. "The Epistle to the Ephesians." *IB* 10.597-749. New York: Abingdon, 1953.

Beet, J. A. *A Commentary on St. Paul's Epistles to the Ephesians, Philippians and Colossians.* London: Hodder & Stoughton, 1890.

Benoit, P. *Les Épîtres de Saint Paul aux Philippiens, à Philémon, aux Colossiens, aux Éphésiens. SBJ.* Paris: Éditions du Cerf, 1949.

Bruce, F. F. *The Epistles to the Colossians, to Philemon, and to the Ephesians.* NICNT. Grand Rapids: Eerdmans, 1984.

Caird, G. B. *Paul's Letters from Prison.* NClarB. Oxford: Oxford University Press, 1976.

Calvin, J. *Commentarius in epistolam ad Ephesios.* CR 15. Brunswick: Schwetschke, 1895.

Cambier, J. *Vie Chrétienne en Église: L'Épître aux Éphésiens lue aux chrétiens d'aujourd'hui.* Paris: Desclée, 1966.

Chadwick, H. "Ephesians." In *Peake's Commentary on the Bible,* ed. M. Black and H. Rowley (London: Thomas Nelson, 1962) 980-84.

Conzelmann, H. "Der Brief an die Epheser." In *Die Briefe an die Galater, Epheser, Philipper, Kolosser, Thessalonicher und Philemon,* 15th ed., ed. J. Becker, H. Conzelmann, and G. Friedrich, NTD 8 (Göttingen: Vandenhoeck u. Ruprecht, 1981) 86-124.

Dahl, N. A. *Kurze Auslegung des Epheserbriefes.* Göttingen: Vandenhoeck & Ruprecht, 1965.

Dibelius, M. *An die Kolosser, Epheser, an Philemon.* HNT 12. Tübingen: Mohr, 1953.

Dodd, C. H. "Ephesians." *AbBC* 1222-37. New York: Abingdon-Cokesbury, 1929.

Eadie, J. A. *A Commentary on the Greek Text of the Epistle of Paul to the Ephesians.* 3rd ed. Edinburgh: Clark, 1883.

Ernst, J. *Die Briefe an die Philipper, an Philemon, an die Kolosser, an die Epheser.* RNT. Regensburg: Friedrich Pustet, 1974.

Ewald, P. *Die Briefe des Paulus an die Epheser, Kolosser und Philemon.* KNT 10. Leipzig: Deichert, 1905.

Foulkes, F. *The Epistle of Paul to the Ephesians: An Introduction and Commentary.* TNTC. London: Tyndale, 1963.

Gaugler, E. *Der Epheserbrief.* ANS 6. Zürich: EVZ, 1966.

Gnilka, J. *Der Epheserbrief.* HTKNT. Freiburg: Herder, 1971.

Graham, E. "The Epistle to the Ephesians." In *NCHS,* ed. C. Gore, H. L. Goudge, and A. Guillaume (New York: Macmillan, 1928) 1.538-50.

Grassi, J. A. "Ephesians." In *JBC,* ed. R. E. Brown, J. A. Fitzmyer, and R. E. Murphy (Englewood Cliffs, NJ: Prentice-Hall, 1968) 2.341-49.

Grosheide, F. W. *De Brief van Paulus aan de Efeziërs.* CNT(K). Kampen: Kok, 1960.

Haupt, E. *Die Gefangenschaftsbriefe.* KEK 8. Göttingen: Vandenhoeck, 1899.

Hendriksen, W. *Exposition of Ephesians.* NTC. Grand Rapids: Baker, 1967.

Hodge, C. *A Commentary on the Epistle to the Ephesians.* New York: Robert Carter & Bros, 1856.

Houlden, J. L. *Paul's Letters from Prison: Philippians, Colossians, Philemon, and Ephesians.* PNTC. Harmondsworth: Penguin, 1970.

Hugedé, N. *L'Épître aux Éphésiens.* Geneva: Labor et Fides, 1973.

Johnston, G. *Ephesians, Philippians, Colossians and Philemon*. NCB. London: Thomas Nelson, 1967.

Lincoln, A. T. *Ephesians*. WBC 42. Dallas: Word, 1990.

Lindemann, A. *Der Epheserbrief*. ZBK. Zürich: Theologischer Verlag Zürich, 1985.

Lock, W. *The Epistle to the Ephesians*. WC. London: Methuen, 1929.

Luther, M. D. *Martin Luthers Epistel-Auslegung, 3: Die Briefe an die Epheser, Philipper und Kolosser*, ed. E. Ellwein. Göttingen: Vandenhoeck u. Ruprecht, 1973.

Macpherson, J. *Commentary on St Paul's Epistle to the Ephesians*. Edinburgh: T. & T. Clark, 1892.

Martin, R. P. "Ephesians." In *BBC* 11: *2 Corinthians—Philemon* (Nashville: Broadman, 1971) 125-77.

Masson, C. *L'épître de Saint Paul aux Éphésiens*. CNT 9. Neuchâtel and Paris: Delachaux et Niestlé, 1953.

Meinertz, M. "Der Epheserbrief." In *Die Gefangenschaftsbriefe des heiligen Paulus*, 3rd ed., HSNT 6 (Bonn: Peter Hanstein, 1923) 50-106.

Meyer, H. A. W. *Kritisch-exegetisches Handbuch über den Brief an die Epheser*. Göttingen: Vandenhoeck u. Ruprecht, 1843.

—— *Critical and Exegetical Handbook to the Epistle to the Ephesians*. Trans. from the 4th German ed. by M. J. Evans; rev. and ed. by W. P. Dickson. New York: Funk & Wagnalls, 1884.

Mitton, C. L. *Ephesians*. NCB. London: Oliphants, 1976.

Moulton, H. K. *Colossians, Philemon and Ephesians*. EpPC. London: Epworth, 1963.

Mußner, F. *Der Brief an die Epheser*. ÖTBK 10. Gütersloh: Gerd Mohn, 1982.

Rienecker, F. *Der Brief des Paulus an die Epheser*. WStB 8. Wuppertal: R. Brockhaus, 1961.

Robinson, J. A. *St. Paul's Epistle to the Ephesians*. 2d ed. London: Macmillan, 1904; reprint ed., Grand Rapids: Kregel, 1979.

Salmond, S. D. F. "The Epistle to the Ephesians." In *EGT*, ed. W. R. Nicoll (London: Hodder & Stoughton, 1903; reprint ed., Grand Rapids: Eerdmans, 1976) 203-395.

Schlier, H. *Der Brief an die Epheser*. Düsseldorf: Patmos-Verlag, 1957.

Schnackenburg, R. *Der Brief an die Epheser*. EKKNT 10. Zürich: Benziger Verlag; Neukirchen-Vluyn: Neukirchener Verlag, 1982.

Scott, E. F. *The Epistles to the Colossians, to Philemon and to the Ephesians*. MNTC. New York: Harper & Bros, 1930.

Soden, H. von. *Die Briefe an die Kolosser, Epheser, Philemon; die Pastoralbriefe*. 2d ed. HKNT 3. Freiburg and Leipzig: J. C. B. Mohr, 1893.

Ströter, E. F. *Die Herrlichkeit des Leibes Christi: Der Epheserbrief*. 2d ed. Gümligen-Bern: Siloah, 1952.

Synge, F. C. *St. Paul's Epistle to the Ephesians*. London: SPCK, 1941.

Theodore of Mopsuestia. "Ad Ephesios." In *Epistolas B. Pauli Commentarii*, ed. H. B. Swete (Cambridge: Cambridge University Press, 1880) 1.112-96.

Thomas Aquinas, Saint. *Commentary on Saint Paul's Epistle to the Ephesians*. Trans. M. L. Lamb. AqSS 2. Albany, NY: Magi Books, 1966.

Thompson, G. H. P. *The Letters of Paul to the Ephesians, to the Colossians, and to Philemon*. CBC. Cambridge: Cambridge University Press, 1967.

Vosté, J.-M. *Commentarius in epistolam ad Ephesios*. Paris: Gabalda, 1921.

Westcott, B. F. *St. Paul's Epistle to the Ephesians*. London: Macmillan, 1906; reprint ed., Minneapolis: Klock & Klock, 1978.

Zerwick, M. *The Epistle to the Ephesians*. Trans. K. Smyth. New York: Herder & Herder, 1969.

2. Commentaries on Other NT Books

Allo, E. B. *Saint Paul: Seconde Épître aux Corinthiens*. 2d ed. Paris: Gabalda, 1956.

Barrett, C. K. *A Commentary on the First Epistle to the Corinthians*. HNTC. New York: Harper & Row, 1968.

—— *A Commentary on the Second Epistle to the Corinthians*. BNTC. London: Adam & Charles Black, 1973.

Brown, R. *The Gospel According to John, xiii-xxi.* AB 29A. Garden City, NY: Doubleday, 1966.

Conzelmann, H. *1 Corinthians: A Commentary on the First Epistle to the Corinthians.* Trans. J. W. Leitch. Hermeneia. Philadelphia: Fortress, 1975.

Dahood, M. *Psalms II: 50-100.* AB 17. Garden City, NY: Doubleday, 1968.

Fee, G. D. *The First Epistle to the Corinthians.* NICNT. Grand Rapids: Eerdmans, 1987.

Furnish, V. P. *II Corinthians: Translated with Introduction, Notes, and Commentary.* AB 32A. Garden City, NY: Doubleday, 1984.

Haenchen, E. *John 2: A Commentary on the Gospel of John Chapters 7-21.* Trans. R. W. Funk. Hermeneia. Philadelphia: Fortress, 1984.

Holtzmann, H. J., ed. *Die Synoptiker. —Die Apostelgeschichte.* HKNT 1. Freiburg: Mohr-Siebeck, 1889.

Hughes, P. E. *Paul's Second Epistle to the Corinthians.* NICNT. Grand Rapids: Eerdmans, 1962.

Knox, W. L. *The Acts of the Apostles.* Cambridge: Cambridge University Press, 1948.

McNeile, A. H. *The Gospel according to St. Matthew.* 2d ed. London: Macmillan, 1915; reprint ed., 1961.

Martin, R. P. *2 Corinthians.* WBC 40. Waco, TX: Word, 1986.

Orr, W. F., and Walther, J. A. *I Corinthians.* AB 32. Garden City, NY: Doubleday, 1976.

Ruef, J. *Paul's First Letter to Corinth.* WPC. Philadelphia: Westminster, 1971.

3. *Periodical Literature*

Aalen, S. "Begrepet πλήρωμα i Kolosser- og Efeserbrevet," *TTK* 23 (1952) 49-67.

Albright, W. F. "A Catalogue of Early Hebrew Lyric Poems (Psalm LXVIII)," *HUCA* 23 (1950-51) 1-39.

Alexander, P. S. "The Historical Setting of the Hebrew Book of Enoch," *JJS* 28 (1977) 156-80.

Ball, C. J. "Psalm LXVIII *Exurgat Deus*," *JTS* 11 (1910) 415-32.

Benoit, P. "L'horizon paulinien de l'épître aux Éphésiens," *RB* 46 (1937) 342-61, 506-25.

—— "Corps, tête et plérôme dans les Épîtres de la captivité," *RB* 63 (1956) 5-44.

—— "The 'plèrôma' in the Epistles to the Colossians and the Ephesians," *SEÅ* 49 (1984) 136-58.

Bloch, R. "Écriture et tradition dans le judaïsme—Aperçus sur l'origine du Midrash," *CSion* 8 (1954) 9-34.

—— "Note méthodologique pour l'étude de la littérature rabbinique," *RSR* 43 (1955) 194-227.

—— "Note sur l'utilisation des fragments de la Geniza du Caire pour l'étude du Targum palestinien," *REJ* 114 (1955) 5-35.

Bogdasavich, M. "The Idea of *Pleroma* in the Epistles to the Colossians and Ephesians," *DR* 83 (1965) 118-30.

Bousset, W. "Die Testamente der zwölf Patriarchen, I. Die Ausscheidung der christlichen Interpolationen," *ZNW* 1 (1900) 141-75.

Bröse, E. "Der descensus ad inferos Eph. 4, 8-10," *NKZ* 9 (1898) 447-55.

Buck, C. H., Jr. "The Early Order of the Pauline Corpus," *JBL* 68 (1949) 351-57.

Cadbury, H. J. "The Dilemma of Ephesians," *NTS* 5 (1958-59) 91-102.

Cambier, J. "La signification christologique d'Éph. IV.7-10," *NTS* 9 (1963) 262-75.

Cerfaux, L. "Influence des mystères sur le Judaisme alexandrine avant Philon," *Mus* 37 (1924) 36-48.

Chadwick, H. "Die Absicht des Epheserbriefes," *ZNW* 51 (1960) 145-53.

Chilton, B. D. "Isaac and the Second Night: a Consideration," *Bib* 61 (1980) 78-88.

Clark, S. D. "La Enseñanza Paulina sobre los Dones y los Ministerios: Un estudio exegético de Efesios 4,7-16," *RivB* 41 (1979) 141-53.

Connolly, R. H. "The Early Syriac Creed," *ZNW* 7 (1906) 202-223.

Conybeare, F. C. "On the Jewish Authorship of the Testaments of the Twelve Patriarchs," *JQR* 5 (1893) 375-98.

Cope, L. "Matthew 12:40 and the Synoptic Source Question," *JBL* 92 (1973) 115.

Cowling, G. J. "New Light on the New Testament? The significance of the Palestinian Targum," *TSFBul* 51 (1968) 6-14.

Cranfield, C. E. B. "The Interpretation of I Peter iii.19 and iv.6," *ExpTim* 69 (1957-58) 369-72.

Davies, P. R., and Chilton, B. D. "The Aqedah: A revised tradition history," *CBQ* 40 (1978) 514-46.

de Jonge, M. "Christian Influence in the Testaments of the Twelve Patriarchs," *NovT* 4 (1960) 182-235.

——— "Once More: Christian Influence in the Testaments of the Twelve Patriarchs," *NovT* 5 (1962) 311-19.

Dunn, J. D. G. "A Note on δωρεά," *ExpTim* 81 (1969-70) 349-51.

Edgar, S. L. "New Testament and Rabbinic Messianic Interpretation," *NTS* 5 (1958-59) 47-54.

Evans, C. A. "The Meaning of πλήρωμα in Nag Hammadi," *Bib* 65 (1984) 259-65.

Finkelstein, L. "The Book of Jubilees and the Rabbinic Halaka," *HTR* 16 (1923) 39-61.

Gandz, S. "Studies in the Hebrew Calendar," *JQR* 40 (1949-50) 251-77.

Garland, D. E. "A Life Worthy of the Calling: Unity and Holiness, Ephesians 4:1-24," *RevExp* 76 (1979) 517-27.

Goguel, M. "Esquisse d'une solution nouvelle du problème de l'épître aux Éphésiens," *RHPR* 111 (1935) 254-85; 112 (1936) 73-99.

Goldberg, A. M. "Torah aus der Unterwelt?," *BZ* 14 (1970) 127-31.

Guilding, A. "Some Obscured Rubrics and Lectionary Allusions in the Psalter," *JTS* 3 (new series, 1952) 41-55.

Hamann, H. P. "Church and Ministry: An Exegesis of Ephesians 4:1-16," *LTJ* 16 (1982) 121-28.

Hanson, A. T. "The Midrash in II Corinthians 3: A Reconsideration," *JSNT* 9 (1980) 2-28.

Harmon, A. M. "Aspects of Paul's Use of the Psalms," *WTJ* 32 (1969) 6-7.

Harrison, P. N. "Onesimus and Philemon," *ATR* 32 (1950) 268-94.

Holzmeister, U. "Genitivus Epexegeticus in N. T.," *VD* 25 (1945) 112-17.

Hooker, M. D. "Beyond the Things That Are Written? St Paul's Use of Scripture," *NTS* 27 (1981) 295-309.

Hunkin, J. W. "The Testaments of the Twelve Patriarchs," *JTS* 16 (1915) 80-97.

Iwry, S. "Notes on Psalm 68," *JBL* 71 (1952) 161-65.

Jaubert, A. "Le Calendrier des Jubilés et de la Secte de Qumrân: Ses origines bibliques," *VT* 3 (1953) 250-64.

Käsemann, E. "Das Interpretationsproblem des Epheserbriefes," *TLZ* 86 (1961) cols. 1-8.

Klauck, H.-J. "Das Amt in der Kirche nach Eph 4, 1-16," *WiWeis* 36 (1973) 81-110.

Klein, M. L. "The Preposition קדם ('before'). A Pseudo-Anti-Anthropomorphism in the Targums," *JTS* 30 (new series, 1979) 502-7.

Kretschmar, G. "Himmelfahrt und Pfingsten," *ZKG* 66 (1954-55) 209-53.

Kuiper, K. "Le Poète Juif Ezéchiel," *REJ* 46 (1903) 161-77.

Le Déaut, R. "Pentecôte et tradition juive," *ASeign* 51 (1963) 22-38. Originally published in *Spiritus* 7 (1961) 127-44.

Licht, J. "Taxo, or the Apocalyptic Doctrine of Vengeance," *JJS* 12 (1961) 95-103.

Lincoln, A. T. "The Use of the OT in Ephesians," *JSNT* 14 (1982) 16-57.

Loewe, H. "The Petrie-Hirschfeld Papyri," *JTS* 24 (1923) 126-41.

McNamara, M. "Targumic Studies," *CBQ* 28 (1966) 1-19.

Metzger, B. M. "The Formulas Introducing Quotations of Scripture in the NT and the Mishnah," *JBL* 70 (1951) 297-307.

Middleton, R. D. "Logos and Shekinah in the Fourth Gospel," *JQR* 29 (new series, 1938-39) 101-133.

Mitton, C. L. "Unsolved New Testament Problems: Goodspeed's Theory Regarding the Origin of Ephesians," *ExpTim* 59 (1948) 323-27.

Moore, G. F. "Intermediaries in Jewish Theology: Memra, Shekinah, Metatron," *HTR* 15 (1922) 41-85.

Morgenstern, J. "The Three Calendars of Ancient Israel," *HUCA* 1 (1925) 13-78.

——— "Supplementary Studies in the Calendars of Ancient Israel," *HUCA* 10 (1935) 1-148.

Moule, C. F. D. "The Ascension—Acts i. 9," *ExpTim* 68 (1956-57) 205-9.

Murphy-O'Connor, J. "Who Wrote Ephesians?," *BiTod* 18 (1965) 1201-9.

Noack, B. "Das Zitat in Ephes. 5,14," *ST* 5 (1951) 52-64.
Overfield, P. D. "Pleroma: A Study in Content and Context," *NTS* 25 (1979) 384-96.
Rönsch, H. "Miscellen," *ZWT* 28 (1885) 102-4.
Rubinkiewicz, R. "Ps LXVIII 19 (= Eph IV 8) Another Textual Tradition or Targum?," *NovT* 17 (1975) 219-24.
Sanders, J. T. "Hymnic Elements in Eph. 1-3," *ZNW* 56 (1965) 214-32.
Schweizer, E. "I Petrus 4.6," *TZ* 8 (1952) 152-54.
—— "Zur Frage der Echtheit des Kolosser- und des Epheserbriefes," *ZNW* 47 (1956) 287.
Smith, D. C. "The Ephesian Heresy and the Origin of the Epistle to the Ephesians," *OJRS* 5 (1977) 78-103.
Starobinski-Safran, E. "Un poète judéo-hellénistique: Ezéchiel le tragique," *MH* 31 (1974) 216-24.
Taylor, R. A. "The Use of Psalm 68:18 in Ephesians 4:8 in Light of the Ancient Versions," *BSac* 148 (1991) 319-36.
Wernberg-Møller, P. "An Inquiry into the validity of the text-critical argument for an early dating of the recently discovered Palestinian Targum," *VT* 12 (1962) 312-30.
Woude, A. S. van der. "Das Hiobtargum aus Qumran Höhle XI," VTSup 9 (1963) 322-31.
Yates, R. "Principalities and Powers in Ephesians," *NBl* 58 (1977) 516-21.
York, A. D. "The Dating of Targumic Literature," *JSJ* 5 (1974) 49-62.
—— "The Targum in the Synagogue and in the School," *JSJ* 10 (1979) 74-86.
Zeitlin, S. "The Book of Jubilees: Its Character and its Significance," *JQR* 30 (1939) 1-31.
—— "The Assumption of Moses and the Bar Kokhba Revolt," *JQR* 38 (1947-48) 1-45.

4. Special Studies

Adai, J. *Der Heilige Geist als Gegenwart Gottes in den einzelnen Christen, in der Kirche, und in der Welt: Studien zur Pneumatologie des Epheserbriefes.* RSTh 31. Frankfurt: Peter Lang, 1985.
Bieder, W. *Die Vorstellung von der Höllenfahrt Jesu Christi.* ATANT 19. Zürich: Zwingli, 1949.
Bietenhard, H. *Die himmlische Welt im Urchristentum und Spätjudentum.* Tübingen: Mohr, 1951.
Bock, D. L. *Proclamation from Prophecy and Pattern: Lucan Old Testament Christology.* JSNTSup 12. Sheffield: JSOT, 1987.
Bonsirven, J. *Exégèse Rabbinique et Exégèse Paulinienne.* BTH. Paris: Beauchesne, 1939.
Bousset, W. *Kyrios Christos: A History of the Belief in Christ from the Beginning of Christianity to Irenaeus.* Trans. J. E. Steely. Nashville: Abingdon, 1970.
Cadbury, H. J. "Note XXXII. The Speeches in Acts." In *The Beginnings of Christianity*, part 1: *The Acts of the Apostles 5: Additional Notes to the Commentary*, ed. K. Lake and H. J. Cadbury (London: Macmillan, 1933) 402-27.
Caird, G. B. "The Descent of Christ in Ephesians 4, 7-11." In *SE* 2 (= TU 87), ed. F. L. Cross (Berlin: Akademie, 1964) 535-45.
Chase, F. H. *The Credibility of the Book of the Acts of the Apostles.* London: Macmillan, 1902.
Dalton, W. J. *Christ's Proclamation to the Spirits: A Study of 1 Peter 3:18-4:6.* AnBib 23. Rome: Pontifical Biblical Institute, 1965.
de Jonge, M. *The Testaments of the Twelve Patriarchs: A Study of Their Text, Composition, and Origin.* Leiden: Brill, 1953.
—— "The Testaments of the Twelve Patriarchs and the New Testament." In *SE* 1 (= TU 73), ed. K. Aland et al. (Berlin: Akademie, 1959) 546-56.
Dunn, J. D. G. *Baptism in the Holy Spirit: A Re-examination of the New Testament Teaching on the Gift of the Spirit in relation to Pentecostalism today.* Philadelphia: Westminster, 1970.
—— "I Corinthians 15:45—last Adam, life-giving Spirit." In *Christ and Spirit in the New Testament*, ed. B. Lindars and S. S. Smalley (Cambridge: Cambridge University Press, 1973) 127-41.

—— *Christology in the Making: A New Testament Inquiry into the Origins of the Doctrine of the Incarnation*. London: SCM, 1980.

Dupont, J. "Ascension du Christ et don de l'Esprit d'après Actes 2:33." In *Christ and Spirit in the New Testament*, ed. B. Lindars and S. S. Smalley (Cambridge: Cambridge University Press, 1973) 219-28.

Elbogen, I. *Der jüdische Gottesdienst in seiner geschichtlichen Entwicklung*. 2d ed. Frankfurt: Kauffmann, 1924.

Ellis, E. E. *Paul's Use of the Old Testament*. Edinburgh: Oliver & Boyd, 1957.

Ernst, J. *Pleroma und Pleroma Christi: Geschichte und Deutung eines Begriffs der paulinischen Antilegomena*. Regensburg: Friedrich Pustet, 1970.

Goodenough, E. R. *By Light, Light: The Mystic Gospel of Judaism*. New Haven: Yale University Press, 1935; reprint ed. Amsterdam: Philo, 1969.

Goodspeed, E. J. *The Meaning of Ephesians*. Chicago: University of Chicago Press, 1933.

—— *The Key to Ephesians*. Chicago: University of Chicago Press, 1956.

Gruenwald, I. *Apocalyptic and Merkavah Mysticism*. AGJU 14. Leiden: Brill, 1980.

Guilding, A. *The Fourth Gospel and Jewish Worship*. Oxford: Clarendon, 1960.

Gundry, R. H. *SOMA in Biblical Theology with emphasis on Pauline Anthropology*. SNTSMS 29. Cambridge: Cambridge University Press, 1976.

Hanson, A. T. *The New Testament Interpretation of Scripture*. London: SPCK, 1980.

Hanson, S. *The Unity of the Church in the New Testament: Colossians and Ephesians*. ASNU 14. Uppsala: Almqvist & Wiksells, 1946.

Harris, J. R. *Testimonies*. 2 vols. Cambridge: Cambridge University Press, 1920.

Hengel, M. *Studies in Early Christology*. Edinburgh: Clark, 1995.

Hermann, I. *Kyrios und Pneuma: Studien zur Christologie der paulinischen Hauptbriefe*. SANT 2. Munich: Kösel, 1961.

Holtzmann, H. J. *Kritik der Epheser- und Kolosserbriefe*. Leipzig: Engelmann, 1872.

Horst, P. W. van der. "Moses' Throne Vision in Ezekiel the Dramatist." In *Essays on the Jewish World of Early Christianity* (Freiburg [Schweiz]: Universitätsverlag; Göttingen: Vandenhoeck u. Ruprecht, 1990) 63-71.

—— "Some Notes on the *Exagoge* of Ezekiel." In *Essays on the Jewish World of Early Christianity* (Freiburg [Schweiz]: Universitätsverlag; Göttingen: Vandenhoeck u. Ruprecht, 1990) 72-93.

Jacobson, H. *The Exagoge of Ezekiel*. Cambridge: Cambridge University Press, 1983.

Kahle, P. E. *The Cairo Geniza*. London: British Academy, 1947; reprint ed., Munich: Kraus, 1980.

Kelly, J. N. D. *Early Christian Creeds*. 3rd ed. London: Longman, 1972.

Kirby, J. C. *Ephesians, Baptism and Pentecost*. Montreal: McGill University Press, 1968.

Knox, J. *Philemon Among the Letters of Paul*. Chicago: University of Chicago Press, 1935.

Knox, W. L. *St. Paul and the Church of the Gentiles*. Cambridge: Cambridge University Press, 1939.

Le Déaut, R. *Liturgie juive et Nouveau Testament*. Rome: Pontifical Biblical Institute, 1965.

Levine, É. *The Aramaic Version of Ruth*. AnBib 58. Rome: Pontifical Biblical Institute, 1973.

Lincoln, A. T. *Paradise Now and Not Yet: Studies in the Role of the Heavenly Dimension in Paul's Thought with Special Reference to his Eschatology*. SNTSMS 43. Cambridge: Cambridge University Press, 1981.

Lindars, B. *New Testament Apologetic: The Doctrinal Significance of the Old Testament Quotations*. London: SCM, 1961.

Longenecker, R. N. *The Christology of Early Jewish Christianity*. SBT, 2d series, 17. London: SCM, 1970.

—— *Biblical Exegesis in the Apostolic Period*. Grand Rapids: Eerdmans, 1975.

MacCullagh, J. A. *The Harrowing of Hell: A Comparative Study of an Early Christian Doctrine*. Edinburgh: Clark, 1930.

McNamara, M. *The New Testament and the Palestinian Targum to the Pentateuch*. AnBib 27. Rome: Pontifical Biblical Institute, 1966.

Meeks, W. A. "Moses as God and King." In *Religions in Antiquity: Essays in Memory of E. R. Goodenough*. SHR 14, ed. J. Neusner (Leiden: Brill, 1968) 354-71.

—— *The Prophet-King: Moses Traditions and the Johannine Christology*. NovTSup 14. Leiden: Brill, 1967.

Messel, N. "Über die textkritisch begründete Ausscheidung vermeintlicher christlicher Interpolationen in den Testamenten der zwölf Patriarchen." In *Wolf Wilhelm Grafen von Baudissin zum 26. September 1917*, BZAW 33 (Gießen: Alfred Töpelmann, 1918) 355-74.

Meuzelaar, J. J. *Der Leib des Messias: Eine exegetische Studie über den Gedanken vom Leib Christi in den Paulusbriefen.* Assen: Van Gorcum, 1961; reprint ed., Kampen: Kok, 1979.

Mitton, C. L. *The Epistle to the Ephesians: Its Authorship, Origin and Purpose.* Oxford: Clarendon, 1951.

—— *The Formation of the Pauline Corpus of Letters.* London: Epworth, 1955.

Moule, H. C. G. *Ephesian Studies: Expository Readings on the Epistle of St Paul to the Ephesians.* London: Hodder & Stoughton, 1900.

Mußner, F. "Was ist die Kirche?" In *"Diener in Eurer Mitte" : Festschrift für Dr. Antonius Hofmann Bischof von Passau zum 75. Geburtstag*, ed. R. Beer et al., Schriften der Universität Passau: Reihe Katholische Theologie 5 (Passau: Passavia Universitätsverlag, 1984) 82-89.

Neusner, J. *Comparative Midrash: The Plan and Program of Genesis Rabbah and Leviticus Rabbah.* BJS 111. Atlanta: Scholars Press, 1986.

Nickelsburg, G. W. E., Jr. *Resurrection, Immortality, and Eternal Life in Intertestamental Judaism.* HTS 26. Cambridge, MA: Harvard University Press, 1972.

Odeberg, H. *The View of the Universe in the Epistle to the Ephesians.* Lund: Gleerup, 1934.

Overfield, P. D. "The Ascension, Pleroma and Ecclesia Concepts in Ephesians." Ph.D. thesis, University of St. Andrews, 1976.

Percy, E. *Die Probleme der Kolosser- und Epheserbriefe.* Lund: Gleerup, 1946.

Pokorný, P. *Der Epheserbrief und die Gnosis: Die Bedeutung des Haupt-Glieder-Gedankens in der entstehenden Kirche.* Berlin: Evangelische Verlagsanstalt, 1965.

Porter, C. H. "The Descent of Christ: An Exegetical Study of Ephesians 4:7-11." In *One Faith: Its Biblical, Historical, and Ecumenical Dimensions*, ed. R. L. Simpson (Enid, OK: Phillips University Press, 1966) 45-55.

Potin, J. *La Fête Juive de la Pentecôte: Étude des textes liturgiques.* 2 vols. LD 65. Paris: Éditions du Cerf, 1971.

Reicke, B. *The Disobedient Spirits and Christian Baptism.* Copenhagen: Ejnar Munksgaard, 1946.

Roels, E. D. *God's Mission: The Epistle to the Ephesians in Mission Perspective.* Franeker: T. Wever, 1962.

Roon, A. van. *The Authenticity of Ephesians.* NovTSup 39. Leiden: Brill, 1974.

Rowley, H. H. *The Relevance of Apocalyptic.* 2d ed. London: Lutterworth, 1947; reprint ed., Greenwood, SC: Attic, 1980.

Russell, D. S. *The Method and Message of Jewish Apocalyptic.* Philadelphia: Westminster, 1964.

Sanders, J. N. *Studies in Ephesians*, ed. F. L. Cross. London: A. R. Mowbray, 1956.

Schildenberger, J. "2 Kor. 3,17a: «Der Herr aber ist der Geist» im Zusammenhang des Textes und der Theologie des hl. Paulus." In *Studiorum Paulinorum Congressus Internationalis Catholicus, 1961*, AnBib 17-18 (Rome: Pontifical Biblical Institute, 1963) 1.451-60.

Schille, G. *Frühchristliche Hymnen.* Berlin: Evangelische Verlagsanstalt, 1965.

Schlier, H. *Christus und die Kirche im Epheserbrief.* BHT 6. Tübingen: Mohr, 1930.

—— *Die Zeit der Kirche: Exegetische Aufsätze und Vorträge.* Freiburg: Herder, 1956.

Schnackenburg, R. "Christus, Geist und Gemeinde (Eph. 4:1-16)." In *Christ and Spirit in the New Testament*, ed. B. Lindars and S. S. Smalley (Cambridge: Cambridge University Press, 1973) 279-96.

Schnapp, F. *Die Testamente der zwölf Patriarchen untersucht.* Halle: Max Niemeyer, 1884.

Scholem, G. G. *Die jüdische Mystik in ihren Hauptströmungen.* Zürich: Rhein-Verlag, 1957.

Segal, A. F. *Two Powers in Heaven: Early Rabbinic Reports about Christianity and Gnosticism.* SJLA 25. Leiden: Brill, 1977.

Simon, U. *Heaven in the Christian Tradition.* New York: Harper & Brothers, 1958.

Stendahl, K. *The School of St. Matthew and Its Use of the Old Testament.* 2d ed. Uppsala: Almqvist & Wiksells, 1954.

Thackeray, H. St J. *The Relation of St Paul to Contemporary Jewish Thought.* London: Oxford University Press, 1900.

—— *The Septuagint and Jewish Worship*. London: Oxford University Press, 1921.

Vermes, G. *Scripture and Tradition in Judaism*. SPB 4. Leiden: Brill, 1961.

Zunz, L. *Die gottesdienstlichen Vorträge der Juden*. 2d ed. Frankfurt/Main: Kauffmann, 1892.

5. General and Reference Literature

Aland, K., and Aland, B. *The Text of the New Testament*. Trans. E. F. Rhodes. Grand Rapids: Eerdmans, 1987.

The Apocrypha of the Old Testament. Revised Standard Version, ed. B. M. Metzger. New York: Oxford University Press, 1957.

Aurelii Augustini Opera. CChr 46. Turnhout: Brepols, 1969.

The Babylonian Talmud: Seder Mo'ed. Ed. I. Epstein. London: Soncino, 1938. *'Erubin*, translated by I. W. Slotki.

The Babylonian Talmud: Seder Mo'ed. Ed. I. Epstein. London: Soncino, 1938. *Shabbath*, translated by H. Freedman.

The Babylonian Talmud: Seder Nashim. Ed. I. Epstein. London: Soncino, 1936. *Yebamoth*, translated by I. W. Slotki.

The Babylonian Talmud: Seder Nezikin. Ed. I. Epstein. London: Soncino, 1935. *Sanhedrin*, translated by J. Shachter.

Bacher, W. S.v. "Targum." In *Jewish Encyclopedia*, ed. I. Singer, 12 vols. New York and London: Funk & Wagnalls, 1906.

Barnes, W. E. *The Peshitta Psalter according to the West Syrian Text*. Cambridge: Cambridge University Press, 1904.

Bauer, W. *A Greek-English Lexicon of the New Testament and Other Early Christian Literature*. 2d ed. Trans. W. F. Arndt and F. W. Gingrich; rev. F. W. Gingrich and F. W. Danker. Chicago and London: University of Chicago Press, 1979.

Bengel, J. A. *Gnomon Novi Testamenti*. Tübingen: Schramm, 1742.

Biblia hebraica stuttgartensia. Ed. K. Elliger and W. Rudolph. Stuttgart: Deutsche Bibelstiftung, 1977.

Βιβλιοθηκη Ἑλληνων Πατερων και Ἐκκλησιαστικων Συγγραφεων, 2: Κλημης ὁ Ρωμης—Διδαχη των Δωδεκα Ἀποστολων—Βαρναβα Ἐπιστολη—ἡ προς Διογνητον Ἐπιστολη—Ἰγνατιος. Athens: Apostolic Diaconate of the Church of Greece, 1955.

Βιβλιοθηκη Ἑλληνων Πατερων και Ἐκκλησιαστικων Συγγραφεων, 3: Πολυκαρπος Σμυρνης—Ἑρμας—Παπιας—Κοδρατος—Ἀριστειδης—Ἰουστινος. Athens: Apostolic Diaconate of the Church of Greece, 1955.

Βιβλιοθηκη Ἑλληνων Πατερων και Ἐκκλησιαστικων Συγγραφεων, 6: Ἱππολυτος. Athens: Apostolic Diaconate of the Church of Greece, 1956.

Βιβλιοθηκη Ἑλληνων Πατερων και Ἐκκλησιαστικων Συγγραφεων, 19: Τιτος Βοστρων—Θεοδωρος—Ηρακλειας—Ἀλεξανδρος Λυκοπολεως—Ἐυσεβιος Καισαρειας. Athens: Apostolic Diaconate of the Church of Greece, 1959.

Blass, F., and Debrunner, A. *A Greek Grammar of the New Testament and Other Early Christian Literature*. Trans. and rev. R. W. Funk. Chicago: University of Chicago Press, 1961.

Bowker, J. *The Targums and Rabbinic Literature*. Cambridge: Cambridge University Press, 1969.

Brown, F.; Driver, S. R.; and Briggs, C. A. *A Hebrew and English Lexicon of the Old Testament*. Oxford: Clarendon, 1907; reprint ed. 1972.

Büchsel, F. "Κατώτερος." *TDNT* 3.641-42.

Burton, E. D. *Syntax of the Moods and Tenses in New Testament Greek*. 3rd ed. Chicago: University of Chicago Press, 1900.

Catchpole, D. "Tradition History." In *New Testament Interpretation*, ed. I. H. Marshall (Exeter: Paternoster, 1977) 165-80.

Charles, R. H., ed. *The Apocrypha and Pseudepigrapha of the Old Testament in English*, 2: *Pseudepigrapha*. Oxford: Clarendon, 1913.

Charlesworth, J. H. *The Pseudepigrapha and Modern Research*. SCS 7. Missoula, MT: Scholars Press, 1976.

——, ed. *The Old Testament Pseudepigrapha*, 1: *Apocalyptic Literature and Testaments*. Garden City, NY: Doubleday, 1983.

——, ed. *The Old Testament Pseudepigrapha*, 2: *Expansions of the "Old Testament" and Legends, Wisdom and Philosophical Literature, Prayers, Psalms, and Odes, Fragments of Lost Judeo-Hellenistic Works*. Garden City, NY: Doubleday, 1985.

Clemens Alexandrinus, 2: *Stromata Buch I-VI*. Ed. O. Stählin; rev. L. Früchtel; 4th ed. with addenda by U. Treu. GCS. Berlin: Akademie, 1985.

Cohen, A., ed. *The Minor Tractates of the Talmud*. 2 vols. London: Soncino, 1965.

Cureton, W. *Ancient Syriac Documents*. London, n.p., 1864; reprint ed., Amsterdam: Oriental, 1967.

Dalman, G. H. *Grammatik des jüdisch-palästinischen Aramäisch*. 2d ed. Leipzig: J. C. Hinrichs, 1905; reprint ed. with *Aramäisch Dialektproben*, Darmstadt: Wissenschaftliche Buchgesellschaft, 1960.

—— *Aramäisch-neuhebräisches Handwörterbuch zu Targum, Talmud und Midrasch*. Göttingen: Vandenhoeck u. Ruprecht, 1938; reprint ed. Hildesheim: Georg Olms, 1967.

Denis, A. M. *Fragmenta pseudepigraphorum quae supersunt graeca*. PVTG. Leiden: Brill, 1970.

Driver, G. R. *The Judaean Scrolls*. Oxford: Basil Blackwell, 1965.

Etheridge, J. W. *The Targums of Onkelos and Jonathan ben Uzziel on the Pentateuch*. No publisher, 1862; reprint ed., New York: Ktav, 1968.

Eusebius Werke, 8: *Die Praeparatio Evangelica*. Part 1: *Einleitung, die Bücher I bis X*. Ed. K. Mras; 2d ed., rev. É. des Places. GCS. Berlin: Akademie, 1982.

Foerster, W. *Die Gnosis*, 1: *Zeugnisse der Kirchenväter*. Zürich and Stuttgart: Artemis, 1969.

Froidevaux, L. M. *Irénée de Lyon: Demonstration de la Prédication Apostolique*. Paris: Éditions du Cerf, 1959.

Goudoever, J. van. *Biblical Calendars*. Leiden: Brill, 1959.

The Greek New Testament, ed. K. Aland et al. Stuttgart: United Bible Societies, 2d ed., 1968; 3rd ed., 1980.

Guthrie, D. *New Testament Introduction*, 2: *The Pauline Epistles*. London: Tyndale, 1961.

Hagiographa Chaldaice. Ed. P. A. de Lagarde. Leipzig: B. G. Teubneri, 1873.

Hennecke, E. *New Testament Apocrypha*. Ed. W. Schneemelcher; trans. and ed. R. McL. Wilson. Philadelphia: Westminster, 1965.

Humbert, J. *Syntaxe Grecque*. 3rd ed. Paris: Klincksieck, 1960.

Jastrow, M., ed. S.v. "מ׳." In *A Dictionary of the Targumim, the Talmud Babli and Yerushalmi, and the Midrashic Literature*. 2 vols. N.p., n.d.; reprint ed., Brooklyn, NY: P. Shalom, 1967.

Josephus, 4: *Jewish Antiquities, Books I-IV*. Trans. H. St J. Thackeray. LCL. London: Heinemann, 1930.

Kautzsch, E., ed. *Die Apokryphen und Pseudepigraphen des Alten Testaments*, 2: *Die Pseudepigraphen des Alten Testaments*. Hildesheim and New York: Georg Olms, 1975.

Kümmel, W. G. *Einleitung in das Neue Testament*. 14th ed. Heidelberg: Quelle & Meyer, 1965.

Landgraf, A. *Commentarius Cantabrigiensis in Epistolas Paule e Schola Petri Abaelardi: 2. in Epistolam ad Corinthios, I^am et II^am ad Galatas et ad Ephesios*. PMS 2. Notre Dame, IN: University of Notre Dame, 1939.

Le Déaut, R. *Introduction à la Littérature Targumique*. Première partie. Rome: Pontifical Biblical Institute, 1966.

Lightfoot, J. B. *Apostolic Fathers*. London, Macmillan, 1891; reprint ed., Grand Rapids: Baker, 1956.

Lutherbibel erklärt: Die Heilige Schrift in der Übersetzung Martin Luthers mit Erläuterungen für die bibellesende Gemeinde. Stuttgart: Württembergische Bibelanstalt, 1974.

McNeile, A. H. *An Introduction to the Study of the New Testament*. 2d ed. Rev. C. S. C. Williams. Oxford: Clarendon, 1953.

Mayser, E. *Grammatik der griechischen Papyri aus der Ptolemäerzeit*, 2: *Satzlehre*. Berlin and Leipzig: Walter de Gruyter, 1934; reprint ed., 1970.

Mekilta de Rabbi Ishmael, translated by J. Z. Lauterbach. 3 vols. Philadelphia: Jewish Publication Society of America, 1933.

Metzger, B. M. "Trends in the Textual Criticism of the Iliad and the Mahabharata." In *Chapters in the History of New Testament Textual Criticism*, NTTS 4 (Grand Rapids: Eerdmans, 1963) 142-54.

——— *The Text of the New Testament: Its Corruption, Transmission, and Restoration.* 3rd ed.
     New York and Oxford: Oxford University Press, 1992.
The Midrash on Psalms, trans. W. G. Braude. 2 vols. YJS 13. New Haven: Yale University
     Press, 1959.
Midrash Rabbah, ed. H. Freedman and M. Simon. *Exodus*, trans. S. M. Lehrman. London:
     Soncino, 1939.
Midrash Rabbah, ed. H. Freedman and M. Simon. *Song of Songs*, trans. M. Simon. London:
     Soncino, 1939.
Migne, J.-P., ed. *Patrologiae cursus completus, series latina.* Paris: no publisher, 1845.
———, ed. *Patrologiae cursus completus, series graeca.* Paris: Garnier, 1862.
Moore, G. F. *Judaism in the First Centuries of the Christian Era: The Age of the Tannaim.* 3
     vols. Cambridge, MA: Harvard University Press, 1927-30; reprint ed., 1946.
Moule, C. F. D. *An Idiom Book of New Testament Greek.* 2d ed. Cambridge: Cambridge Uni-
     versity Press, 1959.
Moulton, J. H. *Prolegomena*, 3rd ed. MHT 1. Edinburgh: Clark, 1908.
New American Standard Bible. La Habra, Calif.: Foundation, 1963.
Novum Testamentum Graece, ed. K. Aland et al. Stuttgart: Deutsche Bibelgesellschaft. 27th
     rev. ed., 1993.
Odeberg, H. *3 Enoch or the Hebrew Book of Enoch.* Cambridge: Cambridge University Press,
     1928; rpt. with prolegomenon by J. Greenfield, New York: KTAV, 1973.
The Old Testament in Syriac according to the Peshitta Version. Part 2, fascicle 3: *The Book of
     Psalms*, ed. D. M. Walter. Leiden: Brill, 1980.
Pesikta Rabbati, trans. W. G. Braude. 2 vols. YJS 18. New Haven and London: Yale Univer-
     sity Press, 1968.
Philo. Supplement 1: *Questions and Answers on Genesis*, trans. R. Marcus. LCL. Cambridge,
     MA: Harvard University Press, 1953.
Philo. Supplement 2: *Questions and Answers on Exodus*, trans. R. Marcus. LCL. Cambridge,
     MA: Harvard University Press, 1953.
Philonis Alexandrini, Opera quae supersunt, ed. L. Cohn and P. Wendland. 8 vols. Berlin:
     Georg Reimer, 1902; reprint ed., Walter de Gruyter, 1962.
Pirkê de Rabbi Eliezer, trans. and annotated G. Friedlander. London: no publisher, 1916; re-
     print ed., New York: Sepher-Hermon, 1981.
Radermacher, L. *Neutestamentliche Grammatik.* 2d ed. Tübingen: Mohr, 1925.
Roberts, B. J. *The Old Testament Text and Versions.* Cardiff: University of Wales Press, 1951.
Robertson, A. T. *A Grammar of the Greek New Testament in the Light of Historical Research.*
     4th ed. Nashville: Broadman, 1934.
St. Irenaeus: Proof of the Apostolic Preaching, trans. J. P. Smith. Ancient Christian Writers
     16. Westminster, MD: Newman; London: Longmans, Green & Co., 1952.
Schneider, J. "Καταβαίνω." *TDNT* 1.523.
——— "Μέρος." *TDNT* 4.597-98.
Schoeps, H. J. *The Jewish-Christian Argument: A History of Theologies in Conflict.* Trans. D.
     E. Green. London: Faber & Faber, 1963.
Schürmann, H. *Ursprung und Gestalt: Erörterungen und Besinnungen zum Neuen Testament.*
     Düsseldorf: Patmos-Verlag, 1970.
Septuaginta, ed. A. Rahlfs. 5th ed. Stuttgart: Württembergische Bibelanstalt, 1935.
*Septuaginta: Vetus Testamentum Graecum auctoritate Societatis Litterarum Gottingensis
     editum*, 13: *Duodecim Prophetae.* 2d ed. Ed. J. Ziegler. Göttingen: Vandenhoeck u. Ru-
     precht, 1967.
Smyth, H. W. *Greek Grammar.* Rev. G. M. Messing. Cambridge, MA: Harvard University
     Press, 1956; originally published as *A Greek Grammar for Colleges*, 1920.
Soden, H. von. *Die Schriften des Neuen Testaments in ihrer ältesten erreichbaren Textgestalt
     hergestellt auf Grund ihrer Textgeschichte*, 2: *Text mit Apparat.* Göttingen: Vandenhoeck
     u. Ruprecht, 1913.
Souter, A. *Pelagius' Expositions of Thirteen Epistles of St Paul: Text and Apparatus Criticus.*
     Cambridge: Cambridge University Press, 1926.
Sperber, A. *The Bible in Aramaic*, 4A: *Hagiographa.* Leiden: Brill, 1973.
——— *The Bible in Aramaic*, 4B: *The Targum and the Hebrew Bible.* Leiden: Brill, 1973.

Strack, H. L., and Billerbeck, P. *Kommentar zum Neuen Testament aus Talmud und Midrasch*. 6 vols. Munich: Beck'sche, no date; reprint ed., 1969.

Swete, H. B., ed. *The Old Testament in Greek*. Cambridge: Cambridge University Press, 1909.

Le Targum de Job de la Grotte XI de Qumrân. Ed. and trans. J. P. M. van der Ploeg and A. S. van der Woude. Leiden: Brill, 1971.

Tertulliani Opera. CChr 1, 2. Turnhout: Brepols, 1954.

The Testaments of the Twelve Patriarchs: A Critical Edition of the Greek Text. Ed. M. de Jonge. Leiden: Brill, 1978.

Tischendorf, C. von. *Novum Testamentum Graece, editio octava critica maior*. Leipzig: Giesecke & Devrient, 1872; reprint ed., Graz: Akademische Druck- u. Verlagsanstalt, 1965.

Tragicorum Graecorum Fragmenta 1. Ed. B. Snell. Göttingen: Vandenhoeck u. Ruprecht, 1971.

Tromp, J. *The Assumption of Moses: A Critical Edition with Commentary*. SVTP 10. Leiden: Brill, 1993.

Turner, N. *Grammatical Insights into the New Testament*. Edinburgh: Clark, 1965.

—— *Syntax*. MHT 3. Edinburgh: Clark, 1963.

Wacholder, B. Prolegomenon to *The Bible as Read and Preached in the Old Synagogue*, by J. Mann. New York: Ktav, 1971; original ed. without Prolegomenon, 1940.

Westcott, B. F., and Hort, F. J. A. *The New Testament in the Original Greek*. 2 vols. London: Macmillan, 1881; reprint ed., New York: Macmillan, 1946.

Winer, G. B. *Grammatik des neutestamentlichen Sprachidioms als sichere Grundlage der neutestamentlichen Exegese*. 3rd ed. Leipzig: F. C. W. Vogel, 1830.

Zerwick, M. *Biblical Greek Illustrated by Examples*. Rome: Pontifical Biblical Institute, 1963.

Zwingli, H. *Huldreich Zwinglis Sämtliche Werke*, 12: *Randglossen Zwinglis zu biblischen Schriften*. Ed. E. Egli, G. Finsler, W. Köhler, O. Farner, F. Blanke, and L. von Muralt. CR 99.1. Leipzig: Heinsius, 1941; reprint ed., Zürich: Theologischer Verlag Zürich, 1982.

INDEX OF AUTHORS

INDEX OF SUBJECTS

W. Hall Harris III (Ph.D., University of Sheffield) is professor of New Testament studies at Dallas Theological Seminary.